FREEING
THE
EDINBURGH
FRINGE

There is no posterity
as amazing as you

Peter Buckley Hill

FREEING
THE
EDINBURGH
FRINGE

The quest to make performers
better off
by charging the public nothing

Peter Buckley Hill

First published
in 2018 by

DESERT HEARTS
www.deserthearts.com

© Peter Buckley Hill 2018

Project-managed by Nick Awde / Desert Hearts

ISBN 978-1-908755-34-6 (paperback)

A CIP catalogue record for this book is available from the British Library.

Printed in Great Britain by
Cann Print, Kilmarnock

To Mel

CONTENTS:

Preface and False Start

I NEVER USED TO READ PREFACES. But now I've ended up writing one.

I feel the irony. Enmity and irony live together in perfect harmony, side by side on my computer keyboard, oh lord, why can't we?

The book didn't originally start here. The original start can be found below the little centred star in a page or so.

I need to explain a few things, though. Otherwise I'm just writing a story from 1994 to the present day.

It's all about the Edinburgh Fringe. The Edinburgh Fringe is the largest arts festival in the world. It's mad, it's chaotic and a lot of people love it.

You may already know all about it. But I can't assume you do. Please skip this preface if you do.

To geographers and train timetables, Edinburgh is a city. But to performers, it's a time. It's usually 23 days in August. We say things like "I'll see you next Edinburgh", which makes no logical sense, but every performer understands it.

In theory, anybody can perform at the Edinburgh Fringe. In practice, the performer needs a venue. So, whoever controls the venues controls the Fringe.

My organisation now controls 52 stages in 32 venues, and therefore gives performing opportunities to 518 shows and over 9000 performances. These were the 2017 figures. That makes us by far the largest provider of venues at the Fringe, and twice as big as the second largest.

So what? Somebody has to be biggest. And outside the Arts, there are many bigger organisations than that.

So this. Until we came along, venues were in the hands of for-profit organisations, as many still are. To get a venue, the performer had to pay through the nose.

Performers left Edinburgh considerably in debt. Thousands, if not tens of thousands of pounds.

But the Free Fringe, which I started, is a non-profit organisation. We don't charge performers. That's the difference.

And that, I humbly suggest, is why this story, the story of the Free Fringe, is important.

Why are so many performing artists middle-class? Same reason so many lawyers are middle-class. Because it takes money to become good at either profession. And only the middle class has that money.

Pay-to-play systems deny many non-wealthy people the right to pursue their dreams.

But worse than that: they don't stop having those dreams. And many will go into debt to back their dreams. And the money they borrow goes into somebody else's pocket.

We've fought against that. We're still fighting.

And even as I proofread this, a good friend has lost a fortune at an Australian fringe festival, where the promoter has not paid the money owing to the artists.

This is the story, with its ups, downs, mistakes, quarrels, bitchiness and occasional ecstasy, of how I, and later we, carried out that fight.

The Free Fringe is a collective, and I was the dictator of that collective. I don't think I set out to be a dictator. It's hard work.

All I know of Tiberius Claudius, I learned from Robert Graves. Not personally; reading his books. Maybe he wasn't really like that. Graves has him wanting to restore the Roman republic. I want to be succeeded as dictator by a republic, or collective. It's the same sort of thing. Perhaps.

Read on, or put the book back on the shelves of the charity shop in which you found it.

Everything in here is true, for a certain meaning of 'true'. A number of names have been changed. It all relies on my memory, and my memory makes mistakes. I have almost certainly put some events in the wrong year, for that reason.

Other people and organisations will remember things differently. Sometimes they'll remember things differently because it's in their interests to do so.

I have been as accurate as I can, and as truthful as I can. But truth is in the eye of the beholder.

Apart from the names. There are a lot of pseudonyms in what follows.

Because it's more about what people did and how they reacted than who they are. I just want to describe what happened, nothing else, and no doubt other people see things differently.

A vast apology in advance, however, if I have chosen any pseudonym that is somebody's real name who's completely unconnected with this story. In fact, that's bound to have happened. Sorry. In my early songwriting years, maybe 1980, I wrote a parody of Me and Bobby McGee; the parody was called Me and Sharon McGurk. Fifteen or twenty years later, I got an email saying: I'm Sharon McGurk and I swear I don't know you. I didn't know how to reply, so I didn't. Sorry again.

A lot of people deserve to have their contribution to the Free Fringe acknowledged. At the very least, by having their names in this book. And yet their names are not here. I hope they haven't bought it to see their names. If that's you, it doesn't mean your contribution isn't valuable. It's just the way I wrote it. A narrative, not an analysis. My story. You're free to write your own story.

*

This is where it started, originally:

This won't be an autobiography. So let's assume I had the usual friendless childhood in isolated places, frequent parental moves, terminal teenage acne and all the other things that turn an almost normal human into a comedian.

Not the best comedian in the world, either. But that doesn't matter much. Comedian is not what you can do; it's who you are. You can tell them in primary school playgrounds. Not the children who have a rapt audience of other children; they grow up to be the pub bore, telling jokes they haven't written themselves. The future comedians are the picked-on, the ones who are laughed at for being odd, until in later years they learn how to control when people laugh at them.

This won't be a book about the theory of comedy, either. Nor the psychology of comedians. There are plenty of books like that.

No, this will purely be a how-I-done-it book. How I done what I done, why I done it and why I shouldn't of done it. And yes, dear editor, I know that's an error of grammar. Sometimes we do them deliberately. That one's passed into the language. I think it was Terry Pratchett who first used it, deliberately, to indicate his character was not very articulate. And that was read by millions of young people who didn't realise what was happening, and assumed it was correct English.

I know this because, despite the comedy, I've marked a lot of essays. Comedy wasn't my only job. I would have starved otherwise. Or do I mean 'would of starved'?

Odd how comedy can change language, though. Before Michael Crawford brought life to Raymond Allen's sitcom character Frank Spencer, the word 'harass' was pronounced differently, with the stress on the first syllable. I still pronounce it that way, but I'm strange.

I also digress a lot. Imagine a butterfly. I wonder if it's the same one as I'm imagining as I write this? We shall never know.

Anyway, back to how I done it. Firstly, we need to establish what I done.

Some would say I saved the Edinburgh Fringe. Actually, when I say 'some would say', I mean 'I would say'.

I'm normally modest and terminally shy (another thing you should know about comedians: we're all shy and have very deficient social skills. Why else would we stand on stages and tell out innermost thoughts to total strangers? Because we can't do it in one-to-one relationships.) But you can't be shy and write a how-I-done-it book.

So how can I make a claim like that?

After all, the Edinburgh Fringe is even older than me. It started in 1947; I was born in 1948, in Burnley, of distinctly non-Scottish ancestry. And my path and the Edinburgh Fringe's didn't cross until 1994.

And this is where the story really starts ....

*

1994

In which our hero discovereth the Fringe.

I WAS ALREADY IN MY 40s. There was a folk circuit in those days, and I did comedy on it. If that sounds pathetic in the 21st century, then consider that this was the same background from which Billy Connolly, Jasper Carrot and several others emerged. It was, as they say, a thing, in those days.

Actually, it was around then that the folk circuit was drying up. It still exists, and long may it exist, but the days of easy availability of work are long gone. With two long playing records (remember them?) under my belt, and a small following at places like Cambridge Folk Festival, I had some self-confidence as a performer. I was proud of the comic songs I had written and reasonably sure I could hold an audience. Where does one go to become famous?

And the answer seemed to be the Edinburgh Fringe.

How was I to know then that I'd made the same elementary mistake as thousands of others before me?

As it turned out, I was luckier than most. I'd taken a year's unpaid leave of absence from the day job. I had something to go back to. In my ignorant and arrogant head, I had a year to get famous. Yes, it would cost me most of my savings. But at least I had some.

And that, I discovered later, is how the Edinburgh Fringe is financed. People spending their savings to finance their dreams.

It comes as a shock to realise that the world's biggest arts festival is almost entirely pay-to-play. And that the payment isn't small. But such is the strength of dreams, people pay it. I'm getting a little ahead of myself here. Let me tell you the story, as far as I remember it.

I knew nothing of the Fringe or Edinburgh. I'd never been to the city, in August or any other month. In 1993 I'd seen a small ad in The Stage for last-minute Fringe slots at a venue on Broughton Street, and was tempted just to take one. Fortunately a friend advised me that this was not a good venue (it doesn't exist now), but I promised myself to do it properly in 1994.

So, I asked the only person I knew who'd been successful at the Fringe: John Hegley. I'd known him on and off since 1980, so went to one of his gigs (Lauderdale House, a Scottish connection that hadn't occurred to me until just now) and asked him what was a good venue.

Hill Street Theatre, he said. It worked for me, he said.

I should have realised: he's John Hegley. Anywhere would have worked for him.

So, Hill Street Theatre it was. 65 seats. £3.50 a ticket (oh, the prices of those days. I priced relatively low; normal was £4-£5 than. Now it's nearer £15 than £10, for a one-hour show). I paid quite a lot to rent the space, all in advance, of course, plus the Fringe Participation Fee that then as now gets you 40 words in the Fringe Programme, plus a quarter-page ad in the same programme.

Plus, of course, accommodation. The venue arranged a flat; me sharing with four complete strangers. Fortunately, by virtue of advanced age, I got the single room. I think they politely looked upon me as a freak, being 20 years younger than me, and they representing the future of comedy. Yet 24 years later I'm still in the business and none of them are. It's cruel. They were nice people.

So, several thousand pounds, paid up front. One gets back a percentage of the box office. So if I'd sold most seats at most performances — say 75%, to be on the safe side, maybe more at weekends — I'd have broken even.

How little I knew.

They say the average Fringe audience is six people and in your first year you mustn't expect to do that well. I hadn't heard that before arriving at the 1994 Fringe. If I had heard it, I wouldn't have believed it. I would have thought, as many do, that the shows with six or fewer people would be those who aren't as good as mine. That eventually, the public was bound to flock to my show.

The first night, I had 19 in. Well, I thought, not bad. Even when I found that most were on free tickets, given out by the venue's PR person (another expense). And I was very gratified when, just before the show, an audience member came in and asked me to autograph his ticket. Oh, I thought, I must be better known than I think.

What I didn't know was that I'd started on a date almost no other shows were running yet. I was, almost, the only show in town. And the autograph person turned out to be attempting the record for the number of Fringe shows seen in one season; the autograph was simply proof of attendance.

Next night I thought it might go up to 30 and so progress to a full house by the weekend. But I got 10% of that. Three people. Next night another three, then zero, zero and two.

This nagged at my self-esteem a little.

I made, that year, just about every mistake it was possible for a Fringe newcomer to make, but it wasn't all that bad.

BBC Radio contacted me. They were interested in my blurb and would like to see my act. Could I arrange a complementary ticket? Certainly, I said, and strode self-importantly to the box office to do that very thing. That night, I waited in the kitchen that served us as a backstage area, willing myself to shine for the BBC. On time, I burst on to the stage. There, in the middle of the front row, was the BBC. And there, on all the other rows, was nobody else.

I got three-quarters of the way through the second number when we mutually agreed it wasn't working. They said they'd be back when the audience situation had improved. I'm still waiting.

There was, however, a world outside my own show. The cabarets. What existed in those days, but no longer does, was the Fringe Club. It was in Teviot House, on Bristo Square (not, as I thought it said for the first two weeks, Bistro Square), home of the Edinburgh University Students' Union.

For £5, the public could buy an evening ticket to the Fringe Club and be entertained by wandering through the three stages, as well as having drink at student union prices and a self-service cafeteria, the second most popular dish at which was haggis and chips. Plus drinks promotions; Newcastle Brown was the chief driving force behind that.

And if you were a registered Fringe performer, you got a discount card with 10% off your haggis and chips. Or indeed your fish and chips, which was somewhat more to my taste. That wasn't the important bit, though. You could sign up at the Fringe Office during the day for a performance slot on one of the three stages, and thus plug your show. Aha, I thought: that's for me. No more zero audiences. They will see my excerpt and flock to the whole show. So I signed up as soon as I could.

They were kind at the signup. They explained that the space officially known as the Wine Bar was more commonly known as the Bear Pit. "But it isn't that bad really". They lied out of kindness to a newcomer.

I was the second act on, around midnight. I don't remember much about the first act. There was no compère, just the sound man announcing the name of the acts. I went on. Conversation did not cease; if anything it got louder. Finished the first number, normally a point at which applause happens. Nothing. Did a couple of gags. Nobody laughed, smiled, nodded or gave any impression of listening at all. And so it went on for the agonising 15 minutes, after which I slunk off to no applause or acknowledgement. I beckoned over one of the itinerant Newcastle Brown salespeople and ordered rather a lot of it. A victim, for the first time, of the Wall of Indifference.

The act after me was a young Australian comic, full of self-confidence or so it seemed. His first words were; "aren't you glad I'm not the last guy?" You bastard, I thought, amid gulps of Newcastle Brown; I hope you die.

(For the benefit of the over-literal, 'die' in comedians' usage doesn't mean actually succumb to a terminal disease; it means precisely what had just happened to me, giving a performance the audience hates).

And that was my first encounter with Brendon Burns. If you had told me that night that we would become friends in the future, I would have spluttered on my Newcastle Brown at the thought.

Pack up, said the inner parent; go home. You've taken on more than you can handle. No, said the inner donkey; I'm toughing this out.

And I signed up again. No Wall of Indifference the second time. Boos, heckles, catcalls, and underwear (male, alas) dropped on me from the balcony conveniently placed above the stage. Not realising quite what had been dropped, I wiped my face on it. It was hot and sweaty on that stage, after all. "Fuck off, granddad" they shouted, and off I duly fucked. They were no nicer to most of the other acts, but occasionally they turned and — for no reason I could discern — suddenly decided they liked somebody.

And the third time, perhaps because it was Tuesday, it was me. I don't know what I did different, apart from having a bottle of Newcastle Brown before going on, but I got them. I got an encore in the Bear Pit. I think this ranks with the birth of my daughter as one of life's high memorable moments. When I walked back to the flat, my feet didn't touch the ground.

But between my set and my homeward float, several members of the audience invited me to perform at other cabarets around Edinburgh. I wondered then, and I still wonder, how many real audience members there are at the Fringe, and how many are show members seeing other shows? But anyway, I had gigs. Not paid ones, but it didn't matter. Even with single-figure audiences, I wasn't hopeless. I could face the three people in my own show with less trepidation.

The reviewers slaughtered me. Try this for size:

Totally lacking in delivery skills is Peter Buckley Hill, a man with a knowledge of 3 guitar chords, a host of banal folksongs and a Shakespearian sketch entitled "Omlette". The songs tended to rattle round an unamused audience whilst the omelette sketch left the stage in embarrassment. Imagine your father doing a talentless act at Christmas and you've got Peter Buckley Hill".

I'm quoting that review because I still have it; I don't still have the Edinburgh Evening News' one, but I remember it was worse. I won't give the name of the writer of the review above; maybe he was right. No, he wasn't: I knew 4 chords then and I played them all. Alright: I googled his name just now, just for curiosity, but there are several people with the same name. I hope he wasn't the one they sent a mountain rescue party for in the Highlands in early 2018.

I now say I got five stars that year — one each from five different publications. It's a sort of gag, but it's also true, although I'm not sure who the fifth was. And yet a whole party came to see me one day, enjoyed it and met me in the bar afterwards. Why did you choose my show, I asked. Oh, we saw a good review, they said. Really, I said, in what? Oh, we can't remember; it was just lying around. The day after, I went to the Fringe Press Office and scoured everything they had, twice. Nothing. Only the lousy reviews I already knew about, and one I didn't. Nothing good. I hunted everywhere, but no. The review never existed. They'd gone to completely the wrong show. But they enjoyed it.

At the end of the four weeks, I had achieved little to boast about, but I was hooked. Despite drinking much more Newcastle Brown and other ales than I should have, I'd lost a stone dashing from cabaret to cabaret with guitar and props bag. I'd heard of emotional roller coasters but I'd never been on one before. Too exhausted to attend the venue closing party, I slept for 15 solid hours until we had to vacate the flat, then took two days to drive home.

I was so exhausted I didn't really stir until October. And the Fringe Box Office sent me a payment for central ticket sales. £98.50, less 7% commission. There were other sales at the Venue Box Office; I don't have that figure any more, but in total I was so far away from the break-even point that you couldn't see it with the Hubble Space Telescope.

Now, there's nothing in this story that other Edinburgh Fringe performers of that time haven't also experienced. Maybe not in detail, but in general. You quickly learn you have to improve your game, and that you're nothing like as special as you thought you were. And it cost most of your savings, but either you'd never look up at Edinburgh Castle again, or you were Fringe-hooked.

One year's experience didn't make me an expert. But it did give me something to think about. And I thought: I'm stuck in a cycle.

I can't go on, year after year, making losses in the thousands of pounds. But that's what's going to happen unless something changes.

What can change? I can get better at what I do. I hope to.

But the best in the world are in Edinburgh in August, and am I as good as the best in the world? Probably not.

And if I were as good as the best in the world, how would anybody know unless they came to see me? Word of mouth will only go so far. Maybe it takes ten years to build a reputation for one's show. Which runs out first: the perseverance or the money?

Because if all shows are about the same price, then audiences will go to see the names they've heard of rather than the names they haven't. Unless one writes an interesting and different show on a theme nobody else has thought of. And everybody else is trying to write precisely the same sort of show.

No; it's a cycle of dreams. As long as people are willing to pay nearly all the money they have in pursuit of their dreams, there will be other people willing to take that money. And when that dreamer's money is all spent, and he or she slinks away to wherever people with unfulfilled dreams go, there will always be other dreamers with more money. And the same people willing to take it.

And it doesn't matter what the people-who-take-dream-money's motivation is. They may, as some people suggest, be profiteers; they may, as others say, merely cover their costs. Nobody quite knows where the money goes. Some say the real gainers are the suppliers: firms who hire chairs, lighting rigs, PA and everything else one needs to make a theatre out of nothing. Others say it's the public relations industry that gains most; shows paying somebody to make their particular leaf stand out, amidst the forest of the Fringe.

Nobody knows where the money goes to. But everybody who does the Fringe knows where it comes from. Participation fee, venue rental, accommodation, leaflets and posters (very expensive in some poster sites), possible PR and extra programme advertising; even for a one-person show, it amounts to much more than you can reasonably expect your share of the box office to cover.

It's a showcase, they say. Expect to lose money. But they said the same about the pay-to-play gigs musicians were forced to play in the 60s and 70s.

And at the end of 1994, there I was, facing a decade of losses until I might just be good enough. But certainly with the potential to have some fun on the way.

Multiply that by a thousand me's, and you have the seeds of a bigger problem.

*

1995:
The Intermediate Year

In which an idea is born

THERE'S LITTLE TO SAY ABOUT 1995. Let's dismiss a complete year. Not much happened other than the death of my ex-partner on Midsummer Day; I hadn't seen her for some time and I didn't know she was dying until she was no longer dying. I went a little mad; some say I remained so.

Well, I say not much happened: I'd taken a year's unpaid leave from the day job. The 1994 Fringe was to have been my launch. Could I make it as a performer? I'd gone with dreams of doing so. The battering those dreams took at that first Fringe, I've described above. The battering was also felt by my savings.

But I'd learned a lot more about the craft of performing and, buoyed up by my lucky encore in the Bear Pit, thought at least I had it within me to raise my game. I settled down to doing gigs, after the month or so doing nothing but feeling exhausted that seems to be normal after one's first Fringe.

The worst part of doing comedy gigs is asking for them. The easy bit — normally, not always — is actually performing them. But getting someone to book you is hard. You have to overcome shyness (and if you're not basically shy, you're probably not a comedian) and ask for spots, giving your credentials without sounding boastful. Boastful is bad and puts promoters off, although not in the USA.

I toted my guitar around such clubs as I could get booked at, mostly for no money but after a while progressing from unpaid open spot to paid 10 minutes to paid 20 minutes. You could do that, then. Do well and you would be re-booked; do badly and you wouldn't see that promoter again. Nowadays it's said to be much harder to do that progression, although easier to ask for the gigs themselves; there was little email in 1995 and one had to telephone.

Obviously, the money wasn't enough to live on. I sold part of my soul to a publisher and got a part-time job sorting out his accounts. There are some people I know who are completely unsuited to any job save that of comedian. If they make it in comedy, great; if they don't, they have nothing. Fortunately I am not one of these; perhaps that means I don't deserve to make it to the top. And, as you know, I didn't.

I had an answering machine in those days, working on two cassette tapes, as they did then. And that sometimes failed. One day I came home to such a message. It said: garble — saw you at Hill Street — garble — a proposition — garble — ring me on — garble. And try as I might I couldn't make out the rest. This was in the days before caller ID, so no way of finding out who had called, thus what the proposition was. Maybe it was The Man With The Cigar. Maybe not. I'll never know. Maybe the proposition would have meant fame and fortune. Maybe he was mortally insulted I didn't ring him back, whoever he was. Maybe that was my one shot, swallowed by a wobbly cassette.

But my plans for the 1995 Fringe evolved, and they involved concentrating my forces. Fine, I thought: some people like what I do, so let's ensure full audiences by doing fewer one-man shows, and at the same time as many guest spots or cabaret spots as I can. And that, of course, will be cheaper in venue rental, although not in accommodation or Fringe participation fee. Gather my people, my audience, together and they shall be mighty. Honestly, I still thought like that.

Good plan. But, like many good plans, completely wrong. I was, perhaps, still thrown by the death of my ex-partner; not only the fact of it but the unexpected news. I had romanticised. Every time I accidentally left my light on and returned home to see it blazing as I put my key in the lock, I imagined she'd come back and was waiting for me. No matter how many years it had been. So, when I was forced to accept this was never going to happen (even though a bit of my mind hoped she'd faked her own death in a Reggie Perrin re-enactment) I took a trip to the bottom of a bottle and stayed there for a while.

I emerged only briefly in the month following that Midsummer-day news. But I emerged long enough to claim my right to return to the day job. If you're going to be bereaved, you might as well have an income. Giving it up for Music And The Free Electric Band, or in my case for the sleazy comedy clubs, the temporary laughs and the few crumpled notes shoved into one's hand at the end, no longer seemed an option.

Whatever I was to do from that point, I would have to do as a semi-professional. I was clearly not going to be able to afford doing the Edinburgh Fringe annually without another source of income.

So be it. Meanwhile, let's see how I fared with my fewer performances (five, scattered throughout the Fringe) and my concentrated audience.

It turned out not to be concentrated. Fringe legend has it that the average audience is six people. It's widely believed, but nobody's ever officially confirmed it. Many shows, by well-known performers, sell out and have audiences in the hundreds. So if the average, the arithmetic mean, is six, the mode must be lower than six.

I got, in my five performances: 11, 5, 3, 0 and 12. So, I suppose better than the notional average.

I did some compering of my venue's open night, that year. And there was a folk singaround in the back room, which was not Fringe-like at all, and I enjoyed playing that, among the regular Edinburgh folkies.

And one of them told me that his old friend Billy Connolly had dropped in, stood at the bar at the back of the main room and seen me do one of my songs, which he had liked. Wow. Good thing I didn't notice him at the time; I might have gone to pieces. I didn't actually meet him; I was just told about it afterwards. Maybe it wasn't true. Oh, but I choose to believe.

Not all stars are as nice. A female singer was booked in for a standard 15 minute spot on my watch as compère. Nothing unusual there. But the unknown singer arrived in the entou-

rage of Famous Female Cabaret Performer. Whom I didn't immediately recognise. And who obviously expected to be recognised, and expected her and her protégée, the actual performer, to be accorded due deference. Where was the sound
man? she demanded. How can Protégée perform without a
sound balance? What, there's no sound man? How can this be?

There were maybe a couple of dozen people in. It was an
informal cabaret, like all such cabarets. Protégée could easily
have done it without a PA at all. Maybe Protégée didn't mind,
but FFCP certainly did, and of course it was my fault.

I sat beside the four-channel mixer side-stage throughout
Protégée's set, and pretended to twiddle knobs. It was all I
could do. I suspect if I'd actually twiddled them it would have
made things worse.

Maybe I'd caught FFCP on a bad day. Some of her own songs
are funny. Some of mine are funnier, but I would say that,
wouldn't I?

What a lovely word 'twiddle' is.

I had just as much fun as 1994 at the cabarets and variety
shows; I could easily find guest spots, although not always
happy ones. The same heart-in-mouth approach to the Bear
Pit. A triumph at Fringe Sunday, but leading to no spinoff audience into my own show.

(Fringe Sunday, another excellent thing that no longer exists, was the Fringe's gift back to the city: an event with three
or four marquee stages and several busking spots in Holyrood
Park, the Queen's back garden, overshadowed by Arthur's
Seat, which is an extinct volcano, or so the Tourist Board
would have us believe. I dream of it springing back to life and
freezing the entire city, Pompeii-like, in mid-Fringe. Archae-
ologists two millennia hence would really wonder at what the
petrified bodies had been doing.)

I had devised a strategy for the Bear Pit. If the Bear Pit represented the lowest common denominator of comedy
(although their cruelty could be sometimes witty, it was seldom subtle) then I would prepare for it using good old British
lowest common denominator comedy.

Just next to Euston Station, there was a shop called Trans-formations: slogan "turning beautiful men into beautiful women", and with some illustrations painted outside to, well, illustrate, as illustrations do. Now, this is not my kink of choice; the moustache rather gets in the way. No disrespect to those whose choice it is. It was obvious that shop would sell what I wanted. I prepared a speech in which I would express my full respect for their kink, explained that it wasn't mine but for completely different purposes.... Oh well. I paced out-side for a long time and then barged in, forgot the speech and blurted out "I'd like a suspender belt and a pair of fishnets, please".

Eyelids were not batted. Certainly, Sir, the assistant said. These will fit you. (And they did). Would you like knickers with that? I said: no, thank you, and scurried home with my brown paper bag.

You will see my fiendish plan. Put the suspender belt and fishnets on under the trousers and then, when things were getting unbearable, drop the trousers and get off stage on a laugh. Pure Benny Hill, or sub-Benny Hill.

Praise be to the gods, or whoever the Muse of Lowest Com-mon Denominator comedy is. The barracking was getting worse, as expected, when a female heckler, and I swear she wasn't a plant, shouted "show us your knickers". In any other circumstance, I would have had no reply to that, but now... Bingo. The laugh happened.

Was it worth the price of the equipment? If you think not, congratulations on being a normal. To a comedian, yes, it was. Or maybe it just showed how Fringe-addicted I already was.

So, I was addicted but conflicted. There was enough about the Fringe to keep me wanting to go for as many years as I could. But I couldn't afford, every year, to hire a venue at the going rates, and play to small audiences thus getting little of that money back. Yes, I could get better at what I did. That might lead to bigger audiences. But the odds are it wouldn't; everybody else would be doing the same thing. Maybe that means the artistic standard of the Fringe is constantly rising. But that's no consolation to the performer.

How, I wondered, do other people manage it? I was relatively well off. I had a day job I was about to go back to after a year. I was based in the UK; I had to pay rent in Edinburgh, yes, but I didn't have to fund a flight from San Francisco or Adelaide, as many others did.

The Fringe was an addiction. More addictive than smoking, and almost as bad for you. And, just like smoking, people continued to do it, in the face of all the good reasons why they should not. And no matter how much it cost, or how bad it made you feel on occasions.

Could I give up?

Did I want to give up?

Or could I mitigate the damage by switching to a cheaper brand?

Well, there were price variations between space brokers. The venues then called the "big three" (Pleasance, Assembly, Gilded Balloon) charged approximately the same, depending on size of room and time of day. Some deals by less prominent organisations were less expensive — indeed, I had already worked with two such organisations. Cheaper, but not cheap enough.

What about raising admission prices? At the time, there wasn't a great difference in price between shows by the most famous people and the most obscure performers; maybe £2 per ticket more. To charge the top rate, I'd have to be famous and good. I certainly wasn't famous. I thought I was good, but not everybody agreed.

If you're a leaf, and you want as many people as possible to admire the beauty of your green colouring and the precision of your veins, where do you go? Not to the forest, where you look too much like the other leaves.

But if you want to be in the forest, among the other leaves, doing leafy things and feeling part of a brotherhood of leaves?

Well, you have to make yourself distinctive some other way. One way to be distinctive is to increase your circle of friends.

Which you can do by buying them. Or rather by doing things for them that they'll appreciate, which is after all a form of buying.

Hundreds of performers were in my situation. Weak audiences at their own shows and therefore bad times at them. If you're a comedian, it's hard to get a laugh out of a large-ish room with four people in it. So, even ignoring the financial loss, you don't have a good time at your own show. You have a much better time at the open shows and cabarets, doing shorter spots to usually bigger audiences. And there's always a chance that people will come from those shows to see your own one-person show.

So, I decided I would become the organiser of a show with a different bill every night.

And I would call it "Peter Buckley Hill and Some Comedians".

When I thought of the title, a finger descended from the heavens and angelic choirs sang a single chord which resounded over the city of Edinburgh. Or so I remember. It wasn't, by itself, a particularly spectacular idea. But it was a way forward.

And then the second thought hit.

I can only buy friends by doing things for them if the things I do for them are the things they like. A bad show is going to impress nobody. What do these performers most want? And I imagined them in their own shows, playing to three or four people, just as I had done, and I knew the answer was: a big audience.

Which is precisely what I wanted in the first place. All this thinking had brought me back to the same place and the same dilemma. My problem was the same problem as almost everybody else had, and yet I felt alone with the problem. And so, I assume, did they.

For in my first two years I had met many excellent fellow-performers, but gained no feeling of support from that; rather, they were rivals. We were competing for audience, and for the audience's money. However friendly things seemed to be on the surface, there was little deep comradeship. And I, at least, felt the need for more support from fellow performers. Hence the need to buy friends.

Round and round the thoughts went, always landing back at the same place. There were no short cuts. Nowadays, everybody knows Jerome McCarthy's idea of the Marketing Mix — the four Ps, although not everybody knows the context or background, or the ideas that have been had since McCarthy devised it in 1960. And we're certainly not going to go into a marketing lecture here. McCarthy's four Ps were, and are: Product, Promotion, Price and Place (distribution, but that doesn't begin with a P).

I had my product. Two products: my own one-man show, and the newly-hatched Peter Buckley Hill and Some Comedians. What could I do about the other three Ps to help it along? (Yes, it's a service, so the seven-P model applies, but let's not go there).

Could it be promoted better? Yes, but it would cost more. And promotion is an arms race. Once one competitor increases their promotional spend, others do the same, and we end up with everybody spending more with no net gain.

Could it be located better? Well, perhaps so, but in a festival with hundreds of venues, I didn't think this was the critical factor. People, I thought, walked happily from venue to venue, within the central area. Later on, I discovered that location was a much more subtle problem, but as far as preparations for 1996 were concerned, it didn't seem too important.

Price, however....

Let's make it cheaper than the norm. A couple of pounds, say. But what message does that send? That says it's worse than the rest. And most venues want all their shows to be within a specific price band; how else can they make money on the percentage of the admission price they charge?

And whatever price you charge, even a pound, you need an infrastructure for booking tickets, checking tickets, getting information from the Fringe Central Box Office, having another local system of booking, making sure the two systems between them don't oversell the venue; you need a whole body of people running that system.

Unless you have no tickets at all.

You used to have half-a dozen people paying £5 each, of which you see maximum £4; a day's pay of £24, and you've worked very hard on street leafleting to bring them in.

If you had 25 people on free admission, and they each put £1 in a collection afterwards, you'd be £1 better off. That's not a significant amount of money. But with 25 people, you'd have a much better show, or at least a much better chance of a good show.

What a pity the venues won't let you do this.

And on that thought, the 1995 season ended. Nice idea. Shame it could never happen.

*

1996

In which the Free Fringe taketh its first faltering steps

THERE'S ALWAYS ROOM for a good *Deus ex Machina*.

At first sight, it was unlikely to be Reggie Schutt, universally known as Z. Nobody quite knew why, but that's not a question one asks in this business.

Z ran several comedy nights in London and Hertfordshire and compèred them himself. A wild and hairy man, now alas dead.

And some of the pubs he ran them in were Firkins. And I'm going to have to explain that one for the benefit of the young.

The Goose and Firkin was a pub with its own brewery in Southwark. When it started, real ale was rare, and people flocked to consume beers like Dogbolter. It was popular. And because it was popular, it expanded, and eventually there were Firkins everywhere, all with names beginning with F; the Fulmar and Firkin, the Fox and Firkin, the Phoenix and Firkin (yes, I know) and so on. They all had ex-church furniture and most had breweries attached. And many of them put on comedy shows.

I had met Z when I did an open spot at one of the shows he ran, in St Albans, at the Philanthropist and Firkin. He liked my act and gave me paid work.

And, rather later, he'd used his initiative to contact management in the Firkin chain (by then owned by a national pub company) and he'd negotiated the right to put on comedy shows in two Edinburgh pubs — the Physician and Firkin and the Footlights and Firkin. Z approached a few performers he knew, and who he thought might get on well, and offered them hour-long slots for their shows for £300 each. I was one of those who were offered a space. I accepted. It was good value. Better than the thousands I would otherwise have paid.

And the miracle I had thought impossible. At that price, I could afford to make the show free.

Z had devised a form for us to give our show details (there were only 18 of us or so; a form wasn't necessary, but there was one anyway). Under 'admission price' I put down 'free'. The experiment had begun. I had been wrong about doing fewer performances and concentrating the audience; let's see if I was any more right about this.

There was some consternation. Did I really want to do this? Why give away something you can get people to pay for? Of all the other shows in the Footlights and Firkin, not one seemed to understand the idea. But they didn't stop it.

The Footlights and Firkin was a basic pub and had its own crowd of drinkers. There wasn't a separate room for the shows; the landlord had found a heavy curtain with which he separated off a performance space. We had to put the benches (former pews) out at the beginning of every show day and put them back at the end, lest drinking space should be lost. My show was an hour long; me compering and two guest performers doing 15-20 minutes each. Not the only free show on the Fringe — all BBC shows are free by charter, and various shows run by religious organisations have always been free, some even throwing in tea and biscuits on top. But mine was the only free show of its sort and, before we started, this had been noticed.

We started on the Saturday, and in my case to the first full house of my Fringe career.

Oh, it wasn't perfect. On Saturdays and Sundays the noise of conversation from the other side of the curtain interfered with the show quite a lot. But the houses stayed full or mostly full, throughout the run.

Fridays were a nightmare. The pub did attract its fair share of heavy drinkers, and Fridays were the days they came and heckled. On the worst day of them all, both my guest acts terminated their sets after a couple of minutes and I was left holding the fort against a barrage of incoherent shouting. There are days you want to give up, and that was certainly one. I came to dread Fridays. But I wasn't alone; the other performers in the venue could be relied on to give support to any

of their number who needed it. With one exception, but I suppose there's always one.

Partly through judgement, but mostly through luck, I'd hit
the right combination. Free admission, of course, but also an
unpretentious space where people felt welcome, no need for
ushering or stewarding, drink at what used to be called popular prices, and a team of fellow-performers who got on with
each other. The informality turned out to be quite important
to the scheme.

Not perfect, but good enough. Full or fullish houses
throughout, reasonably behaved except on Fridays, bringing in
enough bar sales for the management to be happy and putting
enough money in the hat at the end of the show for me also to
be happy. Apart from the time somebody stole the hat. It was a
good hat and I'd had it since 1972. I miss that hat. It was the
sort of German sailor's cap that both Dylan and Donovan had
affected in their early years. I don't suppose it suited me, but I
miss it nonetheless.

Still, you never play the Edinburgh Fringe without losing
something. You just have to hope it's not your mind.

Now, there's a difficult bit. Only despicable people speak ill
of the dead, and yet that's what I have to do. Let me make it
clear that Z was a decent man and I liked him, as did everybody else, as far as I know. I am sorry he's dead, and he died of
a horrible disease that he certainly didn't deserve.

The £300 I was paying for the space, and the same sum that
others were paying, I assumed was being passed to the pub.
Other spaces charged performers at the Fringe; it was logical
to assume the Footlights and Firkin was doing the same.

But it was in a casual conversation with the manager that I
learned otherwise. The pub was not charging us anything.
What was being paid to Z was being kept by Z.

This was a problem. But perhaps not as much as I had imagined. Everybody else who had anything to do with putting on
performances at the Fringe was making a profit on the payments made by performers. Why shouldn't Z? He'd done to the

trouble of finding the space, recruiting the shows and making the arrangements. Did that not deserve a reward?

But I felt uneasy about that. He was guaranteed, by our payments, against making a loss on the Fringe, and yet there he was, appearing to be a performer among a co-operative team of performers. I felt deceived. If I had known before signing up where the money was going, I might still have signed up. But I didn't know, and I felt deceived.

So, obviously, I asked. By telephone, because by then he'd gone back home; he wasn't performing for the full run. He refused to discuss it, and later wrote me a letter. The phrase that sticks in my memory from that letter is: "if you don't like it you can fuck right OFF". I don't quite know why the capitals. I think he may have been suffering from the first effects of the disease that eventually killed him, when he wrote that. I really want to remember him kindly. But I felt I had to ask.

I assumed, after that, I was out of the Footlights and Firkin loop. But I had proved what I needed to prove. Free admission worked; one could break even on a free-admission show. But it needed to be of reasonable quality, and it needed to be somewhere where the audience felt comfortable.

Actually, I don't know whether that first show really broke even or not. I didn't count the receipts, but since I didn't charge accommodation, expenses or Z's £300 against tax, that was all right. It felt like a break-even. That was all I needed, and since nobody else was doing it my way, I didn't have to worry about them. I'd proved the concept, so I was happy, although not happy about Z's letter.

But where was I to find another venue? Well, there was no particular rush.

*

1997

In which we could have been stopped but prevailed

I DIDN'T SEE Z AROUND THE CIRCUIT. His illness was worsening, but I didn't know that at the time. The nature of the circuit is such that you can go a long time without bumping into someone, and you wouldn't particularly notice. Then quite often you do three gigs with them in the same week. It's random.

I didn't know things were seriously wrong until I was contacted by another performer. Let's call her Eleanor Coleman. We have to call her something, and I'm damned if I'm going to use her real name.

Eleanor's message was this. Z was too ill to organise the Fringe at the two Firkin pubs in Edinburgh. He had ceded all his rights in this matter to Eleanor. Eleanor was graciously willing to let me put on a show at the Footlights and Firkin, but I must charge admission. It would not be fair to my fellow performers if I did not.

Looking back, I can see why she might have thought that. Free shows (with the exceptions I mentioned ages ago: the BBC, the religious recruiters etc) had, as far as I knew, only been tried once — by me, in 1996. The idea wasn't established. Even after my 1996 show had been reasonably successful, nobody had really grasped the concept. Perhaps she feared that a free show would force other shows to lower their prices.

In my mind, other shows lowering their prices would be a good thing and wouldn't affect their profit, for two reasons. Firstly, they weren't making a profit. Fringe shows run at a loss, and a break-even is an excellent result. Secondly, as I had shown in 1996, lower price meant bigger audience and thus enough revenue to compensate.

What were the terms, I asked Eleanor.

Same price as before, she said. But I won't let you do the show free. You must charge.

Perhaps I react badly to people telling me what I must do. My £300 had gone into Z's pocket. I liked Z, even if he hadn't been open about what was happening to the money. I liked Eleanor less. Z didn't go around issuing orders. He was a much nicer man than I. Despite our quarrel, we might have worked something out. Eleanor was altogether a different proposition. And there she was, now in charge and issuing ultimatums.

Except — was she actually in charge? Had Z really passed on his crown to her? I could have thought of several more likely heirs. And was it, indeed, his crown in the first place?

So I rang the landlord (or possibly manager) of the pub. He'd taken an interest in the shows, not only because they were bringing in beer sales, but also because he liked comedy. Normally, that's good. But when they like it so much that they want to try it themselves and ask for a spot in your show, that's less good. Anyway, I put the situation to him.

No, he said, I want the free show. It works.

But if you've given Eleanor booking rights in place of Z....

No, he said, I haven't. This is the first I've heard of this. I want your show.

Fine, I said, you've got it.

We agreed a start and finish time for the show. With the agreed freedom to over-run the hour if needed, I decided to book three guest comedians a night rather than the two a night I had had in 1996.

Then I told Eleanor. And she wasn't happy. As ill luck would have it, I was due to play a gig that same night that she was compering. She cut my running time down as low as she could, but I did the gig, and as I remember I had a good audience. One of the audience told her she should book me again. Somehow I knew that would never happen. Oh well.

Meanwhile, I had my venue back and I didn't have to pay £300 for it.

Eleanor ranks as the first in a considerable line of people who have tried to stop the Free Fringe. We'll meet some more of them later.

But meanwhile I found myself in a position which, had I but known it, would cause problems for the Free Fringe 15 years later.

I had saved money. Perhaps not deliberately; certainly as a result of an odd chain of events. But the £300 was saved. What did I do with it?

Spent it on another part of the Fringe, of course. And that's typical Fringe conduct, then and now. Making a loss is so impregnated into the fabric of the Fringe that, if you offer people the chance not to make a loss, they'll spend the money elsewhere and still make a loss.

Here I was offering myself the chance to break even, or even make a slight profit. What did I do instead? Spent the money (much more than the £300) on another venue, so I could do a one-man show as well as Peter Buckley Hill And Some Comedians II.

I suppose I could have asked to do the one-man show at the Footlights and Firkin, but the jolly pub atmosphere wasn't quite right for the sort of show I wanted to do. I wanted them all in seats, facing the stage, and not heckling much. So I took the show elsewhere and paid, starting in the second week so I'd have time to bed the Footlights and Firkin in. For it was only the second year; something might still have gone wrong and I needed to be there to make sure it didn't.

The one-man show was free-admission. I was wedded to the idea by then. And I wanted to see if it would work for a one-man show as well as it worked for PBH and some Comedians. It was a different sort of show; it might not have worked.

I had an undocumented promise from the person with booking rights at the one man show's venue (Southside Courtyard). If it went well at the venue, in consideration of the free admission, he might charge me less, and I didn't have to pay up front. So far, so good.

That's when I learned one of the most serious lessons of my Fringe career. Oh, not "always get your deal in writing". That's another good lesson, but in this case I was prepared to pay the full amount if I really had to.

No. This man, the organiser of my venue and a few others under his own banner, had a lot to do to get his shows lined up, his venues rigged and staffed, his box office systems working and everything else one has to do with a pay-to-play venue.

To get this done, he regularly drove between his home in the West of England and Edinburgh, making more and more trips as the Fringe got closer. And shortly before the start of the Fringe, he fell asleep at the wheel, and was killed in the ensuing accident.

Oh, there was a memorial gig that year and a collection for the family. But over 20 years later, I can't even remember his name, and nor can anybody I've asked.

The Fringe kills.

They'll let you work, as he worked, doing the myriad things you have to do, and they'll pile on the pressure rather than help relieve it. And when it kills you, they'll say "pity" and shrug.

Now the Free Fringe has grown to ten times the size of that man's operation, I think of him a lot, whatever his name was.

I no longer drive the 400 miles to Edinburgh. I nearly fell asleep at the wheel once on that trip, and once can be enough. But when things get complex, and people want what you can't give them and complain publicly about what you do give them, then merely not driving is not enough to prevent a stress-related death.

Whatever it's worth, it's not worth that.

But one can get so tied up in it, and try to keep so many balls in the air at once, and have so many people asking so many questions and making so many changes to their arrangements which require immediate response and more work to fix the consequences of those changes. One does that work against the deadlines. It almost becomes a matter of pride that one can cope with all of it. And then comes the moment when one can't cope with all of it, and the Fringe kills again. The beast makes another mark on the wall of its cave, and awaits the inevitable next idiot.

Well, rest in peace, whatever your name was.

Death was to stalk the 1997 Fringe in other ways also.

My shows went well, apart from Fridays at the Footlights and Firkin. The one-man show was never crowded, but audiences averaged well over the legendary Fringe average of six, although there were a couple of days with no audience at all. The Footlights and Firkin was crowded, happy and mostly what one would wish it to be, apart from the day Matt Lucas got booed off. My fault; I compèred badly. I hope he's forgiven me.

In two years Peter Buckley Hill And Some Comedians had become an institution. And the same people came several times, because the bill was always different. One man, older than most audience members, maybe about 70, came, by himself, every night, on his way back to his hotel after a day of Fringing. He was quite critical of comedy he didn't like, as I discovered when we talked later, but our bills satisfied him, on the whole. That was good enough for me. I thought 70 old, then. I don't now.

I was worried about the disconnection between some of the people of Edinburgh and its Fringe.

Oh, to be sure, some would leave the city for a month and rent out their flats at a profit. But others wouldn't. In these years, when all Fringe communication was on paper and came by post, we would get in the packet of papers an invitation to play at the Craigmillar cabaret.

The invitation was fearsome. Craigmillar was painted as an area of great deprivation, whose inhabitants never went to Edinburgh itself. If we chose to brave the cabaret, they would send private cars for us, there and back, and we should be prepared for this very different and challenging audience.

One year a certain comedian, who shall be nameless — no, of course he wasn't nameless; how could I have introduced him without a name? I mean I shall not name him here. Nameless had signed up for the Craigmillar cabaret and was to be fetched by a driver after having played my show. And Nameless got cold feet. And hid from the driver, which meant that I had to confront the driver and either lie to him or tell him that Nameless didn't want to do the show. I chose the latter, on account of it being true. Driver wasn't pleased.

The next year I signed up to do Craigmillar myself. I'm not sure how that happened. The blurb made it feel like going into very hostile territory, like the sort of American film I never watch because I'm afraid of violence. I think I must have been asked directly.

Anyway, I did the show and it was absolutely lovely. Nothing to be afraid of at all. Great audience. Nice community centre in a converted church.

And Craigmillar was less than three miles from the centre of Edinburgh, and several buses linked, and still link, the two.

Why would the citizens not make that three-mile journey to where the Fringe was? There were no borders, no walls, except those that the mind builds. And some minds had clearly built them.

There and then I vowed to demolish those walls.

No, of course I didn't. That would be stupid and pretentious as well as impossible. I did no such thing. I'm not much of a vower, or a demolisher.

But there was a big disconnect between the Fringe and (parts of) the Edinburgh community. The Free Fringe, over time, has helped to bridge it, or at least I think and hope so. But not in 1997; not yet.

Another manager in the Firkin chain (the Fiscal and Firkin, right in the centre next to Tron Kirk) approached me. Could I put on some comedy in his pub? The venue failed the standard test: the performance area wasn't separated from the rest of the pub. But these were early days. I didn't think so rigidly about separation as I do now. And, of course, it was in my interest to be well in with the Firkin chain.

The hours the manager wanted overlapped my own show; I couldn't do it myself even if I had the stamina. But I found him somebody to compère and organise. Randy Wilson, a Texan who wore a Zoot Suit (should that be in capitals?) and played the trumpet in his act. And a variety show ensued, people taking a chance on getting the audience's attention.

They sometimes did and sometimes didn't, and that's the trouble with in-bar performance. But it wasn't in any programme, and the acts were willing. I even performed myself a couple of times before dashing off to my own show.

The irony was: Randy got paid for doing it. I didn't.

That year, I said probably the cleverest thing I'll ever say, and there was no audience to hear it, and the circumstances are so improbable that I can't even make it into a "and then I said" story.

Oh well, it's my book. Here goes anyway.

One microbrewery served all four Firkin pubs in Edinburgh. And one night, in the Footlights and Firkin, I was introduced to the brewer. Who loved his job. We spoke of beer and comedy. And he promised, the next year, to brew us a special beer for the Free Fringe (which, lest we forget, was only my shows at that point, plus Randy's in-bar spinoff).

Actually, said the brewer, I've brewed a lot of ale in my life, but many of your audience drink lager, and I want to try my hand at a lager. What should we call it?

And without hesitation or thought, I said "I Can't Believe It's Not Bitter".

I'm proud of that one. The promised beer never happened, of course. Free Fringe Ale is still a project for the future, many years later.

There was an Irish comedian. Well, there are many. This particular one liked the concept of Peter Buckley Hill and Some Comedians. He could improve it, he said. How? By featuring him every night. I was not up to the job, in his opinion. He was. He would save the show. Well, at least he was direct. And I think he genuinely believed he would be doing me a favour.

But the show didn't need saving and didn't need him. And I didn't need undermining like that. So I said no. I'm not naming him, but he's no longer performing and I still am. Was I that bad, then? At the time, I couldn't afford to think so. I was shaken by his condemnation, but carried on. Even if I was as bad as he said, the show was obviously working as a whole.

And yet maybe I was that bad. I certainly was when the incident below happened.

Most guest performers considered Peter Buckley Hill and Some Comedians a fun show to do. So there was a happy atmosphere. And as we were coming to the end of the run, Gordon Brunton made a suggestion. Why don't you, he said, let me compère the last night. And you can go on last and thus headline the show. And, since it's the last one, that means you've headlined the series.

This is the sort of thing one likes to hear. So I said yes, and Dave Williams did a guest spot, and two other of my favourite guests. And, because it was the last show, and everybody was getting tired and sentimental, and maybe because they could see the start of the Free Fringe Revolution — no, maybe not that. Anyway, in their sets they all praised me for starting the show. It almost became a tribute show.

And then I went on to headline. And I died a horrible death. After all that praise, my head was in a strange place. I couldn't be funny at all. Everything I said evinced no laugh. I called on the gods of comedy for help, from Thalia to Lenny Bruce, but it was the end of the Fringe and they were sick of being prayed to. I slunk off, in deepest defeat. And that was the end of Peter Buckley Hill And Some Comedians II.

And thus the Fringe was over, on that Sunday, and I intended to relax over many drinks with Gordon and Dave and the others. And they'd put the pub hours back to the non-Fringe times, and we couldn't get a drink, even though I'd brought them massive business over the previous three weeks. That rankled. I slunk back to my nearby flat, undrunk and wishing to be. And that's where death (real death, not comedy death) released its second barrel.

Turn on the TV. Diana, Princess of Wales. First critically injured, then dead.

Very little danger of her name being forgotten 20 years later, unlike the asleep-at-the-wheel venue manager of whom I wrote earlier.

I don't think many of us who turned on the television that night could have predicted the mass hysteria that was to follow. Death, of course, is tragic; sudden death at a young age even more so, whether the victim be rich, poor, famous or obscure. My first reaction was: well, that solves a major problem for the Establishment. My second was: if it had happened a week earlier, what would the Fringe have made of it? There we were, thousands of comedians in the same city, including the finest in the land, and this happens. Imagine the potential for gags. A gift to comedians wishing to be thought edgy, and there were many of those.

We could not have predicted how tragedy-obsessed the nation was to become. We'd seen the unexpected deaths of the very famous before. I was in the sixth form when JFK was shot; everybody went in the next morning. (Yes, fact-checkers, it was indeed a Friday, but we had compulsory Cadet Force on the Saturday). The world should have stopped when John Lennon was shot, and I certainly mourned him with an ostentatious candle, but life went on. The famous die, and it's a tragedy, but things proceed. But that wasn't the case in 1997.

Of these three early deaths of the mega-famous, if I could turn back time and prevent only one, which would it be? Lennon, without a doubt.

And for which of the three would I turn off all entertainment on all radio and television channels? None of the above. I slept fitfully that night, not because of the news, but because one sleeps fitfully after the Fringe. It takes ages to adjust back to normal life; in 1994 I did nothing until November. I awoke after the fitful sleep to find all television channels blocked with news and tribute, except that Channel 4 showed The Waltons, as a last gasp before falling in line with the rest.

Driving back home, nothing but repeated news and solemn music. Actually, driving home an interesting way as I often did, I went over the top of Shap Fell just as the solemn music became Vaughn Williams' The Lark Ascending, and even on my crackly car radio it was a sublime combination of music and scenery. I stopped in Kendal and bought mint cake, for no reason.

The mood of the nation was mad that week. Shopkeepers were threatened with violence for not intending to close during the funeral. Carpets of flowers were laid outside palaces, and people came from miles to see them and add to the carpet. There was no dissent, or rather those who dissented thought it wise to keep very, very silent. This is what a fascist state must feel like.

It was not until later I reflected that this showed how vulnerable the Fringe itself is. When I first heard the news, I thought the Fringe would adapt to it and, like any other event, bring comedy into our perspective of it, although sometimes in questionable taste. But may the gods preserve us from attempts to remove questionable taste from comedy. Comedy gives perspective and balance to a world that may otherwise perish from high seriousness.

But now I know that, had the accident occurred two or three weeks earlier, that would have been the end of the Fringe. And with it the end of the livelihoods of the small businesses in Edinburgh who rely on a good August. And the recuperation of the hundreds of thousands to whom the Fringe is an annual holiday. And the artists, depending on box offices or buckets to shield them from major financial losses.

And today, the much larger Free Fringe is vulnerable to just such an event. Yes, death happens. Yes, accidental death happens. Yes, there are conspiracy theories surrounding that particular one, and others. But what did all the enforced public mourning avail us? If some event causes massive public grief, is there not a greater need for comedy, not a lesser need?

I dread a similar event happening during the Fringe now. Obviously one wouldn't wish any similar events at all, but when they happen, should not life go on as much as it can?

That was going to be the end of the chapter. But another small thing happened during the 1997 Fringe, and it seeded something quite important to the Free Fringe in later years.

I was canvassed. Earl Okin, a musical comedian of whom you may have heard (he toured as Paul McCartney's support once, which is not a bad gig) approached me. Oh, not to praise my act (20 years later, he posted on social media that my act was 'dire' that year; well, it might have been. Apart from using guitars, our acts had and have nothing in common. But I'm glad I didn't know he thought that, at the time.) No, he wanted me (and others) to join the Festival Fringe Society Ltd, which I think cost £10, and vote for him as a member of the Fringe Board.

What's your platform? I asked. And he was surprised, because nobody else had asked that. His main point was that there were no performers on the Fringe Board of Directors, at all. And there had not been, in living memory.

That whole situation intrigued me. I wanted to know more. So I paid my £10, or whatever it was, and went to the Annual General Meeting. And discovered a few things that shocked me. Is 'shocked' the right word? Or 'mildly surprised'? I concluded that Earl was right; things did not seem to be as they should be.

Performers, as we've seen, pay for the Fringe. It's financed by the losses people make to do their shows. Ought they (we) not to be represented in the management of the Fringe?

Did performers care? It seemed not. The AGM was very sparsely attended. In the open discussion, some points were raised, mostly by long-term Fringe attenders. It may have been that Earl and I were the only performers there (one could vote by post for the Board, so attendance wasn't necessary, and the meeting was held at 11am on a Saturday; hardly performer-friendly time. The AGM was pretty stultifying.

If you were throwing thousands of pounds of your money into a festival, wouldn't you want a say in how that festival is run? I would. But obviously that was just me.

Earl got elected. I forget how many votes he got, but it was fewer than 30. A Fringe teeming with many thousand performers, and fewer than 30 could be bothered to vote. And nobody saw anything unusual in that.

I wasn't brought up Socialist; quite the opposite. I acquired some aspects of it in my later years; one doesn't cross picket lines, and one joins the Union appropriate to whatever job one's doing. Was there a Union for Fringe performers? No. Nor was there any solidarity among them. And I found that quite odd.

I stored those thoughts away, and got on with the job. It wasn't the first unexciting AGM I'd been to, at the Fringe or elsewhere, nor would it be the last. But we'll return to this theme.

*

1998

I HAD SECURED THE FOOTLIGHTS AND FIRKIN. We'd brought them the customers they needed, and their takings were very satisfactory (I never found out how much; one doesn't). For once, I didn't have to worry about a venue for what was obviously going to be Peter Buckley Hill And Some Comedians III. The formula worked and I knew I was safe to go to a 90-minute -plus show, effectively an open-ended show, with four guest spots and an interval. The interval is crucial, as I discovered, if you go beyond an hour. It massively increases bar sales and allows for what are euphemistically called comfort breaks, which would otherwise mean people getting up during the show itself.

Simple stuff, but important. Details make a great deal of difference.

I still didn't feel like doing a one-man show at the Footlights. Same reasons as 1997; my one-man show's a lot quieter than compering four guest standups, and I would like something that's a room on all four sides, not with a curtain on two of the four sides, as the Footlights had. But I knew people by then, and found a comfortable berth at W J Christie's on West Port, which had several shows going and a nice simple room in the basement. I had to pay, of course. Same principle as 1997.

There were nice people at W J Christie's. It felt a bit like a com munity in the way that most venues don't. Basically, the more you pay, the less of a community feeling you get at your venue.

What I did feel like doing, however, was using my improved position at the Footlights and Firkin to bring some other shows on board what I could now regard and advertise as the Free Fringe. I'd shown the concept works. I had friends on the circuit, or at least people who would pretend to friendship when they saw advantage in it. It shouldn't have been too difficult to put other shows on.

But it was.

There were two problems; one persists to this day, and that's sport.

Sport and the Fringe are natural enemies. When there are major sporting events, venues want to show them. And around 1997 the world was awakening to bigger and bigger television screens, and you could find one in almost every pub. Not the world I had grown up in, but in that world football was Match of the Day, highlights only, Saturday night only, watched at home (watch with Mother?) only. And not in August, of course. August was cricket, and they don't have that in Scotland. (Yes, I know. Allow me some rhetoric.)

Sport, by that year, could happen at any time, and there were people prepared to watch it. And the Footlights, like any other pub, would show it if they thought it more profitable to do so.

But you can't run a Fringe show and publicise it and have people turn up, only to be pre-empted by sport. And it doesn't necessarily come at neat times that you can schedule shows not to clash with. My own show was safe; it brought in enough numbers to justify itself. Shows earlier in the day would be vulnerable. This problem persists, in some of our venues, to this day.

The second problem was simply that nobody was interested in doing things the Free Fringe way.

Now, I thought I had shown, over the previous two years, that it worked. But I had underestimated the conservatism of comedians. On the whole, they resist innovation and cling to their security blankets. Perhaps because you don't become a comedian if you're completely sane.

In any event, I talked to a number of people about doing a free show, for no charge, alongside mine at the Footlights, but got no takers.

I wasn't, at the time, aiming for world domination. But I was a little disappointed. For I could see the vision. This sounds far too messianic. In those days, commercial firms didn't have mission statements, or they were just acquiring them. The Vision Statement, which sits on top of the Mission Statement and is meant to encompass lofty goals in a single sentence, hadn't been invented yet.

It's all bollocks, of course. If a Company doesn't have a vision to start off with, you'll get nowhere by grafting a vision on, after you've been trading for 20 or 50 years.

The Free Fringe, however, has one. Or rather, I had one. A Fringe in which no performer lost £10,000, or £5,000, or any unaffordable sum of money. And we could do that by replacing the middlemen into whose pockets that money s0eemed to be disappearing.

Now, whether it stayed in their pockets, I don't know. Perhaps their overheads swallowed it all up. Very probably. For, mostly, they were renting space from the University, and rigging every space with rented seating, raked with scaffolding, hiring PA and lights, together with control consoles for both which needed an operator (the performers would pay the operator).

However, most of their shows, by 1998, were comedy. Those shows didn't need that amount of rigging. Money was being wasted. And, of course, the ultimate payers of that money were the performers.

By using spaces like ours, this expense could be avoided. And by making all shows free admission, all the infrastructure of ticketing and ticket-checking could be avoided. And by using venues with a relaxed atmosphere such as pubs, the audience would be better disposed to the shows And since they hadn't paid to come in, they wouldn't be sitting with arms folded demanding that the performer should be good enough (whatever that means) to justify their investment.

That was the vision. A whole Fringe like that, or at least the Comedy section. I wasn't thinking beyond Comedy at that stage, although obviously I knew different genres would have different problems.

But the Fringe was in the mess it was in largely for one reason: all pay-to-play venues were rigged, at some expense, to meet the needs of Theatre, and yet were being filled mostly with shows in the genre of Comedy. Most Comedy shows were therefore paying for something they didn't need.

Of course, the Fringe didn't know it was in a mess. It still doesn't.

And it didn't know it was in a mess because nothing was drying up. The pay-to-play venues, if they thought about it at all, must have assumed that there would be a limitless supply of shows, prepared to pay the going rate to perform at the famous Edinburgh Fringe. And, at the time, they were right.

My vision, the Free Fringe vision, involved happy comedians, free from having to finance a massive loss, free from the grind and stress of having to sell tickets, free from the need for four- and five-star reviews to sustain those sales, free from having to give their audiences "safe" material to make sure they liked it. Fluffy bunnies and sunshine all around, really.

Even now, shattered and battered by everything that's gone wrong since, I believe in the vision. But now I know it's a lot more difficult than I thought in 1998.

It was very disappointing when I couldn't convince a single other show, that year, that the idea was good. Not even convince them enough to try the experiment.

Very well; I'd do it alone. (At this point in writing the book, I searched the web for a good quotation to illustrate doing things alone. But all I got were popup adverts for loans. Which aren't even spelled the same. Not a gag; it happened.)

You might have thought the Fringe Office would not have stood in the way. I had, after all, paid them £495 to list both shows in their programme. I decided to emphasise the selling proposition (sorry, a bit more marketing jargon there) by putting Free in the title. Peter Buckley Hill and Some Comedians — Free. Still Bottom of the Bill in a One-Man Show — Free.

Out came the censors' scissors. No, they said. You can't put Free in your titles. I wrote a letter asking why (ask your parents what letters were). An excerpt from the reply:

    "The reason is that we have to maintain a clarity in the way the programme works and that means using each index for its sole purpose. We do allow people to extend a show title

*by adding a company name [example] but we have resisted
adding other words that are effectively providing extra information"*

Make of that what you will. I thought a show title was to
provide information, but hey ho. Did this answer actually
mean anything? Or were they just throwing random words
together to justify their instinctive reaction against what I was
doing?

They don't like change, up at the Fringe Office. They didn't
then and they don't now.

And yet someone connected with that office had noticed us.
I didn't see it at the time. The cover of the Big Fat Fringe Programme that year featured a montage of cartoon figures, and
at the bottom left was a character holding up a sign on a stick,
saying "FREE". Just like I did. Oh, to be sure, the character was-
n't me; it was female and sported a purple Mohican hairstyle.
But it held a sign like I did. Ostensibly to say the Big Fat Fringe
Programme was free to the public, but I like to think somebody had noticed what I was trying to do. Maybe, maybe not. I
didn't notice it myself until years later.

My one-man show started badly. A first-night audience with
whom I could not connect, and many technical things going
wrong. I can't remember exactly what, and this is probably my
own memory saving me from things I would cringe to remember. Nobody likes it when a performance doesn't work. But we
like it even less when The Scotsman's reviewer is in, as I discovered a few days later. Two stars, and the only good thing he
said was that I didn't give up. And because I didn't give up, he
ended the review with words to the effect of: anybody can do
it when things are going right, but he kept on going despite
everything going wrong, so maybe he's a Titan. Aha. I had a
usable quote. "A Titan — *The Scotsman*". Oh, come on, everybody does it. I used that for quite a few years.

It wasn't a completely new one-man show, anyway. It's tra-
ditional to write a new one-man show every year for Edinburgh, and then that becomes one's material for the next season. I wasn't doing that yet. The songs I'd already written de-

served, I thought, a wider audience and there was little point in writing more until the current ones were appreciated. I did write a few more every year, but not a whole showful. I should have; when I started doing that, in later years, things improved.

Meanwhile back at the Footlights, Peter Buckley Hill and Some Comedians III was gaining more strength, and good comedians were contacting me and asking to play a spot. Word had got around. Stuck in their expensive venues with their high ticket prices, they were experiencing typical low Fringe audiences, and for a comedian a low audience is a much bigger problem than for a Theatre show. The laughter doesn't catch when a room is mostly empty. So when they did a guest spot in my show, to a full, usually happy, audience, they had a good time of the sort they weren't having in their native shows. Of course, there were other places, mostly the late-night cabarets, where they could achieve the same.

One place they could no longer achieve it, however, was the Bear Pit.

The Bear Pit had been getting out of hand, admittedly. It was always hard, as I've described before. But the 360-degree balcony allowed people to drop things, both solid and liquid, on to the performer's head as he/she was performing. There never was a compère to try to control the audience; I don't know if even the most experienced compère could have succeeded there anyway. The drinks promotions continued and Newcastle Brown Ale, sold by wandering vendors from handcrates, fuelled the mayhem. In 1996, the police were called most nights.

In 1997 the Fringe Office had decided to tame the Bear Pit by programming music after midnight instead of the (mostly) comedy that had hitherto been the staple diet. Some comedy continued upstairs in the Debating Hall, which in olden days was a more sedate venue. Naturally, the frustrated bears moved upstairs and the Debating Hall became substantially less sedate. "I hope you die soon" one of them called out, to me, devastatingly in a pause I had unwisely left, and it was clear he didn't mean 'die' in the sense comedians usually use it.

But for every bear that migrated upstairs, more than one didn't come at all after the news got round. They wanted blood and weren't going to settle for cocoa. The bars, formerly full to bursting, became empty. What the takings were, I don't know, but they must have been massively down. The building belongs to the Edinburgh University Students' Union and, in those pre-outsourcing days, I assume the catering and bar profits went to them. For 1998, they (or whoever the decision-maker was) clearly thought they could do better, and gave the whole building over to disco. It didn't even appear in the Fringe Programme.

Well, we can see how that happened. But a valuable thing had been lost. The Fringe Club was the only level playing field at the Fringe. Whoever you were (at least, if you were a registered performer) you were equally entitled to a slot at the Fringe Club and you could use it to promote your show. If you won the Bears over, and there was a chance, you might well get some of them, more sober, in the audience for your own show.

When the Fringe Club went, it was not replaced. And it hasn't been, to this day.

It gave the Fringe Office the opportunity to say: we're not in the business of giving people places to play short spots. And they did say that.

What's the result of that? A performer new to the Fringe, quite possibly from abroad and having few or no UK contacts, has nowhere to go to make those contacts. The Fringe Office helps less. Oh yes, it provides information, but that's not half as good as practical help in the shape of a place to play. Although the Bears savaged me at my first two attempts at the Bear Pit, and in many subsequent ones, it was a learning experience that ultimately improved my work. Without the Fringe Club, and without the friends and contacts I made there, I would have done my 1994 show to small audiences, spent the rest of the evening in bed or in drink, and achieved nothing. And I was not alone in that.

Today, you pay nearly £400 per show Fringe Participation Fee. It is worth questioning what you get for that. I think the opportunity to play at the Fringe Club was a valuable part of that fee, and it no longer exists.

It's the same for Fringe Sunday, but they abolished that somewhat later on, in 2009.

And, to a certain extent, the parade. Festival Cavalcade, it was called, and it used to take place on the first Sunday, going down Princes Street from East to West, and then via Lothian Road, Kings Stables Road, Grassmarket, Victoria Street (very steep) and then down the Royal Mile to Holyrood. As I remember. I think it varied. In 1997 and 1998 the Firkin Brewery had a float and I part-walked, part-rode in the parade. I could do nothing much, but shows in other venues, who had highly visual costumes or dance routines, certainly did good business with their leaflets on parade day and may have gained quite big audiences as a result. I still have the t-shirt the Firkin gave me to wear in that parade.

The parade was abolished in 2011. The parade and Fringe Sunday were ways of giving back to the people of Edinburgh. There was an undercurrent of resentment, at "the English" taking over their city in August with sometimes pretentious art. Events like these helped to defuse that resentment.

All of this is gone now. The Fringe Office doesn't see its role as providing things like that. And arguably that has built up a larger barrier between the Fringe and the people of the city that hosts it. And I would argue that this barrier would be catastrophically high, if the Free Fringe had not done a compensating thing by providing a large number of free-admission shows and thus making the Fringe much more accessible to the citizens of Edinburgh itself.

Then again, I would say that, wouldn't I?

That lay in the future. I was, in this chapter, writing about 1998. And the Free Fringe had three shows, in three venues, one not particularly suitable — hardly the critical mass we would achieve ten or more years later. In 1998 there was no particular willingness on the part of other performers to make it four or more shows.

The one-man show improved slightly from the version The Scotsman saw, and Peter Buckley Hill and Some Comedians filled every night. Not too difficult, if you're the only free show in town that isn't selling a religion.

My one-man show even got on An Itinerary. In those days, perhaps even now, some fringegoers in groups would pore over the printed programme as soon as it arrived in June, and work out all the shows they were going to see, where they were going to eat and drink, and the walking times between them. They would then immediately book tickets, and that was their holiday. They would copy this itinerary to all the members of their party, for obvious reasons. It felt surprisingly good to be included, to be one of the perhaps two dozen shows chosen by that particular group out of the many hundreds of shows they could have chosen. Yes, the same could be said of any individual choosing his/her shows, but somehow the piece of paper and the group made it more thrilling.

1998 was a good year for all those reasons. And I thought myself reasonably secure. Even though I was the only show at the Footlights, I had satisfied them with the takings. They had, they said, done better than when they had had several shows, curated by Z, in 1996.

The manager was leaving. But he would pass on the good report to his successor and all should be well for 1999. (I didn't get any feedback from the Fiscal and Firkin show that Randy was running, but it hadn't been in the Fringe Programme anyway.)

And on that note I drove home, this time undisturbed by celebrity deaths, playing the Lovin' Spoonful on cassette most of the way, which I had used as ambient music in my one-man show and which I now associated with good times at the Fringe. All was well and maybe for 1999 I'd be able to persuade a couple more shows to go free, and feel as good at the end of the Fringe as I now did.

I should have known better.

1999

I PUSHED MY LUCK. It probably would have made no difference to the outcome, but still.

The tills were ringing at the Footlights and Firkin. My show was bringing in much more revenue than they otherwise would have had, in the 23 days of the Fringe.

Like many other Fringe obsessives, I was blind to the fact that the Fringe is merely three and a half weeks of the year, and that business continues throughout the year. We're less important than we think we are.

I asked the Area Manager for a contribution to our costs. We were bringing in lots of extra turnover (but how much? I never had the figures) so would it not be fair to share the bounty? Covering, perhaps, the Fringe Participation Fee and the leaflets?

English or Scots, we are polite nations. He hid his outrage well, but it was there. As if I'd asked to sleep with his wife, which I would not have done, to him or anybody, irrespective of me not knowing if he had a wife or not, or whether I might have found her attractive, or she me, which is less likely, but anyway that's not the point. One doesn't do that sort of thing. It's a faux pas. And so, it appears, was asking for what I asked for. I had pushed it too far, and I should not have pushed it at all. Performers had always been at the bottom of the Fringe food chain. He must have felt he was being savaged by a piece of plankton. If plankton have pieces. I'm not sure they do.

But it would probably not have mattered anyway. What I didn't know was that the Firkin chain of pubs was about to be bought by Punch Taverns. Which changed everything about their policy; by 2001 the Firkin brand was no more and most of the pubs themselves were sold on. Comedy clubs in the Firkin chain shut down almost immediately.

So when the area manager contacted me early in 1999 and told me the Footlights and Firkin would not be putting on shows in 1999, I blamed the request for a contribution. But it was much more likely to be the acquisition, although I didn't learn about that until later.

Suddenly my tiny island of free shows was no more. Something needed to be done. Either give up the Fringe, or just do a one-man show, or pay for a new venue, or find another similar to the Footlights and Firkin.

The last of these would be the best, clearly. But I lived in London, and could only visit Edinburgh at limited times.

And, or so I thought at the time, not many Edinburgh pubs fitted the specification. Because if they did, somebody would already have used them to do what I was doing, would they not?

The best option would be a function room, with its own doors. Operating behind a thick curtain at the Footlights hadn't been ideal, after all. I liked it so much that I had been blind to the disadvantages.

Thinking about it, if you were starting a Fringe Festival now, you wouldn't start one in Edinburgh. A magnificent city, well worth a visit in its own right, with a unique character and more history than you could shake a stick at, if you were inclined to shake sticks at history. But the Fringe came about by chance, and was now suffering from it.

The Fringe had, in fact, started in 1947 by six theatre companies who thought they should have been invited to perform at the new Edinburgh Festival, had not been invited and decided to go anyway, performing in whatever space they could find. What space that was, in those blighted and rationed years immediately after the war, the year before I was born, I do not know.

But if you were going to start a Fringe deliberately, you'd do it in a city with a lot of available space, i.e. where most pubs had function rooms. And in a city like that, pay-to-play venues wouldn't have arisen and middlemen wouldn't rent space, rig it and rent it onwards to performers, driving costs and therefore ticket prices up.

And because pay-to-play venues had arisen, and few shows were in spaces like the Footlights, I concluded that there were few available function room and similar spaces in Edinburgh. That was partly right, but things were not as bad as I feared, although I did not discover that until years later.

My task was to find a pub with a decent function room, from 400 miles away. An uphill task, particularly against the early deadline for inclusion in the Fringe Programme, which would have been about mid- April.

Somebody must have helped. I made several trips which I spent mostly walking the streets of Edinburgh seeing what I could see, and finding nothing.

I tried to fit in some performances with every trip to Edinburgh, in those days. Sometimes I could, sometimes I couldn't. Many people have tried organising year-round comedy clubs in Edinburgh; most of them fold within a couple of months. Probably because The Stand is good and well established. In those days, there was also a Jongleurs in Edinburgh.

One of these clubs happened in The Canons' Gait, run by someone we'll call Ben Lomond, which I think is a nice Scottish pseudonym. If this person had been female, I probably would have called her Bonnie Banks. Or not.

Anyway, Ben booked me for his club on the Thursday, and arranged another gig with a different promoter for me on the Friday, at the Tron Tavern. Which was nice. I did all the business I could do that week, and it was cold, and home was calling, so on an open train ticket (affordable in those days, not nowadays) I took a mid-afternoon train home on the Saturday.

The train was very crowded, and broke down in northern England. After the usual period of no information, they announced that we would be towed into York, where the later train to London had been held up so we could squeeze on to it. And, at York station, just as I was squeezing with guitar and luggage, the telephone rang.

"This is Billy. Where are you?"

"York"

"Why aren't you here in Glasgow?"

"Erm.. why should I be in Glasgow?"

"You're playing my club tonight. Ben Lomond arranged it".

Great. I knew nothing of this. I could have done the gig, if only I'd known. How nice of Ben to arrange it. How not-nice of him to forget to tell me. The promoter, Billy, wasn't pleased. As you can imagine, having a me-shaped hole in his programme which he had 10 minutes to fill. And I knew the club by reputation, and it was supposed to be lovely. I never played it from that day to this; I wouldn't dare ask, having accidentally let him down once. And the train journey was awful; I stood most of the way.

It was another ill omen. But I persisted.

These were the days before social media. And email was rare. I have all my emails from 1999 (never throw anything away; it may turn out useful) and I know that I kept W J Christies waiting for a decision on my slot until the last possible moment. I got one email every few days, in those pioneering years. I must have kept Christies hanging on because I had not yet found a replacement venue for Peter Buckley Hill and Some Comedians IV. So the date at which I sealed the deal, and agreed the time, with W J Christies, April 15th, must have been about the date that I found the Three-Quarter Sports Café.

And, as I say, somebody must have helped. I no longer remember who. There's no email trace; nobody used email in those days apart from my contact at Christie's. But whoever you were, thank you a thousand times.

For the Three-Quarter Sports Café answered almost all my needs. It had only recently opened, in a former church. I had even played a spot in it in a previous year, when it was occupied by squatters who put on shows.

And the function room upstairs was perfect. You could get about 140 people in it, including on the balcony. It had speakers built in to the room; we just had to get mics, stands and a mixer to interface them, and they agreed to hire those, plus some lights.

Perfect, of course, except for sport. It was a Sports Bar. Or Sports Café, for it was licensed as a restaurant, not a bar. It was owned by a consortium of former Scotland rugby internationals. And it was made clear to me that sport took precedence.

So they said we couldn't do shows on the Saturdays. Sacred, I presume, to Match of the Day. Now, Saturday is the busiest day of the week. If I was booking for anybody else, I'd be very reluctant to suggest that deal to them. But it was for me, and I didn't mind. I was within a week of not having a venue at all. Of course I didn't mind. Imperfect miracles are still miracles.

The capacity was about double what we had at the Footlights. Which was a worry, of course. Filling anything over 100 at the Fringe is always difficult unless you're already on television. It's the "average audience of six" belief again. In truth, nobody really knows what the average is, but it would surprise me if it's in double figures, even so.

Neverthless, we were at peak game. And the Three-Quarter was a little more central than the Footlights; it was on the junction of Grassmarket and Kings Stables Road. To get to the Footlights from, say, the Fringe Office on High Street, one had to go through Grassmarket and past what's called the Pubic Triangle — three erotic dance bars on West Port, whose locations did indeed form an equilateral triangle. One of them's moved now, but the name has stuck. Not moved far away; it's still a triangle, but the triangle is now icoceles, not equilateral, which makes it somehow less pubic. Anyway, walking past the triangle it felt a little as if one was moving away from the action. And that's a psychological effect that we always have to pay attention to.

My two shows were still, with the same exceptions, the only free shows in town. The one-man show still operated at a modest, though satisfactory, level, which taught me that free admission, by itself, was not enough. And that became an important point for future years.

The other thing that helped with Peter Buckley Hill and Some Comedians was the quality of the guest acts. I was getting messages from London recommending people such as Bruce Griffiths from Australia, whom I was delighted to have on. A glance at the notes for that year shows that people such as Jimmy Carr, Adam Hills, Hal Cruttenden, Lucy Porter, Robin Ince, Marcus Brigstocke and Tony Law all did standard 15-minute spots that year. Ever since the show began, the running order's been set by where else the performers have had to be. Sometimes they make it with seconds to spare, but they make it.

I left one name off the list of performers above. The night Ross Noble played, we were so jammed that I actually could not get to the stage to compère. People sat, stood and squatted anywhere they could. We must have been well over the fire safety limit. Ross did much more than the 15 minutes of the normal slot length at the show, but what would one expect? We over-ran shamelessly, but we could. One of the many magic nights.

Even now it astounds me that they would give us the space for a single show, even one of such quality. But they had their sport, which also brought people in. And there were a couple of conflicts with that. Once we had to start late, for the sake of half a dozen people watching Manchester United, but the staff were adamant that the full audience had to be held back until the final kick of the match.

The other part of their plan was to have music and dancing at 11 or 11.30pm after my show. Which was a good plan. Live bands were booked. But neighbours complained, as if the Edinburgh Fringe came as a complete surprise to the people of Edinburgh. The music plan had to be killed off.

So, one way or another, enough money came into the bar to satisfy the owners, even with a single show, plus the sport.

And I was wise to keep my one-man show at W J Christie's, which was much smaller and more intimate. If I'd have had to do it in a space as big as the Three-Quarter, it wouldn't have worked. Shows seldom do, if they're a small thing in a big space.

My one-man show got its first five-star review that year. The words were not unconditionally positive, but essentially said that some bits were good and other bits were so bad that they were good, and thus the whole show was unmissable.

Well, five stars are five stars. Unmissable it may have been; the majority of fringegoers missed it anyway.

I can't deny it, though; five stars is a good feeling.

It is, however, a wrong good feeling.

Ever since I started to do the Fringe, I had wondered about the emphasis on reviews. An obsession with reviews and their star ratings seemed to be part of almost every performer's make up.

And it was almost expected of you that you would help other performers improve their reviews. It was a commonplace that you'd meet on the street somebody you (often) didn't know too well, and he/she would say "I've got The Scotsman in tonight; come to my show" and you were expected, if you were available, to come in (free) and to laugh as loudly as you could, in the hope of convincing the reviewer. I don't know if that ever added a star to anybody's result. It might have, though; comedy depends on relatively full rooms and a good atmosphere, and when you're up on that stage, even the sight of a friendly face can give you impetus for a better performance. Little things make a big difference.

But why were reviews considered much more important than entertaining the audience in front of you?

I don't know the answer to that, and I've had every number of stars from one to five. Yes, of course it's a good feeling when somebody says you're good, and puts it in print, but if you're so insecure about your own act that you actually need strangers to praise it in print, should you be performing at all?

Of course, the theory was that good reviews sell more tickets. And therefore anybody with a five-star, or even a four-star, would photocopy the review and laboriously staple it to their show leaflets, spending hours on the task. I didn't do that; it seemed a little futile, and anyway I wasn't selling tickets.

The reviews issue became much more important ten years later. Feel free to skip ahead. I haven't written that bit yet, but by the time you see this, I will have. I broke the fourth wall there, didn't I?

And while I'm breaking that wall, I'm worried that so far this is reading like a puff piece. Like some sporting memoir, listing scores made, cups won and reasons not to be modest. Bear with me, though. The custard pie is waiting round the corner for me and the embryonic Free Fringe. And it's been mostly about me so far, because I was the only one doing it. If it had stayed that way, I'd have no justification for writing this.

But what it's really about, what it will eventually become about, is a whole movement. The emancipation of performers from the pay-to-play world, and the ways in which that ideal can go badly wrong. That happened later.

What it's been about so far is: what I learned in the days before the Free Fringe had many other members. Because that learning's going to form the basis of how the Free Fringe grew.

Anything else to say about 1999? Doesn't seem so. I remember it now with happiness, although there were bad moments.

*

2000

In which we buy a piano and get heckled by a biscuit

MUCH DEBATE WHETHER 2000 was the New Millennium or whether it started more correctly in 2001. I had some flu-like condition on New Year's Eve, but felt I couldn't miss the magnificent fireworks at which London would beat the world. So I struggled down to the Thames and stood just east of Parliament, in clear sight of Big Ben, in a crowd but alone, with the then-new-fangled mobile network swamped and unable to get a line to my daughter, who was somewhere elsewhere in the millions.

And London, of course, cocked it up. Every other city had the sense to put its fireworks on high ground so they could be seen. London decided for a River of Fire, running from Tower Bridge to somewhere that wasn't Tower Bridge, and thus completely bloody invisible unless you were right on the bank of the river, or watching on television. The crowd was more than disappointed. I managed to find a walking route down back streets which avoided the human traffic shepherding, and caught the first bus of the Millennium back home.

It was an ill omen, if one believes in omens.

And it taught me one Free Fringe lesson: you're only ever one cockup away from people hating you and calling you useless.

At least the Free Fringe doesn't suffer from Millennium Domes.

And if I had regarded the disappointing New Year, New Century, New Millennium firework display as a bad omen, I would have been wrong. Perhaps because 2001 was after all the correct start year. Or perhaps because omens are rubbish.

The 2000 Free Fringe wasn't smooth, but we made it.

The Fringe Office managed to print the details for my one-man show under Three Quarter Sports Café and the details for Peter Buckley Hill and Some Comedians under W J Christies, which was the wrong way round.

I kicked up a fuss about that. Well, wouldn't you? They print 400,000 copies of the Fringe Programme nowadays, and I imagine they did then, or possibly more, since there weren't many web sites then. It was people's main source of information. If your show details are wrong in there, it does damage.

And I hadn't forgotten that they refused to let me say Free in the show titles, two years before.

Their response was "mistakes happen". Not very satisfying. Performers make the entire Fringe, but were still at the bottom of the food chain. I may have been wrong, but I didn't get the impression they cared much, if at all. But they laid on much better facilities for the Press. They took performers' money, and performers got a 40 word listing in exchange. And if there was a mistake, so what?

Fortunately it didn't seem to affect audiences at the Three-Quarters very badly; having put up correcting notices at both venues, people managed to find it. And they gave us the Saturdays; no more yielding to Match of the Day.

But it did make me think: how important is the Fringe Programme compared to other means of publicity? It was, and is, certainly inconvenient; it goes to press in mid-April. A lot of standup comedians haven't written their show by then, and therefore can't write a good blurb for it. And, of course, things change between April and August; shows drop out, casts change, people have accidents and bereavements. So the programme can never be fully accurate. The question is: how much does the public care about that? In 2000 there were few web listings and the print programme and the daily diary (which doesn't exist now) were the only sources of information apart from the shows' own leaflets. Nowadays there are web listings, but the print deadline has only got earlier.

We were lucky in one way: every four years, the Fringe gets blighted by Olympic Games. Fortunately 2000's games were in Sydney, and so even in a Sports Bar or Café there wasn't much interference. In 1996 I hadn't even noticed the Olympic effect. Future years would prove less accommodating.

So that was all right, or alright, however one spells it. Good bills at PBHASC; same sort of star names as before. I suppose it was getting formulaic. But the audience didn't mind, and I certainly didn't.

I looked at the email archive for 2000; there isn't much. People were still doing things mostly by telephone. But one emailer was a then-unknown Russell Brand, introducing himself and asking for a preview slot. I think it was his first Fringe. I didn't put him on at PBH And Some Comedians; I know, because his name's not on the Roll of Honour. I really really hope that was because of a time clash or some other good reason.

But still, why was nobody else getting the idea that free-admission shows worked?

I decided to accelerate the process.

We could put on an afternoon show of previews at the Three-Quarter. Any show who wanted could come and do 15 minutes and plug themselves.

Seemed like a good idea. The Fringe was full of people wanting to preview their show, or so I thought. All genres. Everybody's desperate for an audience; why not get an audience in for a relaxed afternoon seeing 15-minute slots? All it would take is a little organising. And the venue would like it; they'd probably sell some food as well as drink.

So I bought a piano. I can't play piano, but I expected that a lot of shows might rely on one. Nearly £1000 for a decent electric piano. But on the other hand I'd always sort of wanted one, and maybe if I had one I'd learn to play it, after the Fringe.

I still have it. I still can't play it. I now have a much greater admiration for those who can, having tried.

And with that piano, plus a cassette deck (yes, it was that long ago) we were set up.

Love is a strange thing. I don't think I understand it at all. And parental love is no exception to this. All those years ago, my parents showed no love for me; if they felt any, they didn't express it verbally or by touch. The relationship ended with my father leaving nearly £600,000; all to my sister, nothing to me. He didn't tell me about this, and nor did my sister after his death; I had to get his will from the public records. I suppose that's why I'm such a lousy father myself; I don't quite know how to be one.

I didn't grow up with my daughter. I didn't know for certain I had one until she was seventeen. A long and extraordinarily complicated story, often sad. I want to share the story with somebody, for the sake of my own head. But this isn't the book for it.

Nobody was to blame for the situation. It wouldn't happen nowadays, now we have DNA testing. But DNA testing didn't exist then.

So in 1997 I'd gone looking for somebody who might be my daughter, and found her, and exchanged letters, and eventually met, and she looked like me, which wasn't the case when she was five, the last time I'd seen her.

So I had a teenage daughter. Which was quite an amazing thing. And even more amazingly, we seemed to get on well. She came to visit me at the Fringe in 1998 and 1999, and we had good times.

Especially at the bar at the old Gilded Balloon, where all the comedians used to congregate after work, and I was talking to her in the crush when a young, brash comedian, seeing me conversing with a beautiful young woman, elbowed me aside and started to chat to her. "Why are you talking to that old sod?" And the perfect timing with which she said "actually, he's my father" was a joy to hear.

I was proud of her. Still am, all those years later, and she's due to give birth to my first grandchild in six weeks, as I write this.

There's a point to all this sentiment.

When I told her my plans, back in London, in February, she was enthusiastic. And asked if she could run the show.

Of course I said yes. What better thing for a father to hear than "I want to follow in your footsteps".

I wasn't a very good father. As I proved the following year, which is a story for another chapter. I suppose, if I'd grown up with her, I'd have learned that fatherhood is about saying 'no' sometimes. But I didn't and I wasn't and I'd lost her once, and had found her again when she was grown up, only a year younger than my first-year students. And the genes, the mighty genes, I thought, would win through. I could make things work without the faintest idea of what I was doing; so could she.

And she did, at least for a week. But she was only 20 and had had no stage time to speak of. So her grasp of what to say when introducing acts was limited. Mine would have been, at that age.

Nowadays I tell everybody who asks: don't do the Edinburgh Fringe until you're absolutely ready. But I broke my own rule that year.

The show went on. But there came a point at which she couldn't. I don't think I helped; I must have put her under too much pressure. Should have kept away from the show altogether, left her to own devices, sink or swim. But by always being around to help, I wasn't actually helping. And one day she just left a note and went back to England.

Any decent father would have chased after her, but to what avail? And the show must go on. It's a cliché, but people actually do it, and I did. I asked around, found some people who would cover her slot in part, even though it wasn't quite the show that was intended, and people still dropped in.

My own father frequently said "blood is thicker than water". That was before he disinherited me without telling me, of course. And in this case, blood won out. With a little help from text messaging. I was angry, of course, but wrongly so. The fault was mine, not hers. Yes, if any other performer had deserted his/her post, I would have been furious. But she wasn't any other performer. She was my own flesh and blood, placed in an impossible situation at an incredibly early age, with no experience to fall back on.

We sorted it out. She's been to most Fringes since.

And the shows went on. PBHASC successfully as before. And the idea of extra shows was proven; all we needed was more experienced acts to catch on.

The performers whom I roped in to do a show subs tituting for my daughter's show, at least, would surely understand the Free Fringe idea now? Or so I thought.

One act who did not feel comfortable was Earl Okin. He resigned from the Fringe Board, citing inability to work with the others, who, he said, were forcing him into stating public agreement with positions he did not actually agree with. Cabinet Responsibility, they called it, or so he said.

There were certainly public disagreements at that year's AGM. And perhaps Earl, being an entertainer, did not have the business skills required. Or perhaps he was made to feel that. I don't know; I wasn't at the Board meetings. But I felt there was clearly an Establishment, doing things in an Establishment way, and that Earl was seen as a boat-rocker. I've always approved of boat-rockers. Earl had not been to London Business School. But I had. So maybe I should put myself forward?

LBS imbues you with a certain confidence in your ability to do things in business contexts. In 1998 I was talking, informally, to a then Board member, complaining about something or other I felt the Fringe could do better. He responded "do you really think you know better than the Fringe management?" I was taken aback by the question. "Of course" I said. And meant it. It never occurred to me that others might not share my perception. Nor that they should not take every opportunity to improve their own organisation, by listening to the people who paid for it.

There was a boat to be rocked. Next year, perhaps. But it was to take much longer than that.

This was the year I was heckled by a biscuit. When compèreing I had taken to offering biscuits to the audience; sometimes passing them round, but when there was a big crowd, throwing them for the audience to catch. Oh, individually, not the whole packet. And one night, I tossed the biscuits as usual, and immediately one landed back on the stage. Not unexpected.

But I picked it up. I knew what types of biscuit I had tossed out, and this was none of them. A Jammy Dodger. Someone had taken the trouble to buy special heckle-biscuits. This showed more wit than most heckles.

And with that thought I packed up the show, cramming PA, guitars, printwork and a host of other stuff into a groaning Fiat Uno, and home to rest.

*

2001

In which we know not how we offended the rugby-ers

RELATIONS WITH THE THREE-QUARTER had cooled. I'm not sure why. I had genuinely thought the place was called the Three-Quarter Sports Bar. But when I put that on the posters, all manner of grief ensued, even though they had said nothing in 1999 and 2000.

It should have been the Three-Quarter Sports Café.

What difference did it make? Well, it appears they were running what was effectively a pub on a restaurant licence. And the word Bar was drawing attention to that fact.

If only they'd said that in 1999. But they didn't.

Anyway, they now only wanted the evening show, my show, and sport in the afternoons. We are a sports bar, they said. Don't you mean café, I said? Wrong thing to say.

But I still had my own show. And it usually packed, so I had some leverage. So that was the agreement. I did in fact have a couple of enquiries about doing shows alongside mine, but the café, or bar, didn't want that.

But I persuaded them to let me do my one-man show there also, that year called One Man and his Frog, in the early evening. As long as I did it Monday to Friday only, and was prepared to be flexible if they discovered some other sport. The show had its own theme song, but was otherwise unremarkable. I'd paid the previous venues for my one-man shows, but now at least I had two shows without a venue charge.

The season started in the worst possible way.

My usual route to Edinburgh was the West Coast one; M1, M6 and then the various ways one can get to Edinburgh from Carlisle; the A7 or the A74, or others. I grew up partly on the left-hand side of England, so it felt more familiar than the wastes of Yorkshire that the A1 would have taken me through. Anyway, I spent five years at school in Yorkshire and hadn't taken to it. Some biographical listings have described me as "educated at Leeds Grammar School" but I don't think I was. I attended; that was all.

But the main point to the West Coast drive was that, half-way, I could slip into Warrington and say hello to my aunt, the only decent member of that generation of my family, and have a cup of tea. Not in an attempt to save the motorway prices, you understand. My aunt was a good people. She didn't judge. She acknowledged my daughter, which my parents didn't.

So, as I had done for many years, I motored into Warrington (unannounced; we were family; that's what we did) and rang the bell. No answer. Odd, I thought; she could be out, but she's over 90 so probably isn't.

So I went the secret way to the back door. And through the back window, there she was, sitting upright on the sofa.

I knocked on the window. No response.

I may have mentioned my own stupidity several times in this memoir. But never was it more apparent than then.

I went back to the front and rang the bell again. Why would I have done that? And a neighbour asked if everything was all right. I don't know, I said. Did I want to borrow his ladder and get in through an upstairs window? No, I said. Was I sure? I wasn't, but still no. She had an intruder alarm. The code was her birthday. I knew that; what I couldn't remember was the date.

I went round the back again, and only then did the obvious hit me.

Her eyes were open.

I telephoned my cousin's widow, whom I knew to have a key. She came, from the Wirral, in about three-quarters of an hour. We entered together.

Yes, dead.

Seated on the sofa as if alive, but dead.

My back-brain had been processing this during the wait for the key. I knew, at least, what the first step had to be. Call the police. So I did, and they came round, and did police-like things.

Actually, they (he) was very good. He told me that if I'd taken the neighbour's suggestion and got in through a window, they'd have had to investigate at great length; it would have made the death suspicious. Well, at least I made one right decision. I couldn't reach her surviving son, my cousin; the police volunteered the help of their network to get the news to him.

Meanwhile, cousin's-widow and I sat next to her, on the sofa, drinking tea, as if she were alive, except if she had been, she'd never have let us make the tea. You sit there, I'll do it, she would have said, and been affronted by offers of help.

And undertakers came, because they had to, and they asked us not to watch what they had to do, and I wanted to, because she was a great person and I thought I owed her that much, even though she'd never know it, but the undertakers shut the door in my face. I should have been angry; I suppose I still am. And away in a body bag she went.

And then cousin came and it was his responsibility as the closest relative, and vicars were called about funerals, and we were rather rudely told to do it through the undertakers, and then called back ten minutes later and asked if we wanted a pastoral visit. I said no, fairly firmly.

And after all that, which took some time, I proceeded to Edinburgh. What else could I do? Onward, onward, ever onward, and there was nothing I could do to make her any less dead.

I had, of course, contacted my sister. We were not close and still aren't. But I had a landline number for her (this was still before the days of universal mobiles) and called it, and got her husband. You realise, he said, that she and I aren't together any more? That's not my business, I said, but would you please get her to contact me on my mobile as soon as you can?

And he did. Her call came through when I was about fifteen miles north of Warrington, back on the M6. I told her the news. She was devastated. A reasonable reaction.

But then she told me why she and her husband were no longer together.

"My daughter found him wearing my clothes. He'd decided he was a transsexual".

Now, elder-brother arrogance is a thing. And it was with that thing I answered:

"Surely you mean transvestite?"

And with younger-sister determination I got my answer:

"I know what I mean. I was married to it."

There's no comeback from that. Yes, she meant transsexual. Yes, he intended to have the operations. Yes, in the meantime he was living as a woman.

But still, it seemed, under their joint roof. I never got to the bottom of that. Wasn't my business.

I felt, nevertheless, strangely vindicated. As an undergraduate I would go to my parents' house for the vacation and have nothing to do and nobody I knew (they'd moved, again). And I brought my London ideals with me, which were not the ideals of rural, money-counting Cheshire. He, Nick, was dating my sister, in his sports car. Why, said my parents to me, can't you be more like Nick? (That's another pseudonym, by the way.)

And that was their constant refrain, until all those years later he became Nicole. When I next saw my parents, they refused to discuss it, only saying "he left her in the most disgusting way possible".

So I wrote him a letter of support. He (she) had come a long way to find himself (herself). I still don't understand how, if you're a woman trapped in a man's body, you don't discover that until you're over 50. But there's a lot I don't understand, and if you don't understand, just accept.

That, of course, didn't happen in the car, pulled illegally over on the hard shoulder, that day. But the tragicomedy of it was welcome after the trauma of finding my aunt. The first time I'd seen death that close, also.

I'm glad I found her and not some anonymous health visitor. She (as I learned) was due such a visit, but had cancelled because she was expecting someone. At her funeral, there was much speculation as to who that someone could have been. I hadn't said I was coming. But I think it must have been me; she knew the Fringe dates, she knew my habits. She was old; she wasn't stupid. She'll have worked it out.

I'm getting sentimental as I write this. Sleep well, Florence Newall née Buckley. Although death isn't a sleep and it's stupid to think it is.

Anyway, I was back on the road. I'd telephoned the landlord of the flat I was renting in Edinburgh; I'd used it before, so I knew him. He would leave the keys behind the bar of a nearby pub which closed at 1am. And if that failed he'd be at work at 5am, baking (which, although I needn't say it, is what he did).

So, right foot down and hasten to Edinburgh, defying speed limits in so far as one can in a Fiat Uno, which is actually not very much.

And I made it with five minutes to spare, and got the keys. And in a state of physical and mental exhaustion, I got to my flat.

My car, of course, was full of stuff. And I couldn't leave it on view parked in the street, inviting break-in. It would take a few trips up and down the stairs, but I had to store it inside. The last thing you need to do when you're exhausted, but there's no choice.

Up went the first load. Back downstairs for the second load. Door shuts with a determined clunk. Where are my keys? The wrong side of the door.

It had not been a good day.

I slept, fitfully, partly in the driving seat of my car and partly in the hallway of the tenement on an abandoned sofa, cursing my stupidity, although I probably chose to call it my luck. But it was stupidity, really.

And I was at the bakery at 5am. But my landlord didn't turn up until well after half past five.

And I shouted at him: what sort of time is this to get to work? You're bloody late.

No, I didn't. That would have been very stupid. But in my mind, I did.

The funeral was on the first Wednesday of the Fringe. I cancelled my one-man show by a notice on the door, and got a

guest compère in to run Peter Buckley Hill and Some Comedians. Oddly, my daughter was on a course at the same time,
based in a hotel between Warrington and Runcorn, so she
could come. And meet her grandparents for the first time.
Who didn't want to know her.

Why?

To this day I don't know.

My aunt had been fine with her. As why should anybody not
be?

Anyway, funeral-type things were done (and I discovered
you don't have to wear a suit or black tie; whom you mourn
and how you mourn them is nobody else's business). And I
made it back to Edinburgh just as my show was finishing under
its guest compère, and people from the balcony called out a
welcome, which was nice after all that. And then I had beer. I
felt I deserved it.

My daughter came up to Edinburgh later that year and
stayed for a few days. The nice man who headed the security
at The Pleasance knew she was coming, and said to me that, if
there was a show she wanted to see, he'd get her in, no matter
how sold out it might be. That was good of him. Even in those
days, the Free Fringe had spread a thin mist of niceness.

So I put it to her. Was there anything she particularly
wanted to see? Yes, she said: Howard Marks. A hero to her
schoolmates when she had been at school. Fine, I said, and arranged it. I met her in the bar afterwards (I had been doing my
show) and asked her how the show had been.

OK, she said, but I didn't get to ask my question at the Q&A.

Well, I said, there he is in the courtyard; do you want to ask
him now?

A jaw that contained 50% of my DNA dropped. "Do you
know him?"

No, I said, but I do know the people he's with in the courtyard, so we can go and join them. And we did. And she asked
him her question. And then he handed her a remnant, and
said: finish this, you two.

So, in a remarkable father/daughter moment, we finished Howard Marks' spliff together.

I haven't smoked dope since that day. Nothing could top that.

But there's a punchline. As I told her, I didn't know Howard Marks. And I didn't see him again for another ten years, when I found myself backstage at a festival where he was giving readings, and I was also performing. And he somehow recognises me, and unprompted says: how's your daughter?

All the social interactions he'd had between those two meetings, and yet he remembers a detail like that. Remarkable. And they say dope destroys the memory.

*

Everything I've written for 2001 has been about me and my family. What, you may ask, about the shows? What about the Free Fringe?

The shows were fine. We'd reached a plateau. In what may well have been the ideal venue, for the times. And yet the owners were getting colder and colder towards me. Nothing was said, but the atmosphere was there.

And when the entire Lockerbie Trials court team turned up, swamped the room and talked loudly all the way through the show, the staff didn't help, which in earlier years they would have. The lawyers were celebrating the end of something; I don't know what, since the verdicts were delivered in January 2001. But something had finished in August, and the celebration killed the show. I had thought lawyers were well-mannered, before that.

Nothing had changed. And yet something had. Hard to know what.

I knew I couldn't count on the venue for 2002. And, indeed, they let me know that soon after. They closed down, and the building remained unoccupied. It may have had something to do with the licence, or they may have gone back to rugby, their first love.

We were homeless again. Three years in venue 1; three years in venue 2. A pattern was emerging.

It was to get worse in due time.

Homeless or not, though, at least one good-quality free show had become a Fringe institution. And with audiences that people who lost thousands of pounds on their shows would kill for.

One of my last memories was being spotted on the steps of my venue, pretty much at the end of the Fringe, by (presumably) somebody who'd seen the show in a previous year. This person said: I've been looking for you all Fringe. Well, I said, I'm in the programme. Yes, he said, but I wish you weren't so far from the centre. Dear readers, this was in Grassmarket. I think I learned from that how little people were prepared to move around the city. The old cabarets I played in 1994 and 1995, in Morningside, on Easter Road and even in Leith, were no more. The Fringe was developing a dense core, like a neutron star. And this is happening to this day.

*

A couple of months after the Fringe, there was the sort of coincidence that can shake one's atheism. Nothing really to do with the Fringe, but still.

My uncle had played the football pools all his life. And for some reason, staying there as a young child, he asked me to pick the numbers for that week's matches. I did. And thereafter he always played my numbers. Why he got them from me in preference to his own two sons, I know not.

He had died a few years before my aunt, as is often the case.

He was a decent man.

In adult life, I went through phases of playing the football pools; not scientifically, predicting the outcomes of matches (I know too little of football for that) but using a standing entry of the same numbers, perm any 8 from 11. Never won anything. Until 2001.

Out of the blue came a payment for £630; some of my numbers had come up.

It would be so easy to imagine this as a message from my dead uncle, saying "thanks for looking after my wife when she died". Only he, she and I would have known about my picking his pools numbers, over 40 years before.

No, I don't believe it. There is no life after death, except in the minds of those who knew the deceased. But you can see how easily one could interpret something like this as a sign of the opposite.

I hadn't really taken care, anyway. Just been the first to find her. Life went on. I spent the £630.

*

2002

In which our tent gets re-pitched in a spiffy new pitch

BACK, ONCE AGAIN, TO SQUARE ONE. A venue needed to be found.

It ought to have been easy. But it wasn't. Even with the help of the friends I now had in Edinburgh. There really seemed nowhere that wasn't in the grip of the pay-to-play venues and had a suitable space.

Would the Three-Quarter not have us back? No; closing down, selling up. Would they recommend us to whoever took over? They didn't know who was taking over; they were gone; nothing to do with them any more. And indeed the venue was shuttered during the 2002 Fringe.

I came to Edinburgh; I paced the streets looking for pubs with function space. Oh, it was there, as I found out later that decade, but I couldn't find it.

On the third trip, I did. And I already knew about it, for I had played Ben Lomond's short-lived comedy club there in early 1999. And yet I must have forgotten on the first and second trips. I no longer remember who reminded me, but somebody did. And it became the most important one of all.

Down the Royal Mile, as the foot-traffic peters out and one feels as if one's walking into mist, even if there's no mist, lies the Canons' Gait.

And below the Canons' Gait lies the almost perfect function room. Holding about 75, more with cramming (as I later discovered). Steps down at the entrance to the pub. Above anything, the room had character.

Now, character's not essential to a room, particularly at the Fringe where shows go on anywhere. But it helps a lot. I couldn't define exactly what character is, but I know it when I see it. A little like love, in that respect. But more permanent.

I spoke to the manager. She wasn't averse to the idea. Could she find a PA? She could. Enough chairs? No problem.

Did they want any more shows? No, let's just try it with these two. I wasn't going to push it. I couldn't see another venue being available; let's nail this one.

And she uttered a sentence I never expected to hear:

"How much would we have to pay you to have this?"

In a city where every performer had to pay for his/her space, it felt that the world had turned upside down. Clearly not everybody in Edinburgh was out to get as much money as they could from performers. (Oh, Edinburgh, forgive me. I know that now. So many people have supported us, now. But at the time it seemed otherwise. In fact, most of the people who were charging performers so much were based in England, not Scotland. But not all).

Oh, how easy it would have been to have named a sum of money and pocketed it.

And I remembered I had asked for money from the Footlights and Firkin, and been rebuffed.

Money, after all, is money. And accommodation in Edinburgh is quite expensive.

So I almost surprised myself by saying no, a payment wasn't necessary. I think I left a door open for a future year, but for 2002 no money was necessary.

And for once I'd made the right decision. Because what happened later would have been quite different.

We shook hands on the deal. I registered the venue with the Fringe Office. I registered my shows for the programme.

And at last I wrote a proper one-man show. All my previous shows had been me doing my songs and standup, with occasional silly props. I wrote a few new songs every year, but the format didn't change much. In time for Fringe 2002, I wrote "My Old Man's a Dustman — A Deconstruction". Fifty minutes taking all sorts of angles on the eponymous song.

This was a proper Fringe show. Something different to my standup act; something different to my musical act. Even using an overhead projector, for people who remember what one of those is. And a campaign of silly email questions. I was very proud of that show. I still am. It may be the best one I've ever done, although others have had better reviews. It took me from December to June to write, in fits and starts, chopping out the pathos after a disastrous preview in Camden, flitting from Delta Blues to biblical times, through Chaucer, Shakespeare, feminism, the Read Army Choir and ending on the Last night of the Dustman Proms.

I loved that show. I still write occasional new bits for it, even though it will never be performed again. As one always is with a purpose- written show, I was excited and apprehensive in equal measure.

And I proceeded in that excitement and apprehension. Up until three days before I was due to start. I had driven, car full of stuff, up the East Coast this time (no aunt to give me tea on the West Coast route) and had reached the bottom of the Royal Mile itself, when my mobile rang. I pulled in and answered.

It was the manager of the Canons' Gait. The new one.

She had noticed, or somebody had pointed out to her, the shows listed in the Fringe Programme. She knew nothing about this. Nothing was in the pub's diary. Would I kindly explain?

Gulp.

I was five minutes away, and I may yet have to turn back and drive 400 miles in the other direction.

Five minutes, I said, or ten. I'm close. Can I please come and talk face to face? So much easier than telephones. (I've always hated them, but for most of my life there was no alternative; thank all the gods for email.)

Now, she was perfectly reasonable when I actually met her. Yes, we could make it happen. Could we put the stage by the door? Oh please don't; it's better at the other end. This nearly became a sticking point, but I prevailed by promising to do all the hauling myself. I was right to insist; a stage right next to the door is to be avoided wherever possible.

She even knew a PA we could borrow, but no mics or leads.

Fine, no problem; I went out and bought.

The venue was rigged. We got it together. But for those ten minutes the earth had opened and I had looked over the edge of a flaming pit of custard.

The Friday before we started, the day before we started, I wanted to see my friend Gordon Brunton's first one-man show, which was on at a pay-to-play venue. It clashed with mine, so that Friday was my only chance, and I wanted to see it because the show's name ("Brunton Disorderly") was my suggestion.

Then Gordon contacted me. I couldn't come after all, he said, because his first performance was completely sold out. Congratulations, I said, knowing how rare an achievement that was, to sell out your first performance of your first OMS or OPS, as I should more correctly say. Ah well, he said, come along anyway and I'll talk to the door people and see if we can't sneak you in. He was so proud of this sell-out, which boded so well for the rest of the run.

I turned up. There was an audience of six, and four of them were at the wrong show. The sell-out was a glitch in the box office computer system.

I felt for him. If it had been a deliberate hoax, it would have been a very cruel one. But of course it wasn't; it was just a major system error. But just as devastating.

I took away from that incident one comforting thought: that the big pay-to-play venues, for all that they painted themselves as professionals and captains of competence, were just as likely to get things wrong as we were. And yet people paid them. That gave me hope for the Free Fringe, even though it was back to only being my two shows.

And my two shows started on the Saturday as scheduled. The people came. The seventh year of the compilation show, so enough knew what to expect and came and found us. There were wild times, and at weekends people standing outside the open doors who could hardly hear the show and yet wanted to be there. A venue just over half the size of the previous one, so I suppose we retained over half of our old audience.

Not too many people came to see the one-man show, but those who did mostly approved. Apart from anybody not brought up in the UK or Australia, who had never heard of the song, and especially the Americans, who don't know what a dustman is. And actually, you lose a lot of the references if you don't know all four verses of the song, which you probably don't if you were under ten years old in 1960. But artistically the show worked. I was more than a comic songwriter, more than a standup. I was a Nartist. At least in the egostorm that is sometimes my head.

A reasonably triumphant year. The tills rang joyously. We were at home in our new home, and it felt like a home. At the end of the run, I discussed improvements: make jugs of beer available to increase the turnover and other collaborative suggestions.

Who could doubt that we would be back in 2003?

And with more shows? No problems with sport here, no conflict of interest.

I felt comfortable. And that's always dangerous.

*

2003

In which our tent is uprooted to no good purpose

NOBODY HAD TRIED TO STOP the Free Fringe for a while, except by closing or changing our venue. So I wasn't expecting the next move.

An Edinburgh-based 'promoter' leapt in. After yet another change of management at the Canons' Gait, he promised them more shows, better shows and shows with an admission charge, so they would be part of the 'proper' Fringe.

And, of course, new manager, didn't know me, didn't get back to me or give me a chance to speak. I don't actually think he had my contact details, even. Just as we nearly lost the venue on the last change of manager, so we actually did at this change of manager.

I should have kept in better contact with them. All seemed well. I shouldn't have trusted that.

And when I found out, the deal had been done.

Annoying, because there could have been more shows in 2002, if the original manager had not said 'only your own two'. And there certainly could have been in 2003. As for better quality, that's subjective, but we hadn't done badly so far.

Being part of the 'proper' Fringe? That's what made me grit my teeth and anything else I could grit. We were part of the proper Fringe. We paid to be in the Fringe Programme, with the same rights as everybody else. The venue got an official Fringe venue number. The only difference was the admission price.

It was all playing on people's assumptions that free must mean inferior. Throughout the history of the Free Fringe, we've battled that. And now, in 2018, we've won that battle.

But in 2003, it was being used nastily against us.

It was always fundamental to the Free Fringe that our shows should be as good as the programmes of pay-to-play promoters. Otherwise, we'd just be creating a layer below the

Fringe. It was to turn out that we'd have to fight this battle again, later in the decade.

But back in 2003, I took the news badly.

I'd had to do a lot of work in 2002 to find this good venue. It seemed to me — wrongly — that there were no others. I had certainly been depressed with the search, before I found the Canons' Gait. A second search was unlikely to turn up anything I hadn't already seen.

The Free Fringe was dead.

Everything had been in vain.

Except, I suppose, that we'd entertained lots of people, I'd made many friends, or at least acquaintances, famous and ob-scure, and I had at least proved the concept. It wasn't entirely in vain. It just felt as if it was.

Obviously venues were the biggest barrier to making it hap-pen.

If I could have seen into the future as far as August 2003, I would have been a lot angrier. Because none of the promised shows at the Canons' Gait actually took place.

We had been blind-sided and the blind-sider had not even delivered.

Meanwhile, there I was with a dead Free Fringe. Clearly I wasn't coming to Edinburgh for Fringe 2003.

What do you do when things collapse like that? Something else entirely. Something that might get you a bit of self-esteem back, in the long run. Something to give you something else to think about, preferably a lot to think about, to stop you brood-ing.

Right, I said, I'll finish my doctorate.

It had been rather on the back burner for a while, and now was obviously the time to get writing and crunching data like a demented obsessive. And then, with a following wind, I'd at least have a title and a silly hat to plaster over the death of the Free Fringe.

And it was so. I wrote like a Dervish, except that I don't know that Dervishes write any more frantically than anybody else, really. In fact, I know nothing about Dervishes. So, I suppose I wrote like a Dervish trying to finish a doctorate in a hurry.

Until the telephone rang, in June.

And on the other end was the former manager of the Canons' Gait, who had been in office during our 2002 shows.

Would I like a venue for 2003?

If she'd have called in March, I'd have been able to have a show in the Fringe Programme, and I'd have been at the 2003 Fringe, and would be undoctored to this day.

But in June?

Well, let's see. My then partner, Mel, who deserves a lot more credit than I have put into this book so far, and who accompanied me on several venue expeditions before, said I should go and see. I'm glad she did, because that's what I wanted her to say. She and I had been venue-hunting in snow and cold, defrosting ourselves on takeaway soup before driving 400 miles south, more than once.

It was summer; no need for the soup. So we drove, from her home in Northamptonshire, up the A1 and back in the same day. Normally she'd do most of the driving, because she enjoyed it more. That day I drove all the journey, both ways, and I don't know why. Some sort of penance or guilt, I imagine.

We got there, and we saw. The former Canons' Gait manager was now managing the social club for the Union of Communications Workers. Which in practice meant mostly postmen and women. And they had a big building, in Brunswick Street.

We looked at the proposed room. It was certainly big enough. Inbuilt bar at the back, high ceiling, some seating in horseshoe bays (which means some audience with its back to the stage) but enough room to put 60 or so chairs out, and a stage on a couple of pallets. A room that could be put to show use.

But Brunswick Street? Physically, easy enough to get to; psychologically, less so. From the Fringe Office one had to cross North Bridge, which by itself gives one a sense of separation. Leave the part of the town where most of the Fringe is, and cross over the railway to where the citizens go about their daily business. And then down the steep hill of Leith Street, past the shopping centres that do not support Edinburgh's reputation as a city of great architecture, past the nightclubs of Picardy Place, down Leith Walk for a bit, and then down a road with no shops.

Not far in distance; less than a mile, but not where you'd expect to find a Fringe venue.

Would it work? Especially for a show that wasn't in the Fringe Programme?

But the lifebelt had been thrown to the drowning man. Clutch on to it and perhaps the Free Fringe wasn't dead after all.

What to do?

Maybe that's why I did the driving. To stop myself sitting in the passenger seat thinking and dithering.

Do I abandon the doctorate and go for another risky show? Do I refuse the venue, thus killing the entire thing? For it would have been difficult to start again from scratch in 2004.

But there was another way. I could send a show to represent us, to blow on the almost-dead flame.

And thus was born the show called Some Comedians Without Peter Buckley Hill.

If we could pull off a show, without being in the Fringe Programme, without me running it (for, in all modesty, after so many years there were people who would follow my show), in an out-of-the-way venue, wouldn't that prove something?

I recruited three good men and true, as I thought, to run it. Basic PBHASC format, with whatever acts they could get. Anything could happen. Who the audience would be, how many there would be, how interested the acts would be and how the members of the UCW club would react: all this was unknown.

Because I was not there, a lot of it remains unknown.

The club's members could have been a problem. Some were accustomed to start drinking as early as 9am (postal workers can work the night shift, so 9am was evening to them) and the Scottish Socialist Party was accustomed to meet in the room where we were doing the shows. But with the exception of one member, it seemed to have been no problem.

The biggest complaint I received from the manager was that a musical act consisting of three very young girls had been allowed to perform, at the insistence of their very determined father. We were taking risks with the club licence as it was; the presence of the under-age made things considerably riskier.

I met the father the next year, and he was indeed hard to say no to. I can understand how it happened.

Had we done enough? Why am I saying 'we'? I wasn't there. Had the team done enough? It would seem so. The club wanted us back.

Now, there were agendas. This large building was under-used and sometimes used by young people on whom the manager was not too keen. Any Fringe activity might change, or raise, the profile. It did not seem to be all about the bar takings.

But whatever the motivation, they wanted us back. With me.

The Free Fringe was lying on the beach, gasping for air. But alive. Like all the cockles and mussels in Dublin's fair city, alive.

*

2004

In which we re-emerge, not drowning but waving

A SOMEWHAT BUSY YEAR.

I was cast in a play, which performed in London, and I could have done a Fringe run with it. But it was too much. At the point when they wanted to vastly increase the number of rehearsals per week, I was on the leadup to submitting my doctoral thesis. It was too much at once. I pulled out of the play and was replaced by somebody more famous and better, for the Edinburgh run. So that was all right, really. I got the thesis in on 29th February, suitably commemorating the leap year, and awaited developments.

Something happened just before I submitted the thesis. One evening in February, let's say 15th because I can't remember the date, I had a fun gig. 60 comedians in 60 minutes again, I think it was. And an email came through that afternoon. Auditions for the University Challenge team in the Union building on 15th March.

Right, I said, I'm there. For despite my advanced age, until (and if) they passed my thesis, I was still eligible. Last chance in my life, ever. I want this. And such is my accumulation of useless knowledge, I fancied my chances. It would be worth making a special trip for the auditions. In my diary it went.

And then a couple of hours later came the second email. It said: we didn't mean 15th March. We meant 15th February. Tonight.

And out of the window went another dream. I'd have got on a train, if I hadn't had a gig. But I did, so I didn't.

This has nothing to do with the Free Fringe. But I'm telling you anyway. I still feel the frustration. And all I can do nowadays is shout answers at the screen, but the contestants never listen.

Anyway, back to the Free Fringe story.

My 2004 return to the Fringe, I hoped a triumphant one but at any rate a return, was boosted by me becoming a playing card.

I'd received a call from an organization, or perhaps it was an email, outlining the plan for a Top Trumps-like card game featuring comedians. Was I interested? I got hold of the wrong end of the stick, as I often do. At least 50% of the time, in fact. Hard to tell one end of a stick from another.

Digressed again, and now my mind is full of sticks. Focus. I told them nice idea, but the Free Fringe has no money to buy in to anything like that. Because obviously it would take money to produce and yet be distributed free. Ah, no, they said: we want you as an individual to be a Comedy Trump.

Well, that was nice. And they gave me scores on my card:

Festival Appearances 10, Awards 1, Snogability 6, Shock Factor 1...

... which meant I could beat Stewart Lee on Shock Factor and the Dutch Elm Conservatoire on Snogability. Not sure that was right, but still.

There are things of which one is strangely, irrationally, proud. And being a Comedy Trump is one of mine. I framed the whole set, years later, and it's on my wall.

Meanwhile, there was a Free Fringe to prepare for. No need to look for another venue. The key was consolidating the one we had, the UCW Club, and for that I needed more shows than mine. The Canons' Gait still rankled. They had said no more than two shows, and then under different management said we weren't providing enough, and dropped us in favour of somebody who promised more and then provided none. That mustn't happen again.

So let's ensure we have a bigger programme of shows.

And that's where I screwed up. Massively.

Oh for a time machine to unmake that mistake. For it is still costing me, and still damaging the Free Fringe.

And it all came about because I was lazy and gullible. Not a good combination. And to a certain extent greedy.

I can make excuses. For lazy, read overworking on the doctorate. For greedy, read tired of making losses. For gullible, read gullible. I had not yet learned to trust nobody.

For I had not yet realised that others saw an opportunity for profit in the Free Fringe, which I saw as a non-profit organisation.

This was my thinking: since the venue was somewhat out of the way, the best sort of show to add to the roster was another show with different acts every night, like Peter Buckley Hill and Some Comedians. People come to see such shows (Variable Bill Shows, or VBS: I may have coined that designation) more than once, as I discovered all those years back at the Footlights and Firkin. That sort of repeat factor might well compensate for the distance of the venue from the main hubs, and indeed from other venues.

So, that was the sort of show we should add. Much more likely to succeed than a one-man show, except if the performer was famous.

The trouble with VBSs is they need organisation. Somebody to book the acts and make sure, as far as possible, that they turn up; somebody to compère the shows themselves and deal from the stage with anything that does go wrong (such as the acts not turning up).

That was a role I performed myself for my own show. Obviously I couldn't perform it for another. So, what had to be recruited was somebody who would prefer to compère and organise, rather than do an hour of their solo material. Just as the three-man team had done when doing Some Comedians Without Peter Buckley Hill in 2003.

So, the 2003 team was the first to be approached. Were they willing? Alas, for one reason or another, they were not.

So the search had to continue elsewhere. I knew plenty of performers by then, but everybody I asked wanted to do one-person shows, ideally closer to the psychological centre.

Among the gigs I was doing in the non-Edinburgh part of the year were the several small clubs in and around London run by Laughing Horse. The two-man team who ran that organisation had seen me at PBHASC in 2000 or 2001, and had offered me paid gigs ever since. I was glad enough to have the gigs, as any comedian would have been, even though these were mostly smaller clubs. At least I was headlining, mostly.

So I had no reason to suspect anything wrong when they volunteered to arrange the sort of show I wanted.

But there were conditions. And that's where alarm bells should have started ringing.

It had, they said, to be worth while in terms of publicity for them. Not for the performers: for Laughing Horse itself.

That's where I should have said no. Where any sensible person would say no. Where it should have been clear that their interests were not the same as mine. Where freeing performers from the problems caused by pay-to-play, the idea that started the Free Fringe, wasn't their objective.

Instead, I thought: well, they're not performers (actually, one of them was). They should get something.

And then, astoundingly, they offered me money.

Another set of alarm bells failed to ring. And they should have. Instead, greed took over, and greed for a trivial sum. I think it was £500.

Why on earth would they do that? That's what I should have thought. Of course, I was used to being paid by them, for gigs; I earned that money fair and square. This, however, was different.

In exchange for their money, they wanted their name on the venue. It wouldn't be the UCW Club for the purposes of the Fringe: it would be Laughing Horse @ The UCW Club.

As I said, I wasn't thinking straight. Let them have it, I thought; it gets me the extra show I want, it puts money in my pocket and how much damage can it do?

I have spent every year since finding out how much damage it could do, and it seems I shall spend even more years knowing that, and regretting it.

The show they put in the Fringe Programme that year wasn't quite the show I remember happening. But although I remember most things clearly, and certainly the problems, I can't be sure about that. And no disrespect to the then-inexperienced act who ended up running it.

My shows were solid. I made a stupid decision (it seems it was the year of stupid decisions) to do two one-man shows, one on even dates, the other on odd. I revived Dustman, and the other was my standard song-based show. I couldn't let Dustman go. An audience-reviewer, in 2002, had called it the best thing he'd seen at the Fringe. That's heady stuff. And it went to my head. One person on the same wavelength as me, but that was enough. I was married to that show. But another, a wonderful dignified old man such as I shall never be, had complained after 2002 that he preferred me doing the Auld Shite. So I wanted to do that as well. (That same excellent man has come over the bridge from Fife to my one-man shows every year since, wherever they were, until 2014, and said the same thing. I hope he's not dead; I fear he might be, and I never knew his name).

Comedians are desperate for praise. No sense of proportion. And that includes me. Why else am I writing this? But praise is simply one person's opinion, not necessarily even sincere. Not something to base decisions on. One learns much more from criticism.

So, my head in 2004 was turned in several wrong directions. And most of all by an organisation (actually, two people) who had convinced me they were in sympathy with what I was doing, and wanted to help. I wanted to believe that. I did believe that. I shouldn't have.

Instead, I felt we were making progress. And I could delegate some of the administration to them, and thus achieve the growth I wanted easily.

In principle, if the Free Fringe was to start achieving what I wanted it to achieve, the emancipation of performers, further expansion was needed, and it couldn't all be Variable Bill Shows.

Time for the dreams of a bigger and stronger base to start coming true.

It was working. People were coming down a dark street, off the Fringe beaten track, and they were seeing the shows. Oh, it wasn't full all the time, by any means. But doing a lot better than the apocryphal Fringe average audience of six people.

Little did I know the fights ahead. All I dreamed of was the expansion. A panoply of free-admission shows, costing the audience nothing and yet allowing the performers to break even.

I'd been nine years in the building. And called mad more times than was strictly comfortable. Now was the time to prove I was sane, or if not that, that my idea was sane.

Now, the UCW club was up for that. As well as the large bar upstairs that we had used, they had a pool room in the basement, and they suggested that the pool room, minus its table of course, could also be a venue.

My eyes lit up. Two stages in the same venue; we would have a hub. People would come to that.

But I was greedy. Nice as the UCW club was, in that position it could only be a peripheral attraction (which is a 1947 Fringe joke).

Which brings us to 2005

*

2005

In which we do a very silly thing

THE SECOND BIG MISTAKE.

I should have thanked the Laughing Horse and sent them on their way. Instead, I was lazy. Could I use them for the cause? I thought I could.

And the way I thought I could use them was to get the Canons' Gait back.

This was my reasoning: if I approached Canons' Gait by myself, they may not trust the approach. They'd been let down in 2003 by an individual. In 2004 they had had no shows at all. It was worth making the best case we could.

And therefore by incorporating an organisation that ran comedy clubs year-round, the proposal might seem more credible. And we'd go for an all-day bill from the outset.

If I couldn't find enough acts, said the LH people, they certainly could.

So, I wrote the letter (it was a real letter, not an email; you don't see many letters nowadays but in late 2004 the world hadn't quite got round to universal emails) and they sent it on their letterhead.

I still have the notes on the letter's content. Before I checked recently, I had forgotten that I did the writing as well as formulating the plan, but it is so.

And the plan worked. We got the Canons' Gait back, for the whole day. Alongside the UCW club, we'd have two venues, and three stages. That was all satisfactory.

I booked my slots for a one-man show and for Peter Buckley Hill and Some Comedians. They intimated they'd want a similar Variable Bill Show before PBHASC, and the one of them who performed wanted a one-man show before mine. OK.

Too excited that the dream was taking a big step forward. Not watching my back, and not ensuring that the dream was keeping true to itself.

And wanting a peaceful life. I hate conflict. The Free Fringe has forced me into more conflict than I ever wanted, and looks like it will do again. I'm a lover not a fighter. No, that's silly. But I will fight, rather than give up what I've worked for.

I should have fought then. I should have started the fight, rather than waiting for others to do so.

I thought I was booking the shows, but they were free to suggest. Instead they did the booking, and presented me with a fait accompli.

The acts they presented me varied in quality. A lot of variable bill shows, which was fine. One act that went on to do very well for herself. One who was an old friend whom I was glad to see. But others less solid, including one who could only get work by running his own club and whose act was generally thought of as hopeless. I would not dream of naming him, for like many others in that situation he was a perfectly decent person. Comedy is cruel.

It was important to the Free Fringe to have good quality shows. Combatting the "free must be rubbish" mentality has taken many years. So every show that falls below a fringe-acceptable standard damages the Free Fringe. And that year, with due respect to their performers as people, there were some.

Now, having said that, I have good news and bad news. The good news is: the below-par shows did not have much negative impact on the Free Fringe brand.

The bad news is: this was because the Free Fringe brand itself had been suppressed.

When I saw the Fringe Programme of 2005, I was shocked. Firstly, both venues been registered as Laughing Horse @ [venue name]. The year before, they had paid me for that publicity. In 2005, they paid nothing and asked no permission; they just did it.

Secondly, my name was nowhere. Theirs was everywhere. Not only in the venue names, but in the performer names as well. In the majority of cases, the performer name was given as "Laughing Horse Comedy".

Only in my own show listings was my name and the brand Free Fringe mentioned.

For everywhere else, I might as well not exist. The work I had done for ten years, building the Free Fringe so it could expand might as well not have happened, as far as a reader of the programme was concerned.

And not everything was free. They were advertising stand-up comedy courses at the former UCW club, on six separate days at £79 per course per participant. And the course members got spots at some of their variable bill shows.

I was annoyed. So much of this was not what I wanted. So much of it was alien to the vision of performers helping each other. I hadn't thought the 2004 situation through; I'd got sidetracked.

I should never have taken their money in 2004, although the gods know I needed it. They obviously thought they'd bought my compliance with everything they did behind my back. They may have thought they'd bought the entire operation.

Grrrrrr.

My temper was not improved the morning after my first show, although once again a valuable lesson was learned. It was a Saturday, and things had been so hectic I hadn't attempted to change the coins in my collection bucket (or was it still a hat then? It was a receptacle of some sort, anyway). I just poured them into my left-hand trouser pocket and walked, rather lopsidedly, to the late bars and thence home.

My intention was to get back to the Canons' Gait for the first show on Sunday. The 12 noon slot was bound to be difficult. In Fringe terms, 12 noon is the crack of dawn. I knew Jasmine of old, when she did a character act, and she made me dinner once. These are ties that bind. So, support was appropriate, as it was for all the team even if most of it was wished on me.

Now the lesson is: don't have a pocket crammed full of coins. Or if you do, don't have anything else in that same pocket. Because whatever it is will swim to the top of the mass of coins and fall out of your pocket, quite possibly in a taxi.

Like, for example, all your credit cards and things of that shape.

Which is tricky.

Because if you're in Edinburgh for three weeks, you can persuade your bank to send you some replacement cards, if you have anything left to prove your identity, which is mostly in the same wallet. And your bank will kindly do that, and send the PINs to your London address, thus rendering the new cards unusable until after the Fringe.

Grrrrr again.

But that was minor compared to the Laughing Horse issues.

A sensible person would have aired the issues at the Fringe.

But I'm not a sensible person. Instead, I tried to make it work.

And reflected. What was at the root of this?

Money. They were a for-profit organisation. I wouldn't have been averse to making a profit on the Fringe either.

But money can come at too great a price.

If I'd have made a profit on my shows, bucket take greater than total expenses, that would be one thing. But making a profit on other people's work? That wasn't the spirit. That was exploitation.

And that would also have been how the pay-to-play venues started.

Suppose we had a sponsor. What would happen then? There'd be a surplus of money. And it would be spent in inappropriate places.

Nobody would be motivated to work for the good of the organisation, unless they were paid. There'd be no altruism in that.

If there was spare money, there'd be display banners, big posters and other unnecessary publicity. We could never spend as much as the pay-to-play venues spend on that sort of stuff, so that money would be wasted.

There'd be extra rigging. The whole point of the Free Fringe was to do it simply. A room a stage, a mic, and away you go. If we started providing extra, such as projectors, people would take that for granted and only want more.

Above all, performers wouldn't feel part of the process. It wouldn't be any sort of collective effort, it would be pay-to-play again.

And finally, suppose we did get a sponsor? These deals don't last for ever. After a certain number of years, maybe three, maybe five, we'd be out on the streets again, and because we'd become dependent on sponsorship money, we'd be flashing our fishnets at anybody prepared to take up the sponsorship bill.

And then they'd own us.

No, the only way to make this work is with as little money as possible.

And making sure the performers knew that, and put in their work instead of their money. What others paid for, we could get free from within the ranks of our performers.

We wouldn't buy PA; we would borrow it. We wouldn't pay minimum-wage stewards; we'd do the stewarding ourselves. We already didn't have tickets, so no need for ticket-checking.

I had thought Laughing Horse understood that. But clearly they didn't.

It was a problem. They'd already undermined.

It was, I thought, a problem for after the Fringe. I had shows to do. Two shows a day is hard enough, without adding conflict and complexity to it.

Indeed, I started the Free Fringe to take stress off. Our way, you didn't have to have the worry of selling tickets and packing them in, nor the worry of making sure they left with the feeling they'd had their money's worth. And that would make the shows better. I didn't want to make my shows worse by doing them under stress.

In later years, I had to do precisely that. But I'll come to that in due time.

Peter Buckley Hill and Some Comedians packed them in, sometimes with crowds holding the doors open at the back. They couldn't have heard very well, but they came.

The one-man show, Stand-Up Tragedy and Other Disasters, went pretty well as soon as I dropped the opening number, which wasn't good. In fact, I was supposed to start that show on the Sunday, but I used the Saturday as a rehearsal. But a medium-sized crowd came (nobody reads the programme accurately) so I told them it was a run-through but they were welcome to stay. And one of them at the end said: don't change anything. So I was encouraged. These small things mean a lot.

And then just when you gear up to addressing the serious organisational issues of the Free Fringe, fate catches you without your trousers. Literally, in this case. In an unfamiliar flat, after heavy sleep and woken by bladder pressure around dawn, it's surprisingly easy to turn left out of the bathroom instead of right and thus find oneself outside the flat rather than back in the bedroom. And thus, separated from clothes, money and telephone, completely dependent on the kindness of strangers.

It's not always like A Streetcar Named Desire, or even the Simpsons' version.

But fortunately, after about an hour, the kind stranger came along. A true Scottish hero, whose office was very close and whose habit was to get in early. Not only did he kindly call a locksmith; he had in his office spare trousers, which he brought to me. Slightly too small, but welcome as a life-jacket to a drowning man, even though covering a different section of the body.

In due course the locksmith arrived, and I promised him half my kingdom, and he did whatever locksmiths do and got me back in the flat, fortunately without having to change the lock. It took me back to 2001 when I was locked out of a different flat after my aunt's death. And, just to show things come in threes, a few years later at the Fringe, my front door key broke in the lock and a third locksmith had to be called.

I never knew the name of the white knight with trousers. I brought them back, obviously, but he wasn't there by then, and I was unable to thank him properly. I should have made a greater effort to thank him. I hope he reads this and accepts my apology for not having thanked him enough.

It's hard to stand on dignity without trousers, especially on a fairly cold morning.

It seemed an omen or a metaphor, but I'm not sure what for. Put everything behind you and concentrate on the job. And then drive home to London and sleep, sleep, sleep. But before that, I was still considering expansion. At last I was getting leads on some further venues.

One I saw myself, the other was the result of a suggestion from an Edinburgh contact.

The Meadow Bar had a couple of performances of one show in 2005. They told me they wanted more. Well, we could do that.

The Jekyll and Hyde had a hidden function room. The shape was difficult, but it could be made to work for smaller shows.

I had hopes for five stages in four venues for 2006. And so it proved.

Call me lazy. Or maybe too pressured doing two shows a day. Or maybe just bitter at the way my name had been wiped from my own organisation. But whatever my motive was, I made another stupid decision. Having made the initial contact with the Meadow Bar, I asked the non-performing half of the Laughing Horse complex to go and see them about the details and to come back with a confirmed deal.

Well, he was doing nothing much else, and getting the credit.

The deal with the Meadow Bar was done. But I was to regret not doing it myself.

Can one be performer and organiser? I thought so. But it's a matter of how much time one spends on both, and how much time is available. Can one be performer, organiser and full participant in the wild drink-fuelled socialising that happens

among Fringe performers? Is that too much? Can one be organiser and yet still enjoy the Fringe?

The next few years were to provide answers to that.

*

Short interval at the end of 2005.

In which we consider how far we got in 10 years (not very)

WELL, THE FREE FRINGE had been going for ten years. How far had we got? Not close to World Domination. Not even enough to march into the demilitarised Rhineland. Three stages in two venues. And only a recent expansion into those.

I had expected more, after ten years work. But we could have died completely in 2003 and nearly did. The concept wasn't dead. It had proved itself by getting audience.

But the sort of acts at whom the Free Fringe was targeted still mostly remained aloof from it. The idea had sunk in among a few. But there was still too much pay-to-play around.

Was the idea gradually taking hold? It didn't seem so. Ten years to go from one show to about thirty, two of which were me.

At that stage, it certainly wasn't worth writing a book about. Or even keeping notes (hence some of the discrepancies in the story that you've probably spotted). At the most, we'd be a small eccentric enclave in a world still dominated by pay-to-play.

The Fringe had got bigger. Admission prices for shows had increased considerably. People seemed to be drinking less (possibly influenced by the smoking ban, which people were still getting used to). The jollity, I thought, was leaking out of the Fringe: no more Fringe Club, Fringe Sunday under threat (it finally expired in 2008, having failed to find a sponsor) and fewer open cabarets. More things happening behind passwalls, separating performers from audience.

Most of these gradual changes should have supported the Free Fringe. Only the decline in drinking worked against us; the less people drank, the worse our deal was for pub owners.

There was still scope. I was disappointed with how slow progress was. But I still believed in the idea. Most of the time.

Just as well I did. I was a prisoner of it. I was so closely identified with it that I could never go back to pay-to-play. Well, they probably wouldn't let me. And it would seem, like selling out.

The pay-to-play venues barely noticed us, or seemed not to. I think they wrote me off as a harmless eccentric, and I was by no means the only eccentric at the Fringe. They, and the Fringe Office, seemed content to think that things would go on the way they always had.

So, in our first ten years, not quite a failure but certainly not a roaring success. A small cluster of mutant cells, not quite knowing what sort of creature it might grow into, if it survived. So small it was beneath the notice of creatures that might otherwise have been its predator.

Did we carry on? A small cluster of mutant cells has no choice.

I didn't do Biology at school, so this bit about cells might be completely wrong. We had to choose between Ancient Greek, Biology. Geography or German. So, we could learn where Germany was or what they spoke, but not both, and not what sort of creatures were in it. As for the Greeks, they didn't bear any gifts so I didn't fear them. Which was probably a mistake.

Especially considering the events of the next two years. Fear not only Greeks, but everybody bearing gifts. If you want the gold, you have to take the myrrh. Whatever myrrh is. I think it's something you can say when you forget the lyrics of songs.

End of interval. Please take your seats for the second half, unless you've slipped out during the interval, thus avoiding the bucket.

*

2006

In which we carry on doing a very silly thing, which biteth us in the arse.

THERE ARE SHOWS YOU WISH you could have put on, but you can't. Mark Watson, when he first thought of doing a continuous 24 hour show, asked me if we could accommodate it. I liked the idea. I enquired, but all venues said no. Licensing; health and safety; staffing. Dammit, I'd have suspended my own show to make this happen. But I had to say no, and watch the show go to a pay-to-play venue. I turned up around dawn and got a name check, but it wasn't the same.

Still, it was good that Mark thought of us first. Or maybe he didn't. Maybe he just asked everybody. Yes, that's more likely. Blast. All the intervening years, I've been thinking that we were his first choice, and now I realise.

Anyway, that was the easy bit.

We had an unresolved problem.

And this problem had the potential to kill the whole thing. I'm very bad at biting bullets. I'd rather dodge them. But sometimes they have to be bitten.

And I trusted people in those days. I don't now. I really thought that anybody wanting to be involved in the Free Fringe must have their heart in the right place, and the rest was just detail.

So maybe things just needed spelling out. Maybe I hadn't made things clear enough.

How many wars have been in my lifetime, and how many have I condemned as futile? Have I not said that negotiation is so much better? Did I not join in with Lennon's Give Peace a Chance, back as the 60s were disintegrating?

43, all of them, yes and yes.

So, I trusted to negotiation.

I now have much more sympathy with the hawks and warmongers.

Emails flew from Kentish Town to Richmond, or was it Twickenham? It doesn't matter to an email, does it? Others flew back. Meetings happened. An elaborate written agreement was drafted, disputed, discussed, re-drafted and finally agreed.

I must have been mad. That level of verbosity wasn't what the Free Fringe was supposed to be about.

I suppose I still had visions of having somebody take care of the nuts and bolts for me, and thought that an agreement like that might allow the Free Fringe to grow under my direction. And I still believed that they subscribed to the ethos. But I was negotiating with the non-performer, and how could a non-performer understand the principle of empowerment of performers?

Indeed, not only that; I was talking to somebody who ran comedy nights and made a profit from doing so. Now, that's not in itself evil. But the whole idea of the Free Fringe was not to make a profit off the backs of performers during the Fringe. Why did I think Laughing Horse would change motivation for one month of the year?

The final written agreement was full of holes. But fortunately this turned out not to matter much.

It did, at least, make me do one obvious and necessary thing: register The Free Fringe Ltd properly as a Company.

Initially, Laughing-Horse-man and I were to be the two directors. And as I duly registered one share each for him and me, a part of my brain cried 'mistake'. And I thought: what if I sneakily issued myself two shares, thus retaining a casting vote?

No, I replied to myself; that's not what was agreed. It wouldn't be honest.

His part of that agreement was to register the domains freefringe.com and freefringe.co.uk on behalf of the Free Fringe. He knew more about domain registration than I. At that time, I knew nothing about domain registration. He was an IT manager in the City somewhere.

Little did I know that he had already done so, and registered them as belonging to himself, thus Laughing Horse.

Although, to be fair, had I studied the 2005 Fringe Programme carefully enough, I would have seen one each of these domains used at the end of two show listings. I didn't. I missed that. And, knowing nothing about domains at the time, I wouldn't have realised the importance.

The other points of the agreement were: they were to manage the venues, and be entitled to call them Laughing Horse@ [venue name], as they had paid for in 2004 and simply done without payment in 2005. All shows, however, were to put / Free Fringe after their performer name in the Fringe Programme. The imbalance of 2005, where their name was all over the programme and mine nowhere, was rectified by this.

Well, not my name. I never wanted my name all over it, although readers of 2018 will find that hard to believe. Just the name of Free Fringe, which was the name of the organisation and the Company. And the thing I founded, and (as I thought) presided over.

It wasn't enjoyable, negotiating bits of my vision away. Aaaarggh. How pretentious was that sentence? My vision, forsooth. I was no Bernardette Soubrious. But, OK, I had seen clearly where I wanted the Free Fringe to go, and what would be necessary to achieve that. And now I was horsetrading parts of that for the sake of a relatively quiet life.

Which I was anyway not destined to get.

I had written, I thought, a promising one-man show for 2006. It was basically one song (or more) for every month of 2006 so far, climaxing on the August song, which was about the Fringe itself. A show I was quite pleased with, although it was a work in progress during the Laughing Horse negotiations, and I wrote each song in the month concerned, except August, which I wrote in advance.

(The next year, I completed the show, and recorded it, and you can download it from the Web. If you're a Fringer, you plug things, and this is a plug. Even though the download is free.)

I was mostly focused on that show. That's my excuse for not paying attention, not standing up for myself in those negotiations. It's no excuse. I read this now, and I know my mistakes.

The contract, I had thought, retained my rights over the Free Fringe name. And my jurisdiction over its use.

It had not addressed — why on earth did I not make it address? Years later I don't know the answer — the issue of how the shows should be booked.

So I suppose I shouldn't have been disappointed when once again I was presented with a fait accompli. This time it included some people I actually wanted on board, especially Pappy's Fun Club in the opening spot at the Canons' Gait. And Yianni Agisilaou in the midnight slot.

That, at least, was pleasing. I knew them from the circuit, and I knew they'd do well. They were, and are, the sort of act that I always wanted on board.

Others, perhaps, less so, with no disrespect to them as people.

We certainly needed the Canons' Gait programme to be solid. Having lost the venue once, I didn't want to lose it again. I was, you may remember, still under the impression that there were very few suitable venues in Edinburgh. Each one had to be cherished.

Fortunately, I could rely on Peter Buckley Hill and Some Comedians to pull them in. And that was immediately preceded by Laughing Horse's variable bill show, with the same format although less carefully selected guest acts. By then I was in a position to attract many established acts as my guests, including that year Glen Wool, Mitch Benn, Robin Ince and Paul Sinha.

What the Free Fringe needed was something to create a sense of unity among the performers.

And thus was born the Free Fringe Programme.

I did it all myself, that year. Which was not as easy as it ought to have been.

I had, in the 1970s, run a backstreet printing works, but was not myself a printer or even a printer's assistant. And in the intervening years, much had changed. We used to do things, in those pre-computer days, all by hand, typesetting on an IBM golfball, stripping things together with paste and tape, shooting negatives in a darkroom, making plates, printing, trimming and finishing. If Caxton would not have recognised the process, at least he'd have understood it. Thirty years later, everything had changed and I knew nothing. All I had was a PC, and no software to speak of.

One thing I was determined of: the shows were to have pictures next to their listings. Because the Fringe Programme itself did not. For your money (nearly £400 nowadays; maybe £300 then, but I don't have the exact information) you got a listing of 40 words plus venue and date details. The 40 words included your show title, and still do.

So, we could offer our members a picture, however tiny.

I emailed; I collected blurbs and pictures. I put them together using Microsoft Notepad, at 72 dots per inch.

Yes, I know now what I should have done. I didn't then. The format was A2, folded twice to make an A4. We had a logo (Laughing Horse designed, without clean edges); we had a map for the back showing where the venues were. I set it at full size and sent it to the cheapest printer I could find.

When they'd stopped laughing at the artwork, they explained, as to an idiot, what the problem was.

And, credit to me as the idiot, I understood. 300 dots per inch was the minimum viable.

What I had thought was: since the public were getting the shows free (or for as much as they cared to put in the hat) they would understand that our promotional materials need not be as good quality as the materials of the pay-to-play venues.

And that thought turned out to be completely wrong. Not only did our shows have to be as good as theirs: so did our handouts.

I don't know that scientifically. But I've talked to enough audience members over the years to be convinced I'm right. At the time, I thought different.

Anyway, the printers were nice about it. For more money, they'd reset the whole thing and make it look good. I gave them more money, and they did.

I now wonder: whose money was it? Did I pay from my own means or did Laughing Horse contribute? Memory fails, especially in that turbulent year. I rather suspect I paid. Certainly Laughing Horse had no enthusiasm for the programme project. I know this because the performers at the Meadow Bar had clubbed together, with the Horse's blessing, and produced a combined flier listing all the shows at that venue. And when they saw the Free Fringe programme, they (or at least the instigator of their combined flier) said they had been told nothing about it.

I wonder what they thought I was collecting blurbs and pictures for?

I know I sold a small amount of ad space in that first programme, and if there's one thing I hate doing, it's selling ad space. Valvona and Crolla, the wonderful shop on Elm Row bought one; so did an envelope manufacturer Mel worked for. And so did a comedian with a water-cooler business, although I'm still awaiting payment for that one.

With the programme was born one of the Free Fringe's main principles: don't just offer the public your own show leaflet, offer them your leaflet PLUS the full programme. That way everybody works for everybody else, and for the advancement of the Free Fringe versus the pay-to-play venues.

I regret to say that I never saw the two Laughing Horse principals handing out the Free Fringe programme, although I saw them often enough leafleting for their own shows.

All the effort negotiating the peace treaty (alright, the collaboration agreement) was in vain.

Doubly so when they crossed the demarcation line again and offered a line of merchandise (baseball caps, t-shirts) with the brand, without the slightest consultation.

Triply so when they emailed saying they didn't want to be a Director of the company after all and would I kindly not issue them a share.

I don't know why they did that last thing, to this day. If they wanted to hijack (as it later turned out they did) it would have strengthened their position.

But as it stood, I was able to give the share in question to the magnificent Mel, who had supported me in all the venue frustrations so far, and to make her the other Director of The Free Fringe Ltd, which she remains to this day, for all that our relationship is now different. And, as long as she and I agreed, control of The Free Fringe Ltd was now in safe hands. And therefore, as I thought, the name Free Fringe was in safe hands, although again time was to show that I had assumed too much.

It was a confusing time. But I had a good venue for two — in all modesty — good shows. Performer-me was satisfied. Organiser-me wasn't. But organiser-me wasn't supposed to exist; the Free Fringe was supposed to be a collective of performers.

What, therefore, was a non-performer doing at the heart of it? And why was he giving me orders? Get your car, take this thing to that place.

That's how I remember it, anyway. No doubt they remember it differently.

But all was clearly not well. And this is how I could tell:

Somewhere in the middle of the first week of the Fringe, one of the bar staff mentioned a meeting that coming Sunday with the owner of the pub, who owned four other Edinburgh pubs also.

What meeting? I knew of no such meeting.

Oh yes, he said, it's been arranged. And he gave me the venue (the Guildford Arms) and time. In my diary it went.

The meeting had been called to discuss an idea the owner had had: to have comedians perform in the main bar of the Guildford, in the intervals between the jazz and blues acts he always booked for August.

This is the sort of thing I don't think is a good idea. Musicians may be able to work with people talking all the way through and paying scant attention; comedians can't. Without attention, the act dies. I wouldn't ask any decent act to do that.

It turned out the meeting had been arranged by Laughing Horse supremo man, and I wasn't supposed to know anything about it. He didn't turn up himself (he was in London at the time); he sent a minion, who was very surprised to see me there.

Later the same day I received a telephone call from LH supremo. How dare I sabotage his private arrangement, which was nothing to do with me?

Well, it was to do with me. It happened on my watch, and it would have committed my Free Fringe performers to work in unacceptable conditions.

There was supposed to be a collaboration agreement. How was this not my business? The reputation of the Free Fringe could have been on the line, for the connection would certainly have been made by audiences.

It's a funny sort of collaboration, doing behind-the-back deals. Whether money had been asked for, I don't know. I don't rule it out.

Looking back on that year, it's a wonder I had the stamina to do three hours stage time a day, publicise two shows and fight these battles, which the agreement should have rendered unnecessary. But the Fringe gives you stamina; the whole thing is so mad that normal laws of physics, biology and civilised behaviour fly out of the window. In my first year, I drank at least five pints a night without fail, at the various gigs and cabarets, and still lost a full stone in weight. There's no logic.

More madness was to come.

At last we were getting some attention. The public was noticing; our programmes were shifting and creating a brand identity. And the press was noticing too.

Now, at the Fringe, one is advised to send press releases about everything. I pity the poor press who have to read them, especially when most shows, however good, have no distinctive proposition. "Comedian puts on show" is not a news headline. Anyway, I had followed this advice slavishly since 1994, with no result. But in 2006 I had also sent a press release about the Free Fringe itself, explaining what we were trying to achieve and how.

That too was ignored, until around the middle of the Fringe I was contacted by Kate Copstick, chief comedy reviewer for The Scotsman. Now Kate, or Copstick or Cop as she largely prefers, was a highly feared person. When she did not like a show, or rather when she thought a show had been given insufficient effort by the performer(s), her reviews showed no mercy and, in the sensitive, could induce severe trauma. I knew of her, at the time; we had not met and she certainly had never reviewed my shows. So the call was a surprise.

What was the Free Fringe about? she asked.

I filled her in, as best I could. Had she not seen the press release I had sent to The Scotsman? No, she hadn't. Could I send it? In those pre-laptop days (or maybe I was just behind the times) I had to go to a cyber café and comb through floppy disks, but eventually it was found and sent. Next day, a call from Murdo McLeod, a name I recognised from numerous Guardian photo credits. Was I available to be photographed? I was.

Oh, the detail that comes back to me as I write this. Everybody spends time on the streets giving out leaflets, or fliers (the American term that's now become part of UK English) for their shows. In my case, I wanted to give out the Free Fringe programme as the main thing. So, I printed up a simple A3 white piece of paper and attached it to cardboard. It said: 69 shows for the price of none.

That simple placard was attached to a wooden broomstick. And on the other end of the broomstick was the original brush.

People saw the brush. They thought it silly. Some even pointed out to me that the brush was attached, as if I didn't know. But when they'd stopped laughing and pointing, they took a programme. Which was the objective. Without the brush, fewer people would have taken the programme.

Anyway, nowadays holding up signs is commonplace when one is leafleting. Then, it wasn't. I don't claim to have invented it. I'm sure somebody else did it first. I'm not sure anybody else did it with the brush on the other end.

So it was holding up that sign that the eminent Murdo pictured me, and a large article duly appeared under Copstick's byline and the header "The man who wants to set the Fringe free".

Which was nice.

Until Laughing Horse saw the article.

How dare I not mention them?

Well, I've just re-read the article for the first time in years (I kept it. You would have.) 23rd August 2006, if you want to search for it. And one of the things the article said, not even in direct speech but in reported, was:

"This is not just a guy bringing a bunch of shows up to Edinburgh, this is something close to a sociopolitical movement. Performers are expected to help each other with their shows, there is no real central organisation, there are no charges, hidden or otherwise."

Ballistic, they went. WE are the central organisation, they said.

No, you're not, I said. Did I say you could be? It wasn't even in the much-broken agreement.

This went on for some time, on the comedy forum chortle.co.uk.

As I said, I've just re-read the article and I wouldn't change a word.

I wondered what else had been going on that I didn't know about. And why the indignation? The context made it perfectly clear what the aims of the Free Fringe were, and indeed still are.

Things were boiling. But let's get the Fringe over before we let them explode, I thought. It's a long and stressful haul, and shows very few of us at our best.

That, however, was clearly not what they thought.

It was the last day but three of the Fringe. It was five minutes before my one-man show was due to start. Some audience were already in.

I was setting up the show. Usually a time when one would let a performer concentrate.

Down the stairs they stormed, the Laughing Horsemen of the apocalypse. Just two of them, though. The non-performer who'd arranged the behind-the-back meeting, and the performer.

We don't want to work with you any more, they said.

I'm about to do a show, I said. This is not the time to discuss things.

Nothing to discuss, they said. We're taking over. We'll run it without you. You're sacked.

What, from my own organisation?

Not your organisation any more.

I may at this point have raised my voice somewhat.

I was angry.

Having delivered their ultimatum, they left, no doubt with feelings of a job well done.

Now, that ought to have meant that I did a bad show, with some of the audience having witnessed the happenings, and me seething with rage and my mind on all sorts of possible ways of action. But oddly enough I didn't. I don't remember every show I've ever done; they blur and merge in the memory. But I do remember that one. My timing and delivery were exactly as they should have been. Perhaps I have a better auto-pilot than I think I have.

But still. Fight or flight? Give up everything I'd worked for over the last ten years? Or struggle?

For I knew intuitively what they'd done and why they'd timed their announcement. The meeting with the Canons' Gait owner had told me that. While I'd been performing and publicising the Free Fringe, they'd been building bridges to the venues, and representing themselves as the people responsible.

At this point, I have to introduce you to a significant character in our saga. His name was, and is, Calum Gunn.

Well, no, it isn't. That's the pseudonym I'm giving him. Now, I'd met him before, many times. But usually as an audience member, and not the sort that you'd wish for in an ideal world.

Large, loud, tall, often wearing full highland dress, and with a tendency to heckle with remarks it was sometimes difficult to understand, let alone answer, as one must when heckled.

A very unlikely white knight indeed. But in Edinburgh very little is what it seems. For all that I don't live there, it's my sort of city; everybody's an eccentric of one sort or another.

I finished both my shows that evening, and was done by shortly after midnight. Strong drink was called for. Ideally where there might be friends, although after the incidents of that day, how was I to know who was my friend and who not?

I went to the Holyrood Tavern, which I knew to be open until 3am and to serve good beer, including sometimes the Red McGregor. They also had a late night show, in which I had often played guest spots. There, if anywhere, I would be in company I could stand being with.

And there at the bar stood Calum.

I saw what happened, he said. I was upstairs.

Alright, upstairs he couldn't exactly have seen, but he could have heard. Such distinctions were not important.

I did not sob on his shoulder. He is a very tall man and I wouldn't have been able to reach it. And any sobbing I ever do, I do in the privacy of my own home, so neither you nor he would ever know. So, for all public purposes, I do not sob.

But I certainly needed somebody to talk to about it. And I talked.

Yes, showing weakness. Dear reader, I'm sure you have no weakness.

This was his response. I know, he said, you started the Free Fringe. Was I not there, in the Footlights and Firkin, and in the Three-Quarter, watching your show? (Yes, and heckling, I could have said, but didn't.) I know what you've been trying to do for Edinburgh, he said. (I suppose I was mostly trying to do it for the performers, I thought, but yes: free shows bringing back good-value entertainment for the people of Edinburgh; that's all part of it.)

They'll take all the venues, I said. I worked to find them. How can I recover from that?

I know a lot of space in Edinburgh, he said. I live here. (He may have said "I stay here", which is the Scottish way of saying the same thing, but means something else in English English.) I know people. I know places. If they take your venues, I can get you better ones. Just give me the authority.

Well, that got me on the defensive. Giving authority to Laughing Horse, or letting them take it uncontested, was what had got me into this mess in the first place.

White knight or clown in a horse costume, I wasn't going to relinquish authority ever again, to anybody.

And I was sceptical. Remember, I'd only ever known this man as an eccentric who had heckled. Very few comedians like hecklers. Mostly we want to deliver the material we've painstakingly written with no interruption other than laughter. Hecklers may be a fact of life, but we don't like 'em. Especially the ones who think they're helping. They're not.

No, I said, not authority. If you have venues, I'd love to know about them. But I need to see them first.

Because the years had taught me a little about what might work and what might not.

He accepted that. Which was good, because as I got to know him better, I learned how hard he found to accept it.

This was progress, but in the Holyrood my mission was to drink. Possibly to oblivion; they sell oblivion in glass or bottle. But only death brings permanent oblivion; the temporary sort that can be bought in glass or bottle achieves nothing.

One should, however, make no major decisions while seeking temporary oblivion.

So I arranged to meet him at a sober time, on the Sunday that concluded the Fringe.

The other person I told my troubles to (the Samaritans would not have understood, and I was never one for biblical references) was the mighty Mel. And her response was: I'll come up on Friday night.

I didn't deserve her.

And she and I met Calum on the Sunday. And our agenda was: is this man a nutter, or can he deliver what he promises?

And our conclusion was: we still don't know, but what do we have to lose?

I talked to the venues, but when I did, I knew that damage was done, except possibly, only possibly, at the Canons' Gait, where I'd done my own shows.

If there was to be a Free Fringe 2007, it would either be a hijacked one, or one with a competitor.

Do I fight or do I flee? Do I stay or do I go?

I've skipped forward. I'm back now in the Holyrood, not crying into my Red McGregor. There are still four days of the Fringe to go.

I occupied them, in part, by a small gesture of defiance. The performing half of the Laughing Horse (perhaps the only pantomime animal with an arse at both ends) was that year advertising a show that was completely 100% improvised and thus different every day. That was the show immediately before my own one-man show.

I took some pleasure in telling my audience that, and then showing them the set list he had carefully blu-tacked out of the audience's sight.

And a good thing happened, amid all this rubbish. I was given an award.

Now, it wasn't the first. But I'm never blasé about these things. I'd previously been given an award by Three Weeks newspaper, but that was just a published thing. The 2006 one was the Tap Water Award.

For which there was a ceremony, and the opportunity, or obligation, to perform a set at the ceremony.

I suppose I need to explain another aspect of Edinburgh Fringe lore. Since about 1980, there had been comedy awards at the Fringe, and these were celebrated at a lavish party on the last Saturday night, with the winners being announced at midnight and (in my time, anyway) broadcast live on Channel 4. And these awards were sponsored by Perrier. The party was a major event, and I had been doing the Fringe for six or seven years before I dared ask for a ticket.

That wasn't the award I won. (Yet.)

Perrier is owned by Nestlé, although it wasn't always. And Nestlé is a controversial company, against whom many people protest. And many times in the past, those protestors had urged Edinburgh performers to boycott the party and ceremony. To little avail; after 23 days of the Fringe, and with a motivation to meet The Man With The Cigar, few performers have much conscience left.

But the Tap Water awards were instigated as a response to the Perrier. Deliberately un-slick, un-corporate, un-sponsored and alternative. My sort of stuff. I wasn't aware of having been nominated. Perhaps that was deliberate. But in any event, I had won one. Spirit of the Fringe.

Among all the low-flying excrement of 2006, I at least had some recognition and something of which I could be proud.

I collected my award.

It was, like everybody else's, a second-hand tap on a wooden base; no plaque or anything. When people visit my flat, which is rare enough, they often ask why I have a tap mounted on a wooden base. It wasn't even individual. As you collected your award, you simply chose the tap you most liked.

My performance at the awards ceremony was abysmal. I had no stamina left that could be summoned.

But at least I had an award. And it reassured me that what I was doing had had some impact, and still had some value. I hadn't sought the award, and yet people had noticed enough to nominate and to give.

If I had thought of not fighting, that would have changed my mind. Even despite my performance at the ceremony. All these years later, I apologise to those who saw it. I was the marathon runner staggering across the finish line, neither knowing nor caring whether he has won or lost, only rejoicing that he has finished.

And I had finished. But was I finished? I was certainly in a bad place. Could I get out of it? Well, I was resolved to try. I had made a big mistake giving Laughing Horse house room, or indeed the time of day. One pays for mistakes. But at least I was rid of them.

The preparation for 2007 would be difficult. But in 2003 I thought I had lost the whole thing, and yet I survived. They tried to stop me in 1997, and I survived.

So much depended on Calum. Could he deliver what he promised? I had no right to expect it. But I was in no position to find venues myself; look how hard I'd tried in previous years. I'd come up with four venues, and now three or all were lost to underhand means.

Home, home, and sleep, but not too deeply, for there is much work to be done.

MacHorse hath murdered sleep.

*

2007

In which we are even freer and bigger, but moist.

2007 STARTED ON 1ST SEPTEMBER 2006. We had to recover venues, performers and status. I hardly had time to throw my things into the washing machine and read a month's worth of accumulated post (much more than there would be now; email was not as widespread as it now is, and we still paid utility bills by putting cheques in the post) before I was back off to Scotland.

It went slowly at first. But I was immensely helped by the owner of the Canons' Gait forwarding to me the email Laughing Horse had sent him, and his own reply. Flatteringly, it said he would be uncomfortable with a programme of shows that did not include Peter Buckley Hill And Some Comedians.

So Laughing Horse replied. They said, to him not to me, that they would be happy to have my show as part of their programme.

Again, I got a copy of that. Would I be happy with that arrangement? he asked.

No, I wouldn't.

I was astounded that they'd even said that. Would it be fair to infer that they would have said anything to get control of all four venues? Win or lose, I wasn't having that.

But if it was lose, I had nothing. Let me at least win that one good venue.

Calum telephoned the owner of the Canons' Gait. He wanted a meeting. It was arranged for 1pm, Sunday 8th October at the Guildford. Mel and I travelled to Edinburgh. I was in a state of anxiety. I pitched our case, as I had never pitched before. Actually, I haven't ever pitched much, so that's accurate.

Field the difficult questions. Keep positive. Emphasise track record and contacts. Make sure LH didn't get credit for what I had done. Answer more difficult questions.

And then he said yes, and we shook hands on the deal. Which in Scotland means it's firm, without the need for paperwork.

We were alive. Back in the game, with the best venue of the four we had had, no disrespect to the others.

If necessary we could just run a full programme there. They would have more shows, but we'd have better ones.

Calum, however, had not finished. He declared that there was much more unused space in the city of Edinburgh than I could imagine. And he was the man to find it.

One of his characteristics was an almost complete lack of inhibition. He would ask people I wouldn't dare to ask.

He took me to a run-down pub with slashed seats and a general air of depressed over-consumption. And a grumpy landlord who might have come from central casting, grumpy landlords division. Why, I whispered, are you taking me here? Wait while I show you, he said.

And at the back, past the toilets, full of discarded furniture, clearly unused for ages, was a function room. Looked like it would seat about 40 people. And it had character. Clinical it certainly wasn't. Stones and an interesting feel, just as you imagine an Old Town Edinburgh place to be.

And 50 yards from the Canons' Gait. I must have walked past it a hundred times.

If we brought in even low audiences for a full day of shows, he'd double his turnover. It wasn't a popular place. And, although it took him some time to cogitate this, assisted by his considerably less grumpy wife, he saw it. And we shook hands on the deal. Two venues in the bag. That was the White Horse.

Calum was full of ideas. Some good, some wild, and sometimes the wild ones turned out to be less wild. He pointed out empty office buildings that we could convert if we could merely get permission to do so. Nothing happened on that front, at least not that year, but it kept the hope up.

There was a restaurant, down one of the numerous wynds that lead from High Street to Cowgate. Therefore, very near the Fringe Office. If it had happened, it would probably have been the venue closest to the Fringe Office in the whole Fringe, and since the audience congregated near there (to pick up their tickets for pay-to-play shows) that would have been a big advantage.

Calum had the vision. They were on two levels; they could carry on food service upstairs and we could do shows downstairs. The manager was doubtful. He weighed up the options. We had several meetings. I even worked out some indicative figures, based on various levels of occupancy. I put them on a spreadsheet so he could change the percentages and see the outcome. Actually, that confused him rather than helped him.

It took some time, but eventually he decided against.

The gods were smiling on us in a mysterious way, for by the time the Fringe came round he'd gone out of business. We'd have had no fallback plan if we had put shows in that venue.

It wasn't the first time I learned how vulnerable our relationships with venues and potential venues are. And it certainly wasn't the last.

We had conversations, some as short as a minute, some considerably longer, with many other potential venues.

I put together an information sheet, stating our case on one side of A4 to any venue that might be interested. And accompanied it by Kate Copstick's article in The Scotsman, which gave us some credibility.

And the work paid off.

Several people were helping by looking out for venues. I should at this stage remember who suggested what and who found what. And thank them, whether they succeeded or not. Which I do, and I'm sure I did at the time, although memory of who suggested or found each has now faded.

Talks extended almost until the last minute. Suggestions came, went, were investigated.

And we ended up with no fewer than seven venues.

Three could be described as central, the other four slightly less so. Actually, they were all easy to get to, but we were hitting one of the Fringe's fundamental problems.

Since the mid 1980s, Comedy had become the dominant art form at the Fringe. The Alternative Comedy boom of 1980 onwards had fed the Fringe, and more and more comedians sought to emulate the success of those pioneers.

The more comedy shows there are at the Fringe, the less inclined audiences are to take a long walk to see one when they could take a short walk to see another. Although some shows were not only excellent but distinctive, many were simply competent and entertaining. And audiences need more motivation than that if they're going to walk any distance to get to their show. Consequently the Fringe was concentrating more and more in a narrow central area, like a black hole at the heart of a galaxy.

Now, I thought that our audience proposition might break that pattern. Audiences had, after all, come to the Communication Workers' Club, which was outside the crucial area. If a show was free, it would repay the ten or twenty minutes extra walk. That, after all, is what you expect in a whole-city festival.

Performers, however, want an easy life. Even the offer of a venue at no cost to them will not be looked gladly upon, if it means they have to do more work to get people in to their shows.

Some excellent rooms suffered, and still suffer, from this problem.

And the rooms that we got were indeed good ones. I'd like to describe them in the order in which we acquired them (alongside all the other things we tried) but unfortunately I don't remember that order.

So, from West to East, we had:

The Mercat Bar, an excellent space near Haymarket Station with a good room in the basement, seating about 70. Owned by a former Wetherspoons manager and his assistant, with a regular clientele and good drinks, it would have been everything we wanted, had it been in another place. As it was, to walk to it from the West End meant eight minutes down Shandwick Place, where there were houses but no shops. The psychological feel was that one was going out of town, although that wasn't true. Edinburghers knew that, but visitors didn't.

The Hudson Hotel, at the West End. A basement, of a somewhat odd shape, but usable for several sorts of shows. The difficulty here was actually finding the entrance, which was not the door everybody thought it was.

The Phoenix, on Broughton Street. The best juke box in Edinburgh was their boast and it was probably true. A good room downstairs with its own entrance, a little long and thin but very viable for shows and I sometimes saw it full.

The Outhouse, on Broughton Street Lane. Another good venue, with a courtyard. That, in the second year of the smoking ban in Scotland, was a big advantage; it was outside, so people could smoke and still be with their non-smoking friends at the same table. The performance room was upstairs and almost square, which is always good. The two disadvantages were that Broughton Street Lane is difficult to find if you don't already know where it is, and every Sunday they held a massive barbecue in the courtyard, the noise of which completely drowned the shows.

In going from West to East, I left one venue out, deliberately until last. I think I found it myself; I certainly negotiated for it myself. It was The Ivanhoe on South St Davids Street; a stone thrown not very hard would hit the Scott Monument. And in the basement it had exactly the sort of function room we wanted, again holding about 50. I had high hopes of it succeeding.

Until three weeks before the Fringe. One of our performers, in Edinburgh on other business, had gone to check his venue, and found it closed. It might, of course, have been closed temporarily. Telephones gave no response. I was in London at the time; I had to ask others to enquire before I could give our performer a clear answer. But I found out eventually. They had closed down; the whole building including several floors of offices above the Ivanhoe had been sold. The pub's staff had been dismissed at short notice. They didn't tell us anything, but honestly I can't blame them; their own livelihood will have been much more important to them.

The building was still there in 2015. It was never been put back into use. Every time I passed, I felt frustrated at that waste of very usable space.

Anyway, crisis time, yet again. We have shows booked in the Ivanhoe from 1315 to 2340, and no Ivanhoe for them to perform in.

If you don't care about performers, you don't care about that. Some people would have said: well, the performers paid nothing for the venue. There's no contract. Performers' risk, if they want to do it that way.

But we weren't going to think like that. These were people we knew; friends, even. We had promised, and if we couldn't deliver exactly what we promised, we'd damn well deliver something, the best we could in the circumstances.

And we weren't going to risk our reputation by letting people down. Oh, how the Laughing Horse would gloat if we did.

Calum in his tireless way saved the day. I went to Edinburgh as soon as I could and met him. He looked around and made contacts. And then he introduced me to Matteo Marino (another pseudonym), who owned several restaurants and a bar. And the one Calum had in mind was Madogs, on George Street. A place known for late-night drinks, in those days; empty (Calum said) during the day.

And five minutes or less from the Ivanhoe. So a notice could be put on the boarded-up window, all shows start times set back by five minutes, and the transfer was neat and complete.

Madogs did not have its own performance space. It would be a question of doing it in the main bar. But could we have exclusive use, we asked? Would they keep people out who had not come for the shows? You can't do a decent job if people are drinking and talking loudly during the show.

Yes, they said, they would.

Now, that didn't happen perfectly during the Fringe. The later shows suffered particularly as more and more drinking and conversation took place; the exclusivity wasn't always enforced. It largely depended who was on duty. The earlier shows were all right. Some were grateful that we'd solved the problem; a couple of others blamed us for the problem in the first place. Rather unfairly, I thought. A good but not perfect solution had been found for a difficult problem at almost no notice.

The Mercat, being in Haymarket slightly out of the psychological Fringe area, needed all the help it could get. And didn't need the 12-hour error it got. The Fringe Office, like most venues and promoters, works on the 24-hour clock, so if you have a show at 11pm, you list it as 2300.

The 2300 show listed itself as 1100, with non-hilarious consequences. I don't know how much difference it made; you can never tell. Maybe a lot, maybe none. There are many hotels near the Mercat; the 2300 show might have been a good stopping-off point for people on the way back to their hotels. The show actually listed at 1100 certainly wasn't a stopping-off point, for there was nothing there. I hope nobody came at that time.

OK, that's the story of the venues, in that year following the attempted coup d'état. There were many more things to do. Shows, people, the programme and some PR work to combat the negatives that Laughing Horse were posting on chortle.co.uk and elsewhere.

I certainly don't claim I did everything myself. But I did cause everything to be done, and I did a lot of it myself. Often not knowing who was on our side and who was reporting our activity back to the other camp.

Sounds paranoid, I know. But after the events of 2006 I had lost many of my certainties.

Fortunately I still had confidence in myself as an organiser, if not as a human being.

And in one particular thing I had confidence, and I still do: I am a better judge of comedy than Laughing Horse. Some of the acts they had wished on us were good, and I knew them; others I thought less so. I could do better.

Yes, they did know a lot of acts. They ran, and still run, a national New Act Competition. By these means, they got to know a large number of early-career acts, some of whom would go on to become famous. Before the backstab, I had judged the final of that competition (as part of a three or four person panel) on three occasions.

But I also knew a lot of performers, and the ones I knew had been around early in my own performing career, in the 1980s. So some of them were very famous by 2007. And others knew me, and knew of what I was trying to achieve. And I had been performing at the Fringe since 1994, so many people knew me from that, if only by osmosis.

I resolved to put quality as far up the agenda as I could, dependent of course on whom I could get. The very famous wouldn't be interested — yet. Although we'd been going since 1996, it still seemed to them a new and revolutionary concept. They thought the Free Fringe idea mad in the first few solo years, and some of that impression still stuck.

If we were going to compete, it would be on our terms. And that would be on quality. We would say, as Laughing Horse could not, that we vetted the quality of all our acts, and that free was not rubbish. We would not necessarily strive to be bigger than LH; we would not necessarily have nicer venues, although we would try. But we would have the quality.

And we would also have the team spirit. We would do all we could to make the acts pull together as a team and support each other.

So, that was the task in recruiting shows.

Competition wasn't what I wanted. As I think I may have said earlier, and I may miss when I come to edit this, competition drives capitalism. But we were a non-profit; we had no resources to waste on competition.

But I was stuck with competition. And if you're stuck with competition, you have to ensure you at least don't lose.

We've never tried to persuade acts to come to us if they seemed unwilling. And even in those critical days, we didn't. I put the word around that we were looking for acts, and when I met people who had been with us in 2006 and who I thought met the standard, I enquired how they felt.

The announcement on Chortle brought in some acts whom I didn't know, and I went round comedy clubs watching them. In these days of YouTube, this is no longer necessary, but in those days it was. It also brought in enquires from people I did know.

I made one other rule. Nobody could work with Laughing Horse and us. And nobody could apply to us and them.

If the public could see the same act under the aegis of two different promoters, where would be the quality advantage we were determined to achieve?

And as for applications: if people could apply to both, then they probably would, and then choose the venue that they preferred. And they would make that choice as late as possible, usually right before the programme deadline. The result would be a programme of shows with huge holes in it.

Our venues depended on the refreshment sales. Holes in the programme would damage that greatly. It mustn't be allowed to happen.

Besides this, we wanted people on board who actually understood and believed in what we were doing.

We would, of course, make an exception for people doing one-off guest spots in LH's variable bill shows. There were so many of those shows that we could never police any such restriction, and performers want to do a lot of guest spots; it's part of the Fringe. And if their name wasn't in the programme, if they weren't a permanent part of the show, it did no damage. It would be petty to go down to that level.

I put this together in an information sheet for performers.

This in later years was to get expanded.

And the enquiries came in, gradually.

I tried to get as many Scottish and Scotland-based acts as I could, since I wanted to have strong connections to the performers who served Edinburgh all year round. We weren't, and didn't want to be, a competitor to The Stand, Edinburgh's year

-round comedy club. Although not free, they gave their performers a good deal.

People I liked came on board. Noel James, probably the best comedian you've probably never heard of, wanted to do three shows a day. I was a great admirer. But three solo shows a day? I knew how exhausting two a day could be; three would require superhuman strength. I counselled Noel against doing so many. But he was adamant. He certainly had enough comedic ideas to fill three different shows a day. And he was a grown-up. He'd never had a good Fringe experience before, and he wanted to try it our way. So I said yes.

Lots of others. Iona Dudley-Ward with her quirky comedy. Ro Campbell, who has done a show with us every year since. Brian and Krysstal. I'd known Brian, who's really a Paul, for ages, and he and Krysstal, who's really a Vicky, met at Peter Buckley Hill and Some Comedians and then married. So I felt some personal interest there.

A show specially dedicated to early-career comedians with walkup open spots. We had a duty to the next generation, I thought. Danny Worthington, tireless worker, ran that.

Tom Bell, now well known and always renowned for off-the-wallness, if that's a valid expression. Kate Smurthwaite. Yianni Agisilaou again. Martin White, like me a regular at Robin Ince's Book Club and one of the few accordion-based acts on the circuit. Viv Gee. Matt Price. And many others, who are now free to be insulted that I haven't mentioned them in these paragraphs.

Not everything was rosy. One act, since much more famous, was down for a variable bill show, and I fear I rather pressured him into running two with not enough space between them. He had a health problem of which I wasn't aware, which didn't help.

My fault, not his. I had to ensure that we had full programmes at all venues, except for the odd programmed day off. So if I saw gaps, something had to go in them. And variable bill shows were always popular. So when it came down to deadline, I had to work to create a gapless programme.

And chances were taken. I discovered that, in booking for a Free Fringe programme, there are always chances to be taken. Any show is a risk. Sometimes one just has to put people in the slot and hope. Under that dispensation, we had Aaron Barschak, better known at the time as the Comedy Terrorist, who had recently served prison time for breaking in to Windsor Castle and gatecrashing one of Her Majesty's functions. This gained him a lot of media coverage, which I thought would be to his and our advantage.

Other people sniffed at the opportunity but didn't bite. One show in particular from 2006 declared they were coming with us, and got a very good slot in consequence. Shortly before deadline, they pulled out and went to Laughing Horse. So, despite our conditions saying "don't apply to both", they clearly had. I suspected this had been a deliberate underhand manoeuvre, but of course one can't prove that. And maybe that was paranoia. Luckily we plugged the gap.

And for the first time we deviated from Comedy; we took on two plays.

It was a very busy year in the leadup to the 2007 Fringe. Lots of other stuff to do, learning some of them as I went along.

One of the things on the agenda was to get our domains back.

Laughing Horse had registered the domains freefringe.com and freefringe.co.uk as theirs, as I mentioned earlier. And this was likely to confuse applicants. So far, the real Free Fringe, the company The Free Fringe Ltd, had nothing.

It took somebody else's suggestion for me to register the domains freefringe.org and freefringe.org.uk for myself, although I should really have done it for the Company. Without that kind stranger's suggestion, I wouldn't have thought of registering those other domains.

So we at least had the potential for a web site of our own. And I put descriptions of the venues on it for the benefit of potential performers. But not much else.

And then I set about getting the domain freefringe.co.uk back. I would have tried freefringe.com as well, but it appears the procedure is completely different for .com.

It cost over £800 to instigate the procedure. My own money. But I thought the case was solid; we were after all The Free Fringe Ltd, a company, in the UK, and that's what .co.uk stands for.

Besides, they had a mediation/negotiation procedure, which they said was highly acclaimed, which had to be gone through before an adjudicator made a decision.

Well, it wasn't highly acclaimed by me.

The mediator contacted me once for an initial position, which I gave, then only contacted me again 14 days later, saying this was the last day of mediation and did I have anything to add?

So it went to adjudication. I should have known that it would be problematic. Laughing Horse man's day job was as an IT manager in the City somewhere. Quite possibly he'd done something similar before, although I don't know. To me the rightness of our case was obvious.

But not to the adjudicator. He decided in their favour. And commented how badly prepared our case was. The adjudication's on the web.

I was furious. Perhaps with myself for not writing it up in better detail, but also with the verdict itself, and with the procedure. By their own admission, Nominet asked Laughing Horse a supplementary question, received their answer and believed it. They didn't give us a chance to present counter-evidence to that answer. Doesn't sound like correct procedure to me.

The appeal would cost £3000, of my own money. So I decided not to.

It still makes me angry. If they traded honestly under their own name, we'd have far fewer problems. And anybody applying to them, or us, would know precisely whom they were applying to. Now, they don't. Every year I encounter shows who claim to have played the Free Fringe when they haven't, and they frequently reply that they applied via a "Free Fringe" web site, presumably freefringe.com.

And Laughing Horse are still at it. In 2014 they registered the domain freefringe.uk, as I discovered in 2016.

Maybe I should have appealed, after all. Or paid a solicitor.

But it was quite a lot of money.

The other main thing I had to deal with was the printed Free Fringe programme.

The 2006 experience had taught me much I should already have known. I bought a graphics package, for not very much money. I made sure everything was set to 300dpi this time.

Chris Lincé designed us a new, simpler and altogether better logo, which with a change of year we've used ever since.

Canons' Gait's owner bought two ad spaces, one for Canons' Gait and the other for the Guildford Arms's jazz festival. A Scottish comedian who ran an agency bought an ad space for that agency. It wouldn't have been fair if anybody could buy ad space for their shows themselves, but this ad wasn't.

I thought we could re-use the 2006 map and re-locate the venues on it. But there was, in very tiny letters which I at first overlooked, a copyright on it, attributing it to Laughing Horse's main man. So that couldn't be used.

One of our comedians volunteered to do a substitute map. It took him more time than I'd expected. When I saw the artwork, I realised why. It was entirely hand-drawn; not only that, but freehand. It looked like no other map I'd seen.

I asked advice. Some said we couldn't use it; looked too amateurish. It certainly gave an informality to our look. But anybody who looked at our programme could tell the rest of it wasn't done by a professional designer either; it was me, making it up as I went along.

I thought we should go with it. After all the work our comedian had put into it, it would be a slap in his face not to. And anyway the programme was about the information in it, not the design. And maybe it would reinforce, to the public, the idea that we had no money to waste and that we, the performers, did everything to do with the Free Fringe.

I had, however, to make one change. The Mercat Bar was shown in a cutout. And that venue was the most distant, and distance was a worry. Showing it in a cutout would make it look even more remote than it was. We had to connect it to the map.

I can't draw. In some countries, you have to pass every subject in the primary school syllabus before you can proceed to secondary. If that were so in the UK, I'd still be in primary school, repeating drawing for the 56th time. No hopes there.

But I stayed up all night, wrestling with my graphics package, extending the map to Haymarket, copying and pasting the cross-hatching from elsewhere in the drawing, fitting letters down the streets and trying to make it look somewhat like the rest. It would have taken a decent designer ten minutes. It took me eight hours. With a magnifying glass, you can easily see the bits I did. It was a lash-up. But I'm strangely proud of it, because I faced up to something I couldn't do and nevertheless did it. And got it to print on time.

I also spent a lot of time chasing up people's pictures and blurbs. In two cases, when they weren't forthcoming in time, I wrote the blurbs myself. Again, anybody who reads the programme can tell which ones.

It was, now I look back on it, an exhausting year leading up to the Fringe. As well as all the things I've described, I kept the day job going, and I also recorded my fifth live CD. And was present at all the numerous edits of that CD, although I couldn't actually do much. And it was also the year Robin Ince's Book Club played the Hay-on-Wye literary festival, so I got backstage with all sorts of literary giants, and I held the door open for Doris Lessing. Why that should be such a point of pride, I don't know, but it was.

A boost came in Spring when the Free Fringe won two Chortle awards, for best off-stage contribution and for innovation. Both of these were decided by popular vote.

We won cleanly; often, when people are nominated for an award with a vote, they pressure everybody they know to vote from them. Not only did we not do that; I didn't even know we were nominated until invited to the ceremony, and I had so little anticipated winning that I had no speech prepared. Only 15 seconds before the envelope was opened, I suddenly realised that a speech would be needed if we won. The speeches I actually made are still on YouTube somewhere, but please don't watch them.

The champagne was top price but not top quality. But worth buying, all the same. The awards came with no cash — why should they? But the trophies looked good next to the tap-on-the-plinth from the Tap Water awards. And, of course, I was able to take an amateurish picture of the three trophies and put it in the Free Fringe Programme.

The work was done; I had a Free Fringe stretching over seven venues with 61 shows, which seemed at the time unimaginably large.

How would it go? I was very apprehensive. Six new venues, and a large number of acts who were first-time Free Fringers, and a very recent change of the seventh venue (but we managed to get the change into our printed programme).

So much potential for disaster.

And it started badly. Not our fault; nature's.

For the first week, it rained.

Not slightly. Torrentially. And constantly. Far too wet for anybody to stand on the street leafleting for their show. I know; I tried.

And that in turn meant that people weren't walking when they could avoid it. Which means fewer people were coming to our shows. Especially the ones which required longer walks.

At one stage I did my one-man show barefoot, with my shoes and socks drying at the back of the room.

The Canons' Gait weren't happy at the amount of money we weren't bringing in. I was summoned to a meeting at the owner's offices, with the manager of the Canons' Gait also in attendance.

They had showed trust in me, they said, by giving me the venue against Laughing Horse's strong counterbid. How had I repaid them? By putting on shows that brought in low audiences.

And why were audiences low? I suggested the rain; they weren't having that. No, they said. Poor artistic quality.

Comedy's very subjective, but I knew that accusation not to be true. We had a solid programme; I'd picked it.

As an example of poor quality, they cited "the woman who was in your (i.e. my) one-man show slot on your day off on Wednesday". She, they said, was awful. Not funny at all.

Oh, I said. You mean Josie Long?

Is that her name? they said. She wasn't good.

I was, at least, able to point out that she'd won Best Newcomer at the Edinburgh Comedy Awards (Perrier Awards, then) the previous year 2006.

They were still not happy. The yellow card was waved emphatically in my direction.

It's a funny business. It didn't feel funny, that day. Nor did I. Not for the first or last time, I felt everything I'd worked for slipping away. But one thing I did know; Josie Long was, and is, funny.

The weather got better. It had to. Worse would barely have been possible. And when it did, audience numbers improved and full houses came back to Peter Buckley Hill and Some Comedians, and to other shows.

Sighs of relief were breathed.

We were getting noticed. I was invited on to Tommy Sheridan's Sunday morning radio show, and we spoke of Free Fringes and reviewed the Sunday papers and this and that. And all was doing well, until I was asked about interesting shows, and I mentioned Martin White and his accordion playing.

It was as if I had said Martin played a dead baby instead.

Or so I felt at the time. The atmosphere changed.

The accordion, it seemed, was too closely associated with the bands that perform for sectarian parades in Northern Ireland and the West of Scotland.

And to me, it was just an instrument Martin used. Clearly I had not explored the implications of having an accordion on the Free Fringe. May the gods preserve me from flutes, in that case.

How did the Free Fringe go in general that year? Mostly well, but certainly not completely well. The later shows at Madogs suffered from drinkers talking, and the exclusivity of use we'd been promised hadn't really happened. Matteo had gone to Italy, so couldn't intervene. Noel James' attempt to do three full shows every day was costing him his health; the strain was apparent. The shows at the Mercat bar were bringing in mostly a local audience, no bad thing in itself.

And we had been suffering from dropouts and last-minute changes. In the opening slot at midday in the Canons' Gait we had to put a compilation show, getting people to do bits from their own shows and drum up an audience. This was an emergency stopgap when another show dropped out shortly before the Fringe, and it didn't always work. Shows like that don't get publicised well, because no single person is in charge, and the contrast between that show and the much more successful lunchtime shows at the Canons' Gait in 2005 and 2006 didn't go unnoticed by the owner.

It would really be good if we had a reserve show; a performer standing by whose show could plug any short-notice gaps that arise. But no performer worth his or her salt would volunteer to be in that position, when they could have a confirmed show elsewhere.

With bigger numbers, we could do more to alleviate problems like that. And the more people thought and worked as a team, the easier the solutions would be.

One show dropped out after three performances and didn't tell us at all. That was embarrassing. If we don't know there's a problem, how can we fix it? And it wasn't the last year in which that happened.

What had we learned from the 2007 Fringe?

Well, we learned that we were better off without Laughing Horse, but we already knew that.

We learned that the more we do to bring people together as a team, the better the results are. The Free Fringe's emphasis had to be on mutual support.

We learned that the more we spelled out what was expected of performers, the more they would understand it.

But mostly we learned what we already know: that managing the Free Fringe is a matter of constant troubleshooting, and never knowing where the next problem was coming from. It was never going to be smooth. It's an informal atmosphere, and that can sometimes get out of hand.

But the audience made it for us. Amid all the troubleshooting it was easy to forget how much better it was to perform to our audience than a paying one. They were, and are, much more open to different types of show and experience. And while we still got a number of idiot hecklers, their number was diminishing.

It had been hard work, but we were getting somewhere. I was still financing things out of my own pocket, though. And we needed a better system for keeping track of the data. I'd used a simple spreadsheet, but it needed to be more complex. And incorporate some way of generating the printed programme. If we got any bigger, we'd need a better system. I could write a lot about the data processing system that's been developed since, over the next several years. I'm an amateur, but I can make spreadsheets do things many people can't. There are bits I'm quite proud of. Describing them, however, would be incredibly and cringemakingly tedious. I'm tempted, but I shall resist.

It had been hard work. The Free Fringe was taking my life over. And I still had two other jobs: performing and the day job

I· needed a rest, but wasn't destined to get one.

*

2008

In which our hero commits indecent exposure

SOME PARTS OF THE FREE FRINGE STORY are easy to write. Some less easy. In some cases the memories are so bad that I have to take the laptop down to the pub and do the writing there, fortified by strong drink. You can tell which times these were; the typeface is blurred.

In a mixed comedy bill, you can always tell who are the relative beginners. They use the phrase "I'll tell you a little bit about myself." As if that were some sort of treat for the audience.

I'll tell you a little bit about myself.

I thought I was just a panicky, evil-tempered bastard. A set of characteristics that I hated myself for. But it turned out I had Tourette's Syndrome, and that was the explanation for both these problems, and a few others. I was diagnosed in the late 1990s.

Now, many, perhaps most, people don't know what Tourette's Syndrome is. They think it's constant involuntary swearing. It can be, but in most cases it isn't. And it isn't in my case.

Tourette's is the constant subject of comedians' material. I even have had a couple of gags about it myself. Well, I've got it; I'm entitled.

One of the ones I frequently hear, from non-sufferers, is: I wish I had Tourette's Syndrome; I could tell everybody at work to fuck off and they couldn't touch me for it.

If that ever provokes any laughter, it should be hollow laughter.

For it was in October 2007 my life collapsed. And that affected the Free Fringe.

I was always happy in the day job. I lectured, and in my own biased opinion I lectured well. I was put in charge of things; courses, timetabling and initiatives to reduce the dropout rate. I was on the top pay grade below Head of Department.

It all collapsed in a single moment. I lost my temper with a student, and went into an attack of uncontrollable rage, as we Tourette's sufferers sometimes do. We can't help it. That's what uncontrollable means. If you don't have it, you won't understand.

I will mention that the student concerned was no shy and disadvantaged 18-year-old woman, but a male mature student, from no ethno-cultural minority (which should not matter). Nor was he one of my own students; he wasn't even in my Department. He stood in my seminar, preventing it from happening, accusing me and my students of being in the wrong room which we were not, and demanding to know where his own class was, which was information I did not have. When my polite reply was met by a further demand for information I did not have, I lost control.

And having remembered all of that, although I never really forgot it, I don't want to dwell too much. The point is I was suspended from the job I loved, and spent the next four years trying to clear my name. Through all sorts of medical and capability assessments, sometimes on sick leave, sometimes on non-teaching duties, always under great stress but at least on full pay.

The bottom line was, although unhappy, I had more time available to devote to the Free Fringe. The longditudinal research into student assimilation I had been doing was killed; I lost the continuity and never got it back. Clearing my name and running the Free Fringe were my two occupations, and I did both obsessively.

It may have helped, or it may have hindered, that 2008 was the year in which I became 60. In Germany, where I worked a lifetime ago, they had a tradition of celebrating people's 60th as a milestone. I was going to import that tradition, come what may.

60 comedians in six days was the plan. Or rather 59, and the sixtieth would be me, doing a one-man show on my birthday itself, March 3rd, a Monday in that year. Of the six mixed-bill shows, four were to be in London and two in Edinburgh, at the

Canons' Gait. I was looking forward to it; performing was the thing I liked to do best, and why should I not do that on my milestone birthday?

Plans, as I should have known by then, never work out as they should.

All of the comedians who had agreed to play were working performers, many quite famous. They had, often, spouses and children to feed, so if paying work came along, of course they had to take it. Not all of them made the gigs. Audiences were also variable. In fact, of the 60 (or 59) booked, only 43 turned up and played. I claimed that this by definition made me only 43 years old, but that did not reduce the wrinkles.

Was it paranoia, or did I draw from this situation a conclusion that I was less popular than I thought I was? I had sort of assumed that doing a lot of things for a lot of performers (although far fewer than there later would be) would put a few good-guy points in my bank. But it never works out that way. Remember when you tried to pay off your bullies at school? That sort of thing.

Truth is, one never knows.

On the morning of my 60th birthday, I went to the Post Office to claim my free bus pass. And the person who served me said "happy birthday". Which was nice.

I looked forward to travel without cost on all London's buses, tubes and other transport thingies. When I have leisure, I thought, I shall travel from one end of my city to the other. For that was the limit of the pass, in those days.

But later that month, I discovered that from 1st April 2008, my pass would be valid (between 9.30 am and 11pm) on every local bus in the land.

And the light bulb pinged above my head.

Right, I said: I'm going to Edinburgh.

I contacted the Guardian and they said they'd print a diary of my journey, and pay a small sum for it, and send a photographer to see me off and another to catch me arriving. All I had to do was acquire the huskies, the pith helmet and the native trailfinders. No, they didn't say that, and neither did I. I wrote that in the pub.

If this goes well, I thought, or even if it fails spectacularly, I have my one-man show for the 2008 Free Fringe.

I wrote up the journey in some detail and put it on my Myspace blog, which I cannot now access. I should have kept a copy. I could just have pasted it here, and bulked out this book a little. But that would have been cheating. So I'll have to summarise.

The Guardian did send the photographers and I sailed forth on the first legal bus of 1st April, photographed for several stops, to the consternation of my fellow passengers who knew I wasn't famous but yet I was being photographed by an obviously professional snapper.

The Guardian, however, never paid me or published the thing. It turned out that their travel section had commissioned exactly the same thing from somebody else. No liaison between sections. And, as I should have realised but didn't, on the first day of the universal bus pass, practically every over-60 in the country was attempting to travel as far as he/she could on their pass. I wasn't the only one with the idea. D'oh.

To cut quite a long story short, three days, 27 buses and one major cheat later, I arrived at the door of the Canons' Gait at 4.38pm. Such is the friendliness of Edinburgh, the driver of the final bus, a 35, held up the rest of his passengers so the photographer could take several shots of me getting off. Such was my state of mind, I wished the photo session would be over so I could get inside and consume a pint of something, followed by several more of the same.

Very little happened on the journey, from bus to bus to bus. The rule I set myself was not to consult timetables in advance, but only to decide the next journey from the buses available when I had got off the previous one. Hardly arctic exploration, but at least not mechanical.

But enough happened to make a show out of it. No slide projection, even though I had photographed each bus (only one driver objected, in the vicinity of Leeds; perhaps he spotted me for a native Lancastrian). Just talking through the journey, including three gags and four lies, immediately admitted to when told. And a small amount of statistics, with the mean of the bus route numbers on which I had travelled (132.4), the weighted mean and the standard deviation.

It shouldn't really have worked as a show, but it did, especially when audience were in who lived along the routes of the buses I'd taken.

And may I recommend the seats on the 36 Leeds to Ripon, and the scenery on the X15 (or 501, as it then was) Newcastle to Berwick-on-Tweed. And not the 5 from Darlington to Bishop Auckland, which goes down every side street in between the two, sometimes twice. And do not believe bus drivers never get lost or take wrong turnings, for on the way from Ripon to Northallerton both happened.

I was happy with the show, because it meant I could tell a story happily enough, without having to twist and wrench it to accommodate gags. I was pleased, and although few fellow comedians came to see it, many heard of it and remember me for it. Or they did, then.

I am getting ahead of myself. Wind the tape back to the preparations for the 2008 Free Fringe, the second year after the Laughing Horse backstab.

We had over 100 shows, a big leap over 2007.

And 2008 marked the first appearance of the Wee Blue Book itself, although it wasn't called that then. But it was a book (or a booklet, A4 folded and stapled to A5) and it had a blue cover with the logo, and the venue map on the back; the same format as we have used ever since.

And this time it was professionally designed and laid out. A vast improvement on what I had been able to cobble together with my limited (indeed, almost vanishing) graphic skills. Duncan Bolt, a performer, had taken charge and had done a proper job. The pictures lined up with each other. The venues were colour-coded in the listings. There were headers and footers. And a tiny flying pig on the cover. I'm not sure what that was meant to symbolise: perhaps the impossibility of the whole enterprise?

The format's remained the same except for one decision I made in 2009. Let's face it, I had unwillingly become boss of something, so I had to make at least one decision. But not yet; we're still in 2008.

We had eleven venues. Back in the old solo days, I didn't think there were 11 viable venues in Edinburgh. But there were, and many more to be discovered. Finding them was almost as exciting as the Great Bus Trip.

Some venues that you think will probably not work, do work. And the other way round. Odd shapes with difficult sightlines ought to be a major problem, but actually aren't so much. The oddness helps to produce an ambiance or atmosphere. Whereas sterile rooms seldom work. We went through a phase of looking at hotel function rooms, but, even if they had been available, they would have been devoid of atmosphere.

The most important question one has to ask in looking for new venues is: where are the toilets?

I discovered, and Calum showed me, several pubs with function space but which disqualified themselves by having the pub's only toilets in the function space. Sometimes both sexes, sometimes one. But either way you can't run a show with people constantly walking through it to find the toilet. And back a few minutes later. But it's even worse when they look at the scene with confusion, and then interrupt the show to ask where the toilet is. Any such venue we had to rule out, however promising it otherwise was.

But we ended with clusters. Two venues in the vicinity of Haymarket Station (Mercat Bar and Voodoo Bar), two on George Street close to the Assembly Rooms (Madogs and the Standing Order), Nicol Edwards on Niddry Street (now the Banshee Labyrinth), our pair on Canongate (Canons' Gait and White Horse), the Phoenix in isolation on Broughton Street and the Arts Complex on London Road, which we used for Theatre.

We were beginning to snowball, or do I mean avalanche? Same substance; different degrees of control and destruction. Avalanche, therefore. Two of these venues had been found or recommended by a third (the Mercat, and thank you Graeme).

Calum had found and arranged the Arts Complex. We were getting several Theatre applications and I wanted to book them; it seemed to me fatal to confine ourselves to Comedy. We were about all the arts, if they could be done using our system. Theatre required a different sort of space, and it wasn't easy to find. Church halls would have been ideal, but all the churches that were willing had already been tapped by pay-to-play promoters.

Arts Complex was a large former Government office block which was being used for arts purposes, and I'm glad to say still is. It was somewhat out of the Fringe area, requiring a bus trip more usually than a walk. But there was so much empty space in it. If it had not been for the Laughing Horse, we could have put the whole Free Fringe there, and said to the public: if you want good free shows, take this short trip. But we couldn't, because there were rival free shows that didn't require the trip.

As I may have said before, people will travel further for Theatre than for Comedy. And so it, mostly, proved.

I'm dwelling on this one; I'll come to the rest in a minute. But to me it was important. I wanted to establish that we could do Theatre as well as comedy, and apart from the two plays in the previous year, that hadn't yet been proved.

I salute Chris Lincé, playwright, who designed our logo. Chris had a play in the 2008 programme. And to make it succeed, he brought with him Nic Watson, theatre technician extraordinaire. I had known Nic for a while, but when I saw how he had transformed a huge empty space in Arts Complex into a comfortable theatre of the right size, my jaw dropped. And it dropped again when, in a dispute over which floors we did and did not have permission to use, he took it all down and put it up again in a different place.

I don't remember the details of that dispute, but it was major. It delayed the opening of the shows by a few days and that I spent ages driving Calum, Nic and Chris around in vain attempts to find the decision-maker.

And one other thing. Before the Fringe, I received an email. Its author said that we had no permission to use Arts Complex whatsoever, that Calum was deceiving us and that he was a "serial fantasist" who was not to be trusted. If we persisted, said the email, we would only be disappointed.

This wasn't anonymous, or even malicious. The author clearly believed what he wrote and was, as he thought, doing us a favour by warning us of disaster.

What do I believe? Whom do I believe? What contingency plans do I make?

For certainly, if you meet Calum for the first time, he seems like a bullshitter. And he certainly has more ideas than can possibly be brought to fruition, and sometimes quite fantastic plans.

What people are is not always what they seem. And sometimes people are what they seem for some of the time and not for the rest. Does that make sense? Well, life doesn't, and nor did that situation.

I had no plan B, and no mans of drawing one up. Having decided in the first place to trust Calum, I stuck by that decision. And it wasn't misplaced. He delivered. But all the renegotiations, and the finding of the decision-maker, and the car journeys of the first few days, were stressful and did lead me to doubt.

The Free Fringe needs certainty about venues. But we seldom get it, and perhaps we never will. The stress of the uncertainty is such that I wouldn't recommend anybody to do my job, anywhere in the world. You may let a large number of people down through no fault of your own, and even if they'd paid nothing (as Free Fringers don't) they'll still hate you. And I understand why they would.

The first week of that Fringe was almost all about Arts Complex, for me. But it was sorted out, and things went ahead, and

audiences took the bus trip. I wouldn't base a future round
that venue, though, good though the space itself was. And the
lifts became non-operational, which meant that wheelchair
access wasn't what we said it would be, to the frustration of at
least one potential audience member.

When something's doomed, it stays doomed.

One of the theatre groups involved, doing a piece related to
street culture, took it upon themselves to spray-paint the
space with street-like graffiti, towards the end of their run.
And they left that in place, looking for all the world as if genuine graffiti artists had broken in and tagged (is that the right
word?) the place.

Naturally, I got a complaint about that from the venue, after
the Fringe, with a demand that it should be made good. And
that was fair.

I contacted the group. Haha, they said: the Fringe is over.
You can't touch us.

This was a harbinger. I learned from that: it only takes one
rogue to completely damage the Free Fringe's reputation. And
if they don't get the ethos of co-operation, so much damage
can ensue.

That theme was to recur in future Free Fringes.

But meanwhile, that problem was to be faced. Two fingers
had been waved in my face. Was I to accept that?

Those who know me might suspect not.

The group were, as I found from their application (in those
days not on a form, but all done informally by email) students
at the University of Redsnow. That's obviously not its real
name. It's a famous and highly ranked university. An institution with a great history of performing arts and other things,
where a famous televised comedy duo had met. And, although
this has nothing to do with the performing arts, where I had
completed my doctorate.

And who had been my doctoral supervisor? One of the Pro-
Vice-Chancellors, that's who. Professor Millicent Ford, CBE,
and that's not her real name either. And I had met the Vice-
Chancellor himself, Professor Sir Jeremy Rhymer, through her,

and that's not his real name either. I'm hopeless at pseudo-nyms. (Actually, he may not have been Sir Jeremy at that point, but it was fairly obvious he would be eventually, and he now is. Doesn't matter. Vice-Chancellors are gods, knighted or not).

Knowing that if necessary I had contacts at god-level in the University, I emailed these students' Head of Department.

Small thermonuclear devices exploded. And very soon a cheque from the students for the full extent of the damage came my way, along with a letter of apology I never bothered to open. Apology changes nothing; forced apology even less. But the Redsnow Faculty were most keen to defend their reputation, and for that I am most grateful.

It did reinforce my role as Mr Nasty (not Mark Kelly's Mr Nasty, who is a much nicer Mr Nasty than I shall ever be). To do this job properly, I had to accept that I would do things that made enemies.

And that was not what I had set out to do. I had attempted to buy friends. Still, although friends have to be bought, enemies are free. And frequent.

Well, that was the Theatre section. I'd learned that the demands of many Theatre companies could be heavy, and although you explain to them that we're only going to provide a basic space with no facilities, they don't always listen.

In the event, and thanks to Nic, we provided much more than that. And we even managed to borrow top-of-the-range chairs for the audience — another Calum deal. Both of these weren't going to be repeated in future years. And we'd have to make damn sure that theatre groups knew that. There are some people so out of touch with reality that they expect to get a fully rigged and staffed theatre for no money, and then when they don't, it's somehow our fault. We'd have to work harder on our information in future years.

So, back to the Comedy section. As I said, I'd rather neglected that for the first week while we sorted out the Arts Complex. I did my own shows, of course, but I had been doing no troubleshooting in the Comedy venues while the Theatre problems took centre stage (see what I did there? Oh, never mind).

This was wrong because we had many new venues in the Comedy section. And new venues need reassuring.

Troubleshooting is the order of the day. When audiences start to dip, as they will in on the first Tuesday and Wednesday, they lose faith and can do silly things.

All our venues had advantages and disadvantages. And, if shows are absolutely dedicated to making them work, they will work despite any disadvantages. But, as I was to discover, not all shows are dedicated to making their venues work.

I had, to an extent, forgotten what I learned in 1994 at my first Fringe. It's difficult, it's demoralising, you don't know where to turn, and it's easy to give up and go home. Or just go through the motions for the full three weeks, without really trying. And, when you see for the first time how good everybody else (well, most other people else) is, you do undergo a crisis of confidence that can kill your show.

I knew that, but where I should have been is among the newcomers and the new venues, spreading that message. Not debugging the Theatre section, important as that also was.

And, if I couldn't do all that myself, which I clearly couldn't, I needed to ensure we became a self-supporting community where the experienced passed on encouragement to the less experienced.

The two venues near Haymarket Station needed support. One was new, the other was the Mercat. Relatively isolated from fringegoer traffic, these two had to support each other. Some shows did; some others blamed us for putting them in isolation, as if we had snubbed them deliberately rather than work with whatever viable venues we could get.

I don't blame the shows for losing heart. Not all of them did, and both venues came back the next year, so many good things also happened there. But, because the Free Fringe makes things so much easier for performers, I had lost sight of the fact that it's still hard, and always will be. And, when it doesn't work, as it will not for many, they'll blame any factor they can see, including and especially the people who worked hard to get them a venue for nothing.

The Standing Order was going great guns. If guns can ever be great, which given their propensity to kill people may not be the case. They had a room at the front, facing George Street, which packed for almost every show. Passers-by could see the shows through the windows and came in. And, of course, they benefited from Wetherspoons' low prices for real ale, a big advantage in a sometimes expensive Fringe.

No, in an always-expensive Fringe, with occasional pockets of cheap.

If it had not been for the man, still around in Fringe circles and therefore not named here, who persuaded me to book a rather punkish and sweary act who had a cult following on cable, or YouTube, or something. Now, nothing against that act. Not my cup of tea, but I didn't have to like everybody, just know that they were competent in their own ways.

The mistake I made there was not insisting on speaking to the act himself.

So, when the intermediary, or manager, told me at very short notice that the act couldn't come, I was screwed.

Ah, but the man had a solution. He'd find another show to fill the gap.

I had no choice. I couldn't have a gap. Not in a new venue that we had to impress.

The show he gave us was — himself.

Had the originally booked act ever even known that he'd been booked?

Was this a con of some sort? How could I tell?

And in the last week, I was approached by a completely different person. Again, somebody who's still around, so I won't name him. He thanked me for the opportunity and could he please have the artwork for the logo?

Erm, what opportunity?

Person A had other business in the last week, and so had sub-contracted his slot.

Now, Person B was innocent here; he'd accepted in good faith. In later years, he was to have much to do with faith and doubt. But at that time, he was an unknown quantity. I had to accept him; he was not guilty of anything, he kept the slot filled and I had nothing else waiting,

But I wasn't happy. We couldn't have people trading their slots. How would we know money had not changed hands? How would we assure the quality of anything arriving by this route? We already had a rule against it happening, but we needed to reinforce it.

Also at the Standing Order that year we had the Fringe's only fart act: Mr Methane. Part of a long and noble tradition that encompassed Josef Pujol and, er, Mr Methane, and as far as I can see, nobody else. Josef Pujol was on the cover of Sergeant Pepper. Mr Methane wasn't. Perhaps he should have been. Keep flatulence British.

In the end, our attempts to keep the Standing Order were in vain. The accountants, far away from Edinburgh, compared our takings to what they might have achieved from food service, and claimed that comparison worked against us to the tune of £28000. Or so I was told, a couple of months later, by the Standing Order's manager. Now, this number is arbitrary. They couldn't estimate how much drink was served over the main bar because of our shows; they couldn't estimate how much food would otherwise have been eaten in the same space. But clearly the numbers didn't work out for them, and especially not for the manager, who had enjoyed the shows but not the feedback from Head Office on his figures.

It was a good try. We did what we could.

The way the Free Fringe works, for venues, is by turning dead space into live space. Not live space into a different sort of live space. Our targets were otherwise-underused pub (and other) function rooms, and nightclubs during the day. Adding to their business, not cannibalising it. And we can almost never compete against food service, which is almost always more profitable for the venue than our shows.

One of the triumphs of that year was Robin Ince.

Now, I'd known Robin for years, and he'd known what I was trying to achieve. He'd played Peter Buckley Hill and Some Comedians every year except the first. I counted him as a friend, if anybody's ever a real friend in this business. I'd been part of his core team at the Book Club, which was a wonderful thing.

He was less famous then than he is now, but he was a cult.

He also became one of the reasons we became an option for higher-profile artists.

We have to speculate a little here. I don't know this stuff for a fact. Nevertheless, I believed at the time that the major pay-to-play venues, the so-called Big Four, did not always apply their tariffs equally or impartially for all applicants.

If you were famous enough, I believed, you got a deal that was not available to the non-famous.

If your name was big enough, you could make a profit on your Fringe run. Not only would your name sell your show out, but you could also, as I believed but without concrete evidence, get a deal that cost you less for venue space.

Other shows at the same venue would be on a full-cost deal and would therefore not usually make a profit.

For that reason, I thought, we would not get famous acts on board. Good ones, certainly. But the very advantage that we offered to performers would be no advantage to those in a position to negotiate preferential deals with the pay-to-play venues.

Robin, however, had not been happy with the deals he had previously had at the money Fringe. Nor did he particularly like the atmosphere of the Fringe itself; late-night boasting about one's audience and eternal contact-making was not for him. Actually, he's not alone in that. Mostly, doing that stuff is people's way of being part of a community of performers.

He wasn't going to commit for a full run, lest he be equally miserable. Instead, he set us, or rather me, a challenge. Could we cram as many performances of three different shows into a 48-hour visit to the Fringe?

We could. I could. As long as it wasn't a weekend. We just make maximum use of other performers' days off. People often take one day off a week, and believe me one needs it.

So, after due discussion, we settled on eight hour-long shows in two days, plus guest slots in Peter Buckley Hill and Some Comedians, and a few others he arranged himself.

I turned up for Robin's first one-man show, at the Beehive. Nice and early, but the queue was already spilling out on to the street, for a 60-seater room. I counted them down and had to inform the people at the end that they stood little chance of getting in. They were disappointed and sometimes annoyed. But that's first-come-first-served for you.

I learned that we'd have to be careful of our door procedures in the case of highly popular shows. But, because I managed that queue, things proceeded fairly smoothly.

He went straight from that show to his second, at the Dragonfly. I didn't follow. I was due to do a show myself, so I couldn't. I'd have to rely on our other shows at the Dragonfly to do what they were supposed to.

As I later learned, they didn't. Nearly 80 people got into a 30-35 seater room. Fortunately there wasn't a fire. The Dragonfly used to be called the Old Fire Station, but that wouldn't have saved it.

Tighten up on the briefing. Make sure everybody understands that they have to do door duty for the shows before and after them, and that includes controlling the size of the crowd against the fire safety limit.

Many shows saw that need immediately. Some didn't. And to this day we have a problem with shows that don't.

But Robin enjoyed his flying visit, and that raised our profile. As I've said before, people's natural reaction is to think that free equals rubbish. With a name like Robin's on board, that shook this belief. Yes, we'd already built up an audience by then, but there were still many fringegoers who were reluctant to try us or believe in our quality.

We had some good other shows that year also, including one future Perrier winner.

We were well set up. We'd recovered from the attempted coup; we'd spread to a then record number of venues.

Nicol Edwards on Niddry Street was doing splendid business on two stages.

And a delight happened. The owner of the Dragonfly asked if I'd be interested in seeing another venue he owned. Of course I would.

And he took me to the Voodoo Rooms. Would I be interested in programming the smaller room for 2009?

Was the Pope Catholic? Was the Moderator of the General Assembly of the Church of Scotland a Rangers supporter? Yes.

It was a sort of vindication. This was a famous Fringe venue when it was the Café Royal. It had since changed ownership (the ground floor pub is still the Café Royal, but now has no association). And years earlier, I had been invited to a small private party there, during the Fringe, to celebrate somebody's birthday. But because I'd been on stage, I arrived late and they'd all gone. I ate the remnants of the party food, and the most obnoxious and rude Dutch barperson in the world threw me out, refusing to believe I had been invited. Edinburgh is a friendly and tolerant city, so what she did rankled several degrees deep. I hadn't been back since.

But now there were new owners, and I had a chance to programme this brilliant space. Did I have the acts to justify it? Oh yes, I assured them. Because it was true.

If we had famous Fringe venues like that, and Nicol Edwards, how could we go wrong for 2009?

So after the bad start to Fringe 2008, all seemed well. A few things were wrong, but I was too stupid to see them at the time. I assumed everybody on board believed in what we were trying to do for performers. I should have known better. Some were taking what they could get and giving nothing back.

Vigilance. Eternal vigilance. I wasn't doing it, eternally or otherwise.

Still, Robin may not have been doing the rounds of the bars where performers go to wind down and lie about how well their shows were doing, but I was. It could have been duty; it could have been pleasure, or it could have been a simple addiction to drink. Whatever it was, I went to them.

Those were the places where one could meet people whom one liked, or who could be useful, and sometimes they were even the same people. I filled up the guest slots on Peter Buckley Hill and Some Comedians that way, and got some good and famous acts.

But, in the Loft Bar, the act I remember was Sean Lock. And I don't think I'd actually met him before that night; if I had, it was only fleetingly. But he approached me and told me he liked what I was doing for performers. Well, I wasn't going to tell him to stop saying that, was I?

And then he came out with it. Book a theatre for a benefit show, he said, and I'll headline it.

Bingo. I accepted.

This was all the more welcome, because we had no income other than the sale of advertising in the Wee Blue Book. And of course that didn't cover costs, let alone the increasing number of trips I was making to Edinburgh. The loss was coming out of my own pocket. Well, yes, of course it was a tax-deductable loss, but still a loss.

With Sean's idea, we could perhaps break even.

You won't believe me when I say: I'd never thought of a benefit show. I'd thought of sponsorship, but dismissed the idea for many reasons. But that approach I hadn't considered. Other famous comedians had in the past praised what we were trying to do: Stewart Lee and Richard Herring in particular. But until Sean spoke I hadn't thought of converting that goodwill.

With money worries likely to be alleviated, there was good reason to look forward to 2009.

So I could finish the run on a big mistake. The last day, I felt light-headed. The job was almost done. My shows, at least, had gone well. Foolish things happen at the Fringe. So, for my last show, I bought a cheap kilt and had myself piped on stage.

Not entitled to a kilt. Not Scottish. But it was a gesture. And an experience I had not so far had. Scots had spoken to me of the swagger they felt when walking in a kilt. This experience shall be mine, I thought. And a sort of tribute to the host country. And it was a cheap kilt, not a £600 job, for that is what the good ones cost.

I wore the kilt for the final performance. Which was all very well. And I wore it as it should be worn, or as I had been told it should be worn. It's probably a myth. No problem thus far. But one of the things in my act at the time was a parody of Wonderful Tonight. In which I did a mock guitar solo. And struck a mock-guitar-solo pose. Which normally involves putting one foot on the monitors, or failing the monitors (which indeed we did not have) on a chair.

I forgot I was wearing the kilt. The pose gave the audience perfect visibility right up it. The front row, as one person, moved three feet backwards without leaving their chairs, or so it seemed.

I gather quite a number of web sites are dedicated to so-called upskirt shots. I wouldn't know anything about that, of course. But now I have some idea of how the involuntarily-pictured skirt wearers feel. And I grossed out the entire last-night audience. If only I had worn the comedy stockings of the 1995 Bear Pit. But they were deliberate, and the Great Kilt Exposure was accidental.

Honestly. It was. I had enough problems without adding potential charges of mass indecent exposure to them. Take me back to England where the kilts are few.

*

2009

READER, I MARRIED HIM.

No, I didn't. That doesn't even make sense.

2009 was the year things worked best. 2009 was the year we should have stopped. We attained a peak. We could climb no higher, but we didn't realise that at the time. Excelsior, we cried, not realising how strange our device was.

Well, that's spoiled the tension. And the Tennyson.

I, of course, was still wrestling with the day job, trying to clear my name and have my disability recognised. If I can't help it, which I can't, then they can't sack me for it. But in defiance of their own medical advisors, they refused to believe I couldn't help it.

So I wasn't exactly un-stressed as I went into the 2008/09 academic year, therefore the 2008/9 Fringe season.

As always, we tried to fix our venues as soon as possible after the Fringe. As always, our venue owners hesitated, changed and sometimes went out of business.

My dreams of a series of venues that would be with us year after year faded somewhat. I was coming to the conclusion that all venues had a limited life with us, although obviously we'd try to keep them as long as possible.

At that time, we were still gaining more venues than we were losing. But I felt very keenly every one we lost. It made me doubt that we had a good model for our business (if indeed we can call it a business).

And of course I would feel that we'd let our venues down. That's never a good feeling. I think some people would be indifferent to this, and maybe people like that make better promoters. I'm not indifferent. I don't like the thought of people not liking us.

It wasn't that much of a problem, in the season leading up to the 2009 Fringe. The Standing Order went, to my great disappointment. Yes, we had packed it out, but as I said earlier, compared to food service they claimed to have lost a five-figure sum. Nothing to be done about that.

And the Arts Complex was no more, for us. Too politically complicated; too far away from the epicentre of the Fringe, and too reliant on a theatre being specially rigged. Nic had done a great job in 2008, but we couldn't rely on that every year, particularly with the difficulty of bringing all the equipment from London.

We still wanted a Theatre section, though. And we achieved one.

But in a way that wasn't a natural development. Even the least complicated of Theatre pieces require some staging. And our whole concept was not to provide staging, since we had no money to do so. The simpler a show is, the easier it is to stage in the way the Free Fringe does things.

There was one art form that fitted our concept much better. Spoken Word.

Spoken word was the Cinderella of the Fringe. Except that it couldn't get in to the Ball no matter how many wands you waved over its pumpkin.

A Spoken Word show fitted nowhere in the Big Fat Fringe Programme. Anybody doing a Spoken Word show, be it poetry or storytelling or something else, had to describe him/herself under one of the existing headings: Comedy, Theatre or Events. Assuming they didn't come under Children's or Dance or Music.

And yet it could be good stuff. I'd seen one excellent poetry show back in 2001, and it was well attended. There was a market, and the possibility of doing a good job, if it was well curated. There were, of course, people who wrote 'poetry' as therapy for themselves, and we didn't want those. But there were also good Spoken Word artists, who could engage their audiences well.

So, when I got an application from such an artist, I immediately called for a meeting with him. Could we build a whole section of Spoken Word shows, despite their having no heading in the Big Fat Fringe Programme? He was enthusiastic. I, on my part, thought that the omission of Spoken Word in the BFFP could be easily rectified. Little was I to know how many years it would take.

He jumped. He had the contacts on the performance poetry scene. By putting the word around, he could deliver several shows, enough at least for a full-strength trial. We would put a Spoken Word section in the Wee Blue Book, and agitate for such a section in the BFFP. Hands were shaken on this deal.

We now had three genres. We weren't just a Comedy institution any more. We were active in several arts. That was the way we needed to go. Our Comedy section was merely bringing more comedy to a Fringe that already had a great deal of it. But with Spoken Word, we were taking a leading position.

I asked one of the Fringe's Board Directors to spearhead the movement for a separate Spoken Word heading in the BFFP. Back came the reply: he'd spoken to the Fringe Office, and they didn't think it was worth it. Why, I said; surely it could be done at zero cost? Oh no, he said; they'd have to reprogramme.

Then as now, the Fringe Office doesn't like their system being shaken up, and the maintenance of the system takes precedence over the needs of performers. Systems were written, and still are, around the needs of pay-to-play venues. Even as I write this, I face demands to approve each of our shows individually so they can be listed on-line as soon as possible. And yet that early on-line listing is meant to facilitate the sale of tickets, which does not affect our shows. In earlier days, all listings appeared at the same time, which is a much fairer system. But pay-to-play venues asked for a system of early listing and ticket sales, and this was done.

Funny how things are done at their request but not at ours.

And the deadlines; far too early for an operation like ours.

The Fringe Office has a cutoff point for the BFFP in early April, and a discount deadline a month earlier. At that stage of the year, we're still recruiting venues.

And, of course, at that stage of the year, we're still vulnerable to venues going out of business or being sold. And the

BFFP can't be changed. This is not a problem for the pay-to-play venues, who rent from the University with performers' money, and therefore know what spaces they have by Christmas. But it's a problem for us. I'm sure the Fringe Office would be happier if there were no Free Fringe at all.

Oh, and while I'm ranting: our shows pay for a box office system they don't use. Our shows pay nearly £400 for a 40-word listing, the same price as anybody else, whether their venue seats 30 or 1000.

So, the absence of Spoken Word wasn't the only thing that needed to change in the Fringe organisational setup.

But it was, at least, something we could campaign for, and meanwhile take a lead in providing good shows in that genre. And we recruited them.

Another piece of expansion was less successful. I was often asked: do you run (Comedy) clubs in London? Performers new to the game needed stage time to work on their craft, and many assumed that, because we had such a high profile at the Edinburgh Fringe, we would have a London operation also. We didn't. But why shouldn't we? It would give our performers the chance to try out material that might form part of their Fringe show.

It would also give us the chance to see performers in action, if we didn't already know them.

So, we tried it.

A deal was struck for a twice-weekly show in a pub in Leadenhall Market, in the City. At first, one of these shows was to have been a paid one (we had, after all, to raise money) and the other free. It soon became obvious that we needed to make both free-admission.

For the following we had built in Edinburgh proved not to be very transferable. Although the Edinburgh audience contained many Londoners, few were willing to come out and see us during the year. We had occasional good audiences, but mostly not.

Was it the right venue? It was lovely, but perhaps too much in the City, where people either go home after work or drink and talk until closing time.

Over the course of the year, it fizzled out, alas.

We had better luck with the benefit gig that Sean Lock had proposed, back in the Loft Bar. I booked the Bloomsbury Theatre, a place I had performed in several times and a general favourite among comedians, on a date in January. They gave us a reasonable deal. By which I mean: straight takings split, no guarantee or upfront payment.

It took, I admit, more organisation than I had expected. For it wasn't a question of Sean doing a whole show. You couldn't reasonably ask that of him. There's a standard format for these things, and it involves getting several, say eight or ten, acts to do shorter sets. We had to find the others. Robin Ince, enthused by his 48 hours at the Free Fringe and already signed up to do a full run in 2009, helped a great deal in this.

And in the end a wondrous bill was put together.

The poster highlighted four acts: Sean Lock, Dave Gorman, Robin Ince and Milton Jones. And in smaller print, although deserving of larger, were Wil Hodgson, Tony Law, Lucy Porter, Gavin Osborn and Waen Shepherd.

It sold out. It was a great show. The Daily Telegraph sent a reviewer and give it four stars, although it was worthy of five. Maybe he/she knocked a star off because of the compère, who I regret to say was me.

And we had revenue. The expenses of trips to Edinburgh would be covered, as would buying PA if we couldn't borrow it, printing backdrops, and a good slice of the print bill for the Wee Blue Book.

It meant that revenue would, of course, have to go through the Company. It was no longer a case of me financing the Free Fringe personally. Things would be on a proper footing from here on in. My accountant agreed to do the accounts at a rate reflecting the non-profit status of the Company, but of course he still had to charge something.

That may be the most boring paragraph I've written so far. But these things had to be considered. And, of course, it meant that the Free Fringe's losses were no longer allowable against my personal tax. As against that, I would have a substantial equity in the Company, so any surplus up to that equity amount would belong to me. In the light of the money I'd poured into the Free Fringe over the years, that's fair.

Oh, and it meant that anybody could see the statements of account, so they would know there was fair play.

So much for high finance.

Meanwhile, some of the high finance was being spent on trips to Edinburgh in the eternal search for venues.

Some of the ones we found, or rather persuaded to come on board, were excellent. One was disastrous. We had a total of 19 venues in the end, a figure I thought remarkable.

Some of these are still with us. Bannermans, at the corner of Niddry Street and Cowgate, still is. Essentially a music pub, and an excellent one, but willing to let us use their music room during the day. It had, of course, PA and a stage, two things which were not always guaranteed at other venues.

We also made arrangements with both of Edinburgh's piano bars, Fingers and the Rat Pack. In Fingers we scheduled much of the Spoken Word. We guessed that they would need something distinctive, and that mere Comedy wouldn't suit them. That was only partly right, but we did well enough to continue into future years. The Rat Pack was one of those frustrating shapes into which you could pack well over 100 people, but wherever you put the stage you could only get 30 people who could actually see it.

We pushed ourselves geographically. One venture was into Tollcross, at a pub delightfully named The Illicit Still. Very near the newly -opened Royal Bank of Scotland headquarters, before the scandals. Perhaps bankers would come to shows after work? The landlord was keen; there wasn't a separate space but he curtained the bar so we had three-quarters of the pub, and attracted a local audience. The afternoon shows didn't pull in as many people as we'd hoped, and where there isn't full separation of shows and drinking area, there are always problems. A good atmosphere, nevertheless.

No, that wasn't one of the year's two venue headaches. Both of the headaches stemmed from a change of management, or ownership, at Nicol Edwards. Did I say that this is the venue known nowadays as the Banshee Labyrinth? Well, it is. And our contact from the previous year had moved on, leaving it managerless. And, in the event, it didn't open. One of those situations where we couldn't find who to contact, nobody contacted us, nobody we asked knew anything and we just had to hope.

It's a wonder I didn't turn to religion, especially the pagan ceremonies for the manipulation of minds. But I believe one needs some nail-clippings or similar from the person one's trying to manipulate. We didn't have a name, let alone nail clippings.

And they stayed closed.

But Calum charged to the rescue once again. Just up the street was The Globe Bar. I had walked past a hundred times. Backpackers, I said to myself; no ale, not our sort of place. But I, of course, am an idiot. Calum went in and looked. Two good arch spaces, each opening on to the bar, each of which could be curtained at the open end. Two stages, replacing two at Nicol Edwards, a minute away. Once again, the miracle was ours, at short notice; once again, audiences were diverted by a notice on a closed venue. We managed to change the Wee Blue Book listings.

But what of the man who had managed Nicol Edwards?

He contacted me. He had a venue to propose.

It was around this time that our applications started vastly outweighing the number of stages we had to accommodate them. It's stayed that way ever since, except sometimes in June or July, but those are stories for later.

I hate to turn a good show down. And for that reason I have sometimes taken venues I should not have taken.

But never, never, one with as many problems as Cruz.

It was a boat-bar. Two decks. One clear function space which would have been fine for our shows. That wasn't the problem.

It was in Leith.

Anybody reading this who doesn't know the geography of Edinburgh? Alright, you can put your hands down now. For you, then, Leith is the old port of Edinburgh; a separate city, or cultural entity. Where the police used to patrol in pairs and fear and trembling, and where the red light district still is. A fearsome reputation, between the wars. Populated by dockers and seamen and similar, not that I want to say anything against them. Like Wapping, but Scottish and not Edinburgh. There's a point halfway down Leith Walk at which one becomes the other, and even now you'd better know which you're in. In local government terms, however, they've long ago been amalgamated.

But we're writing (we? When did I become Queen or Pope?) about 2009. What happens to areas like that in the 21st Century? They gentrify, that's what. There were upmarket developments in the former warehouses that contained Scotland's imports. The old population mixed with the new. And the now decommissioned Royal Yacht Britannia is parked there.

All my Edinburgh-resident friends would say: there are some good usable rooms in Leith; why don't you put some shows down there?

Visitors to Edinburgh for the Fringe didn't tend to go to Leith. But many Edinburghers, sorry, Leithers, lived there. There might be an audience.

And so I was persuaded, by the former manager of Nicol Edwards, to schedule a full slate of shows in Cruz.

Reader, I really wish I hadn't married him.

Could we have complete, uninterrupted use of the function room (or was it a function deck?), I asked him.

Absolutely, he said. We have no other bookings. See, I'm marking it in for you now.

And he promised to buy a full-page advertisement in the Wee Blue Book.

We cherish venues who do that. But in this case we cherished wrong.

I tried to programme many of our Edinburgh-based applicants into that space. I thought their local following would tie in well with the more local audience we would expect. Clearly there would be a problem bringing Fringe visitors down from the safety of the Royal Mile. But how good would it be if visitors learned to use the whole city for shows? Maybe we could take a step towards that.

Wrong thinking on my part. Very wrong, very very wrong. Our contact left his post before the Fringe started. We were in the hands of strangers.

And those strangers had another diary. Not the one our contact had looked up and pronounced the room clear of bookings. A different one, in which there were PLENTY of bookings.

And on those many days, they set up the shows in the bar itself. Where people were drinking and talking and ignoring the shows.

And they said the stupid thing that many people say; the thing that, when I hear, I run a mile from that venue.

"If your comedians were any good, they'd be able to handle that".

Yes, we really love talking to people who aren't listening. Yes, those non-listening people are really going to give generously to the bucket. Yes, we've worked for a year or more writing a show that's different from anybody else's, just so we can stand in the corner of your bar dying.

Aaaaarrrgghhhh.

All these years later, there are still some Scottish comedians who won't speak to me because of what I wished on them at Cruz.

And, after the Fringe, when I tried to collect the payment due for the advert they had taken out, they threw me off the boat. Admittedly, not into the water, but still.

Most experiences have a redeeming feature. It's hard to find such a feature in our Cruz experience.

No more geographical experiments. If the Fringe chooses to squash itself into the middle of the City, then we shall have to squash with it.

Maybe, sometime in the future, if they build the tramline to Leith, Leith might become viable. Although even now there are perfectly good buses. Why will people ride trams and not ride buses? Discuss.

Losing Nicol Edwards before the Fringe was a nightmare. But Cruz was a nightmare, daymare, twilightmare and any other mare you care to name, and not one that would ever win the insert-name-of-mares'-famous-horserace here. I know nothing of horseracing and Google isn't helping. Horseracing is known for blaming the poorly-paid man with the flag for a screwup by much higher-class people. I wish I had a man with a flag. Cruz was my screwup. The danger signs were there. I ignored them. I was blinded by a nice room and an ad sale.

Sorry, sorry, sorry.

So far, this is not sounding like the good year I said it would be.

Another new venue for 2009 was Jenny Ha's, at the bottom of the Royal Mile near Holyrood. Another geographical experiment, if you like. The Royal Mile is one of the most famous streets in the world. But like another famous street, New York's Broadway, it has an end that is less well visited.

Under another name, Jenny Ha's was destined to become another staple Free Fringe venue. But in 2009 it was an experiment, and again one that did not work perfectly. It split naturally into two areas, and we were promised the larger, but again management changed (actually, twice) and new management would only give us the smaller. We made do. We put some Shakespeare down there, with a cast of 25, most of whom had to wait outside in the rain for their entrances. Still, Shakespeare himself was used to putting on his shows in pubs that weren't necessarily designed for it. The drama students involved should at least learned from that. I hope at least some of them are now in the RSC. They deserve to be.

I have to mention also that more competition had emerged, in the shape of the Five Pound Fringe. Four or five venues in which tickets were a flat-rate £5, less than half the prince of a ticket at the "major" venues. Some quite good acts, also. We weren't sure what the impact of that was going to be.

So, after all that stress and all those changes and all these pre-fringe problems, you can imagine I arrived in Edinburgh in a frazzle. Friday is always setup day. So I sit, or sat, all day in the Canons' Gait, with all the Free Fringers coming to me and being sent out again on rigging tasks and similar assignments. Surrounded by PA, sending two mics here and some speakers elsewhere and backdrops everywhere, and the questions. Oh, yes, the questions. Answered ten times over in the email briefings to all shows, but asked again anyway.

Enter, stage right, Kate Copstick.

I may have mentioned her. She wrote the article in 2006 that led to the Laughing Horse's attempted coup. She had a reputation. She was the lead Comedy reviewer for The Scotsman. And if she did not like your show, she would review in unforgiving terms. Famously, she once said that she would rather cut out and eat her own ovaries than watch another minute of a certain show. I have no ovaries; I therefore don't know how they taste. She has ovaries, but I bet she doesn't know how they taste either. Probably like scrambled eggs, unless removed carefully. The phrase begs many questions. The point, however, is nothing to do with ovaries. It is to do with the vehemence of print criticism, and the goalkeeper's fear of the penalty.

Now, I knew her, of course. One can't be around the Fringe for as many years as I had been, and not. She had written about me. But I did not know her well. I knew nothing of her admirable charity work, for example, until many years later, and because I did not know that, I thought less of her.

To my shame, I thought of her as I thought of many critics; people who dared not face the bulls but criticised the cape and sword work of those who did dare.

But on that Friday in 2009, as I say, she entered. And spake thus:

"I have come to review your show".

That would be my one-man show, scheduled at five past six.

Ah no, I said, you haven't. It's not on today. Observe the Big Fat Fringe Programme; observe the Wee Blue Book. It starts tomorrow. The error, dear Doyenne of Critics, is yours, not ours.

I probably didn't say that last bit. I might have, years later. But then, not. She was feared and I should have been feart. Her words could kill. (Note clever use of the Scots dialect to make a point two sentences earlier. Memo to self: don't do that very often. You're not Scottish.)

I knew nothing of her work among the marginalised communities of Kenya, then. Neither, I think, did many other performers. All I knew was her reputation as a negative reviewer. Yes, of course she gave positive reviews also. The ones that got talked about, however, were the negative ones.

Very well, she said, acknowledging her scheduling error. I'll be back tomorrow.

Just what I needed. Even a problemless Free Fringe setup is stressful; a setup that has involved last-minute changes of venue (Nicol Edwards to Globe) and an incipient disaster (Cruz) is considerably more stressful.

So, the most-feared reviewer at the Fringe is coming in on my first night.

And I haven't rehearsed the show. I've been much too busy shooting problems.

Not only have I not rehearsed it; I don't really know what it consists of. Yes, I have some idea. I'm not that unprofessional. But my shows have always been informal, and change from day to day. I'm not like (insert name of famous televised comedian here) who says exactly the same thing every time, but rehearses his delivery so it sounds like new.

My show in 2009 consisted of a number of different, but new, bits. Some of them I'd tried out at Old Rope at the Phoenix. Some, I hadn't. I had a set list, and a few reserve bits. It was the first show in which I had no songs. I always thought of myself as a comic songwriter, and most of my past shows had several songs in them. All shows had had at least one, except the bus show. This, therefore, was my first pure stand-up show. (The bus show counted as a storytelling show; there were no real gags in it).

And I'd never run the show as a unit, and now the most feared critic on the Fringe was coming to the very first performance.

And the organisation of 170 shows is weighing on my shoulders. Come on, oh you gods, do I need this? Do I deserve this? Was I a senior Nazi in my last life, that this shitpile of karma is being poured on me?

Well, in theory I could have been, if you believe in reincarnation and karma. I was born in March 1948. Adolf Hitler himself, dead in the bunker on April 30th 1945, would have had time for a nice rest in limbo before being reconceived as me sometime in June 1947. But I don't think I was him. He liked dogs and was unfailingly polite to his secretaries. Maybe I was some minor, but karma-deserving, Third Reich functionary? Or maybe I'd just trodden on a butterfly in 1417 and changed the course of history. Or introduced Mary Stuart to Lord Darnley. Or not.

I might have deserved Copstick in a past life, but I hadn't so far deserved her in this one.

I suppose it was my own fault for playing the system.

The show was called "40 Words". The idea behind the title was that, for your Fringe Programme fee (nowadays £391; proportionally less then) you get a listing in the Big Fat Fringe Programme of precisely 40 words, including your show title.

There's not much you can do with 40 words. And yet you're encouraged to make them as distinctive as possible, so that you can stand out from 2000+ other shows in the Big Fat Fringe Programme.

Stupid, stupid, stupid. It can't be done.

These were the days before there were any pictures in the Big Fat Fringe Programme. In fact, the Free Fringe had put pictures in the Wee Blue Book years before, precisely because the Big Fat Fringe Programme didn't. It now does.

The best effort I'd ever seen with the 40 word limit, several years previously, was from the "fierce and funny" comedian Ian Cognito. His show was called Ian Cognito. Two words down, 38 to go. His blurb consisted of his name, Ian Cognito, repeated 19 times.

Mine based on that idea. If they gave you 40 words, in a sequential listing, long words would take up more space and therefore be more noticeable. So, the blurb I submitted was:

Llanfairpwllgwyngyllgogerychwyrndrobwllllanty-siliogogogoch anti-insurrectionists contradistinguishing counterrevolutionary interdenominational establishmentarianism, incomprehensiblise institutionalisations, intellectualisations, journalistically, jurisdictionally, neurophysiologically, overenthusiastically: overapprehensiveness. Weltanschauungen? Wholeheartedness? Ultramicroscopical microminiaturization transmogrifications psychopathologically zoogeographical, zoophytological. Vernacularize valetudinarianism, weatherstrippers! Oversimplification? Over-diversification? Overindustrializing? Incandescence thermoluminescence. Pseudointellectuals pseudo-philosophically pontificate, disenfranchising straightforwardness. Or not.

The Fringe Office didn't like that.

They're not big on liking things, on the whole. Or helping performers.

A long correspondence ensued, which boiled down to how many of those words were 'real' words. For the Fringe Office claims jurisdiction over the English language, as they did for different reasons in the year following also. If I want to put squngaludic in my blurb, I should be able to. It's my money.

They refused to accept anti-insurrectionists. Under pressure I altered it to insurrectionists, thus giving the sentence the opposite meaning. They also didn't approve of pseudophilosophically, and that got changed to philosophically.

They tried a few other words also, but I was able to find instances of the words used in various publications.

All this at a time when they were dealing with thousands of programme forms. What a waste of effort.

Anyway, the blurb got me noticed, which is hard to achieve in the Big Fat Fringe Programme with its endless pages of shows. I had hoped that the title, 40 words, would have taken me to the top of the listings, as it would have on a straightforward ASCII sort. But no; it was listed as if spelt 'forty' and one can't argue with that, really.

Anyway, the listing ruse had brought me Copstick, who hadn't actually seen me perform before. And she duly turned up again on the Saturday, the first actual performance of the show. The first ever performance of the show as a unit. Some people do 20 or 30 previews in London and around the country, refining, rewriting, cutting out the dead wood. I didn't. Too busy replacing Nicol Edwards and similar problems.

Those whom the gods would destroy, they first grant their wishes. I don't know who said that. I googled, but it's only quoted as 'ancient wisdom'. But other people claim the gods destroy people in different ways, by making them mad or calling them 'promising'. I suppose it's safe to assume the gods are out to destroy you, no matter what you do.

I did a surprisingly good performance, considering I had little idea what I was doing. That can happen, sometimes.

And one should always play to the audience. I've seen people, when they knew a reviewer was in, addressing their entire show to the reviewer and ignoring the rest of the audience.

Anyway, my bucket holder ....

No, that sounds too pretentious, as if I had my own staff of flunkies and doers of demeaning but necessary things. I have no such staff. The Free Fringe system is that each show holds the bucket for the show before them, unless other arrangements are made. So the bucket-holder was in fact the next show.

My bucket-holder said that Copstick had apologised for having no change for the bucket, but would four stars do?

Yes, I thought, it would.

And the Scotsman contacted me later, and said could they send a photographer. Yes, they could. She came and pictured. And I got on with my business and waited for the review to come out, which it did on Wednesday, my day off.

It wasn't the whispered four stars. It was five. Maximum and limit. Full house. Bingo. VC and bar. Big splash, with picture.

Now, there's a hierarchy in these things. I'd had five stars before, just as I had had four, three, two and one. Nothing if not inconsistent. But it does depend on the publication, and five stars in The Scotsman outranks virtually all other publications. Only seven shows that year got five Scotsman stars in the Comedy section.

As far as I know, only one Free Fringe show had in the past got five Scotsman stars — Martha McBrier. I had a feeling we'd get another in 2009. But I had never dreamed it would be me.

There was a huge queue for my next show. Which was gratifying, but also intimidating.

Now, Copstick's review had been flattering, but was also a fair description of the show itself. However, that only came out once. What The Scotsman did, and still does, was print the star ratings of 5- and 4-star shows every day until the end of the Fringe, but with no further description.

And, strangely, that rather killed the show.

People would come, following the stars like the Magi of old, but not bearing much in the way of gold, frankincense or myrrh, whatever myrrh is. Presumably they expected some young thrusting comedian as soon to be seen on BBC2, with the best knob-gags in Edinburgh. And instead they got me, talking about Physics.

I shall never forget the lady who spoke at me indignantly after the show, saying "If we knew you had to know things for this show, we'd never have come".

I had let her down badly, creating expectations I did not actually create of a show that cost her nothing to get in. The guilt still lingers.

Reviews. Yes, getting a good one makes you feel good for a while. But so do drink and drugs. One still has to ask: do they do one any good in the longer term?

At my first Fringe, back in 1994, I had wondered at the attention people paid to reviews and reviewers. It didn't occur to me to have reviews as a major objective, and yet so many Fringe shows seemed to, and do to this day. And my sudden unexpected catapult into the major league of reviewees didn't change my view.

In particular, what good are reviews to free-admission shows?

Reviews used to exist for good reasons. When a man (it was a man, in those days) toiled for six days at exhausting labour in the shipyards or mines, to earn the necessary shillings to take his best girl to the Music Hall on a Saturday night, he would have wanted to know that the show was worth his investment. Show your best girl a bad time and she quickly became somebody else's best girl, or so my grandfather told me when I was too young to understand sexual politics and way before feminism had been invented.

That man, quite possibly my grandfather, would want to know that the entertainers were going to put as much effort into their sets as he had in the heat of the enamelling furnaces. Yes, my grandfather was an enameller. 50 years at the Richmond Gas Stove Company and a gold watch. Why am I telling you that?

Probably relatively few enamellers attend the Edinburgh Fringe nowadays, and their best girls pay their own way and are proud independent women in their own right. And almost none have hatpins, as my grandmother had.

So, why do Free Fringe shows need reviews? Shouldn't we be encouraging people to try different shows and make their own mind up?

Are they written to inform the public at all? Or are they written to satisfy (or otherwise) the performers? Is a review the medal you take away from the Fringe?

There are web sites that only exist to review Edinburgh Fringe shows. In several cases, the reviewers are not paid. In some, the reviewers have no expertise in the genre they are set to review. It has been said that anybody can review Comedy. I dispute that.

And yet, at the Fringe, reviewers expect deference, and used to get it from the pay-to-play venues. I have lost count of the number of people who have contacted me with conversations like this:

"I want to review show X. How do I reserve a seat?"

"You don't. It's first come first served for everybody."

"But I'm a reviewer"

"Then you will wish to report on the authentic experience of the public coming to the show, including the queue."

"But what if I can't get in?"

"Then the show will already be a success and will have no need of your words to make it more so."

Now, that's where it normally stops. Because they don't dare come out with the real agenda:

"But I'm more important than the general public."

"No, you're not."

Frankly, if our acts strive to suck up to reviewers more than they strive to entertain their audience, they're striving wrong.

I think the Fringe has lost its way on this one. But I have attended many Fringe Road Shows for potential performers, and without being asked, the 'expert' panel has always addressed getting reviewers as a primary concern.

Screw that. They're wrong; I'm right. Reviews used to sell tickets and this make a difference between losing a small amount of money and losing a fortune. But under the Free Fringe, they don't. And more importantly, a poor review, however ill-informed, makes the performer give up. And you should never give up. With my five one-star reviews in my first year, I had learned that.

If a show's free-admission, people should take a chance on it. If the public are encouraged to go only to safe, guaranteed, un-experimental shows, then why is the whole festival called Fringe?

To quote a five-star review I had before The Scotsman's one "The essential Fringe experience consists of seeing at least one very good show and at least one very bad show. Peter Buckley Hill's show combines both experiences in one, and thus is un-missable." Yes; that reviewer understood.

I have gone on at some length about this. I think it's important for the Free Fringe. Our shows have been copiously reviewed in the subsequent years, at all levels and by all manner of media. But my views remain unaltered.

2009 was a strange year and I had arrived in Edinburgh exhausted. Cruz exhausted me further. Not all shows were working at the Illicit Still, and the afternoon shows blamed me. I still get that a lot, even though I don't make the who-goes-where decisions nowadays.

I forget that I've been around the Fringe since 1994, and I've seen a lot of nervous breakdowns. The majority of Fringe shows fail; not in artistic terms, to be sure, but they fail to fulfil the dreams of their performers. And nothing hurts more than your dreams being shattered. Actually, I wrote that because it sounded good; in reality, many things will hurt more. The proverbial poke in the eye with a sharp stick, for example. I bet that hurts a lot.

But when a show fails in those terms, its performer looks for something or somebody to blame. And that's often me. You want a venue at no cost? I have them. You want a miracle key to success at the Fringe? I'm out of stock of those.

We have survived because enough good performers have understood the whole complex system, and because enough good performers, against all the odds, have indeed had a good time.

Three such performers in 2009 were James Acaster, Nick Helm and Josh Widdicombe, all subsequently very successful, who were doing 20 minutes each in a three-hander, and I had (I don't think deliberately) stuck in our furthest-out and probably least-comfortable venue. I hope it was because they'd applied late, or something, but it might just have been because that venue was the one with space for them when they applied. From their lofty heights now, they have all forgiven me. I haven't forgiven myself. But that's the sort of thing that can happen when you're scheduling.

The Speakeasy at the Voodoo Rooms was going well, as it should, because in terms of sheer stage quality and equipment, it was our best venue.

Several shows had dropped out in July. That's about the worst thing you can do to us. We can't have a show that doesn't happen. If they drop out earlier than July, then you rearrange the schedule and move the dead slot to the first or the last of the day, and tell the venue that you couldn't fill that slot because it was too early or late. But never have the venue's staff on duty, with no audience to sell drinks to. They hate that.

What with venues dropping out, and shows dropping out, and the two never matching, it's a wonder I'm not gibbering in a straitjacket. I'm the wrong person for my job. The person who should be doing it is somebody who doesn't care what people think.

Better and worse was to follow. The Fringe took its course. The excess audience for my one-man show had settled down to a more reasonable number by the third week, and I had shot what trouble I could at the other venues. Peter Buckley Hill And Some Comedians, may the gods be thanked, was getting its usual full houses.

And we motored slowly, through the mists of exhaustion, to the final weekend.

Now, the Perrier award party had always been the climax of the Fringe. It was big. It was full of drinks promotions and exhausted performers who would drink anything free. I think they always kept a stretcher party on hand.

Actually, in my memory, the party was usually fuller of promotions staff and non-performers than of performers themselves. You'd think that anybody with a show eligible for the Perrier award (and that was almost all shows in the Comedy section) would get an automatic invite. But no. It took me six years to get one, and I had to be helped with knowing whom to email. They were much sought after, although the pay-to-play venues never seemed to be short of tickets for their ancillary staff.

Let's be clear. I don't look down on ancillary staff. Even that term ancillary is wrong. Techs, ushers, box-officers: all are an essential part of the Fringe. But if they get tickets, so should the performers.

Anyway, it was a big thing. It was always a Saturday night party, and the winners of the three awards were announced at midnight. Often with a live broadcast feed to Channel 4. Exciting, what?

But in 2009 all changed.

Perrier had pulled out of the sponsorship. And there was no replacement.

The instigator of the awards, Nica Burns, decided to proceed without sponsorship. And good for her.

But this meant that the lavish midnight party had to be replaced. It became a lunchtime affair with the winners announced at 1pm.

My daughter, whom I may have mentioned, was coming up for the last weekend of the Fringe.

So when I asked for my own ticket, I asked for an extra ticket for her. As I would have got in previous years, when it was sponsored and had the midnight party. She had been with me to that party once before, although not having two guest tickets at the time, we left her then boyfriend in the pub. Where he was perfectly happy. I remember meeting Jimmy Carr on the way in and chatting amiably with him, interrupted by some strange press reporter who turned his back on me to address his questions to Jimmy. And Jimmy had said to the reporter: do you mind, I'm talking to Peter. A perfectly normal interaction, but daughter, in her younger years, seemed impressed.

Anyway, I asked the Perrier people for a guest ticket. No, they said. We're cutting down. You can't have a guest under this new regime.

That was disappointing. But at least my daughter and I, together or separately, could use the Saturday morning to better effect.

And so it was. Until my mobile rang on the Saturday morning. For once, I answered it. I don't, nowadays. It's usually bad news, and if it isn't they can send me a text. But that year, I answered. It was Nica Burns, whom I'd never met nor interacted with. Was I going to be at the awards ceremony? Please say yes.

I consulted daughter. She was happy by herself. There was a whole Fringe to explore and only a weekend to do it in.

Alright, I said, I'll go.

Please bear in mind that this was about 10am. A time that does not normally exist on the Fringe. If you want clear thinking, that isn't the time to ring. Actually, I hate telephones so much that no time is the time to ring. With email, you at least have a little time to think about your answer. The correct answer would have been: "only if my daughter can come".

But I wasn't thinking about the correct answers. Nor, crucially, why Nica Burns, whom I did not know, would have asked me that question. Nor where she got my number from (the answer turned out to be Robin Ince, as it so often is, whatever the question).

Yes, it should have been obvious. But I promise it wasn't. Maybe she wanted me to introduce the winners? It was the first year of the new stripped-down lunchtime format; anything was possible.

So I went, sans daughter, who went to see a few shows. Greeted at the entrance by Nica Burns, or I guessed it was she, for as I say we'd never met. And ushered on to the main floor, not the modest persons' balcony.

Even then I didn't know what was going on. It was the last Saturday of the Fringe. I was exhausted from the organising stress, the performing and the drink. What proportion of each component accounted for my exhaustion, I know not, but I was up much earlier than a Fringe person normally is.

It was not until Tim Arthur (then editor of Time Out) spoke on behalf of the judges in the leadup to the announcement of the Panel Prize, that I twigged.

This sounds like me.

Oh fuck, it is me.

That's my name he just said.

Just like the Chortle awards in 2006, I had to make a speech I hadn't even considered writing.

Still, years in standup prepare you for that sort of thing. If you can't speak off the cuff, what are you doing in the business?

I don't quite know what I said, but it's on YouTube somewhere. I'm fairly sure I said: this award belongs not to me, but to all the Free Fringers. On the other hand, I'm keeping the trophy itself.

I also said, I think, that I was glad to get the award in a year with no sponsor, because the Free Fringe was about not being dependent on funding, and neither should the Fringe be. And I have the feeling that Nica Burns interrupted at that point.

Would I like the trophy engraved? she asked. Eventually, maybe. Today, I show it to the team. I'm looking at it now; it still isn't engraved. Huge Perspex thing.

Now, if five stars in the Scotsman turns you into an arsehole, then imagine what a Perrier can do. It doesn't bear thinking about.

I had tried not to be an arsehole about the The Scotsman review thing, but sometimes you can't help it. I remember on my day off, quite some distance from the Fringe epicentre, thinking I was among normal people, but suddenly somebody, rather intrusively I thought, leafleted me for a show. And I said: "how many stars in The Scotsman did it get?" That is the sort of arsehole it turns you into. Building up slagheaps of bad karma.

I tried not to. But honestly, what would you have done? At the end of that long, strange and arduous day (performing my shows with the trophy left discreetly on the stage, another arsehole thing) I went with a bunch of Free Fringers and, I think, daughter, to the Loft Bar, of which I have spoken before.

The Loft Bar is behind a passwall. I don't have a pass. But most of the staff know who I am and let me in. That night, I got the one who didn't.

You can't come in without a pass, he said. Do you have a pass to show me?

Out of the Waitrose carrier bag came the Edinburgh Comedy award in all its purple Perspex glory. And out of my mouth came the most arseholeish three words I have ever enunciated:

"Will this do?"

It's a terrible world. People cross trenches amid cannonfire to bring humanitarian aid to those displaced by war. They seek no trophy. They do what's right in vile circumstances. But people like me wave their award baubles around, gloat and drink without having fed a single starving person or dressed a war-amputee's wounds.

And the rest of the vacuous people look on, congratulating on the surface, wishing underneath it was them instead.

Did I deserve it? Only by the standards of the stupid world in which comedians move. It's not the only stupid world in the world. But what really matters? Cue Bohemian Rhapsody.

It made an appropriately strange end to the Fringe. Except it wasn't actually over.

I tried to hold a meeting of Free Fringers on the last Sunday, so we could discuss and learn from everything that had happened. But people were so exhausted that it barely happened. If you've done the Fringe properly, you're too exhausted to party on the Sunday, or often to think either.

But the Free Fringe had, in 2009, taken everything the gods had thrown at it, and still survived. The award had in a sense set a seal of official approval on us. We were already over 10% of the Fringe itself, but now nobody could call us a peripheral movement or a flash in the pan.

I had arrived in Edinburgh exhausted. I left even more so. The kind people at the Canons' Gait gave me a bottle of champagne to celebrate the year. Thank you.

So I sat on the train (I'd given up driving to Edinburgh after I nearly fell asleep at the wheel in two successive years). I was over 60 then, so I had a Senior Railcard, which meant I could travel first class for the price of second. And that was cheaper than the petrol for the drive, if one booked early enough in advance.

So I sat in glorious state in first class, with my bottle of champagne on my table. Winding down in a serious way. No, I didn't put the award on the table as well. That would have been too much, even for a Fringe-distorted ego.

And an email came in on my Blackberry. I should have switched it off; I really should. Beware what you say or do at times of heightened emotion, be it elation or despair.

This email, paraphrased, said this:

"I went to the Fringe. I am massively talented and I deserve to be seen. I was given a small venue without the lighting and other facilities I had asked for. I had a terrible time. I shall not be coming back to Edinburgh. Unless I can secure as my venue the Voodoo Rooms. I would like you to book me for that now."

And rather more in that vein, or vain.

Lest you think otherwise, he hadn't been one of our acts; he'd been with Laughing Horse.

Anyway, that email seemed to me to represent the opposite of every quality we would want to see in a Free Fringe member.

No deep breaths, no counting to ten. No pausing to consider that he was from New York, and they don't do Brit-like modesty or reserve.

I emailed back, saying "Congratulations. You are the first applicant to be rejected for Free Fringe 2010."

I shouldn't have done it. A couple of years later, it came back to bite me. The owner of the small café in which he had done his shows had been mightily impressed with that man's act. He and his wife even went to New York to see him again.

Fair enough. But when that couple bought the White Horse, our shows were out and Laughing Horse's were in.

One can't predict these things, or perhaps one can. The custard pies of the gods wait round every corner.

More immediate problems were to hit. I got back home, having finished the train-champagne. And collapsed into a deep sleep. The morning after, I checked on my stuff, as one does after nearly a month away. Where would we be without stuff?

It was at that point I discovered my car was not where I had left it. I went to the police to report it stolen. They checked. No, it hadn't been stolen. It had been towed away and impounded. Why? The residents' parking bay had been suspended. When? On the very day I had left for Edinburgh. How much would it cost to get it back? £1360. Accumulated daily storage charges, plus towing charge and fine.

Welcome home.

The car itself wasn't worth that sum, but I paid anyway. You know how Tourette's can give you attacks of rage? That.

When I'd finished raging, I started researching. I appealed that bastard. I went on web sites, checked the parking regulations and precedent cases, and took it to the parking tribunal, with 13 different points of appeal. I spent a lot of time preparing that case.

I won. I got the £1360 back, around March of the following year. But it was a bummer to come home to.

I wonder why I now say 2009 was a good year?

It taught me that many things were always going to go wrong. Sometimes as a result of my mistakes, or the team's; more often as a result of the gods' custard pies.

That's never good. When things go wrong, one has to work frantically to minimise the damage, and then face the people who have been affected by it. Sometimes they're polite, sometimes not. But basically they hate you if you can't give them what they expect.

Perhaps the Free Fringe carried within itself the disease of which it might eventually die.

I increased the bureaucracy for the 2010 season. As organisations become bigger, one has to.

What I did was ask all 2009 shows to write a report on how their show went, and publish it on a bulletin board on the Web.

And this was because I could no longer rely on my own perception of how things went at each venue. We had to hear from the performers themselves. If one doesn't know what's wrong, how can one take remedial action?

This was rammed home to me by being told about a show dropping out after three days. Annoying, as I've said before. But as I found out later, the person running that show had done exactly the same the year before. Nobody had told me. So when she applied again, I assumed she was a veteran Free Fringer in good standing, and she got an offer. Which she would not have done had I known about the dropout. Nobody had said anything, the first time. That obviously couldn't continue.

So, show reports were born. We want all shows to do one. Not all of them do. But when they do, it helps us to discover venue problems and to discuss them with the venues themselves. The more information there is, the better communication can happen.

Of course, a couple of people wrote reports, not realising that the venues themselves would read them. Such report-writers wanted more than a free venue, but services and facilities that we never said we would provide. There are always some.

The reports had another advantage. When applicants asked for a detailed description of the venue they had been offered, we could refer them to the previous year's reports. Even to this day, there are applicants who expect us to provide detailed technical drawings of each space before they graciously decide whether to accept their offer. We don't do that. We can't.

The reports from 2010 and onwards are still on the web, and can be read by anybody interested. They're probably a better history of the Free Fringe than this book is.

*

2010

In which applications flood and the system creaks

WHAT IS IT THAT MAKES a question a silly question?

It's very much in the eye of the person who has to answer it. If I know the answer and you don't, then I may be tempted to call your question silly. But it's probably not.

I suspect people call questions silly when they don't want to answer them, or don't want to spend a lot of time explaining the answer. So to a person with great patience and love, no question is silly, and all answers are clear, reasonable, detailed and at the level of the questioner's understanding.

I can almost see the wholesome drawing that would accompany that statement in a tract. It's so easy, on paper, in a world of infinite patience and love. And I admire the calm teacher-figure in that drawing. Such people make excellent teachers, especially with a pupil/teacher ratio of 2:1 or below.

When I was at primary school, the pupil/teacher ratio was 55:1, and there were no such things as classroom assistants in those days. To progress from one of the graded reading books to the next, one had to queue up to read to the teacher. I was too shy to do that, so for a whole term I read the same book over and over and over again, and nobody spotted it. They had me slated as a backward reader, when they eventually audited which pupil was on what book.

I didn't mean to say that. One gets flashbacks.

They didn't do calm, then. They did shouting. It was supposed to be good for children. It kept them out of the way, at least.

The point is: like that poor teacher I had then, if you are overstretched you don't have the resources to check on things properly as you should. You have to let some things go and hope they'll be all right in the end.

And yes, I could already read. I still can. But how strange old habits are. I still re-read familiar books for comfort, in preference to the excitement of discovering new books.

This isn't about books.

It is about the burdens of responsibility, and questions, and taking the time to explain to people concepts with which they may not be familiar.

It was around the 2010 season that my ability to do all those things took a dive.

We ended up for 2010 with 3500 performances of 220 shows, almost all scheduled by me personally.

Now, if you do a rough estimate of 10 questions asked by each show, whether they be sensible or silly, that's 2200 questions over the 11 months of the Free Fringe preparation time, or say 10 months, because there's not much in September.

220 questions a month. 7.3 questions a day, every day, often the same one from different people. Plus, of course, the questions from applicants who eventually didn't come and, most importantly, questions from venues.

Doesn't sound like too many, put like that. But the constant drip of them can wear one down, particularly if one's naturally irritable.

It was getting to me. We were getting too big to run the way we, or I, had been running it. We needed more system.

But how to get more system, without becoming a bureaucratic machine?

It's a question I'm still wrestling with.

If one doesn't have the resources or patience to answer questions exhaustively, than one gives quick answers which may be wrong in those circumstances, and can certainly seem abrupt if not rude. On the other hand, we are not running a customer service business. Our performers are getting something for nothing, which would otherwise cost them thousands. They shouldn't expect deference, and they should put up with my moods.

There's a contradiction here.

Gradually I'd been codifying the important things about the Free Fringe into a statement of performer behaviour that would eventually become our Ethos and Conditions. The sort of thing that would constitute the terms of the contract between us and the performers, if the relationship were one of contract. It isn't, of course. A contract must have consideration, i.e. the passing of value from each party to the other. In our case, we were giving but not taking, so no contract could exist in Law.

(That nearly became a problem in 2015, but that story is for another time).

But whenever you formulate things, you miss something out, and only experience teaches you what. If you have a list of Frequently Asked Questions, as is the modern fashion, you get just as many questions which are not on the list. I get impatient when the same thing is asked for the twentieth time, but of course the questioner doesn't know it's the twentieth.

I was overworked. Not, perhaps, in terms of the actual amount of work I had to shift. But in terms of the amount I worried about whether I had got it right, and how people would react if I hadn't.

At the beginning, applications were informal, by email, and sometimes even telephone. So each applicant chose to describe his/her show in a different way, and their emails were scattered over several different accounts. One could lose important information easily under a system like that.

I think it was for the 2010 season that we first introduced an application form. And I was worried about that, because it would make the process much more impersonal, at a stroke. But I just had to hope that people would understand.

The data processing system got quite complex. Mostly based around Microsoft Excel, it had several features of my own devising, which were designed to make the production of the printed programme easier. I wasn't bad at Excel, but I was learning to program this particular set of complications as I went along. The important thing was to have a visual grid, so one could see at a glance which slots were free and which occupied.

And that meant giving each show an entity code, or show number.

And that in turn meant an auto-acknowledgement system. And we had to start saying to the very famous: look, it's the same system for everybody, so you too have to do this. At the beginning, actually, there were a few acts I didn't force into the system, but did their entries by the back door. There's a big difference between somebody so good that they can have their pick of our slots, and someone doing their first one-person show.

I shouldn't have started with that. I should have started by delegating a lot more of the work I was doing myself, to a team of other people.

But that team, really, was just building. And one couldn't trust everybody. As I later found out, to my cost.

I had to build An Organisation. Yes, with the capitals.

And I had to, as a business-wise friend pointed out at the time, have a Succession Plan. With one of those in place, I could walk under a bus any time I chose, but without one, I couldn't.

As long as it wasn't the 36 from Leeds to Ripon, I didn't mind which bus.

There was a time, between Christmas and New Year, when I would look for a bus to walk under. For that was the time when I took all the applications and made the first attempt to put them in slots. And it did take four or five days. 25th December was my favourite day to make a start, undisturbed by anything else, while the rest of the world was stuffing itself.

Sometimes I felt isolated doing that. I was estranged from my parents; indeed, I think my mother died on 25th December 2010. It certainly was one 25th December. I don't remember exactly which. The last words she said to me were "Marks and Spencer". No, it might have been 2008. Maybe even 2007. I don't know the year she was born, either; she'd never say, even when asked. I'd seen her the day before she died; if I'd have known she would die that quickly, I would have stayed over.

My daughter would usually go to her mother's for 25th, although in earlier years we had spent it together, usually having Indian vegetarian food in Tooting, where many restaurants and cafes were open. I used to enjoy that.

Anyway, 25th was a good day to do work on, and the first round of show offers was a major piece of work. And even more work when reactions to the offers came back, many scornfully claiming that their offer did not reflect their status on the circuit.

I'm being slightly unfair. Many were indeed grateful, and appreciated what we were trying to do. But the bigger we got, the more prima donnas we sucked in.

Scheduling, for us, is an elaborate business. Any form of gap has to be avoided. We have to aim for full occupancy of all slots, else we lose the venues.

Venues were, as always, the issue. I'll have said, several times, that the idea was to get all the venues lined up before Yule and then all the shows put in the slots after Hogmanay. I'll have said that so many times that I'll have to delete this paragraph when I edit the thing. Or is editing for wimps?

I'll also have said that this scheme was never achievable in practice.

Now, Laughing Horse did it a different way, and as far as I know still do. They simply give most of their applicants a choice of venue and time. Which is vastly easier to organise. But it leads to programmes that don't necessarily suit their venues, and isn't helpful to applicants, especially first-time applicants. We take more trouble, but the result is better.

Calum was as always playing a blinder in his own inimitable way. Indeed, few would want to imitate it. Free Fringers mostly exhibited hostility to him, and I could see why. More worryingly, some negative feedback was coming from venues, specifically about him. But nobody, not even myself, was more firmly dedicated to the cause. He was, in a way, the devil we had sold our soul to, in order to achieve the riches of the world, or at least a dominant position at the Edinburgh Fringe.

It was he who told me the Cabaret Voltaire had changed hands and that the new management might be amenable to our ideas.

Now, it gave me a frisson to work with famous Fringe venues. The year before, we had started working with the Voodoo Rooms — not a famous Fringe name then, but call it the Café Royal, as it used to be, and it had a massive Fringe history. Similarly Nicol Edwards was a famous long-term Fringe venue and had come to us, although closed in 2009. Cabaret Voltaire was an equally famous Fringe name. Imagine getting that as a Free Fringe venue. Our Fringe credibility would soar. This was worth some effort.

And some effort it took. The right person proved difficult to find, as is so often the case, and access to him was limited. Only one day was available. Very well; first train up from London, last train back. I'd done that before. Relatively expensive, but the prize was worth it. A cold winter's day, but clear as dawn broke over the first train out of Kings Cross. By the time we hit Yorkshire, there was snow. And as we pulled into Newcastle, the Tannoy announced that we would not be proceeding any further North.

We were to wait on Newcastle station for further instructions. We did; there were none.

I asked staff. They did not know. I waited for announcements. None came. I paced. That was futile. I asked again. There might be something on one of the other platforms. Would they honour my ticket? They didn't know. I walked. A tiny train, compared to the vastness of the East Cost monster from which I'd debarked. I sat in it and made "I'm going to Edinburgh no matter what" body language gestures. They checked. Yes, they'd honour my ticket, because emergency conditions prevailed. They didn't know if they'd get to Edinburgh or when. It was my risk. I'll take it, I said.

And into Edinburgh I eventually got, several hours late. Time to get to Cabaret Voltaire and have a 20-minute meeting, after which I had to get back to Waverley Station and the last train that would run that day.

But in that 20 minutes, subject to an exchange of emails, I secured that famous Fringe venue for the Free Fringe. There were many other details to iron out, but it was there.

The last train, of course, wasn't the one scheduled, but at least I caught it, and it was duly delayed further by the same weather problem. It was a long and arduous day. But such were the delays that I was entitled to a full refund of the fare, so at least I had saved the Free Fringe's funds to that extent. I wouldn't want to do it again, though.

Not as bad as when I took the overnight coach from London to Edinburgh, did a day's work and then the overnight coach back. However much money that saves, I'm never doing that again.

The decisions you make come back to haunt you, years later.

For both Cabaret Voltaire and the Rowan Caves I decided to have simultaneous starts on both stages. That's not normal. Normally, you'd stagger the starts, to even out the load on the bar and thus maximise sales, and also to avoid any confusion with the public not knowing what show it's going to. This happens quite often. And sometimes it's fun. Remember the large group that came to my very first Fringe show thinking they were going to something else, and yet enjoyed it? Of course you don't. I do, though.

I decided on simultaneous starts because of the architecture at both places. Both had their origins in the incredible network of caves and subterranean arches of which the Old Town in Edinburgh consists. These caves can form natural performance spaces, and they're all along Niddry Street, including Niddry Street South. But they link and echo, and the noise from one of them can interfere with shows in the neighbouring one, if not controlled.

Audiences getting in and coming out can be a considerable source of noise if the architecture is of that sort. There are occasions where you want to control that by getting each show in at the same time, thus minimising the disruption. Shows often create tension and release; I've done it myself. You want the audience hanging on every word while you do that. And external noise is the last thing you need when your show has a moment of tension.

So, we scheduled the two downstairs rooms at Cabaret Voltaire to start simultaneously, and that worked well, for a number of years.

Until, many years later in 2016 (but I'm saying this in the 2010 section, just to complete the story) under different management, they decided to drop us in favour of Laughing Horse. And part of their reasoning was: we were too stupid to stagger the start times, thus maximising the bar takings.

It's a tradeoff. We cared about the shows; Laughing Horse didn't.

But Cabaret Voltaire could have asked us, instead of assuming.

No wonder I scream at nights. My neighbours think we have banshees.

2010 was also the first year we used Whistlebinkies, and that was a coup. I take no credit for this. Whistlebinkies is another famous Edinburgh venue, but not for Fringe shows; for music. And also for late nights. In 2009 we had done shows in the Royal Mile Tavern, where there was a tiny back room holding 35 at a crush, but we had done well there and generated an atmosphere. The person I took to be the area manager, but whose position was in fact somewhat different, had interrogated me very closely on the plan and how we managed without dedicated door staff. I got the impression that he wasn't completely convinced, but had decided on balance to give it a trial. And it worked in 2009.

I knew he was also in charge of Whistlebinkies, but I had never considered that as a venue. In my mind, it was a music place. And I thought the separation between bar and performance area would not be good enough.

But Gaz, for such was his name and still is, knew his business much better than I. He had good PA (of course he did; he put on bands every day of the year) and he had a heavy, thick curtain. It would work, he said. And it would boost his turnover until it was time for the bands to start in the evening.

A classic Free Fringe deal. Turn dead space into live space, and everybody benefits.

And it was certainly a nice stage. What about the toilets in the space? No problem, says Gaz; there are several others in Whistlebinkies; we'll take the ones in your space out of service. You can use them as dressing rooms.

Dressing rooms, however toilet-like, are a wonderful luxury on the Fringe.

He had been sceptical about us in 2009; I was sceptical about Whistlebinkies in 2010. After the Cruz fiasco, I was losing some faith in my own judgement. But both our scepticisms were wrong. Whistlebinkies was a jewel. Except for the one fairly quiet show I put in there, a mistake that was not repeated. It's the sort of place where the performer needs to be on-mic at all times. Basically a standup venue.

And more good news on Niddry Street: Nicol Edwards re-opened with new ownership, and re-named the Banshee Labyrinth. And it was clear that the new owners were in it to stay, and they made efforts. We tried to help by getting them a few shows outside the Fringe. One of their rooms was so difficult, under old management, that we couldn't use it. But the new team re-shaped it and re-equipped it and turned it into the best room in the venue.

You never know where the next problem is going to come from or what it's going to be.

The bit below wasn't the biggest issue in 2010. But it's the one that sticks in my mind the most.

We'd got Jenny Ha's back after its first year in 2009, although management changed again, in fact several times. I always liked the place.

Because I had lived through the early days of the Free Fringe, I always forget that others haven't. People new to the Fringe, and especially new comedians, don't know how it was in the 1990s, or indeed how difficult it was, and still is, to get venues. Consequently, they easily turn their noses up at perfectly good offers. And Jenny Ha's, lying as it did almost at the foot of the Royal Mile, near the Palace of Holyrood and the Scottish Parliament, was often dismissed as 'not central enough'. As if we were insulting performers by offering the space.

That, however, wasn't the problem in March 2010. I'd sent out an offer for Jenny Ha's to a performer, based in Glasgow. The reaction I got was: she would never perform in a Fascist pub, and I should not be offering her or anybody else space in such an unacceptable venue.

Hmmm. The place had changed management several times, but I never thought to question any manager I met about potential Fascist sympathies. Well, one doesn't. If I was seeking political disagreements, no doubt I could find many grounds to disagree with my venue contacts. It didn't seem the best thing to do, on the whole.

So I asked the performer. What makes you think Jenny Ha's is a Fascist pub? It's been used as a meeting place by the British National Party, she said.

I went on line (am I ever off-line, really?) and checked. This is what had happened. The English (not the British) National Party, in collaboration with a Scottish right-wing group, had decided to march in Edinburgh. Being an England-based organisation, they had travelled independently, mostly by train, and needed a rendezvous before marching. They had picked Jenny Ha's, because it was the last pub on the Royal Mile in that direction.

Now if I were a Fascist marcher, I would tend to do it the other way round and choose the nearest pub to Edinburgh Castle, at the other end. That way, my march would be downhill. Actually, I recommend that strategy to anybody contemplating the same, no matter how odious their ideology. Downhill is better than uphill, especially after a few pre-march pints, especially in Edinburgh. It is a city in which one treasures one's few downhill moments.

But anyway, the ENP had picked Jenny Ha's. But, and this is crucial, without any collaboration from the pub itself. It appears they came in in small groups, and the management didn't realise what was going on until too late.

Where there are Fascist demonstrations, there are inevitably antifascist counterdemonstrations. It's like Newton's Laws of motion. Action, reaction. And duly the counterdemonstrators arrived, along with more police than you could shake a stick at, although shaking sticks at any number of police is never wise. And a standoff ensued, with the BNP kettled inside Jenny Ha's singing songs of defiance, and the counterdemonstrators counter demonstrating outside, and the not-very-thin blue line, or blue-and-hivis-yellow line, between them.

And eventually after several hours the demonstrators were herded on to buses, not having marched, and were driven back out of Scotland, although not over a cliff which wouldn't have been fair on the drivers, and peace reigned once more.

Now, I wasn't there; that story's a public one. But I did talk to the manager and did ask, as tactfully as I could which is never very, whether the pub was in any way complicit in being used as a rendezvous. And I was very emphatically told 'no'. They had had no warning.

I passed this back to our applicant, who seemed only half convinced.

I spend a lot of time worrying about all the things that might go wrong at the Free Fringe, but I never predicted that one.

Jenny Ha's never really recovered. When mud is slung, some sticks. As the Free Fringe itself was to discover in 2015.

Because, how do you prove innocence of that sort of thing? When people believe you're bad, nothing shakes that belief.

Jenny Ha's did not do it well. They declared they would contribute the proceeds from their next monthly quiz to an anti-racist charity, and that furthermore that quiz would have a special anti-racist theme, and that anybody who doubted Jenny Ha's innocence was welcome to come to the quiz and see what jolly anti-racists they are.

Which reminded me of an episode of Father Ted.

How many questions can one devise with an anti-racist theme? And wouldn't the answers be quite easy to guess?

Our shows did not go ahead that year. Yet more changes of management ensued in the light of the ENP fiasco, and the new people didn't want us. Yet again I had to move all the shows we originally had booked there.

The pub itself was later sold, this time to somebody who already had considerable experience in running Edinburgh pubs, and refurbished, and repurposed, and renamed The Kilderkin. But that all happened in 2011.

Applications came in. I'd noticed, both before and after 2010, that not all applications were exactly what they claimed they were. Now, everybody's show is informed, to a greater or lesser extent, by its writer's opinions. And of course these are mostly not the same as mine. Agreeing with me isn't one of the selection criteria. We are a broad non-church. I'm not a Christian. Some of our performers are. That's not a problem.

It becomes a problem when a show seeks, not to entertain, but to proselytise. And every year there seemed to be at least one applicant show which, when probed, seemed to exist to sign people up to some belief system or another. There always were such shows at the Fringe; there's a mission hall on the Royal Mile that has an army of uniformed leafleters driving audience into its shows, where they are given tea, biscuits and Jesus.

Fine, but I made it a fundamental principle. If a show entertained, in the broadest sense, then we considered it seriously. But if a show set out to convert its audience, we didn't want it. And it wasn't only Christians; other faiths tried the same thing, and in one year I refused an avowedly Socialist show because it too intended to convert its audience. Same principle applied to everybody, as impartially as I could.

Under that dispensation, I ruled against a 2010 applicant, who was indeed a comedian but seemed to work only the Church circuit and to be involved with a conversion/faith-reinforcement project outwith the Fringe.

He sought me out during the Fringe, differentiating his comedy work from his proselytising work, and I said, as I had to say, that I made the best decision I could in the light of the information available to me at the time.

Was it the right decision? he asked, as we walked towards the late performers' bars.

I didn't know then and I don't know now. In the absence of the sort of all-knowing, all-seeing god in which he believed and I didn't, who can say if any decision is right? A decision had to be made; I made it, and that's all that can be said. But our policy remains in place: any show whose primary intent is to convert people is not a show we want.

He was calm and reasonable about it, I think. Not an awkward performer. But there's always one. And every time there is one, I think: is this my fault? Did I do enough to explain how things work?

In 2010 the one-there-always-is was scheduled in Bar 50. A comedic one-woman play. And in June, I got this email from the venue:

> We have been bombarded with phone calls from [the one], with varying wild requests including:
>
> – giving out free alcohol on our premises (not possible due to agreements with our suppliers and the tenacity of the Scottish licensing laws at the moment)
>
> – asking us to store this alcohol for the duration of the festival (not something we can accommodate in high season, or indeed at any time)
>
> – asking us to store her lights and stage equipment (something we cannot do) and guarantee their security and the fact "no-one would lay a finger on them"
>
> – asking my team to arrange housing for her
>
> These are some of the examples. She has been told, politely and then far more firmly, why these requests cannot be granted. When told by one person she then persists in trying to speak to various members of the team by calling the hostel constantly. She contines to pester anyone and everyone she manages to get on the phone, forcing them to repeat themselves while she ranges from begging to screaming down the phone at my team.

This repeated insistence on taking up my teams time, especially as we are now into high season and incredibly stretched on the floor, means that I have no option than to request that this performer is relocated to another venue.

Bearing in mind the stress and time consumption already experienced with her I can only imagine that actually having her on the premises will be an operational nightmare.

In the eighteenth century, many novels were written entirely as a series of letters between one character and another. It occurs to me, far too late, that I could do this book just by making it a series of emails between people. Genuine ones, unlike the ones in the novels. I've had some major cringe-emails, some of which I don't dare to re-read even now.

Anyway, we tried conciliation, but they wouldn't conciliate, and I don't blame them. So we had to remove her, at short notice, and fill the gap and, most importantly, placate the venue. Venues are much more important than performers.

She took it badly.

I did make one Good Decision for the 2010 season. Yes, it deserves the capital letters. And that decision was that henceforth all shows in the Wee Blue Book would be listed strictly in order of start time, no matter what genre they were. No more separate sections. Anybody who wanted to search by genre could use the colour codes we introduced, or go to the Big Fat Fringe Programme. Best decision I ever made. That was the way people used the Wee Blue Book; you could see them. They'd have tickets for maybe one or two paid shows every day, and work their schedules around that. We set out to answer the question: what's on when I, the fringegoer, have time to see something? And, if the first thing I choose is full, what else is on at the same time?

It's better than the way the Big Fat Fringe Programme does things, and more suitable to our audiences. And another thing: it encourages people to try shows they've never heard of. That's what we want to happen.

And the time order also helps fringegoers to try shows outside their genre. Looking for Comedy? Yes, but that show at half past three sounds interesting, although it's marked Spoken Word. Well, let's try it. This is the sort of thing we want to happen. We're about all the arts, or at least all the ones we can accommodate.

The Wee Blue Book itself was getting better and better. Duncan Bolt wasn't doing the Fringe that year, so the design had been taken over by Henry Baxter (another pseudonym) and much of the work was done by Isla Cromartie (yet another pseudonym); in my ignorance I don't know who did how much of each, but both appeared equally exhausted at the end and both had put in much more work than I initially envisaged when I thought there should be a Free Fringe Programme.

Henry designed the cover and sent it to me for approval. The correct thing to do in those circumstances is to praise the work of the designer and to let it go unaltered, unless there's some factual error. But like almost every design client, I couldn't resist meddling. "That building that looks a bit like Edinburgh Castle? Can we have a Free Fringe flag on it?" Henry produced one. I looked again. Maybe too much ego. "We'd better have the Saltire flag of Scotland on there as well". That made it look better.

But my main problem was with the two Lego or Fisher-Price -looking children in the basket of the balloon, about to land on the meadows and saunter to the Free Fringe for endless fun. Two problems with that. Firstly, I thought them twee. And secondly, we had nothing like enough children's shows to make children the cover focus. It was misleading. We always had a problem putting children's shows on, since most of our venues were and still are licensed premises.

So Henry took the children out of the balloon basket, and replaced them.

With a sort-of-Lego-or-Fisher-Price figure that was unmistakably me. Guitar in hand, tiny Free Fringe badge on my shirt, and all.

No matter how many times I have sworn that the Free Fringe was not a massive piece of publicity for myself, that programme cover stands in flagrant contradiction.

Bad enough that my initials are on the whole thing. That wasn't supposed to be, either; it was fallout from the Laughing Horse fiasco. But the picture also? On top of that, people were starting to refer to the whole organisation as "The PBH" or even just PBH.

In later years, we actually got performers, our own performers, who said "I didn't realise PBH was a person; I thought it was just a name".

I promise you, it wasn't meant to be that way. But I don't blame you if you don't believe me.

I was stuck with being a figurehead. Still more a dictator than a constitutional monarch; Charles I rather than Charles II. And we know which of these benighted Stewarts ended up worse off.

I believed my touch could cure scrofula, though, and that must count for something?

Speaking of monarchs with miracle touches....

Calum had been, as usual, doing a wonderful job looking for and drumming up venues. He had, at least on the surface, an absence of shyness or diffidence, and would march up to anybody asking information as if a person of authority. That helped us to get a lot of venues. I could never have done that.

It's fair to say that most performers didn't understand him and that he was regarded by performers as a liability to the Free Fringe. Wrongly. But Calum could never resist suggesting or even imposing improvements on situations where it wasn't really his place to do so. In other words, telling people how to do their own jobs.

People don't like that, on the whole. I knew how to handle it. My father had been the same, so I learned to bend with certain winds. I could shield the performers against Calum telling them how to perform and how to run their stages; in many instances, he was right. Tactless, but right. And those three words describe me also.

But telling venues how to do their job? That was starting to be a problem.

So much so that, at midnight in the middle of the Fringe, I received a call from a major venue. Now, I'd just come off stage. Not a time when one wants problems. But some calls have to be taken; the name on the screen ensures that.

And sometimes one has to endure the rage at the other end of the line. Normally I'm the one who does rage; it's part of Tourette's. But when I hear "tell that [particularly Scottish expletive deleted] he'll never set foot in our venue again, and it's shaking our faith in you guys and your shows" then I know I have a problem. And winding down is not going to be on that night's agenda.

The details of that incident are still in dispute. And they don't matter. There are very few circumstances in which the will of the venue doesn't trump every other card. It seems to have been thus: Calum observed a show about to start without the Free Fringe backdrop in place. He asked, or insisted, the performer put it up. The performer refused. Altercations started to the discomfort of almost everybody. Security was called. Calum is not an easy man to eject from anywhere if he doesn't want to go; he's big and strong. And that night he didn't want to go. He was, in his view, right, and had a point to prove.

Well, yes, of course every Free Fringe show should perform in front of a Free Fringe backdrop. That's why we have them; that's what they're for. But there are always circumstances to consider. I wasn't there; I don't know what all the considerations were. I knew only this: that I had a venue expostulating into my phone, and Calum on call-waiting, ready to expostulate in the other direction.

As I say, the venue trumps all other cards. But I have to deal with the cards that are trumped.

Calum could find us venues, better than anybody else. But unfortunately he was also losing us venues, often the same ones.

His wonderful enthusiasm was completely swamping his discretion. Indeed, did he ever have discretion?

As I write this, I see myself in him. I don't compromise much either. For me, things have to be right. And when our performers break the rules because they can't be bothered or because they don't understand why the rules exist, I get angry.

If the Free Fringe was ever to revolutionise the Fringe, it required performers to do things the Free Fringe way. And yes, it was mostly I who defined what that should be. As an organisation, we're very far from anarchist. More Socialist, really. The workers controlling the means of production. Clause IV. And to achieve that, one needs Party Discipline. No scabs. One out, all out. Solidarity.

Why did I ever dream that one could get that level of solidarity among performers, most of whom would sacrifice at least one limb for a five-star review in The Scotsman, such as I had unexpectedly received in 2009?

And indeed, the same people would sacrifice at least a digit for a four-star review in The Scotsman, such as Copstick kindly gave my one-man show for 2010. And the fact that I've mentioned that here shows I'm not immune, no matter how much I rationalise.

Almost any other body of workers has better potential for solidarity than entertainment workers. In 2015 and 2016, attempts have been made to unionise comedians in the UK. Even given obvious benefits, such as an approach to a major national chain of clubs who is not paying its acts for work done, the unionisation process is slow.

I haven't really described the 2010 Free Fringe, have I? It was blessedly free of trauma like Cruz, at least. I felt we were getting somewhere. We had major venues and an excellent programme, spearheaded by Robin Ince in the opening slot at the Canons' Gait, with queues round the block before noon. That in Fringe terms is massive. And we were similarly lucky in the Voodoo Rooms Ballroom, a big space which you couldn't possibly expect to fill in the noon slot. But Thunderer, the show we had there, a sitcom based in a Victorian newspaper office which had just employed its first lady journalist, packed from the outset. I made a point of seeing it, and jolly good it was. I think it got onto Radio 4 later, and it deserved that and more. For the next few years I emailed the writer, Bryn Mills, to ask if he had anything else for us, but alas he never did.

When you have shows packing at noon, you have something special.

2010 was also the year that John Otway first joined us. Which I mention, not to boast of what famous people we have on board, for there have been many others I haven't mentioned. But because it reminded me of years before; I forget exactly which year. There were bookable spots in the Ross Bandstand, in Princes Street Gardens, that year; open air show, and the citizens of Edinburgh came to watch. And I was scheduled for one, and when I arrived, saw the running order, and I was on immediately after John Otway. Ouch, I thought; difficult one for me to follow. But he was late, so they swapped the order and I went first. I'd been keeping Mel up to date by text (text messaging was new in those days), and texted her about this, and got one back saying "You are much better than Otway". I never deleted it until the phone itself died. It's not true, but the message was lovely.

And years later there he was, on our team, and delighted to have him.

But there was also despair. On Tuesday 17th I had finished my show, and was upstairs in the bar relaxing and talking to a member of the audience whom I knew, and looking forward to my day off on Wednesday. And then, around half past midnight, word came that I was urgently needed in the performance space downstairs.

In the midnight show, which was like mine a Variable Bill Show, one of the guest performers had had an altercation with an audience member and assaulted him. Put the heid on him, as the Scots expression goes; headbutted him on the bridge of the nose. Kerfuffle ensued, as you might expect. Ambulance and police were called. The victim left in the ambulance. The perpetrator left insouciantly on foot, and it fell to me to persuade him to come back and interact with the police.

This could have been publicity we did not need. Audience member gets gratuitously assaulted at Free Fringe show. Or so, in my mind, screamed the headlines. It took a long time for the police to take the statements they needed. I had not witnessed the incident itself, but a full audience had. We, that is the team running the midnight show, me and the Canons' Gait staff, then repaired to Whistlebinkies to drink away the stress until 5 am.

Even now, I emphasise that the assailant wasn't one of our own performers, but doing a guest spot, as is the lifeblood of variable bill shows. Still, I had the next day to email all our shows and ask anybody who had booked him as a guest to cancel the booking. And then to face the owner of the Canons' Gait, and assure him that this was not something that would ever recur if we possibly could help it. My day off didn't happen, of course.

The case came to court later that year. He could have, as they say, got the jail. But instead there was a substantial fine. The victim, resident in Holland, had declined to return to Edinburgh to give evidence at the trial. And nobody made anti-Free Fringe capital out of the case. But we could have done without this. Could have happened at any Variable Bill Show, anywhere, but it didn't; it happened at ours. Nobody's fault but the perpetrator. But that's no consolation.

At the end of 2009, I had felt foolishly ecstatic, despite all the things that went wrong. At the end of 2010, there was no ecstasy. There was the sense of a job well done. We had, after 15 years, become established.

Things, however, were falling apart on the periphery. And, as poets say: "Things fall apart, the centre cannot hold".

There was no champagne on the train back. But at least my car was where I left it. Outside my daughter's flat, way away from residents' parking schemes. I didn't trust them after 2009.

I wrote everybody an email, that September, asking people to stop asking me questions: I was taking a holiday. I told them I was exhausted. But I didn't take the holiday, in that or any other year. Perhaps I should have done. But holidaying by yourself is a waste of money. As they say: everywhere you go, you always take the weather with you. For weather, read worry.

Speaking of money: Income Tax was first introduced as a temporary measure to finance a war. I think it was the Napoleonic, but I can't remember. Britain against France, the latter standing for Liberty, Fraternity and Equality. I forget why Britain was against those three things, or what our ancestors were in favour of instead.

That's not the point. The point was: as we were growing, we needed money. In the first phase of the Free Fringe, I had paid. In the second, we had benefit shows and I sold advertising (well, three adverts in 2010. I am hopeless at selling anything, doubly so adverts). But the print bill was less than £5000 in 2009, printing considerably fewer copies than we now do. Clearly it had to go up.

Phase three of financing had to dawn. There was a limit to the number of benefit gigs we could put on, and a limit to the number of people who would come.

Many performers advocated an easy solution. Sell advertising in the Wee Blue Book to performers themselves, they suggested. Individual shows will be happy to pay; indeed, many shows said they would.

And others said they'd rather buy the advertising space themselves than sell to strangers.

So, we had an easy solution. But easy solutions aren't always the right ones. And, in my opinion, this one wouldn't have been.

Well, now. Was this a democracy or a dictatorship? The majority seemed to want to buy ads. Although that was just the majority opinion at one meeting with fewer than 20 people there. We hadn't asked the full membership.

It turned out our organisation was a dictatorship after all.

I decided not to do it.

All members were equal (except me, of course). I thought then, and I still think now, that having shows buy advertising space would introduce inequality. Those who could afford would buy. Those who could not afford would either have to buy also or have a show that appeared second-class. We'd be acting like the pay-to-play venues.

But we still needed money, unless I carried on financing the whole thing (minus benefit shows).

So we had to bring in an Income Tax to finance our wars against the French and their garlic-ridden ideas of liberty, equality and fraternity. Or just the printing of the Wee Blue Book.

With great reluctance, the Voluntary Contribution was born. £3 per performance. But absolutely, completely voluntary. And after the shows were over. And as a temporary measure until we got a team who could sell enough advertising to, erm, advertisers.

Years later, we still have the Voluntary Contribution. And I hate it more than ever. And I hope it doesn't stick around as long as Income Tax.

What I wanted was: no charges to performers, not even voluntary ones. That was even an early slogan. And now we, I, broke it.

In mitigation, nobody was obliged to pay. We only wanted the money of people who had had a good time at the Fringe. Nobody was pressured. And when fewer than half paid, we did not panic. With the benefits, we still had enough. We didn't want a surplus.

But by all the gods, I wish we didn't have to do it. If I were rich, I'd finance it. But I'm not.

It's the least-worst option. Selling ads to performers is discriminatory and starts an arms race; sponsorship means you lose control and you have to sell yourself on the streets every time the sponsorship deal expires.

Sell ads to enough commercial companies and the problem goes away. But we've never been able to do that, and it's an awful job.

I hated writing that bit. I need tea. I really hate having to ask our members for any money, even at the rate of £3 per performance. Even those who have post-show buckets over-flowing.

*

2011

In which we get quite huge

YOU CAN'T PLEASE EVERYBODY. And I never realised until just now that this phrase has two meanings.

1. Some people are always going to dislike you, and

2. No matter what you do, some people will not be satisfied with it.

The meanings are close to each other, but somewhat different. One is to do with who you are, the other with what you do.

And Ricky Nelson (as well as the Stone Canyon Band) sang: you can't please everybody, so you've got to please yourself.

2011 may have been the year in which we tried too hard to please everybody and did not please ourselves.

We started by making a good decision that pleased a lot of people. Up to 2010, we had made it compulsory for all our shows to go in the Big Fat Fringe Programme. When I say 'all', I mean all those we'd been able to find space for before the early-April deadline for the BFFP. Not the ones we allocated after that.

There was some resentment, because some considered it not worth the money, and some didn't have the money at all. And in those days the Fringe Office charged the full three-week fee if you were doing three or more performances.

And one otherwise good Free Fringer accidentally-on-purpose did not get his payment in on time in 2010. Were we going to cancel his show? And replace it with something less good, which would also not be in the BFFP? No.

So I decided that henceforth shows could choose whether to be in the BFFP or not. In the early days, we'd needed a lot of listings to build credibility. Well, we had that now. And it's not as if the Fringe Office provided good service in exchange for the large fee. There were good reasons to be in the BFFP; there were good reasons not to be. Let the people choose. And that's what we did. It was the right thing. To this day, shows debate heatedly the merits of being in the BFFP versus the merits of not being.

This had a consequence I did not fully see when making the decision. Until then, "what was in the BFFP" and "The Fringe" were almost synonymous terms. From now on, they wouldn't be. The Fringe was, and is, whatever happens in August that isn't explicitly part of some other festival. And that's the way it should always have been. Otherwise, in what sense is it a Fringe?

I believe in Canada someone's copyrighted the term "Fringe" and uses it for merchandising purposes. That makes me sick.

Applications to the Free Fringe were getting ridiculous. Not in their artistic quality, which was better than ever, but in their quantity. There were, as there always are, a few that didn't make the quality standard, and they were as always difficult to say no to, but we had to do that for everybody else's sake.

Those few weren't the problem. The problem was the good ones we didn't want to say no to.

And that meant getting venues.

So, when I looked at a venue that might be successful and might not be, my inclination was to believe that it would be successful. And when that success depended on the performing team at that venue working particularly hard, my inclination was to believe that they would.

After all, that was the idea of the Free Fringe. Not to have the best venues (the best venues would probably sell themselves to pay-to-play promoters) but to make the best of whatever venues we could get.

Unfortunately, or rather fortunately, we had got some excellent venues that required little or no work by the performers. And perhaps because of that, we had some performers who didn't get the idea of putting in that work. In their minds, we were just as responsible for their well-being as we would have been had they paid us thousands of pounds.

That wasn't everybody. I don't even think it was a majority.

But these were the people I noticed most.

We took on some venues for 2011 which with hindsight we probably shouldn't have.

When there are separate rooms, things are easy. There's a room in which shows take place, and there's another in which people can drink and talk. All we have to do is make it clear which is which, and keep the cross-pollution of noise between the spaces to a minimum. Which mostly involves negotiating for background music to be switched off in the non-performing area, but can also involve other things.

In Bar 50 that year, there were problems. Calum had quarrelled with one of the deputy managers on setup day. Bar 50 was one of our most difficult spaces, because it required three partition walls to be erected, and there was a dispute about where the agreed location was. Tempers were lost, it appears on both sides. Calum knows nothing of the tactical apology; instead, when he thinks he's right he maintains his right against the world, sometimes years later. So things escalated that need not have done.

One of the avoidable outcomes was therefore that our space was next to a pool table heavily used by young people. One doesn't realise how much noise these things make until one tries to do a show next door to one of them.

So performers started giving up in the course of their run. Oh, they'd turn up to do their shows most of the time, when it suited them, but they did not publicise enough, and they didn't do the door duty from half an hour before their shows to half an hour after, as we'd stipulated in the conditions. So the public were turning up and were left to wait, without anybody giving them information or any gesture of welcome.

That wasn't the way things were supposed to be. But it's the way things were at Bar 50 that year. A pity. But after the setup day fracas, I knew we would lose it for next year while Calum remained part of our team.

And that wasn't the only venue problem.

When we talk to landlords about being a venue, we encounter several where there isn't a separate space for performance.

But venues will sometimes say: instead of having a separate room, we'll keep anybody out who hasn't come for the shows, up to a certain time.

Now, that ought to work. But it tends not to.

Managers change, and outgoing managers don't always pass messages like that along to their successors.

And sometimes our shows have low numbers in, especially midweek. And along comes a large group of friends who clearly want drink. A manager, or often a simple member of bar staff, sees potential sales, compares them to the numbers in our show, and lets them in.

Occasionally, they then ask to watch the football. And occasionally that same manager or barperson puts it on for them. Abandon show.

I can understand exactly how that happens. I understand the motivation of the staff. Even though it's a direct breach of the agreement. And even though it means I get shouted at by the shows.

It's not a good deal, because it's not enforceable. And we shouldn't do deals like that. But sometimes we have to, or we won't get enough venues. Or, in one case, we have to take on the deal for the sake of other, better venues under the same owner.

If we do take on a deal like that, we have to ensure the shows will always fill, with an audience that will trump anything else the staff may be tempted to let in. And we can't guarantee that; we can never guarantee that. Our most popular acts will demand 'better' venues, and if we have a late dropout we have to put the best available thing in the gap, whether it's suitable or not.

There are too many unknowns for exclusive-use deals to be sustainable.

But we still have to take them sometimes, and we're still tempted to take them when the waiting list gets immense and the 'where's my show offer' emails get too many to bear.

In 2011, we had this problem at Dropkick Murphy's. There was an elaborate scheme. A large room, with a throat around the entrance. The plan was to curtain off and erect a satellite bottle bar at the throat, thus providing service to people waiting for their shows and to anybody who'd come to drink. Their main business was late night, so not many of the latter class were expected at our times.

The satellite bar never got set up. People instead were let through the curtain for service at the main bar, during the shows. Which could at times be disruptive.

The owner was angry. I'm not quite sure at what, except that he had engaged staff during some of our shows' days off. And two shows, not liking the look of the venue, had pulled out and not told us.

I was told, with what truth I don't know, that another promoter had space at one of their best venues (due, I think, to some of their own shows dropping out) so had no hesitation in persuading our shows to jump ship.

That, of course, led to even more dark time in the venue, and even more fury on the manager's part.

Why were so many shows dropping out? Audiences seemed down across the board that year, particularly in the first week. I don't know. It happens. The money venues were suffering equally. Except that, because of the way they're paid by performers, they're immune from major loss, or losing their venues.

Our whole scheme relies on performers fulfilling their commitments. A dropout immediately before the Fringe does great damage; a dropout during the Fringe does even more. And if they don't even tell us, we're powerless.

Many people thought at the time we should introduce more draconian systems, like requiring shows to give us a returnable deposit. In the face of the Dropkick Murphy's problem, it would have seemed sensible. But to me it was the opposite of what the Free Fringe was supposed to be. It was supposed to be a community, based on trust. If that wasn't working in patches, then perhaps it was my fault for failing to instil that sense of community. After all, weren't the advantages of the Free Fringe model obvious?

Clearly, no. Not to everybody. Wave a 'better' venue under the noses of some people and they're gone, even though they lose the value of their listings in the Wee Blue Book and the Big Fat Fringe Programme. Even though they know they'll never get an offer from us again. Actually, they don't know that; we say it, but they don't believe it. They're still thinking like customers, not members.

Of course, if we did introduce a returnable deposit system, they'd act even more like customers and not members. Write the deposit off and go wherever they please. The culture of making a massive loss on the Fringe is so ingrained that they would hardly notice it.

And that leads me to another issue: spending the money we've saved them, which I'll discuss later.

The other problem with a returnable deposit, or any form of charge, is that it needs human resources. We'd have to have a bookkeeper volunteer. And that's not a popular job. Not only keeping track of what's owed, but also driving in the payment itself, sending it back out by the numerous methods people would ask for (not everybody's based in UK; not everybody has a bank account). And more than that: dealing with the negotiations if we had reason to withhold a deposit. A game of blame and counter-blame. A recipe for really bad feelings.

It would strike at the heart of the Free Fringe itself. And it would certainly have excluded one of our prizewinning Spoken Word artists, who had come to us with her very last money and written me one of the few nice emails I get, saying that we'd given her an opportunity she could never otherwise have afforded. She's won a few more prizes since; she's still not rich, but we helped her to what she now is.

No, deposits and charges aren't the answer. As soon as we have a compulsory charge, we've taken an irrevocable step on the way to becoming a pay-to-play venue. In 20 years, we'd be the Pleasance. The temptation to increase the charge, build up a reserve of cash, and then gain venues by using that cash as rent, and then increasing the charge still further to be able to rent more and more venues — that's the vicious spiral.

Not even, necessarily, paying rent. Sometimes a backhander to a significant person in a venue would be enough to persuade them to switch from one promoter to another. Off the books; untraceable including by the venue's owners or higher management.

Start that game and you never stop.

Don't play that game and you will lose some venues to those who do play it.

It's not a dilemma; we can't lose our principles. But we may die not losing them.

The venue search continued to throw up interesting opportunities, but perhaps they were becoming more and more off the wall as the more obvious spaces had all been explored.

There was a wonderful large basement under an Indian restaurant. Exactly what we wanted (apart from the pillars in the middle, and there are always pillars; Edinburgh is a propped-up city); nice and rectangular, good visibility, well separated from the restaurant, its own little bar and a proprietor who understood the idea. And stood to make some money from food service before and after in the restaurant section, without disrupting the shows with food. People often eat where their shows are, so it was a good prospect. We negotiated; we got; we put good shows in, for it was quite a large space and well located. On the main pedestrian route between Gilded Balloon and Pleasance, in fact.

And once again, we were thwarted by change of ownership. The old owner needed to make some urgent repairs for which he couldn't raise the capital, so was forced to sell. Or that was what I was told, anyway. Well, now, perhaps the new owners would honour the deal? We asked; they wouldn't. They traded under the name of the Mosque Kitchen. They couldn't, they said, have Mosque in the name and serve alcohol, even though they themselves were not a Mosque.

And indeed, there was some dispute as to who owned the name Mosque Kitchen. This continues, I believe, to this day.

The original Mosque Kitchen is a splendid institution, where at open-air tables in the grounds of the Edinburgh

Mosque you can have a bowl of curry and rice at a remarkably cheap price, and I have often availed myself of that. I have also had food at the new Mosque Kitchen that was going to be our venue, and that's very good too. They're both still there.

I'm not going to get involved in the role of organised religion in the Free Fringe. We have had some advantage from religion. Both the Catholics and the Salvation Army have lent chairs for our venues in the past, and we have been suitably grateful. We approve of chairs.

But obviously losing that good venue was a blow. If we'd have known from the outset, perhaps we could have put some Theatre or Children's shows in there that might have done well without alcohol sales. The shows we had actually programmed, under the old agreement, would not have. Comedy audiences like to take a drink in with them.

Calum, once again, did not give up. Five minutes away, he discovered an excellent Italian restaurant, Ciao Roma, who had a basement space that was completely unused. I imagine they must have had occasional functions in the basement, but nothing regular. It was an excellent substitute and we still use it. Still, once again we had to put large notices on the old venue, because our shows were in the Big Fat Fringe Programme, and re-direct audiences down the road. That's never a happy situation.

The Big Fat Fringe Programme should look at its policies, which haven't really changed since the 1970s. They think that most performers have a venue contracted by March and that nothing changes. And that doesn't sit well with us. When we started, we were one show, then two, then a handful, and they could afford to ignore our needs. But now we're between 15% and 25% of the Fringe, depending how you calculate it. And the larger we get, the more certain it is that there will be late changes.

Ciao Roma worked well enough, but of course the shows they got were not the shows that we would have programmed there if we had had the venue from the outset.

And no matter how well a venue does, there's always a thought in their mind: could I do better with another promoter? Could I get money up front from such a promoter?

We can never relax.

We firmed up relationships with many venues, but we can never relax.

A better venue experience was found by Frank Galbraith, and without him we'd never have discovered it.

The Royal Antedeluvian Order of Buffalos had a club premises. And it was on the same street as the Voodoo Rooms. Through a door marked as the entrance to a hostel (which it also was), up one flight of stairs, knock three times and give the password. No, I lied about the password. But few people knew about it. It was, after all, a members' club.

As it turned out, with few members. The Buffalos, alas, had seen more prosperous days and membership of similar organisations, with mutuality and ceremonies and secrets, was on the decline everywhere.

A cynic would say the club premises were a little run down and in need of reupholstering. But in addition to the general bar, they had a meeting room which was exactly the right shape for us, and held about 50 people. They were at first reluctant; they didn't know us, they didn't know how their own members would react to a turnover of strangers watching shows next to their space. The members may not be on our wavelength at all. But there were few members, and therefore little revenue.

I showed willing by drinking lager with the Secretary at 11.30 am, which is early for me, and with Frank's tutelage we shook hands on the deal.

I was worried. A number of things could have gone wrong, and I feared the Buffalo members' hostility. They did not seem to be Fringegoers; indeed, some seemed like the sort of Edinburgh citizen who resents the Fringe, on the grounds that Londoners swamp the city, behaving pretentiously and giving nothing back. That does sometimes get said, even though the Free Fringe has, I hope, done a lot to defuse that attitude.

The chances of failing at that venue, I thought, were quite high. And indeed a couple of shows did fail and one dropped out mid-run, my pet hate.

But what I had not seen was the comfort of the bar itself. And the late opening, and the low prices for basic drink.

What happened was: without any prompting or planning from me, the Buffs Club became a sort of Free Fringe club-house. Many of our shows would go there after they'd finished performing, and drink with each other at the cheap prices, and talk of things that performers talk of.

I didn't know this was happening. I'd been having my late drinks at the performers' bars on Bristo Square. Where people go to be seen and to lie about how well their shows are going.

Robin Ince told me about how the Buffs Club had developed. He was never one for the boast bars, the up-your-arse bars, the be-seen-here bars. The Buffs Club suited him. So one night I went, and it was packed with Free Fringers. I entered, and the Free Fringers broke into applause.

Now that's the sort of thing that makes you want to carry on, no matter how many nasty things you have to face during the year, no matter how many venues you have to change at short notice, no matter how many applicants curse you for not giving them venues that match their egos.

That was the Free Fringe as I had wanted to see it, as I had imagined it. Oh, not applauding me (although I'd never say no to that) but being a team of equals, communing together, working for each other, swapping offers of help.

A clubhouse. That was what we were missing. Somewhere where the ego-inflation of the rest of the Fringe didn't prevail.

Oh, I thought, let us hang on to this venue. It gives us something that I hadn't realised we needed.

And I wish we could have hung on to it.

We did, for one more year, and then it had gone.

We brought in a very satisfactory sum in bar takings. Enough to rescue the club. But then there was a dispute among the officials. Buff A said that Buff B had absconded with most of the money we had brought in. Buff B was reported to have said that he was owed that money and more from previous transactions with the club. I have no way of knowing the truth of any of these things. But the upshot was that the Buffs Club itself had to be sold; it wasn't viable. But with what we brought in, it might have been. And some of our members had plans to put shows on during the year as well.

If it were not for a dispute which was nothing to do with us, we might be there still; we might still have our clubhouse. I miss it.

And we would be so much stronger with a social venue we could call our own. Even though it wasn't our own; it was the Buffs'.

They sold the space. It became a hostel. Another hostel. I asked our friends at the Voodoo Rooms if they might not wish to take it over; after all, it was connected by the usual Edinburgh network of labyrinthine passages. But they couldn't afford to buy, and the Buffs would not rent.

Oh well. This helped me to realise that everything at the Fringe is transitory. Just because The Pleasance had rented the same space from the University for thirty or forty years didn't mean that we, who paid no rent, were entitled to the same degree of permanence. We are, by our nature, nomads. Or perhaps Travellers in the Irish sense. Move along at the landlord's whim; go, move, shift. That's a quote, but I'm not sure from what.

And be grateful for wherever we're allowed to park our caravan, however temporarily.

There used to be a bar in Edinburgh called the Penny Black. As you might guess from the name, it originally catered to postal workers (rather like the UCW Club that we had used in earlier years, which saved the Free Fringe in 2003).

It opened at 6am. And this was important. For the hour between 5am and 6am was the only time you couldn't get a drink at the Fringe. If you'd been drinking until 5am, you'd usually got beyond the point at which you wanted to stop. Or could stop, in many cases.

I may have mentioned before that the Fringe is stressful for performers. Especially if you've hung all your dreams on a success that clearly isn't happening. In those circumstances, drink plays a big role. Especially in the company of people who understand, or are in the same boat.

So, in August, it was commonplace to see a queue outside the Penny Black, waiting impatiently and sometimes moistly for the 6am opening. That queue would consist of alcoholics, deadbeats, dropouts and many many comedians. No postal workers; they have more sense.

The Penny Black itself was on the first floor, and it was a dump. I only went there once. I had an excuse: I was meeting somebody off a bus in St Andrews Square later that morning, and I knew if I slept instead that I would not get up. This was back in the 1990s, and although I feel fairly robust (or equally alienated) in most circumstances, that queue scared me. Fortunately, shortly before opening time, there hove into view Ed Byrne with several women in tow, so I knew I'd have at least one friend in the maelstrom. I went, I drank, I talked and vowed never to go again.

I'm told it had got much worse since my one experience of it, and drugs were being injected with little attempt at concealment. And eventually the police closed it down.

I do not know nowadays whether it's still possible to drink for 23 straight hours in Edinburgh bars; I think there may still be somewhere in Leith. I do not propose to find out. That isn't the point.

The Voodoo Rooms told me they might have a third space, but the conversion might be delayed right up to the start of the Fringe; no chance of seeing in advance what it might look like.

As usual, we were desperately short of venue space. So I booked up the new space, sight unseen, and gambled on it being OK. And then spent anxious months hoping that the Voodoo Rooms wouldn't suffer delays beyond their control. Yes, they're professionals; I knew I could trust them, but one still worries. And, of course, all I could tell the acts was a rough room capacity, no other information.

And at the last possible moment, we got the all clear. It would happen. It wasn't until I saw the new space, with the Voodoo Rooms' management busily hammering cladding into place, that I realised the new space was the former Penny Black. The buildings connected, but I never realised that.

Of course, the space was transformed. The Voodoo Rooms is upmarket; the last thing they wanted was any possible connection to the Penny Black, its clientele or reputation.

I don't think people realise even now that the spaces are the same. The old street entrance is permanently closed and the public now enters through the main Voodoo Rooms door. If the ghosts of a thousand drink-shattered dreams still haunt the space, they do so discreetly.

But if they hadn't for any reason opened the new room as scheduled, if I'd had to disappoint the acts, then I would have gone back to 23 hour drinking, whether the Penny Black was closed or not.

We were developing a presence around Picardy Place, which was risky. When we'd worked with The Phoenix and The Outhouse, audiences complained of distance, even though they're quite central. So when The Street wanted to come on board, with a downstairs room that was quite a difficult shape, I was worried that we might not do well enough. However, the bar was lovely and the management more than enthusiastic. And that counts for a lot. So we agreed that we should mostly book gay-friendly acts, since The Street is on the corner of Broughton Street, the LGBT epicentre of Edinburgh.

I suppose that was the birth of our Cabaret section, which is now a very strong feature. Or maybe it was born earlier. Hard to say exactly when.

We also needed venues for the Theatre section, and again Calum delivered from an unexpected direction. Princes Mall, a shopping centre above Waverley Station, wasn't normally where one would look for Fringe shows.

I knew the Mall only as somewhere to pass through. Until recent years, the North exit from Waverley Station was up a long and murderous flight of steps, not unnaturally called Waverley Steps. Not the easiest thing to drag a heavy suitcase and guitar up. But if one got halfway up, one could nip into the Mall, through the food court, pausing for tea if needed, and up in a lift to Princes Street level. And that useful lift was all I knew of the Mall.

Calum, however, had spotted that there were vacant shop units, and spoken to the management. There was a possibility of using two of these units. It was a little baffling; they'd never done anything like this before and I couldn't see what would be in it for them. But they were willing to give it a try. So we programmed, mostly with Theatre-section stuff.

And later on the management asked us: were we sure all our shows were family-friendly? We weren't, because they weren't. It wasn't mentioned at the initial discussions at all. And too late to change things around.

The whole affair illustrated our strengths and weaknesses. We held a meeting for the Theatre section, in London. I was encouraged; it looked like teams were building. And in one of the two vacant shops, the team got together and brought lights and other stuff from London, and took the time to rig the spaces, deciding among themselves where to put the stage from among the several options. They worked together, and got good audiences, and the staging was exactly as we would wish it, making something like a theatre out of an empty space, and creating a real Fringe experience. They posted people around the Mall to direct the public to the space.

And in the other shop unit, these things did not happen, and the shows suffered as a result. And the performers blamed the space. It wasn't perfect, but was a better shape than the other, more successful one. It was too near the Food Court and there was some noise pollution. All true, but the Fringe as a whole suffers from noise pollution.

All in all, at the Fringe you get out what you put in.

We do tell performers this, but often they don't realise it. Having set up many venues myself in the past, with neither knowledge nor training, I have always assumed that anybody could do the same. But perhaps not, after all?

Jenny Ha's was in new hands and re-named the Kilderkin. We suggested that they hold off the renaming until September, since all our publicity including the Big Fat Fringe Programme referred to Jenny Ha's. But such was their anxiety to dissociate from the past that they went ahead with the renaming anyway. It caused a little confusion among our acts and audience, but we got through it. The pub's still there, still The Kilderkin, and I love the place.

So, the venues of 2011 were a constant headache, as well as an opportunity.

Well, what did I expect when there were 31 of them?

We were at the point where we couldn't even count the venues properly. We had a walking show. Did the start point, David Hume's statue, count as a venue? We put it on our map, but we didn't count it towards the 31.

And there were times when we had to take the rough with the smooth. Most of our venues were part of chains in some way, although you couldn't tell from the outside. Very different places but turning out to have the same owners. And, for the sake of getting a good venue, we'd sometimes have to accept a marginal one as part of the package.

I won't be specific about which venues those were, except that we ended up running an open mic on Sundays in a space we didn't really want, but which was organisationally connected to a space we very much did want.

Sunrise, sunset.

Just under 5000 performances of 326 shows was what we ended up with. And to think we started with 22 performances of a single show. People spoke of the "Big Four" venues, but we were bigger than all of them, in fact bigger than any two of them put together.

They, however, had employees. We just had me, plus Calum on the venues, and a few volunteers.

It was time to make better use of the volunteers. Put that under 2012's mistakes.

I've lost the plot here. I intended to tell the story of the Free Fringe, and what I've been doing in the 2011 story is telling the story of the venue search.

You get no idea of how the Free Fringe itself was going. Classic amateur writer's mistake. Because things are prominent in my memory, I assume they're important to you. My head is cluttered with detail. You might want to know the big picture.

After 15 years of trying, we had made an impact on the Fringe. We were anything between 12% and 17% of all shows, depending how you measured it. And if you added in the Laughing Horse's free-admission shows, at least 20% of the Fringe was now free-admission.

The citizens of Edinburgh liked that, at least.

The Wee Blue Book was a magnificent asset. It had become known. Normally, if you're doing a Fringe show by yourself and just giving out your own show leaflets, you can't give them away. Most people say no. Especially on leafleters' alley, in front of the Fringe Office, where most people give out their leaflets, near where the excellent street entertainers perform.

And where a lot of Edinburghers, including many lawyers, go about their daily business, fighting their way through crowds of Fringe performers who think their shows are more important than those lawyers' fights to keep their clients out of prison. Saughton, I believe, is a good place not to be in.

No wonder they despise us, sometimes.

Anyway, leafleting for yourself, you can't give 'em away, but hold up the Wee Blue Book and people come up to you and ask for it.

That's what 15 years of work achieves. Actually, the Wee Blue Book wasn't 15 years old, but even since 2007 we'd achieved a presence with it.

And with that presence, the Free Fringe was established. The citizens of Edinburgh and most regular Fringegoers knew about us.

Not all Fringegoers. An old friend of mine (we did our Masters' together in 1973 to 1975) turned out to have gone to the Fringe almost every year since, but seldom left the complex of shows run by the Pleasance and I never knew he was in Edinburgh. He was surprised to learn of us. Well, the quality of shows run by the Pleasance is indeed very good and I would never say otherwise. And I think he could have afforded their ticket prices. The Fringe can be enjoyed in many ways.

We were getting bits of press and bits of radio, despite having little Public Relations operation. I was interviewed on Radio 4, not for the first time; I don't know what I said but it was probably banal.

And then there were the prizes.

If you're a comedian, the big prize is the Perrier. And I know it hasn't been officially called that since 2008, but that's what we still call it. They gave me the Panel Prize in 2009, as I said earlier, but that wasn't the issue.

There are three winners every year. Panel Prize, Best Newcomer and Best Comedy Show, the last of these being the big award with twice as much prize money. Only two winners for pure comedic excellence, therefore. And yet almost every comedian at the Fringe fantasises about winning the big award. Or at least being on the shortlist of nominees.

The eligibility criteria, since time immemorial, have been to perform a show of at least 50 minutes duration on at least five days of the last week (but in practice a run embracing all three weeks, else the judges would not have chance to see you). And your eligibility was taken from the Big Fat Fringe Programme.

It was amazing the extent to which people's behaviours were altered by those criteria.

We had acts putting themselves in the programme for a 49 minute show, so they were not ineligible for Best Newcomer the year after.

We had people filling in other shows' days off so they made the minimum number of performances.

And, importantly, we had people who could barely scrape together the nearly £400 it cost to be in the Big Fat Fringe Programme, doing so in order that they should be eligible for a prize which, realistically, they were not going to win.

The Perrier organisation had just assumed that the programme in the Big Fat Fringe Programme represented the entirety of the Fringe. As it used to. But of course, with us around, it didn't any more. We'd released people from the need to be in it. Oh, they could choose to be in it; there are many advantages to doing so. But they could also choose not to be.

2011 was the year in which the Edinburgh Comedy Awards, or as I still call them, the Perriers, accepted our list of shows as qualifying for a visit from their judges. No more did a show have to be in the BFFP to qualify.

And coincidentally 2011 was the first year in which one of our shows was nominated for Best Newcomer. Cariad Lloyd, with Lady Cariad's Characters. She didn't win, but a nomination itself is a big award and shows you as an act to be taken notice of. She could easily have won. Almost every nominee will tell you: anybody on the shortlist deserves to be there.

So, me apart, we had our first nominee. And I made damn sure she had a Free Fringe badge to wear at the ceremony, in case it was she who won and made the speech.

We'd broken through. If the Perrier recognised us as a legitimate source of eligible shows, then we were no longer on the fringes of the Fringe. We were the establishment.

And if we were the establishment, then we were vulnerable to being ousted by people like the people we used to be. That's how it goes.

The pay-to-play venues also started out with the idea of helping artists. And then they became Organisations. And an Organisation's main goal becomes self-perpetuation. We had to stop that happening. Of course, we were a non-profit, and that helped. But still, we could be outflanked by people who were even more collaborative. Should we object to that? I suppose not, but we're human.

Back in 1996, I never imagined we'd get this big. But I imagined the free movement as a whole would get this big. In 1996,

I envisioned several different groupings of performers, each non-profit, each doing its own thing along the same sorts of principle.

What I hadn't considered was people like Laughing Horse, charging performers to apply and setting up as for-profit organisations. And doing so off the back of the reputation we'd worked hard to earn.

That, I thought, had to be fought.

People like the Scottish Comedy Festival were fine. They were run by an ex-Free Fringer and who had taken over the Beehive after Laughing Horse's one non-productive year there. They were doing the same thing as us in a similar way. They had a defined niche, and if the Edinburgh Fringe can't find a home for Scottish Comedy, what hope is there? If some Edinburgh comedians were avoiding us after the Cruz fiasco, well then, let them do the Scottish Comedy Festival with our blessing.

But for-profit organisations on our turf? That's another thing entirely.

There were, as always, performers who presented problems, and I don't mean the one who dropped out shortly before the Fringe because he needed dentistry and he couldn't afford both, although that also happened. I have some sympathy for that, having spent a lot of money on teeth myself over the years. No, not him.

We insist all our shows' leaflets have our logo on. It helps reinforce the team and the brand. Very occasionally, some of them forget, or even worse, don't want to. And we have to ask them to get stickers printed and affix them by hand.

But when we discovered that one of our shows had not been turning up regularly, we needed to investigate. That can't happen; if a show is advertised, then there must be a show. So we investigated, and found this man's leaflets. And prominently, where our logo should have been, there stood the Laughing Horse's logo.

He blamed his printer. But we blamed him, and, after giving him a chance to have his say, filled his slot with another show.

Coke is Coke and Pepsi is Pepsi, and never the twain. Probably a bad example. Anyway, he hadn't been turning up either.

*

A Bit about the Board

Which requireth no subheading

NOW, THAT WAS WHERE I FINISHED writing the 2011 chapter. But looking over it, I realised I'd left something major out, and I had to go back and add it. Ah, the wonder of word processing. Medieval scribes didn't have this luxury. Although Chaucer gave up writing several Canterbury Tales, presumably intending to go back and finish them, and he never did.

Would Chaucer have done better with a word processor? Or would he have been burned for witchcraft? I don't know. All I know is, one of our set texts for A-Level English Literature was the Squire's Tale, one of the ones Chaucer never finished. You don't give 16- and 17-year olds a love of literature by making them dissect a story without an ending. There are better Tales, even though in those more puritan days they felt they had to censor many of them.

It's bad enough studying anything at 17 when your main worries are finding cures for virginity and acne, the two being somewhat related.

But I digress. Perhaps because I don't want to remember the thing I have to write about in this section.

I was finally elected to the Board of the Fringe Society. There's a lot of background here. It was something that had been in my mind since Earl Okin's tenure around 2000. I was indignant that one could win a seat with as few as 25 votes. Or, as in 2001, with as few as 11 votes. Or with 22 votes in 2004. This showed how uninterested performers were in the organisation that managed their Fringe experience. And which set the dates and the participation fees.

For some time I'd been trying to make performers aware of this problem. Very few cared. And because of that, I felt that the Board was dominated by interests other than performers' interests. This, I thought, could change if performers would increasingly stand and vote for the Board.

There was a certain amount of performer unrest around 2006. I wish I could remember more. There was even a meeting organised at which performers could vent their concerns, moderated by a man who didn't introduce himself. At the time I thought things would change for the better. Where there's anger, there is a force for constructive change.

But it was not to be.

I'm going to quote here my unsuccessful manifesto for election to the Board in 2006. There was a slate of five performers standing that year, and had they (we) been elected, the Fringe story would be different. Looking over what I wrote then, there's not much I would change now.

I have been bringing shows to the Fringe for the last 13 years. I estimate that I have spent £35000 of my own money doing so. I know many people who have spent more.

The Fringe is financed entirely by the losses made by performers. Yet the Board has never contained more than two performers out of 14. This must change. We who finance the Fringe should run the Fringe.

No more Board members with a vague interest in the Fringe. No more journalists; no more amateurs; no more men in blazers. Performers have been at the bottom of the Fringe food chain for too long.

Policy should from now on be created with the needs of performers uppermost. Without our contributions, both artistic and financial, the Fringe would not happen. No other interest group can say the same.

I am qualified to serve as Director not only because of my long experience with the Fringe and my commitment to it. I have also encouraged the talent of others, providing performance opportunity for over 250 comedians in my show, and creating the Free Fringe which in 2006 has brought 69 shows to the Fringe, each free of charge to the public. Creative thinking made this revolution possible, and the creative thinking was mine. I am also qualified to understand the business side of the Fringe (MBA, London Business School).

Please vote for me and for other performer candidates.

There was a slate of four performers that year, for the five vacancies (a fifth considered standing, but then decided not to). It was worth a push. Especially since that year the Chair was one of the directors up for re-election, and not re-electing her would have made a strong statement.

I tried to rally people to join and vote; there had been some unrest. I put this statement round:

VOTE FOR PERFORMER CANDIDATES FOR THE FRINGE BOARD

What is the Fringe Board?

The Fringe is really a charity. It has a Board of Directors, 14 strong. This Board doesn't do the day-to-day running of the Fringe; that's the job of the Fringe Director, Paul Gudgin. The Board of Directors sets policy, manages the assets and chooses the next Director when there's a vacancy.

Why does it need reform?

Because performers make the Fringe. We provide all the artistic input; we also provide all the money. The Fringe is financed on the personal losses made by performers. And yet there have never been more than two performers on the Board. This means that, when decisions are made, the interests of performers are low down the list of priorities.

We need at least a majority of performers on the Board.

We pay. We should govern.

What can I do about it?

Vote for the four (possibly five) performers who are standing this year. These are [names]. All are known comedians in their own right; all have brought shows to the Fringe at their own expense in the past; all know exactly how it feels to face a massive personal loss on your show, and to have to hustle for every member of the audience. They are also outspoken, and will say what they think in Board meetings.

How do I vote?

This is the most difficult bit. The Board itself decided to impose a charge on voting, some ten years ago. To vote, you have to join the Festival Fringe Society Ltd. This costs £10. Not only that; you have to join by certain deadlines if you want to exercise your vote. Not only that, but if you go to the Fringe

Office, the odds are that nobody you see will know anything about this. They'll confuse it with things like Friends of the Fringe.

You can vote in two ways: by post or by attending the Annual General Meeting. We recommend you attend the Annual General Meeting. This is held on Saturday 19th August at 1100 in the Apex Hotel, Grassmarket. It is worth getting up for this. And if you vote there, you can be sure your ballot paper has not been lost in the post or elsewhere.

If you want to vote by post, you have to join the Festival Fringe Society Ltd by a date they haven't given us so far. It's an early date, because the voting papers are being sent out on Friday 11th August.

How do I join?

Get a membership form (available by email from [address] or downloadable in Word format from my website on [url]) and return it to [name], the Company Secretary, at the Fringe Office. Doing this in person is best. Experience shows that other staff at the Fringe Office will not be informed and will not know what to do with the forms.

What I said about the Fringe Office staff being unbriefed was entirely accurate at the time; it has since got better.

The slate did not get voted in. Not enough performers cared. This was taken as a sign that the slaves were happy on the plantation; listen to them sing. Did people not want emancipation? Well, clearly not, at the time. Or the other pressures of the Fringe proved to be greater priority.

I lived in Switzerland when a referendum was held on whether women should have the vote in national elections. This was 1970 or 71. And there were women who went on television and argued against their own enfranchisement. Ludicrous, you think. But I felt there was a parallel between that and Fringe performers and their Board.

Up to about 2010, voting for the Board was relatively simple. You had to know about it (they didn't tell you much); you had to get an application form, pay £10 and return it. The

Fringe Office staff, mostly, didn't know about the system, and would often give people the wrong form, to become a Friend of the Fringe (I may have the title wrong) which also cost £10 but didn't give you a vote. Now-famous comedians did their best to join but were somehow or other put off.

But each Board member rotated after three years and could stand for re-election. The Single Transferable Vote system was used, and the vote could be postal or cast in person at the AGM, always held on the penultimate Saturday morning. Members of the Fringe Office staff would take the votes into a separate room and count them, unscrutinised by the candidates or by any neutral observer. They would then return and announce the result.

So, if you could get yourself nominated and enough people to pay £10 and vote for you, you could in theory get elected. If you really wanted to be elected, in the early days, you could pay the membership fee of 25 people yourself, and bingo, that was enough votes; for a mere £250, a seat on the Board would be yours. In 2001, six votes would have been enough, although the lowest-placed elected candidate actually got eleven, and I'm certainly not suggesting any of the votes were bought. In 2001, even the highest-placed candidate got only 22 votes.

But, of course, your nomination had to be valid. And accepted. And not get lost on someone's desk. Over the years, some nominations were ruled out for non-receipt, signature in the wrong place, or non-arrival on time (in one case even though hand-delivered to the Fringe Office, or so it is said: I can't source this one).

One candidate was humiliatingly disqualified at the AGM itself because his proposer had not attended the AGM, even though the nomination was duly signed. In later years, another forgot to sign her own nomination, and was assured by telephone that this did not matter since she had shown clear willingness to stand. In the light of that call, she did not travel to Edinburgh to provide the missing signature, which she was willing to do. And then, after the nomination deadline, her nomination was ruled invalid after all. On another occasion,

two candidates who had intended to stand in different constituencies were forced to stand in the same constituency
against each other; a clear clerical error which the returning
officer (Fringe Director/CEO of the time) refused to rectify.

It's not surprising to know that the nominations thus
treated usually belonged to people outside the ruling clique.

I'm not saying there was gerrymandering. I am saying there
was considerable scope for gerrymandering. The system
lacked transparency and independent scrutiny.

And there was no legal recourse, even if one could afford
lawyers. The position of Board Director (or Trustee: the terminology's changed over the years) was unpaid, and so by one's
nomination not going forward, one made no financial loss.
And the Law does not recognise an unquantifiable loss.

When the natives started getting restless, the Board felt it
had to act. My contention was that, since performers finance
the Fringe and make the Fringe happen, they (we) should also
control the Fringe and make policy. Obviously they couldn't
allow that to happen.

The constitution hadn't been revised since 1969. So, there
was a constitutional reform.

Instead of saying the three people with the most votes
(after vote transfers under STV) should be elected, they made
constituencies. The three categories were Venues, Performers
and General. And they were clear about this: the objective was
to ensure there was never a majority of Performers on the
Board.

To counteract this, there was to be a Performers' Council,
an advisory body with no direct powers. This idea did not survive the proposal. Instead, it was converted into a Participants'
Council, again with three constituencies, again with a guarantee that performers could never have a majority on it. At time
of writing, it's dead; nobody has recently stood to be on it.

It seemed to me, and still seems to me, that this represented
an attempt to hold on to the status quo at all costs. Instead of
seeing the Free Fringe as the institution that rescued the
Fringe from high ticket prices, performer exploitation and

class discrimination (low-income performers couldn't afford pay-to-play prices, which especially affected our Spoken Word performers) we were seen as a threat to the good order of the Fringe. Since we weren't going away, despite what was said behind our backs, we had to be contained.

If you're going to contain something, at least do it effectively.

By presenting winning candidates in both the Performers and General categories, we could still gain a majority of the Board. But that wasn't all. The Free Fringe is a collective. So everybody is involved in the management of venues. Therefore any of our members could stand in the Venues category also. They didn't like that, but couldn't stop it immediately. They tried later.

But why be concerned with the Fringe establishment stopping performer power, when we made such a wonderful job of stopping it ourselves?

I want to make it clear. We've never said to Free Fringe members: you must vote for a particular candidate. That would be pushing it too far. Even though nationally, if one joins the Labour Party, one has to commit to voting for the Labour candidate in one's constituency, no matter what one thinks of him/her or the brand of Labour policies he/she espouses. Labour do that; we don't.

But we have said to them: you must join and vote for the candidates of your choice.

And, year after year, they have failed to do that in their droves.

What is a drove?

It would be a good name for a model of car. Drive a Drove.

Better than Duster, at any rate.

Assuming we presented performer-friendly candidates in all constituencies, there should be a clear majority of performers on the Board by now. And there isn't. If there were, there would be reform of the participation fee structure. And of the too- early deadline for the Big Fat Fringe Programme. And of other policies which present advantages to shows with money-

backing over shows without that backing. But these things
have not happened, and cannot until there is performers' control of the Board.

I am not a politician. I don't do tact'n'diplomacy. I can't. It's
a Tourette's thing.

At the first Board meeting I attended, I presented a scheme
for adjusting participation fees to benefit shows in smaller
venues with shorter runs. At that time, all shows except one-
off performances paid the same flat fee. Five days in a thirty-
seater cost the same as a 24-day run in a 200-seater, as far as
the Fringe Office were concerned.

It's not so much that this proposal was defeated: it was that
the issue was of little concern to most Board members. The
business of the Board seemed mostly to do with the management of elaborate documents: risk assessments and the like.
The welfare of performers did not seem to be perceived as an
issue.

I have been on Boards before, in the private sector, and they
have been concerned with the efficient running of their firms.
I have been on numerous committees with exotic names
within Higher Education, which is a world allegedly strangled
by paper, bureaucracy and red tape. But even the heaviest paper exercise within Higher Education made perfect sense compared to the activities of the Board of the Festival Fringe Society Ltd.

I felt impotent. Frustrated. Incapable of breaching the dis-
connection between the Fringe Board and the Fringe itself.
Even though I was not alone; there was already one Free
Fringer on the Board, and later some others were elected.

My term of office yielded nothing positive. Well, apart from
the grudging introduction of a reduced participation fee rate
for one-week long performances, which I suppose was an improvement. The Board actually debated whether one week
meant seven days or five. And decided it meant five. Anybody
doing six days had to pay for the full month (or else, as many
did, list themselves for five days while actually performing for
six or more).

Which reminds me of the jolly jape, one with a point, perpetrated by Gareth Morinan, Free Fringer, original Participants' Council member and later Board member.

Alongside the five-day rate they had also introduced a rate for two performances (there was already a rate for single performances). Gareth spotted that the cost of twelve such two-day listings was in fact less than the price of a full-page advertisement in the Big Fat Fringe Programme. Accordingly, he listed his show twelve consecutive times, and thus got more notice than a full-page advert would have yielded him.

Now, this makes a point. Something was structurally wrong if this was the case, and Gareth was entitled to take advantage of it, which he duly did. But there were demands that he resign from the Participants' Council (presumably for being too clever). Instead, he stood for the Board itself. The office, meanwhile, made a regulation that the same show could not have more than one listing.

As if they could judge what 'the same show' is. One of my own shows had different guests every night. I could have claimed it was a different show every night, had I wished. And what about Improv, of which there were many good troupes on the Free Fringe? The very essence of Improv is that it's always a different show.

I think my point here is: they'll defend "that's the way we've always done it" at any cost. It was the same with my own "40 Words" show in 2009.

They don't see changing conditions or the Fringe's need to adapt to them. The model that seemed to work in the 1970s is essentially the same model that is still in force in 2018.

Little positive emerged from my time on the Board except the election of a few more performers. But radical reform will not happen until performers are in a majority.

I claimed no expenses for being on that Board. Even though expenses merely cover travel and accommodation, I felt I did not deserve even that. And I refused to attend any lunches for Directors which were paid for by the Fringe. I felt we had no right to be junketing at performers' expense. I did drink the tea that was provided at Board meetings and, occasionally, I had a biscuit. There was blood on that biscuit.

I had joined the Board with high hopes of effecting change, but was able to effect nothing major. It seemed that most members did not see that there was a need for change. Over the years, the few factors that even slightly levelled the playing field for performers had gone: no Fringe Club, no Fringe Sunday, no opening procession.

Before my first year at the Fringe, I attended a London meeting for aspirant Fringe performers. It consisted of a panel of promoters, agents, press and occasional performers, answering questions put by the chair, with a limited number of questions from the floor, followed by all venues present being given about two minutes to pitch themselves, i.e. sell potential performers their space, followed by those same venues taking more detailed questions at tables.

24 years later, that same format is still being used. Something wrong there. The Fringe has changed. Performers' needs have changed. Performers pay their venues thousands and pay the Fringe Office £390 (although that includes VAT). Yet they're not regarded as customers. I think they should be.

I'm prepared to be wrong. But as far as I know no systematic attempt has been made to ascertain these customers' actual needs, whether in information or support. Yes, they have asked performers how satisfied they are with the services that they do provide. But not, as far as I can see, asked what services ought to be provided. Or who regrets the lost of the services that were once provided and now are not.

I do not look back on my time on the Board with any satisfaction. I felt I'd failed. But I also felt that performers' needs would never feature as largely on the agenda as they should, until there was a majority of performers on the Board. Over the years, more have been elected, but there is still no majority.

Too much Board time is spent on figures, five-year plans and risk assessments and not enough on improving the Fringe. Oh, and speaking of risk assessments, one of the risks emphasised in one of the numerous risk assessment documents was that a certain faction, unnamed, should gain majority control of the Board. Could that faction possibly have been 'performers'? The people who make the Fringe happen?

These were the years in which the Labour Party abolished Clause IV. Which, if you don't remember it, committed the party to workers' control of the means of production. Well, that's what I think we ought to do at the Fringe. It wasn't fashionable in Labour politics since the election of the vile Blair, but there are signs it's coming back. I hope it does. You may think different. Write your own book if you do.

Back to the main timeline.

*

2012

THE FREE FRINGE WAS ALWAYS supposed to be a collective of performers, sharing the work. I'd said that to the press and the broadcast media; I'd made that statement at many presentations to potential applicants.

I'd said it so often that I believed it. If you believe in things, don't they exist? Father Christmas is real.

But actually it wasn't true. It was like many Communist countries; in theory the power lay with the people, but in practice with a tiny élite. And I was that tiny élite.

And in fact by 2012 there were few Communist countries left. I live in the past, and dream of futures that have been tried in the past and failed.

September 2011 saw my final severance from my day job, which I had loved but which had gone wrong as I described above. They paid money to be rid of me. Being me, I could easily have spent all that money on the Free Fringe, subsidising other performers, but I decided not to. It would have meant that the Free Fringe wasn't actually viable without external finding. Besides, I'd put enough of my own money into it in my early years.

I resolved to keep the severance money for myself and perhaps buy a Rickenbacker 360/12v64, an exact replica of the one played by George Harrison on A Hard Day's Night. I don't normally desire material objects. That was an exception. I still haven't bought it; maybe I should. But the difference between George Harrison and me is: he could play. Although by September 2011 he hadn't for ten years.

So maybe that's why I didn't. I still could. And leave it to my grandson, who was born on February 25th 2016. Same birthday as George Harrison. Spooky? No. Everybody's got to be born on some day or another.

But I digress.

A team could perhaps take over the scheduling of shows?

We already had one person doing the Spoken Word and another the Theatre. But Comedy was the big task, and I'd always done that myself. I was doing fewer and fewer circuit gigs, and I wasn't really in touch.

But delegating isn't as simple as you think.

Now, I had my theories about delegating in general, and they were wrong theories. I thought one should empower the people one delegated to completely, and ensure they made all decisions. Not interfere, not steer, not complain when they do something I disagree with.

I think there might even be management textbooks that say this.

And maybe that works within business organisations, where people work 9 to 5 and are paid, and come in to the office every day. But volunteer organisations are something different.

A team volunteered. I tend to trust people, which is another bad characteristic of mine.

The first thing they did was change the system I had been running.

Now, it wasn't a good system because it was mine. Well, maybe it was. But it was a good system because it had evolved to do the things we needed it to do. And you should never change a system without running the new one in parallel with the old one, otherwise screwups result and you can't recover.

Now, I mentioned that we vet shows. We do. We get a lot of applications, many from people we don't know. They have to be checked out. Because some applications, with the best will in the world, can't result in shows. People apply for one-person shows too early in their career; sometimes people with no comedy experience at all apply, convinced they can do it by sheer force of personality. They can't; it takes practice. And sometimes we get applications where we can't tell if it's genius or madness, or both.

We're always going to get some of those decisions wrong. The way I used to do the scheduling was: save it up until Christmas, where we might have a reasonable idea of what main venues we had, and then spend the seven days between Yule and Hogmanay putting them in slots. I did this work in the pub quite a lot of the time. Every time I made a decision, I imagined the performer's reaction to it, and often feared it might be negative. Trying to please everybody, you see. Clearly some shows were bankers.

So get the excellent ones, the ones you're sure of, in first, at least the full runs. I'd put a little P for Priority against those shows, but they didn't know that. And then I'd fit the other full runs whose applications I liked around them, in venues I thought would suit, bearing in mind that it's better to be full in a small venue than half-empty in a big one. Each venue had its own characteristics, and that had to be remembered also.

And there were always many shows left over, and we had to wait for more venues to come in. And the part-runs had to be matched with other part-runs to make a full run, because we couldn't afford to leave the venues with one or two weeks with a show not happening. Hell, they even objected to shows' single days off, sometimes.

So, that was the system. But when the 2012 team took over the job, they changed it.

I don't know if it's because I'm old, but people always assume I know nothing about data processing.

So they looked at my complex spreadsheet and they thought they could write a better one. The one member of the team who processed data for a living was overruled by the others. And they produced something that would have done some of the job, but would not have produced the Wee Blue Book in the way mine did.

But worse: they formalised the vetting.

Now, it's nice for everybody to know where they stand. And yes, if you have an application that is an obvious case for rejection, then it should be rejected straight away, in fairness to the applicant. Normally, such an applicant won't accept the verdict and will often complain that we, or I, can't tell quality when we, or I, see it. Well, that may be true, despite years of experience. Dick Rowe turned down The Beatles. But nobody ever remembers the hundreds, probably thousands, of acts he also turned down because they were not, in his opinion, good enough for Decca. His job was to make decisions, and he made them. Everybody thinks: if I had been Dick Rowe, I wouldn't have turned them down. But you weren't, and if you had been, you might have.

Nobody thinks they're Dick Rowe. But everybody thinks they're The Beatles. And nobody is, apart from four or five survivors. (I should check. You're screaming: TWO survivors. But what about Chas Newby? Jimmy Nicol? Tommy Moore? Pete Best, certainly still alive at time of writing.)

It doesn't matter. I'm not writing about The Beatles. That's not The Point. Which would have been a good band name, but nobody's used it so far. Or have they?

So, I used to let the rejected know pretty soon after their application. But the non-rejected would just get their application acknowledged. And that gave us flexibility.

What the 2012 team did was to email people saying they had been accepted, by which they meant: passed the quality scrutiny.

Most of our applicants pass the quality scrutiny, because most are indeed good enough. And those that aren't often get counselled into something suitable. For example, a standup comedian who's not yet ready for a one-person show gets advised to become part of a four-hander and gain further experience that way.

We try to help. But Dunning-Kruger Syndrome is strong. If we tell someone they're not yet ready for a one-person show, they tend to regard that as an insult and go to Laughing Horse, who usually give them a one-person show, or go to the pay-to-play venues and wave money at them.

That's not the point.

The point is: if you tell somebody they've passed the scrutiny, they expect an offer.

And you may not be able to give them one for other reasons. How many offers we can give, and what they are, depends on what venues we have, and when we have them. And whether any individual show gets an offer depends not only on its quality but on its attitude. We want people on board who know what the Free Fringe is trying to achieve and who support it. People who believe that, if performers support and work for each other, things are better for everybody.

We need a prima donna filter. There are plenty out there who really believe that we're doing it because their (the Prima Donnas') shows are so wonderful that we sacrifice our time to get them the fame they deserve.

Honestly.

And still others are using us as an insurance offer. I've mentioned this before. We're not going to hold down a prime slot in an excellent venue right until the deadline, so that an act has an insurance against not liking his/her offer from a pay-to-play venue. And then they go pay-to-play and don't even tell us, so we then to have to fill a prime slot with what may be a sub-prime act.

So, for all sorts of reasons, we don't tell people they've passed the quality scrutiny. We do tell them if they haven't. That's only fair. And we try to counsel them. I've said that. I'm going round in circles. The Free Fringe organisation goes round in circles, trying to learn from its mistakes and sometimes being persuaded to make the same mistakes again.

I do remember rejecting one show in 2012, and I'm telling you about it so you get an idea of what we sometimes have to deal with. This applicant boasted of having been banned from the Guardian's "Comment is Free" web site for "telling the truth". A phrase that usually makes me suspicious. What is truth? A question Jesus refused to answer when it was put by Pontius Pilatus, or so the story goes. This applicant also boasted of having been banned by the Daily Telegraph and the Daily Mail, and yet in her application volunteered to write press releases for us. She also claimed to have done a previous show for Laughing Horse and had made a complaint to the Fringe Office when one speaker on the PA failed.

Trouble all the way, in other words. So I told her no and fielded the barrage of very nasty email that was subsequently thrown. Give me what I want, it said effectively, or I shall publicly accuse you of discrimination. Erm, newsflash: when you select acts, you discriminate. By definition. There are the ones you want and the ones you don't. And we cheerfully discriminate between applicants on those grounds.

It turned out that the "truth" she had told was holocaust denial, and as I write, years later, she's on trial for offences relating to that very thing. And somebody else gave her a show in 2016, and protests ensued; in my view, rightly. Did you know Anne Frank's father forged her diaries for publicity? No, nor did I. I still don't, because I have seen no evidence. But that's what this applicant contended, and that's not the worst. Excuse me; I need a bath.

Now, of course, you too would reject an applicant who came goosestepping up to you singing the Horst Wessel Song. But they don't do it like that. They apply for shows which, on the surface, seem similar to other shows. One has to look for the warning signs and dig a little.

So anyway, our show scheduling team collapsed.

I'd send them the applications and I got fewer and fewer allocations back. And more excuses that they didn't really have time to do a good enough job. Until in the end there was only one person left on the scheduling team.

Could she do as many allocations as she could and put them on the spreadsheet?

She hadn't learned to work the spreadsheet. But surely she'd been part of the team and seen how the spreadsheet worked?

Yes and no. She'd given her opinions on the shows, but had not troubled to see how the data should be recorded. And she too was under stress from other sources.

I put on my Winston Churchill hat and said "very well, then, alone". And sent in the army to shoot some miners. Because that's what you do if you're Churchill. It's not all speeches full of aphorisms. Although I could have done with a bomb-proof bunker at that point.

Back to doing it myself. And facing some shows demanding where their slot was, having been told they'd passed the scrutiny, but we still had no slot for them.

That was Comedy. At least I had someone reliable programming Spoken Word.

There's some bitterness here, because some of the members of that scheduling team, having let us down once, were to do greater damage later.

So by March I was back to doing the Comedy scheduling by myself. And no doubt I made mistakes in the process. The biggest mistake you can make, however, is to give space to a show who will not tough it out and see his/her run through to the end. Because that almost invariably loses us the venue.

The bigger we got, the more vulnerable we became.

Back in the 1990s we were the only free shows in town. People came because of the admission price and stayed because of the quality. But by 2012 there was so much free stuff that 'free' was no longer a sufficient selling proposition.

We had to be free, good, and dedicated to publicising our shows tirelessly.

And there were plenty of shows around who were merely free and not good. Some of them were our mistakes. But mostly they were Laughing Horse shows. Laughing Horse were, I believed, determined to beat us, after the events of 2006. Since they couldn't be better in quality, they were determined to be bigger. And by 2011, they weren't. They boasted of 6000 performances; in fact, they had 5100. I know this, because after the Fringe I went through their programme and counted. We had more. Their programme was padded out with disco. When their venues stopped having live performance, when they reverted to DJs and dancing (as many of ours also did) they would list that as a performance. We didn't.

We tried as much as we could to distinguish our shows from theirs. We pushed our brand and logo. But they had captured the domains freefringe.co.uk and freefringe.com, and many shows thought they were applying to us when they were applying to them. They didn't scruple to use phrases like

"Edinburgh Free Fringe Festival" to describe themselves. And the public, hearing the cry of "free shows" on the street, largely didn't distinguish us from them.

Some of their shows were good. Of course. Law of averages. Some of ours weren't; same reason. Although what defines whether a show is good or not? Genius or madness? If you want a five-star review, be prepared for a one-star. Do reviews matter? I've always said not.

But chortle.co.uk had done an analysis in 2010, and our reviews were, within statistical significance, as good as those of any of the pay-to-play venues. And Laughing Horse's were a full star below that, on a scale of five stars, and the worst of any promoter with a significant number of shows.

It's not an absolute. Reviews don't matter much and many reviewers have insufficient knowledge of the genre they're reviewing. But I'm human and when an analysis supports what I believe, then I also believe that analysis.

And I still believe that Laughing Horse were putting on too many poor shows (not all their shows are poor, and I never said otherwise) because they were too concerned with filling space, and because they don't really know what's good and what's not.

Does anybody? We also don't. But we have a better idea, with our experienced team of performers as Artistic Directors.

I hoped the public would follow our brand. Keep their eye on the big red 50p logo and the Wee Blue Book. These were both brands and we were building them up. But in truth some went to anything that was free and did not distinguish between us and them.

Some did. The wonderful group of young people who would queue for the Canons' Gait for the noon show and still be there at the end of the midnight show. What great people. Even I wouldn't do what they did, despite the excellence of the bill at the Canons' Gait. I'd need to stretch my legs.

Goes to show, though. Canons' Gait was always Venue Number One. So much so that many press and web reports say that the Free Fringe started there, as did Wikipedia until I corrected it. It was headquarters; it was where I did my shows and where I could mostly be found, hogging a one-person table and dealing with crises by email on the very computer on which I am now typing this, and which was my long-service reward from the University.

My grandfather got a gold watch, a canteen of cutlery (why is it called a canteen?) and a long-service ceremony. My father was dined out and given a presentation, even by ICI, his competitors. I was just told to choose a present and shoved out of the back door. The ceremonies used to show that the employer valued your long service. Getting you to choose your own gift and sending them the bill basically means they don't give a fuck about the loyalty you showed. It's not about the gift. My grandfather already had enough cutlery.

This sort of thing is what makes you a comedian, and look for love from drunken strangers ranged on seats in front of you.

So, I'm typing this on my long-service reward laptop. And I would sit in the Canons' Gait answering streams of emails on the same laptop, and dealing with crises as they occurred. At my isolated table where people would occasionally come to meet me or interview me or simply talk. And I could view the queues ready to go down to the shows, which was quite satisfying.

I would, of course, occasionally stand up and help with the queue management, do the door duty and hold the previous show's bucket.

I know many wonderful Americans. But sometimes they conform to their national stereotype, and that doesn't mean they're armed.

While I stood at the entrance, an American couple came in, saw the show list and asked about the upcoming shows.

Yes, I said, the one starting in 30 minutes is very good, as is the one after that. So you can see two excellent shows in succession. But I'd avoid the third after those two, because the compère's rubbish.

Now, if you're British, you know exactly what that means. It means that I, who speak, am the compère of that show. As indeed I was.

One forgets that these things are not always understood. They thanked me profusely for warning them against that show. And left.

I was a lot more dodgy later. Our acts came from almost everywhere, and we had an international comedy show, where the theme was that each comedian would represent his/her country in a mock battle. Now obviously there were more people available to represent England than any other country, even Scotland, but because I was Big Chief of the Free Fringe, I was sometimes invited to perform as England's representative. And because the organiser and compère was German, I'd naturally do stuff about Germany and the Germans. I'd lived there; I spoke the language; it was a comedy mock battle. I could do that stuff. The audience was international. I did my stuff about the Germans, and then, prompted by something somebody else said, I remarked "Nigerians are the Germans of Africa".

The audience was shocked. And one said: isn't that racist? Indeed it is, I said. But I started being racist when I talked about "The Germans". You only objected when I talked about "The Nigerians".

I thought I had a point. All generalisations are racist and all racism is bad. And anything that's divisive is not good for society. But now I wonder: is comedy itself possible without being divisive? And is all divisiveness based on hate? I certainly didn't think so when I took on my German friend in this mock battle, which was his idea and not mine. But should we not avoid comedy based on divisiveness? And, if we do, how much comedy is left?

Not the sort of thing you want to start thinking in the middle of an Edinburgh Fringe run. You survive by sticking to the script and keeping your head in the sand. You're not Bernard Manning or Roy 'Chubby' Brown; you're a well-meaning person. But is that even close to enough?

It was easy to forget that the Fringe had transformed and I was the instigator of that transformation. We'd made it an affordable way of spending the summer, although we could do nothing about hotel prices. We'd brought the buzz back to the streets.

2012, however, was remarkable for lack of Americans; the couple I mentioned above were two of the very few that got through, and normally there are many. Including hobby-bagpipers, who presume they can march into any pub and immediately start piping. Well, one American. Let's not generalise. Euphoria at playing the instrument of his ancestors in the land of his ancestors. No matter whose show he drowned out.

But I digress.

2012, of course, was the year of the London Olympics, and it was said that almost every flight to the UK from the USA and Canada had been booked up by Olympic contestants, officials and spectators. It was noticeable. They say that the atmosphere in London was exceptional, and total strangers spoke to each other, which hasn't happened since the Blitz. Fortunately they've now stopped. I saw nothing of this; my duty lay 400 miles North.

But sport did touch us in a way I hadn't expected. Many comedians like football and some play it. Almost like normal people, really. One of our acts that year was such a person, and mooted the idea of raising a team and challenging somebody.

Sounded innocuous enough. But nothing's innocuous in this game.

To issue a challenge, you have to have somebody to challenge. Pretty obvious. But whom?

(I pause to remark that at the end of the sentence above I have written precisely 66,666 words. And by telling you that, I have broken the symmetry of that ultra-satanic number. As no doubt I shall again, by editing this. I like numbers.)

Anyway, we settled on a challenge to the non-free Fringe in general. The Free Fringe versus the paid shows. Bad challenge, because the challengees weren't banded together in an organisation. Nobody actually spoke for them as a collection of people. It was like challenging the left-handed, or people called George, or owners of large Chinese vases. Whom do you issue the challenge to, and how do they raise a team?

But a pitch was hired and a referee engaged, and I even looked at spending some of our scarce money on shirts and shorts, perhaps in a nice mid-blue like the Wee Blue Book, and maybe even screen-print the Free Fringe logo on. As long as I didn't have to play myself. And naturally, some of the women in the Free Fringe demanded the right to be selected. Which would have been fine by me. Actually, when I said 'some of the women' I meant 'one of the women'.

And then the press got hold of it. And what they printed was: there would be a grudge football match between The Free Fringe (they said PBH's Free Fringe, which was becoming the most common way to refer to us) and Laughing Horse.

No, no, no. That wasn't supposed to be happening and, much as The Scotsman might have liked it, it wasn't going to. Our issues with them were serious and still are. Not to be reduced to the level of sport.

As far as we were concerned, this was 1944, not 1914.

At that point I told The Scotsman that we weren't doing it and that they had misunderstood. I think the truth will have been more complicated and that more than one person thought the Laughing Horse match would be a good idea. Some sort of game took place eventually. I don't know whom it was against, or indeed if the team represented us in any way. I didn't attend.

Because normally at the Fringe one is too exhausted to do extracurricular stuff like that, except drinking. There's usually time and energy for that.

Calum, meanwhile, had not ceased to be a complicated story. If I were writing fiction, you'd dismiss him as an unbelievable character. In 2012 in the lead-up he had proposed Malone's as a venue. I looked. It wouldn't work for comedy, at least not during the Fringe. You'd need a very large audience every day, and if you didn't get one, they'd let drinkers and talkers in to a not-very-well-separated area, and/or the balcony above it.

I said no. Calum was annoyed with that. But I have to trust my own judgement. He put me under quite a lot of pressure to come round to his way of thinking, and that caused tension.

It's possible that, in his mind, he was running things and I was the figurehead.

In my mind, I was trying to maximise the benefit from his strengths and minimise the effect of his weaknesses.

I did agree that Malones would be suitable for a programme of music. Not merely suitable; ideal. Now, I'm not saying musicians don't mind if you talk all the way through their shows; of course they do. Who wouldn't? But music acts are used to that happening and don't require the total focus on their show that comedians, poets and theatre people do. Malones had a good stage and the right equipment, so we agreed to put on a full programme of music, 12 hours a day. And thus the Music section was born.

Now, this was a very rich mine of support. Edinburgh was full of bands and solo artists. Quite how many, I hadn't realised. My mind was on the sort of venue one needs for Comedy and Theatre and the other genres we worked in. We'd had a couple of music-genre shows in the past and they hadn't worked well.

Why not? Because our other genres could at least write blurbs and fliers that would bring people in, focussing on the unique aspects of the show. Make it sound interesting and different enough, and people will come. But only rarely can you do that with Music. The best singer-songwriter in the country, in the world, can only be a singer-songwriter on the printed page of the programme and unless you know his/her work, there's nothing to attract you to the proposition. Hadn't I myself started with a show of comic songs? And how difficult was that to sell? And in my second year I had worked in the Acoustic Music Centre and seen the difficulties experienced by most others. Unless people had a personal following, drummed up by massaging their contacts, audiences were low. The exception that year was a troupe of South American pan-pipers, who would do a lot of street shows and bring audiences in that way.

Music had to be handled differently from the other genres.

We had to book it by the gig, not by the run.

And that meant we couldn't list each individual music gig in the Wee Blue Book. Otherwise we'd have to go to twice the size, and we couldn't afford that. And anyway, we wouldn't know who was in what slot sufficiently in advance.

We needed somebody on the ground who would take care of the bookings and look after the venue, including the sound-mixing, on the ground.

Now, Calum wanted to be that person. In his mind, there's nothing he can't do and nothing he's too busy for. But that was wrong on many levels. He was not himself a musician. He could not therefore have a performer -to- performer relationship with the acts. And he's about my age. That's not a complete barrier, but the music scene changes and, if your taste was formed in the 1960s as mine was, it's difficult to keep up. Furthermore, he doesn't do detail, and detail is precisely what one needs on this.

But he doesn't give up. And when he saw, in the middle of the Fringe, that the Tron Kirk was open as a bar, he saw an opportunity there.

Now the Tron Kirk is a famous building and under all sorts of preservation orders. It hasn't been used as a church for some time, and as far as I know hadn't been used during the Fringe before. I might be wrong about this. I think it just stood there as a monument, its clock reminding generations of Fringe performers that it was time to stop giving out leaflets and start getting ready to perform. I'd never seen it open before, but maybe I hadn't looked.

Calum, of course, knew the people who had opened it. And wanted us to arrange the music in there. They'd already booked some entertainment, but Calum boasted to them that we could get better, and that they'd play for a bucket collection.

And of course we could do both those things. I just had to reassure the management that we could. The people we already had doing gigs in Malones jumped at the chance to do more gigs, in a venue that was heaving with audience. The very location of the Tron Kirk guaranteed that, where the Bridges met the Royal Mile.

So that was done, halfway through the Fringe, and we got some signage up in the venue, which boosted our visibility and gave us a central space in which to give out the Wee Blue Book.

It was a very popular space, for all that it was in no programme. And there were many of the Edinburgh establishment who objected to the use of this formerly sacred space for a profane purpose, like people having fun. John Knox would certainly not have approved. But we did.

I think we were popular among established comedians. Not because we did anything for them, but because we would have done if we'd have been around when they were starting out. They mostly had bad memories of losing large sums of money before they became famous. I've told you how Sean Lock came in to do the first benefit show (it had become an annual event by now, with many major names supporting it, like Stewart Lee and Richard Herring, Lucy Porter and many others). Phill Jupitus had been plugging us on his Radio 1 show, or was it Radio 2? I didn't actually listen myself, but I was told. He'd said that someday he would perform with us. He said that to the public, but never to me. So I just let it go.

I had had talks with the Jam House on Queen Street. Now, that was big. It held at least 300, and if you can regularly pull an audience of 300 at the Fringe, you had to be famous already. Or so I thought, then. Now, I know different. So I was pessimistic with the manager of that excellent venue (although Queen Street wasn't a well-trodden Fringe path). And then Phill finally got in contact after several years of telling everybody but me he was going to.

We met in the lobby of Broadcasting House and thence in an adjacent coffee shop.

And several times again, because his plans changed. A children's show at one stage, then an anonymous show in a small venue, then something else.

I didn't know where to put him, because I didn't know what show he'd end up wanting to do. But when the Jam House came along, I thought finally I had the one act with a big enough national reputation to fill it. And so that deal was done, and he was the only Free Fringe show in the Jam House in 2012. Despite that, they were pleased, and asked for more like that in 2013. Because that's easy for us, of course. Alright, slight sarcasm there, and completely unjustified, because it turned out we could do it after all.

Nevertheless, the already-famous were one of the few groups to whom the Free Fringe offered no advantage. If you can fill a large venue in your own right at full price, why should you not do so?

Now, I do not know what sort of deal you get offered by the pay-to-play venues if you're already famous. But if I were such a venue, I would not make famous performers pay anything at all for their venue space. Their very names bring in audience, and that audience stays for other shows. And the non-famous performers gain prestige from association with the famous, and that would motivate them to pay whatever I demanded on my schedule of hire charges. The famous would be the loss leaders, or judas goats. And, if my charges were structured in such a way that I took a percentage of box office, I needn't even make a loss on the shows of famous performers.

That would be the way I'd do it, anyway. How they do it, I don't know.

So, the famous who play the Free Fringe are relatively rare, and they're usually making a political point by doing so. Our scheme offers a major financial advantage to the non-famous, but not to everybody.

We weren't, of course, immune from prima donnas. At Chiquito, one theatre group decided they wanted a blackout during their show. Not just any blackout: the blackest blackout there could be. Total darkness. So they gaffa-taped several thicknesses of black bin bag over the emergency exit signs. The fire inspectors told them not to, but the next day they did it again. The fire people then closed all our shows in Chiquito down for 24 hours. Rightly, although it punished the innocent other shows in the venue. One does not take risks with safety, and if the fire brigade has requirements, one conforms without argument.

And another prima donna thing. There was a double booking at one of our Spoken Word venues, not our fault. The Banshee Labyrinth kindly offered to open up a room we didn't normally use (Bar 13, informally known as the Pole Room) to break the deadlock, and so we moved a couple of shows there.

And then I got a brief email:

Hi Peter

Just to let ya know, I have cancelled [name]'s show in bar 13, I had caught her and her friend taking a few bottles of beer from behind the bar and putting them into her bag, on closer inspection I then noticed that she had also helped her self to a bottle of wine. Ta for now

If the Banshee's team had not been so on-side with us, we could have lost the whole venue because of this theft. Clearly caught on CCTV. And who would be so selfish and stupid as to jeopardise her show by a trivial low-value theft, and not even think that venues have CCTV? Well, I know who. I'm not going to tell you. But another one for the 'never again' list.

The Free Fringe can only work if its members are honest.

And ideally not stupid. That performer failed on both fronts.

Of course I offered the Banshee full reimbursement from the Free Fringe's funds. I waved the cheque book at them. But they wouldn't accept it. Yes, we were bringing in a lot of custom, but still I'd have been happier if they'd accepted the reimbursement I offered.

Like 2011, 2012 ended on an Edinburgh Comedy Award (formerly Perrier) nomination for one of our shows: Sam Fletcher. Alas, he too didn't win, but it showed we were getting there. Or at least that Sam was. How much credit do we, the

Free Fringe, truly deserve when one of our shows gets nominated? Probably not a lot. The performer does all the work; all we do is select and find a venue. But despite the illogicality of it, the award nominations do reflect well on us, and people notice.

And anyway, Sam's show was excellent, as had been Cariad's the year before. And excellence ought to be its own reward. Come to the Fringe to get a major award, and you'll be disappointed unless you're very very lucky. Come the Fringe to do the best show you can, no matter what the outcome, and you have a good chance of enjoying it.

It's so easy to forget that. Because so many other things at the Fringe are telling you different. Every Fringe roadshow for new performers, that I've ever been to (and that's a lot of them) has answered, without being asked, the question "how do I get reviews?" And "how do I attract Industry Professionals?"

There's nobody more important than the public; the audience sitting in front of you. Every year the Fringe Office would send us a list of Accredited Industry Professionals. And that list would be several hundred people long. I think the idea was that they should all be given VIP access to anything. That's not our way. And for everybody on that list who belonged to a reputable newspaper, there were five with an unknown website or agency.

And you're meant to grovel to the people on that list. Screw that.

The Fringe Office had excelled itself in another way, that year. I've mentioned the 40 words you get in the Big Fat Fringe Programme for your nearly £400. By that time, they'd introduced web listings. And you got another 100 words on the web. Luxury.

So I wrote my 100 words describing my one-man show for 2012. I can't remember what I had called the show. Which may seem odd, but I shall explain. The 97th word of the web blurb I submitted was 'shite'.

When the proofs came back, they'd printed 'sh*te'.

Shite is, I think, the most commonly used word at the Fringe. Comedians use it as a sort of quasi-Masonic code word; if you say 'shit' instead, it means you haven't been to the Edinburgh Fringe.

I objected. Not only did I object, but I went through the 2011 printed Fringe Programme (the big fat one) and listed this:

p 40 pissed-up
p 43 pissing about
p 65 lesbians
p 74 fisting a nun
p 77 poofs
p 89 arseholes
p 102 I am a dick
p 105 drawing of a penis
p 119 sod it
p 121 bell-end and slag
p 122 scissor-kick life in the balls
p 126 professional dick-kicker
p 132 poof
p 140 christ
p 140 talking cock
p 153 spank
p 155 twat
p 163 knickers
p 165 picture of nearly naked woman

... and recalled that in 2004 I had called my show "Miscellaneous Shite", which was at the time a minor catchphrase of mine, and they had checked it then, and reported as follows:

We have checked previous programme information and the word Shite, spellt s-h-i-t-e has indeed been in the programme before, therefore your 'miscellaneous shite' will go into the programme in full. There is one thing though, you will not be able to get that in italics.

I never understood why *shite* could not be in italics, but let it be. In 2012 they stuck to their guns. Odd guns to stick to, but still.

They said they had to maintain a U-certificate standard in their web programme. That being the World Wide Web, on which you can find every filthiness and perversion you can imagine and thousands more that you can't. Who was being shielded here? For if any were offended, they had better not open their ears on the streets of Edinburgh, during the Fringe or at any other time.

Or did they think that the asterisk instead of the letter i so obscured the word that nobody could guess what it was supposed to say?

I argued; I took it to the CEO; I raised it at a Board meeting (but too late for it to be changed). They were adamant before the deadline, but at the Board meeting they said they might have been applying policy too rigidly. But only one show had asked for its money back.

I knew that. It was me. There they were, boasting of being the biggest open-access arts festival in the world, and yet being so mealy-mouthed that they leapt on chairs, gathering their voluminous skirts around them, shouting 'eek, a mouse' at the word 'shite', not even in a show title or a printed blurb, but on the World Wide Web. Describing a show in an 18+ venue.

Yes, indeed I asked for, and got, my money back. And changed the title of my show to "This show isn't sh*te, it's shite".

And it went in the Wee Blue Book and on my fliers that way. And nobody fainted.

*

2013

In which our author perpetrateth another false start

IN REAL LIFE, NINE MONTHS HAVE ELAPSED since I last picked up my pen.

I'm not using a pen. I'm typing this on a laptop. It's a symbolic pen. But by the time this comes out, if it ever does, will anybody know what a laptop is? I'm reading a mid-Victorian novel at the moment, not a famous one, and they talk of how stagecoaches were before the coming of the railways. And I can't understand the terminology. Did they really put straw on the floor of the coaches, or is that a metaphor? And what was Tenerife? From the context, a wine of some sort? I don't know. Sillery, which is mentioned a lot, is a form of Champagne, as I find on lookup. It's over 150 years since that book; things change.

And in the last nine months, things have changed for me. This is probably breaking the fourth wall, but not having been to Theatre School I've never quite known what that means. I have always pretended to know. So, I'm not only ignorant of the social conventions of 150 years ago; I'm ignorant of my own business now.

Why such a long layoff? Dear reader, I shall explain. And then, I hope, get on with the story.

I knew I was going to have to stop writing until September. The sheer pressure of getting the Free Fringe rolling means it becomes a full-time job from April onwards. And when I say full-time, I mean all-consuming. If you're not doing something about something, you're at least worrying about it. Or talking to people, or emailing them, or sticking plaster over wounds, or filling holes that people create by dropping out, for good reasons or bad.

And 2016 was going to be the year in which I started the handover. Get the next generation to do the work; form a proper Committee, get as many performers involved as possible so that the work is shared. So 2016 was going to be my last year as CEO and there'd be a new team for 2017. I'd probably remain as Chairperson, though, and carve myself out a role as the old buffer who used to be someone but now annoys the management team by making bad suggestions and telling long boring stories of how things used to be. I thought I'd probably enjoy that role, although others wouldn't.

But this is the Free Fringe. Things never work out as they should. Oh, the plan was there. A meeting with the Edinburgh team on Wednesday 14th September; a meeting with the London team on Sunday 18th, both to get the new structure rolling. The Edinburgh meeting happened and was fine. I took the last train back on Thursday 15th.

By the morning of Saturday 17th I was in hospital, blue-lighted in an ambulance, which is less exciting than it sounds. Hospital wasn't the only thing I was in. Pain is what I was mostly in. Lots of it. One day I was healthy, if not actually fit; the next day I was screaming, helpless and unable to do anything for myself.

And on Sunday 18th I was getting messages: why wasn't I at my own meeting? Why is nothing happening? We are not impressed by this, said the message-senders. And I don't suppose I would have been, if I had been them.

What this turned out to be was severe acute pancreatitis. The word probably deserves a capital letter, but I'm not going to give it one. I spent about half the remainder of 2016 in hospital and much of the rest not being able to walk more than 20 paces or stand up for more than two minutes. I live by myself, so that made doing most things difficult.

And of course that also meant I couldn't manage the Free Fringe the way I used to, and nor could I oversee the plan for the next generation to take over. The next generation had to do it by themselves, and fast.

Fortunately the core team was in place. The Artistic Directors for each section, and the venue finding and liaison team, were already in office. They could do it, if they took greater autonomy. And they did, or they have so far.

So perhaps you understand why I haven't carried on writing this tome (is it a tome? I want it to be a tome. It's a good word) as I should have.

Up to this chapter, I wrote a lot in the pub. I like writing in the pub; I've written many one-man shows, songs, bits of general standup and over half a doctoral thesis in the pub. I like being surrounded by the noise of others, and the second pint stops me thinking "no, no, I don't dare to write that down". It works for me.

I should have said "it worked for me". For with pancreatitis I can never drink again. Drink is, or rather was, a large part of the fun of the Edinburgh Fringe. I'm sounding like a hopeless drunk. I wasn't. I drank moderately, although perhaps less moderately in August.

I have to find a way of writing without the pint at my right hand. At least there's less danger of keyboard damage due to spillage. I don't know if that's a significant point or not.

So today, 14th January 2017, I take up the writing again, under these new conditions. And having brushed a little with Death. I have no wish to brush again, but it seems there must be at least one other occasion in the future.

And I have to have at least two more operations. I didn't have to tell you that. But somehow I wanted to.

And having explained that, I revert to the Free Fringe's tale in sequence. I have now made it sound like Chaucer. I await April's sweet showers, by virtue of which the flower is procreated. Maybe I'll have time to notice, this year.

*

2013 (again)

In which we embrace popups and win gongs

I MAY HAVE SAID THIS BEFORE. Competition is bad. Oh, not always. Between small for-profit businesses, competition can help drive up quality and/or keep prices to a reasonable level.

This is a situation that doesn't apply to us.

I did put some thought into the Free Fringe model before going live with it. I didn't predict everything, but it wasn't a shot in the dark either.

The Free Fringe was supposed to be a collective of performers, taking collective and collaborative action against the worst aspects of the Edinburgh Fringe. These included the high cost of venues, the power of promoters over performers, the over-importance of reviews and thus the culture of grovelling to press and media.

If we (performers) stood together against these things, we would improve conditions for all performers.

And when Laughing Horse set up in opposition to us, it forced us to divert energy into competing with them. Had we not had to do this, then the energy could have been fully concentrated on our primary purpose — making things better for performers. And, of course, for the public via our zero-charge system; the two are inextricably linked.

Laughing Horse had striven to be bigger than us. Obviously they couldn't outdo us in quality of shows. Well, it's obvious to me, anyway. Maybe it isn't to you? Let me explain, then.

Laughing Horse run a nationwide New Act competition, with heats all over the UK and a final in London. And most comedians, at the beginning of their careers, enter competitions. Even though the number disappointed far exceeds the number satisfied with the outcome.

I myself have never been happy with the concept of comedy as a competition. It tends to increase animosity among performers. But more importantly it suggests that there is only one style of comedy a performer should adopt if he/she wishes to succeed. Anything seriously off the wall is less likely to appeal to audiences, hence judges. But that's just what I think; I also think that anybody who wants to enter competitions is welcome to do so.

So, a lot of comedians pass through Laughing Horse's hands on their way to full professionalism. And many get their first paid gigs in their weekly clubs, although there are fewer of these now than formerly.

This should be a big advantage for Laughing Horse when competing with the Free Fringe, but oddly it's not.

I can only speculate why. The Free Fringe gets considerable loyalty from its members. I don't understand why their competition participants, or at least the finalists, don't show Laughing Horse the same sort of loyalty. A few do, of course.

I wish they'd stuck to their competition and their year-round comedy clubs, to which one cannot object in the slightest.

But, if independent performers wish to alter the conditions of the Fringe to avoid the massive losses they would otherwise make, then it is better that independent performers should speak with a united voice.

I learned over the years that that voice cannot be mine. I think I have the right ideas. But not the right personality to make them credible.

Nevertheless, I am sick of being dismissed. There's a general feeling that, if I can do something, then anybody can. And if I can negotiate a series of free-admission venues, then anybody can. It's seldom realised that there are many more aspects to the Free Fringe than that, and that the whole scheme depends on each element being correct.

Why am I saying this again now? Because the 2013 season sowed the seeds of further fragmentation, although they only sprouted a year later.

We had blossomed in many areas. Our one show at the Jam House had turned into several. I had feared not being able to fill a 300-seater, especially on Queen Street, which has little walkpast trade.

But both the Cambridge Footlights and the Oxford Revue have a long and distinguished history at the Fringe. Pedants will point out that the most famous such show, Beyond the Fringe, with Alan Bennett, Peter Cook, Jonathan Miller and Dudley Moore, was not actually a Fringe show but belonged to the Arts Festival. True. But the sketch shows of both universities have for many years been Fringe features, and one of the few shows who always get full houses and thus presumably operate at a profit. Now, we didn't host the main sketch shows of either university. If they can make a profit elsewhere, they have no motivation coming to us. Their casts, however, and other students from the same universities, wanted to do standup comedy also. And both applied to us for these shows. We put them in the Jam House and a substantial audience followed them, in the way people do not follow the many other universities who perform with us. Including my own undergraduate home, UCL.

And it was in those circumstances I had one of my best ideas. It never happened. But it's still available if they want to take it up. And it is this:

The Oxford-Cambridge Joke Race.

I don't normally approve of competition in comedy. There's more than one way to be funny. And, some day, I hope to find one of these ways for myself. However, if you're a member of one of two élite universities who compete in every other field, you might as well compete in comedy. And there are many boat-race parallels one can bring in to make the show interesting. Winners for every performance and an overall tally of which university has won at the end. Voting by audience showcard. A referee in a silly cap. Or do I mean umpire? Umpire sounds posher. Why?

That would have been an audience-puller. Oxford, that year, were all for it. Cambridge weren't. I have punted it every year since, and one or other of the two has declined. A plague on both your houses. At UCL, we have our founder's mummified body on display in a box in the Cloisters. You haven't.

Anyway, they did well at the Jam House, but not as well as the magicians. We'd had a few Magic shows before, but this was the year they took off. I described the Jam House as a 300-seater, but capacities are variable and they could seat more if there was demand. And Young & Strange, a top magic act, were turning audience away, even at that capacity.

Unprecedented, at the Fringe. By carefully choosing what act might go in what space, we'd picked a lot of winners. Of course, we didn't always get it right.

Applications greatly exceeded the number of stages we had for them. And that in turn increased the pressure on us, or specifically me. More and more shows were chasing information on what had happened to their applications. Sometimes they even chased politely, but too often they were not so polite. They were behaving like customers, but they weren't customers.

It was a year of venue problems, once again.

We had acquired the use of a wonderful four-stage venue, as central as one could possibly wish for. It was being refurbished under its new owners, who also owned some of our other venues, and would be ready in time. (How often have I heard that, and sweated right up to the start date for shows?) It had previously been owned by somebody else and booked by another organisation.

All well and good. We booked shows into these four excellent stages. And I went away and worried about the many other things I had to worry about.

Until one of my confirmed acts contacted me. I have a friend, he said. And that friend has been offered exactly the same space as I have accepted from you, at a similar time.

How could this be?

He was offered by the organisation that had booked it in the previous year.

It turned out that this organisation had made, or was in the process of making, offers for all these same spaces; had confirmed the shows and had received money from the shows to seal their contract. The other organisation had called the venue by a different name, and used different names for the individual rooms, so the Fringe Office hadn't picked up the clash.

I screamed, for neither the first nor the last time.

The other organisation discovered the situation at the same time as I, and made noises to reassure its acts. But they were in trouble. They had had an agreement with the previous owners; we had an agreement with the current owners. I suppose the previous owners had not told them that they'd sold it.

But both of us had booked full programmes. One of us was in very serious trouble. And they and we were equally determined it wasn't going to be us.

Both of us sought meetings with the current owners. They got in first.

They offered money, knowing that we could not and would not. Up to £30,000 was suggested, or so I heard.

And, of course, this was performers' money. A direct conflict between pay-to-play and the Free Fringe ideal.

It was a hard meeting for me and Calum. How could we counter the offer of cold, hard cash? The owners were in business; business exists to make money.

We couldn't make a counter-offer. We had no money. I had some personal money, but was I going to throw it in the ring? No. I'd never see it back, and I'd spent enough of my own money on the Free Fringe.

And, of course, if we paid one venue, even in this emergency situation, other venues would hear of it and also expect to be paid.

We had no cards and yet we could not bluff. All we could say was: we shook hands on the original deal. And your bar takings will be greater with us than with them.

They asked: can you give us a guarantee on the bar takings? No, we couldn't. Same reason as before. Calum wanted to give them such a guarantee. I said no.

It looked grim, but the new owners were, and are, good people. They decided to stick with us and honour the agreement. This did not go down well with the other organisation, who allegedly increased their offer. They were panicking. I would have been panicking had the decision gone the other way.

But the difference in our situations is clear. Our obligation to our performers, who pay nothing, is a moral obligation. But the other organisation's performers pay for their space. That means that their obligation is contractual. They can be sued.

When, to my immense relief, the decision finally went our way, I rejoiced that we were dealing with men of their word. And I still do. But there was another factor I didn't consider.

I said the renovation was not complete. And it wasn't. Shortly before the Fringe I was informed that the biggest of the four rooms would not after all be ready. There were good reasons. But the reasons wouldn't be important to the performers.

The owners' solution was simple and elegant. The shows in the biggest room were to move to the next-biggest: number two to number three, number three to number four and the shows originally for number four were to happen in the bar.

Obviously we don't like shows happening in the bar. There was a vacant shop unit nearby; could we perhaps use that for number four? They enquired, but no. The shows in the bar had to contend with drinkers, and so were in a much more difficult position than they had expected. Shows in the other three rooms, however, were perfectly happy with the arrangement.

And maybe that was a factor in the owners' decision. It's contracts again. They might have known there was a chance the big room wouldn't be ready. If so, there was no contract between us, just goodwill. But if they'd have taken the other side's money, there would have been a contract. And the owners could have been sued for damages consequent on non-performance.

With us, at least they knew they'd be safe from that threat. We were glad enough, and the shows went ahead and did well, except those in the bar. But the year after, with all works completed, money prevailed and we lost the four rooms, at least for the time being.

I have to thank two people I never met for creating an important piece of Free Fringe lore and terminology.

I'd always called our programme the Free Fringe Programme. Which, of course, got confused with a lot of other things that are programmes, and a lot of other things that are free. The blue cover came from the first design in 2008, by Caroline Mabey; that was the first year it was actually a stapled brochure. The designers of later years' covers kept the blue theme.

Isla, in 2013, overheard two Edinburgh-based fringegoers talking in the street, and one asked the other "have you got your wee blue book?" And she told me about this later, and everybody around the table said: yes. Of course. That's what it's called. That's what it is. That's always been its name, but we never realized.

And from that day onwards it has been the Wee Blue Book, or WBB.

And before then the "official" Edinburgh Fringe Programme, the one that costs nearly £400 to be in, had become in our Free Fringe jargon the BFFP, short for Big Fat Fringe Programme.

Are there any other specific Free Fringe terms? Bucket Speech, perhaps, meaning the bit at the end of your show when you encourage the public to put money in the bucket. And VBS, Variable Bill Show: the sort of show that has different guests every night, such as Peter Buckley Hill and Some Comedians.

The Royal Navy has an official dictionary of official slang. I don't think the Free Fringe has got that far yet.

Meanwhile in the wider political world, Edinburgh City Council were selling off assets. Squeezed by government, like most other UK cities, they needed cash.

And one of the things they sold was the storage space below the Central Library. Like many Edinburgh buildings, it went down three stories deep. The library's entrance is on George IV Bridge; the storage goes all the way down to Cowgate, where there's an unmarked door. When I first saw it, it was full of dusty, discarded but massively interesting books, and for some reason antique printing machinery. I think a lot of this material was dumped; a pity, but not my business and nothing I could help.

They sold the storage space off. And it was bought by Riccardo (Ricky) Marino. We had done business with his son Matteo. Ricky Marino rented the space during the Fringe to Charlie Bruce (another pseudonym, but an important man in our story), who then asked me if I could put shows on. Calum had a hand in brokering this deal.

But by that time it was June. We had lots of applicants still technically on our books, but we knew that most of these applications wouldn't be active any more: they would either have found venues with other promoters or decided not to come. Officially, they should have emailed us withdrawing their applications, but people tend not to do this.

Could we fill five stages from noon to midnight on three floors in a month and a half? And could we get PA and chairs to make this happen?

It was a tall order. When we were asked, we were shown no floor plans of the interior. We knew that Charlie's workpeople would partition and convert, but we didn't know into what shapes and sizes. All we could do (for we had no access until the lease was signed) was specify approximately what we would be happy with, and hope we got something close to that. And then we had to book shows in, and they would ask what the spaces were like, and we couldn't tell them.

That was the spirit of the Free Fringe taken to extremes. I told Charlie I'd do my best, but at that notice he couldn't expect a full programme with no gaps. And I and the team set to work. And we got a programme together with about 80% occupancy, which was not bad. Chairs came from everywhere we could scrounge them from; PA we bought.

The beauty about spaces like this is that we could programme regardless of genre. Normally a venue is dedicated to Comedy, or Theatre, or Cabaret, or Spoken Word, and the genre suits the venue. But in a big multistage popup like this, you can programme without restraint, mixing all the genres in together. It gives us flexibility we don't normally have.

But the difficulty is management. We were used to working with venues who had a single stage or two, not five. And with no permanent bar staff on hand. We had to adjust, and we had to do it at short notice.

Now, we have a system. Quite a few systems, actually. The Free Fringe looks simple from the outside, but we have to get every detail right. The public don't see those details, on the whole. All the work is done by performers, and we have to trust those performers to do that work. When they don't, the house of cards collapses.

I'm mentioning this in the context of the Cowgatehead venue (for so the storage space under the Library came to be called) because it presented us with several problems. We couldn't plan well, because we couldn't see the space as it was being worked on. But we trusted the workers. More importantly, we needed to know we could trust our own performers.

For a few years now, I had instituted a system of Venue Captains. One performer in each venue would agree to be Captain, and he/she would liaise with management, sorting out any problems that arose in the course of the Fringe. If a performer, in the stress of the Fringe, said something he/she should not have said to the venue's staff, it was the Venue Captain's job to re-establish good relations. If there was a problem with managing the queue, it was the Venue Captain's job to work out the best solution and to implement it, collaborating with the rest of the performers.

So, we would seek as Venue Captains people who had done the Free Fringe before and who knew how we worked. People of some maturity, despite a Fringe where few people act maturely, including me. People who were able to negotiate with venues, if needed.

But what happens when you try to fill five stages in June? The regular Free Fringers on whom we relied to be Venue Captains all had their slots at other venues. We would have to get

Captains from among whoever applied at this late stage, and this would mean they had no experience of the job.

New venue, new situation, new captain, temporary infrastructure; what could go wrong?

Lots did, but we patched it, and even used the spare slots to provide some extra performances for shows that needed them.

The major problem, when it came, came from a completely unexpected direction. When does it not?

It came in the Tron Kirk. Again, under Charlie's management, with others involved. He had asked us for music, on the same pattern as 2012, and we were happy to oblige with that. We knew how to make that work, and it did.

But Charlie asked for one more thing. He wanted a free burlesque show, at around 10pm. All part of the deal.

Could we do that? Well, of course. There is nothing, I arrogantly thought, that we couldn't do. Anyway, burlesque had given me one of my best true-story gags.

The previous year, I had had to mediate a dispute between two shows, one following the other in the same venue. Both run (this is relevant) by women. The first a variable-bill variety show. The second a show of politically feminist standup. The first show usually had some burlesque performers as part of the entertainment. The second show's audience complained at the sight of burlesque performers at the changeover. Burlesque, they said, demeaned women and made them objects. No, said the first show: burlesque done voluntarily by women is empowering and liberating. There was a standoff.

I suggested that the owners of the shows concerned settled it by three rounds of bikini mud-wrestling.

Well, you either find that funny or you don't.

The point was, I suppose, that because of that incident I was aware we had contacts with burlesque performers, so I knew we could somehow fulfil the requirement for a burlesque show at the Tron Kirk. And we could, and we did.

Now, burlesque requires a space for the performers to change. These are not consumes in which you would wish to walk on the Royal Mile at midnight. Such a space was erected, by partition, and as is the nature of these things used for several other purposes as well, mostly storage of drink and glasses. And people in the know would leave stuff in there, to be collected later.

Stuff is always a problem. I wish people didn't have stuff. The particular piece of stuff that exploded on this occasion was a long stick resembling a shepherd's crook. It has a role when you're in full Highland Dress, which I never am. But Calum is, frequently. He delights in wearing the full kit and being conspicuously Scottish for the visitors to Edinburgh, sometimes loudly. That's just him.

The shepherd's crook, however, had been left in the changing alcove for safe keeping. And one night, he went in to get it, without knocking. Just as the burlesque performers were changing.

I wasn't there. I don't know exactly what happened. I can only piece it together from what I was subsequently told. And, as you shall hear, I was subsequently told a lot.

I mean, who has not barged through the wrong door on one occasion or another? I myself find it hard to tell one picture from another, so you will frequently find me studying toilet doors while I work our whether the symbol is meant to mean Ladies or Gents. And even standing there working it out can itself look creepy, if the symbol turns out to mean Ladies. I wish they'd use words instead. But, even in the worst case scenario, you go through the wrong door, embarrassment ensues, profuse apologies are issued and things are smoothed over.

But not in this case. The performers were livid, and so was Calum. He said that the dressing room had been built at his suggestion and furthermore it was his (very valuable) Highland stick, and he could not do his thing without it. To the performers, it was sexual harassment, pure and simple. (And they pronounced it har-ASS-ment, as is the modern way, not HAR-assment, as I consider correct. Actually, that's a tribute to the power of comedy; the word was pronounced correctly in the UK before Michael Crawford's character in Some Mothers Do 'Av 'Em pronounced it with stress on the middle syllable, to indicate that his character was uneducated and odd. The sit-com and its lead character were massively popular; the pronunciation caught on.)

I have digressed again.

The great Dressing Room Incident exploded until the blast could be heard in Hiroshima. The performers refused to go on until satisfaction had been received. Calum was, by the licensee not by me, forbidden the premises after 6pm and banned, under what powers I know not, from being outside.

The performers came to me the next day and demanded I should hold a formal enquiry into the incident. I listened at great and deafening length, but eventually had to say that I had no powers to do any such thing. Calum was not an employee of the Free Fringe. Nobody is. If you don't get paid, then you're a volunteer. Employment Law does not apply. Everything is done by goodwill and negotiation.

I had neither the powers nor the resources to hold any such inquest. I had to tell them that, if they considered themselves to have been assaulted, their proper recourse is to the police; they have the investigatory powers and resources that I do not.

And at the same time (not literally, obviously, but I met both parties that day and cannot now remember which meeting came first) Calum maintained his innocence, the goodness of his intentions and his right to fetch his property whenever it pleased him. There was no question of an apology on his part, sincere or otherwise.

I cringe whenever things like this happen. I try not to show the cringes to the outside world. But these incidents do shorten my life. There was the time when a performer (not one of ours, somebody doing a guest spot in one of our shows) assaulted a member of the audience. I may have described that incident above. That was stressful, and many other things have been over the years.

But there is a good reason why I'm going on about this, and it will emerge in the course of this narrative. Did I just write 'in the course of this narrative'? Humph. That's a terrible phrase.

Calum had form on things like this. No, not alleged sexual harassment necessarily; just barging in to things. Usually with the best of intentions. He won't change. I'd spare his feelings, but that would mean not publishing this book at all. Many things about him aren't believable, but they're all true.

Calum had been banned or warned, over the course of time, by many of our venues. Like me, he hates to see things done not as well as they should be. But often that perception is incorrect. He was banned by the Voodoo Rooms when he went to see one of our shows. I've described this already, in the 2010 chapter. For some reason, the Free Fringe backdrop was not up. It should have been. But instead of noting that fact, he allegedly barged into the dressing area, five minutes before the show, and insisted that the performer find the backdrop and put it up. The performer refused, as I find understandable shortly before she went on; that is not the time to bring problems to people. And that is why Laughing Horse chose precisely that time, five minutes before my show, to inform me they were taking over, in 2006. No, one does not bring problems to performers five minutes before show-start.

Anyway, Calum did, and things escalated, and he was ejected from the premises (he is a very large and loud man, and difficult to eject if he doesn't want to go) and I was telephoned and told to keep him away. And again, where are my powers to do so? I can only try.

What can you do about somebody who goes everywhere telling people how to do their own jobs? They resent it. Of course they do.

And then there was the Moon Walk. An all-women event, at night, raising funds for breast cancer research, if I remember rightly. And this happened to be on while I was in Edinburgh, walking back with Calum from seeing a possible venue he had suggested investigating. We were on the Royal Mile. He dashes into the race (no, it's not a race, it's people running, but what's a good word for that?) and yells loud encouragement almost in the ears of a group of participants. When he got back to the pavement, I suggested him that one simply does not do that, especially at an all-women event. He replied that, on the contrary, he could and ought to do it, because he was a basketball coach.

You could not invent this man. I last saw him at the scene of a minor street fight, after the police had arrived, telling the police what to do and how to deal with the incident.

And it may well be that we lost our cover designer for the Wee Blue Book because Calum objected to the design featuring ice cream. I remain baffled by that one.

He has told performers how to perform. He has told venues how to keep their bars. But he has found venues we would never have found, and he has supported the Free Fringe very loyally.

Performers have said to me, many times: who is this man, and why does he interfere with our shows? And others have gone further, and said to me: why don't you just tell him to fuck off?

My answer has always been: off is a direction in which he does not fuck.

And he has done a lot for us, and means well. No, that's too weak. We would not have survived into 2007 without him. He was, and I think still is, absolutely dedicated to what we're trying to achieve. We owe him.

But the Great Dressing Room Explosion became a turning point. He felt he had been unjustly handled by me. I should have defended him more, he thought. I should have contested his ban from the Tron Kirk, in the light of all he had done for us.

The pressure from the burlesque performers was equal and opposite. Why did I not sack him? I did make the point that he wasn't actually employed, but such was the strength of feeling that nothing I could have said would have eased their anger.

But when he brought out the argument "they're going to be nearly naked on stage in a few minutes, so what's the difference?" I despaired. If he did not realise there's a very big difference, I don't think anybody could have convinced him.

He felt betrayed. Or such is my analysis of the situation.

And the time bomb started to tick.

Why do people say that? There may have been an era in which time bombs ticked, when run by clockwork. Not any more. There are silent electronic timers one can link to detonators, if one is a time-bomber. Which I hope one is not. But such have been the atrocities perpetrated by bombers in our time that I remain surprised that nobody's tried it at the Fringe. When the Edinburgh Military Tattoo is on, the security services close and search neighbouring businesses in case of lone bombers. But not the Fringe.

I have just depressed myself with those thoughts.

2013 was once again a successful year, performance-wise. To about 90%, and that's about as good as it can get, although that shouldn't stop us aiming for 100%. We lost a number of venues for various reasons, and that's always a pity, but Cowgatehead made up for a lot of that. And it was right at the heart of the Old Town, which meant we didn't have to listen to shows complaining that the New Town isn't really Edinburgh. Something that still grates with me. Compared to when I started, we've made it much easier for performers.

Oh, and we had our third successive Perrier (Edinburgh Comedy Awards) nominee, after Cariad Lloyd in 2011 and Sam Fletcher in 2012. John Kearns was nominated. And this time our guy won. Was this the Rule of Three working for us? Well, I was overjoyed either way.

John gave a great acceptance speech, critical of the corporatism of the Fringe. Normally, acceptance speeches are videoed and put up on the Web. Mine was, although I don't know if it's still there. John's was videoed. But it wasn't put up on the Web.

At the time I was as happy as if I'd won it myself. I went to the press room where the winners get photographed and interviewed. And just before I left, I shouted — no, I didn't, I said loudly and chose my timing — "Anybody want a statement

from the Free Fringe before I go?". As if I had a statement prepared, although I didn't.

Oh, the success was John's, not ours, as I said about our previous nominees. But I felt justified. We had helped; we had facilitated. And it showed the world we had a standard as good
as anybody else's.

There's probably a lot more success I should mention.
That's the Fringe way. Plug, exaggerate and big up everything
you do. But I've never been happy with that approach, and
anyway by 2013 I was getting really worn down. Other people
were having good times, but I was troubleshooting all the
time.

I hadn't seen the last of 2013's troubleshooting, had I but
known it.

I had programmed a little hubris. The last few days of the
Fringe were usually parties of various sorts. But there was
nothing on the Sunday. So I booked the Jam House for an
event. It was provisionally called "The Free Fringe invites the
World" and was a party for all Fringe performers, even those
from other free-admission organisations we normally keep
aloof from. Our quarrel was with the organisations, not the
performers. I thought this would be a suitable peace-laden end
to a Fringe at which performers gave their all.

The idea stemmed from history: the culminating event of
the Fringe used to be the Perrier Party, held on the final Saturday, crammed with comedians and (largely) so-called industry
insiders, and with the winner announced at midnight, sometimes broadcast live on Channel 4. And that had often happened at the Jam House. So now we had the Jam House, I
thought it would be a good place for a party. Even more: I
pitched to the Edinburgh Comedy Award organisation that
they could bring the party back to the Jam House. They said no
to that. Pity.

As it turned out, people were too tired and it wasn't too well
attended, but the bands were good. We tried it in 2014 also,
and then abandoned the idea. Maybe the other organisations
thought the olives on the olive branch were poisoned. Oh well.

2014

In which we have much ado with insurgency

JUST BECAUSE YOU SAY SOMETHING isn't something, doesn't mean it's not that thing.

That's quite an obscure and enigmatic sentence.

Most racist utterances start with the phrase "I'm not a racist, but ...".

On the other hand, Magritte's picture of a pipe is not a pipe. As he clearly stated. There are many things which are not pipes; far more than the number of things that are pipes. I am looking at two pipes now. I don't smoke; I bought them for a gag that didn't work, and now I have two things that are pipes and a large number of things that aren't.

Where is this leading? Patience, O reader, and I shall tell all.

For a few years now, nobody had tried to stop or hijack the Free Fringe. I suppose we were overdue for another attempt. Periodically, the sun must eclipse, otherwise the gods are not appeased and a giant snake swallows the Earth. Or something.

So I shouldn't have been too surprised to receive something that said it wasn't an ultimatum. Just like Magritte's pipe. It looked like one. But it couldn't have been an ultimatum, because it said it wasn't.

I'd better reproduce it in full. I've spent my life writing things with word limits, so quoting things in full is a good way to exceed those limits. But here it is. The names are all pseudonyms.

> *Written by; Sebastian Fisher, Lennox Cunningham, Dieter Holzmann, Henry Baxter, Oliver Kelly.*
>
> *Dear Peter*
>
> *The Free Fringe is a wonderful organisation which has created enormous opportunities for performers and audiences alike. Its impact on the Edinburgh festival has been positive and beneficial and is great testament to your vision and tireless hard work. You have consistently held the organisation together through many storms and we have all learned so much*

from you. The FREE FRINGE has expanded far beyond what any of us could have imagined.

Having all been such a big and productive part of the fringe over many years we wanted to express our increasing concern about the workload that an expanding free fringe is placing on your shoulders. Many times you have expressed the desire to step aside and allow the team to take over more responsibility leaving you more time to perform and enjoy the fringe. Plus, it is no longer feasible to continue without a contingency plan in place should you for any reason be unable to take your customary leading role in the Fringe. Crucially, so much knowledge and information resides with you alone that a failure to disseminate this more widely and plan for your potential absence would in all likelihood lead to the whole organisation fragmenting.

FREE FRINGE Comedy and the arts in Edinburgh is a big part of a very big and serious business. We feel it is increasingly important that structure of the FREE FRINGE reflects performers' needs and continues to deliver a product which maintains industry respect through these tough and changing times.

With that in mind we would like to propose a few changes for you to consider that would facilitate this:

1. Committee definition. In order for you to step back a little and remove some of the burden you have carried for so long we respectfully suggest establishing a clearly defined committee structure with you as Chairman. That will allow others to take more responsibility and be accountable for the progress of the FREE FRINGE into the future. Each committee member would be assigned a clearly defined role and allowed to make the decisions necessary to successfully achieve their goals. In other words, the committee can make policy changes and you would have the swing vote in the case of a hung decision. Micro managing every aspect of the process is often counter-productive, time intensive and stressful for all parties.

2. Quality Control. As the Free Fringe currently stands, and as you have often said too few people are doing the bulk of the work whilst many stand idly by and watch. We worry that the focus on expanding the FREE FRINGE will compromise the quality of its output, the festival experience for the performer and the overall satisfaction of the venue managers. We fear ultimately this will lead to a drop in the creative and artistic expectations of audiences and critics alike. We would like to see a reduction in the number of venues and performances with firm emphasis on maintaining excellence. This would be facilitated by the establishment, where possible, of hub venues with multiple performance areas. This strategy would enable us to bring performers closer together, literally and figuratively, and maximise foot traffic. At the same time, with more shows in one venue we would be better able to monitor the quality and progress of shows through the festival and year on year, and ensure that the best/most popular shows and performers get the venues their efforts merit.

Quality and a real eye for detail should be our priority, not an arms race with competitors simply to generate statistics. Like you we think the FREE FRINGE should give both performer and visitor an experience that is way above any of our competitors regardless of the numbers of shows we have versus our rivals.

3. Accounting & Transparency. It would make things simpler for you if there was absolute transparency of FREE FRINGE accounts. This would also help your Committee to get used to managing the finances of the organisation ready for the day you eventually decide to step back.

Transparency is key in any operation, especially in an operation this big, where so much money and so many people are being 'moved around.' The FREE FRINGE needs transparency both in terms of finances and the organisational structure which also includes quality control, deadlines and the process of venue assignment.

4. Performers' Pack. We would like to provide extra support for acts with a performers pack to take them step by step through the whole festival process. We will produce an information pack for both performers and venue managers. We would also like a performer's pass which gives them discount in

the FREE FRINGE venues thus encouraging them to buy-in to the organisations which support us.

5. Subscriptions. We still want to keep open the discussion surrounding subscriptions. Whilst we have the greatest respect for the principles under which the FREE FRINGE was founded, performer's attitudes and circumstances and even the business itself have changed immeasurably since it began. We strongly suggest an upfront subscription of £100 per show (for a full run) to help cover design and print costs for the programme, performer support and full venue rigging by paid help. This way there will be a vast decline in last minute drop-outs, less financial stress, less performer stress, more harmony within the ranks (there is always resentment generated due to the many individuals who simply avoid helping).

6. Advertising. We want acts / shows to be able to advertise in the brochure. This we feel fits perfectly with your founding ideologies as the performers who are more successful will, via advertising fees, be supporting the newer, less successful acts whose bucket will be lower.

This is a good way for the acts that are most successful to support the newer generation of performers and therefore sponsor and grow the FREE FRINGE quality and loyalty from within. It truly makes no sense for the more successful acts to be forbidden from spending their advertising pounds with us.

It would also be expedient to employ an experienced advertising sales person who would work on a commission only basis to sell the rest of the space in the brochure.

7. Communications. We would like to see a single communications officer appointed who sends out all correspondence to both committee and performers alike in order to remove some of the immediate emotion that we have experienced with previous correspondence when you (often justifiably) feel when a performer has let you down or betrayed you. Similarly we feel that centralising communication with and promotion through the media in one office would benefit the FREE FRINGE greatly.

We represent a number of your hardest working, most loyal and most experienced members of the collective. We have al-

*ways been completely loyal to you. We want the best for the
FREE FRINGE and the best for you and this wonderful organisation that you have sweated blood to bring this far. We do not
want to contemplate a future without the FREE FRINGE but the
current structure and rules must adapt to ensure its survival
and ensure it survives to allow future generations of FREE
FRINGE participants to fully benefit from the Edinburgh experience.*

*We feel it is imperative and urgent that we prepare the FREE
FRINGE for the future. We need to start making changes immediately or we will quickly lose ground. The business is getting
really tough in so many ways with clubs closing nationally,
lower fees and greater competition. Not forgetting that in Edinburgh the Paid fringe which is struggling to sell tickets is using
ever more dirty tactics to stay ahead.*

*Without change the legacy you have worked so hard to
guarantee risks imploding in the hunger to get ahead. The
FREE FRINGE was set up as a reaction to the Paid to give performers free and equal access to the festival. Our proposals seek
only to enhance that vision using our vast experience out there
at the sharp end of the show business and performing world.*

*We ask that you receive these proposals in the spirit in
which they are intended. This is not an ultimatum but it is an
expression of our firmly held belief that only immediate radical
changes will ensure the future of the Free Fringe*

Right. There it was. It makes me angry, even now.

It was sent as an attachment to an email, in the early hours
of 14th October 2013. On the same day as he sent it, before I
had replied, Sebastian Fisher registered pbhfreefringe.co.uk as
his own domain, although I didn't discover that until over four
years later.

I'd better tell you who the authors were.

Briefly: Sebastian had done a few shows with us, had at one
time held the PA brief until I had to take it back and do it myself. He had also stood for the Board on our non-slate, unsuc-
cessfully. Lennox had done shows with Sebastian and ran a

comedy club in London. Both those two had been on the show-scheduling team in 2012 before it ceased to function. Dieter was a performer; Oliver had I think only ever done one show with us, and neither he nor Dieter could claim to be part of any committee. Henry, on the other hand, had designed and put together the Wee Blue Book, and done it very well.

They were not part of the Free Fringe's Executive Board, as they would later claim. There was no such Board.

Now, what you must not do when sending ultimatums like this is use Microsoft Word.

Because the recipient can use the Track Changes function to see what you originally wrote and how you modified it in the course of composition, especially if you've been discussing it with one another.

I won't go into details of the things that didn't make it to the final draft. But the most interesting change was at the top, in the list of the names of the senders.

In the final, there were five names. In the drafts, there were six. And the deleted name was Calum Gunn.

I said he wasn't happy after the Great Dressing Room Incident. And some of the sentences and proposals in the Ultimatum (in my mind, it has a capital U) could have come from nobody but him. The "hub venue" proposal, for example. We take whatever venues we can get who are willing to work with us, if we think we can make them work. Calum thought he could negotiate almost any venue, and indeed as I have said before he has succeeded in many cases. But we weren't going to base a whole strategy around a hope that he could negotiate such venues.

I said I wasn't going to deconstruct the Ultimatum in detail here, but careful reading will show that it's about power, me stepping back and them, with their vaunted (and exaggerated) experience and expertise taking over.

But I would say that, wouldn't I? Maybe they did have the expertise of which they boasted. Well, two years would prove them wrong, as I shall relate in due time.

Meanwhile, I had the ultimatum to deal with. Five Free Fringers (four and a half, really) had expressed, clearly, their views. By withdrawing his name, Calum had forfeited any right he may have had to an answer.

So, I thought, why should not all the other Free Fringers have a say? What distinguishes the Gang of Five from all our other performer -members? This is supposed to be a community of performers. I have tried to keep it that way, although it may not always look like that. If the Gang of Five have spoken, then so should everybody else.

So, I sent this email to all our 2013 performers:

This email goes to everybody on the 2014 Free Fringe mailing list.

I have received an ultimatum from five performers. I'm attaching it.

They say 'this is not an ultimatum' . That doesn't make it not an ultimatum.

Please be clear: what they demand is not going to happen.

The Free Fringe does things the way it does for good reasons. Every part of it is linked with every other part. If the authors of the ultimatum don't understand why we do things the way we do, that's their problem, not mine.

There are demands within this ultimatum which are completely unacceptable. There will not be a charge to be part of the Free Fringe. There will not be a mouthpiece stopping me using my own words. I am not going to be pushed aside to become a figurehead. There will be no committee except of people who have proven themselves by undertaking a major responsibility and seeing it through to the end, such as the section Artistic Directors. There was a proto-committee in 2012/13. It collapsed and I had to pick up the work myself. You don't get to set policy until you have proved your worthiness by doing a job.

Rather than have people trying to take over and change the principles, I will cancel the whole event and wind up the Free Fringe Ltd. Anybody attempting to start their own organisation will do so from scratch, with their own money, as I had to all those years ago. You can't use my name or initials without my consent.

The logo belongs to The Free Fringe Ltd, as does all the PA and all the money in the bank.

You will have noted the subtle smear in the ultimatum. The demand for "more transparency" in the accounts, which suggests that accounts are being concealed, probably because I'm doing something underhand. I quote from the Ethos and Conditions: Our finances are open to any scrutiny. No member of the Free Fringe gets paid for the work they do for the Free Fringe. We get no kickbacks from suppliers, venues or anybody else. In fact, nobody has ever asked, including the authors of the ultimatum. I am attaching the last annual accounts of The Free Fringe Ltd.

You will have noticed a second smear. That we're more concerned with growth than with quality, and therefore have no quality control. We have quality control. We have grown precisely because we accept good quality applicants and try to find space for them. The implication that we have no quality control, in a year marking the second Edinburgh Comedy Award to one of our members, is completely incorrect. If we had had enough venues in April 2013, we could have had even more shows without losing quality.

In short, the ultimatum is written in sheer ignorance, and displays the logic of creationists ("I can't see any transitional fossils, therefore evolution doesn't exist"). I have addressed only a handful of the errors; people bitch about the length of my emails, so I shall not address the rest.

I presume the people behind this ultimatum will now want to form their own organisation and start charging for membership so they can pay themselves for their own work, just as they propose in the ultimatum. And in order to do that they'll capture as many Free Fringe venues as they can.

If I consider it worthwhile, I may decide to continue the Free Fringe with the venues that are left to us. But I do not have to. I have put in more money, time and stress than the signatories of this ultimatum can imagine. They've never organised the Free Fringe and don't know the details, and yet they already think they can do it better. I'll carry on if there's support for the real principles of the Free Fringe. Venues may be difficult, as I already said

2014   281

they would be. If there is insufficient support, then I shall wind the Company up.

I have written a brief paper detailing the things that must not happen to the Free Fringe, and attach it. If any of these things happen, they would change the whole principle of the Free Fringe. Therefore they will not, no matter how many people think otherwise.

This will not be the subject of a protracted email correspondence. If you have views, post them on freefringeforum.org for all to see.

Regards
PBH

I attached to that email the Ultimatum, the latest accounts of The Free Fringe Ltd and another short statement. I'd better paste that as well:

Some things about the Free Fringe ethos are negotiable; some are not.

What are the things that must not happen?

- No payments to venues
- No sponsorship
- No charges to performers (1)
- No performers to be paid for the services they give to the Free Fringe (2)
- No performer to be a customer and demand rights in that capacity
- All performers to contribute to the collective according to their abilities.

This list is not exhaustive. It merely represents the difference between slight negotiable changes and fundamental changes. The Free Fringe may evolve, but if it violates these principles it might as well die.

The way the Free Fringe works is this:
Never become dependent on a source of income.

Don't raise money in order to spend it. Instead, obviate the need for spending it. Become as little dependent on spending money as possible.

Instead of raising money to buy services, get each performer to do those services for themselves and all other performers.

Once you start raising money and charging, you never stop. And in no time, you have become just another pay-to-play venue. The Free Fringe will not do this.

FOOTNOTES

(1) Yes, I'm aware we have the voluntary contribution of £3.50 per performance, to pay for the programme. This is something we don't want to continue. It was an emergency measure to ensure the programme got printed. If everybody raised money by benefits and/or selling advertising for the programme, the contribution would not be necessary, and I hope in future it will not be. It is against the spirit of the Free Fringe and was selected as the least bad alternative. Even now, it remains voluntary. Shows can refuse to pay it, and many have done so.

(2) Except by way of legitimate expenses. The materials for printing backdrops, for example, would be chargeable.

Now, you may have handled the affair differently. Perhaps better; who knows? But this was the way I handled it. I'd like to say that a lively debate ensued in the open forum, as a result of which everybody felt better informed and that they had an opportunity to have their say. That would have been a good thing. But it didn't happen.

The threat, however, was serious and I took it very seriously. Calum had negotiated many venues for us. We kept them, when we did keep them, by doing a good job. But still it was possible, probable in some cases, that we would lose venues.

The Ultimateers were furious that I had shared the Ultimatum with other members. To this day I do not understand why. If their intentions were honest, then they had nothing to fear. If they were not, then their anger at the Ultimatum being shared could only expose their intentions.

Oh, and did I mention that they demanded a signed receipt for the Ultimatum and a response within three days?

I have to tell you that no such undertaking has been received, and that consequently this country is at war with Germany.

Oops. I was thinking of another timed ultimatum.

There was clearly a tactic at work here. They wanted secret negotiations. In the course of which, as happens in most negotiations, they would get some but not all of their demands. And, after a decent interval, be in a stronger position to make further demands.

But there was a principle at stake here. Several principles, in fact. And once you start compromising on principles, they're not principles any more; they're negotiating points.

Once you start charging for membership, or indeed for applying, everything changes. You're on your way to becoming a pay-to-play venue; in fact, you have just become one. You've stepped off the cliff. Just a question of how far down the water is.

And when you start charging, two other things happen. Firstly, they become customers. They behave like customers, not like members of a community effort. They make demands in return for their money. Secondly, you create a contract in Law. Consideration has been exchanged. We are obliged to deliver.

Oh, of course we want to deliver, anyway. But suppose something goes wrong and we can't? That's happened many times, and we've always found a substitute, but if they start having contractual rights, it puts us in a weaker position. And if we have to terminate their show because of their unacceptable behaviour, the legal position is also difficult. Now, it's easy; we can just do it.

If you're shuddering at the paragraph above, I don't blame you. It's the sort of thing a dictator would write. But to the best of my recollection we've only had to apply this ultimate sanction four times, all except one at the insistence of the venues themselves. If a venue bars a particular show, then we have to fall in with that.

But we're not a for-profit promoter. And frankly, I can't imagine a circumstance in which a venue wants rid of a particular show without that show having contributed to its own downfall. And I say this after having mediated between shows and their venues on many occasions. I shouldn't have had to. The stress of the Fringe sometimes makes performers behave unreasonably.

Without principles, the Free Fringe is nothing. It's no better than Laughing Horse. I would not stoop so low.

I had nothing to gain from entering into compromise, and I had something to lose. My integrity. Oh, by compromising I could have salvaged something called The Free Fringe, but would it be the Free Fringe as I envisaged it?

I thought not. I was not going to let them undermine the principles. If they were going to walk, let them walk.

And walk they did. And this is how they spun it, in an email to many of our 2013 shows:

Hi,

You may have heard that there has been a problem within the ranks of PBH's Free Fringe. It is true and we have been forced to start a new organisation and we would like you to be a part of it.

Briefly, PBH's executive board, of which I was a member, collectively wrote a private email to him suggesting changes to improve the organisation. His response was to go public and call us all cunts and black list us. The Free Fringe is a collective where everyone is expected to chip in. In reality, it has been like a building site where there are 20 people standing around drinking tea watching one guy with a shovel. We are the people with the shovels. Our group includes the man who gets all the venues, the fund raisers, the brochure designer, the venue programmers etc.

Having been forced out of the organisation we loved we decided to start a new one. We would like you to join us. We have most of the best central venues on Cowgate, Nidry St, Blair St and will have the Tron Kirk, the big church at the corner of the Royal Mile and North/South Bridge, as our main hub.

We have created a new model for a free fringe organisation from scratch.

There was no "executive board". If there had been, the Gang of Five certainly would not have been the sole members of it. They were not blacklisted, or at least not before the email above; blacklisted from what, precisely? I doubt I called them cunts in a public statement, although I cannot say the same about private communications to my own friends.

The trouble with half-truths, as those who tell them well know, is that if one says "this is not true" they can point to the half-true elements and discredit one's denial. But take apart each statement, explain which bits are true, which are false and which have been spun to mislead, and you enter a piece of analysis which is immensely boring to the reader.

Certainly a large amount of spin, to put it at its politest, is evident in all their communications above, particularly that last email.

Lest I be accused of selectively quoting, here is the rest of that same email:

Below is our mission statement:

Quality is our main priority.

Emphasis will be on well managed high quality shows in central Edinburgh venues, so that public, performers and venue managers all have the best experience possible. We aim to provide full arts coverage including comedy, music, spoken word, theatre and more. A dedicated venue manager will monitor and oversee all venues throughout the run.

For the performers.

Rooms will be set up and ready, complete with lighting, backdrops, PA and soundproofing when the performers arrive. Performers will benefit from ongoing support from application to show time, including a Performer's Pack for acts and venues, with all the information they need to survive the Festival. We operate an open door policy to all groups and performers. We are happy to have our performers appearing on other Fringe platforms. All shows from experienced performers including half hour and one

286	Freeing the Edinburgh Fringe

off shows will be considered. Performers will receive a discount card for our venues and we are examining proposed accommodation discounts.

Fee or free?

A non-refundable show registration fee of approximately £80 may be necessary, depending on sponsorship, to pay for equipment and professional services, such as advertising and marketing. Shows will be free to enter using a bucket and/or Paypal for donations with other possible advanced paid reservation options still under review.

Sponsorship, advertising and marketing.

Sponsorship and support from local companies will pay for a quality brochure print which is distributed to every house in Edinburgh and handed out at train stations and bus stations during the fringe. Acts will be able to advertise their own shows in the brochure. A dedicated communications officer and an efficiently managed, regularly updated social media presence will both be on hand to publicise your shows and further the brand. The brand will be extensively marketed around Edinburgh and in the press before and during the Festival. We are also investigating potential partnerships with external PR companies to get performers discounts on PR management and production.

The organisation.

This is a fresh and energetic organisation dedicated to creativity and quality, and run professionally by people with many years of Edinburgh Fringe Festival experience. There will be no figurehead or central personality. A board of directors will take charge of operations and there will be an open AGM. We will be transparent financially, so you can see where your fees are being spent and we are open to co-operation/collaboration with other groups to further the arts, including the paid venues.

Do you want to join us?

Regards,

Lennox Cunningham

A programme distributed to every house in Edinburgh? Heady stuff. The population of Edinburgh is 494,000, so to get a programme to each citizen they'd have to print that many copies, more than the official Fringe Programme itself. Let's be fair, though; they say 'every house', not every citizen, so maybe 200,000. Quite a big print bill, not counting the cost of door-to-door distribution. And keeping some back for the visitors, who are about 70% of Fringe audience according to the Fringe Office.

Without getting ahead of my story here, I can reveal that this, like many other things, did not happen as they promised. The only copies of their programme, when it happened, that arrived in Edinburgh houses or flats were taken there by the dwellers in those houses or flats. Or delivered with pizzas ordered by the flats.

Now, all this happened before December, so it didn't make a very promising start to the 2014 season. Lost Calum; that would make finding new venues harder. Lost some venues: I didn't know how many; that would have to emerge in the course of time. Lost the designer of the Wee Blue Book: that was indeed a blow. Henry had produced excellent designs in the past, and had worked extremely hard up to print deadline to get the WBB out. Design was his business. I think he had to turn down paying work so that he could give time to the WBB. And, of course, that's not how it should be. I never asked him to do that.

And yes, there was some truth in the Gang of Five's assertion that a minority of members were doing all the work and the majority not contributing to the collective effort. I suppose that will always be so; Pareto's Law is hard to fight against. There should have been more workers on the WBB, to ease the burden on whoever is the lead producer.

The others didn't matter. They could go as far as I was concerned; we would have better performers to replace them. And Sebastian had at one stage held the 'organising PA' brief, which he had done badly; the week before that Fringe (I think it was 2013 itself, can't be sure) I had had to remove the portfolio from him, come home early from the Cambridge Folk Festival and work all night doing the analysis he should have done. I then had to buy more PA, but fortunately we got it delivered in time. So, no big loss there, compared to the potential problems with our venues.

But even if they had been more valuable, they would have been dangerous. The principles were and are more valuable than any individual. No, I didn't blacklist them, whatever they meant by that. They walked. Not only walked, but tried to take venues with them. And only one person could have delivered the venues they promised.

Well, the future is always unpredictable, as the cliché goes.

We needed more venues in case we lost many. And we needed Edinburgh-based help to get them.

But did the appeal by the Gang of Five to performers have much impact? If we got venues, could we get shows?

And if only few shows deserted us for them, what would they do? They'd have to fill their venues in order to justify having them. So, if they couldn't poach many of our shows, they'd have to fill their venues with the sort of shows we wouldn't take.

And once again, that would mean the public would equate "free admission" with "poor quality". Which is something we'd been fighting against all along. Laughing Horse had done enough damage on that front; we didn't need yet more below-par free-admission shows in Edinburgh. You can always get plenty of applications like that.

I'm being harsh. "Poor quality" may be an accurate description of the shows I mean, but Poor can be a station on the way to Excellent. We all have to start somewhere. It takes time to become good. And practice. We recognise that. But if you try to climb the ladder too fast, you can fall off it. So, to be concrete, we've tried to make sure that comedians don't do a one-person show until they're ready. And we try to tell them so kindly.

But if they don't take the kindly advice, they can get their premature one-person show from Laughing Horse. And now from the Gang of Five, or Freestival, as they chose to call themselves.

The last time we had faced an attempted coup like this was in 2006, when Laughing Horse had tried to take over. Then we were only four venues strong, and we lost three of them, but thanks to Calum we found more and better. Now we were much bigger. And better known among the licensees of Edinburgh. And, to be brutally frank, Calum had found many venues, but he had also annoyed many of their managements. On one occasion, he and I were negotiating a venue, and he promised them an increase in turnover which was unrealistically high, and quite at variance with my approach, which was to be realistic and make no promises.

It would take a lot of work, but we could have hope. I had despaired in 2006, and I despaired again in late 2013, but — I was going to say I pulled myself together, and thus sound like an iron-man hero (or, in Scotland, an Irn-Bru hero). No. I was sustained by the faith and support of people in Edinburgh, particularly Isla Cromartie (pseudonym) and Frank Galbraith (real name).

Isla and Frank were long-time supporters of the Free Fringe, and supporters of the Arts in Edinburgh generally. I had first met them at the White Horse, when that was our venue. It was one of those miracles. Frank knew licensed premises in Edinburgh well, and Isla was a graphic designer. These were the two main skills we needed, no that we no longer had Calum or Henry Baxter.

Application numbers did not go down.

So, either that meant the Gang of Five's appeal was not getting much resonance, or people were applying to them as well as us.

Looking back on it, I wonder if people were defying our rule that they could apply to no other promoter of free-admission shows, or — just as likely — that we didn't change the wording in time, so that it only said "don't apply to Laughing Horse". I simply cannot remember, amid the rush and stress of combating the situation itself, when we changed the wording.

This might be the point at which I explain this rule. Or I might have done so earlier. Perhaps editing will tell me which.

It's an obvious objection: why can't people apply wherever and to whomever they want? And that is a very fair question.

Is it because you're just being vindictive to Laughing Horse? No. Although it's tempting. But we're trying to be professional here, and vindictiveness isn't professional.

The two main reasons are:

If shows were permitted to apply to all free-admission organisations, and at a time when we have many more applications than space, then it would be rational behaviour (as the economists term it) to apply to them all. And choose from the offers that you get, according to what you think best for your show. That's how capitalism works. But that doesn't account for the effect on us, in a world dependent on deadlines. The rational consumer (economists again) would hold on to all offers until the last possible moment, and then choose. And this would mean that we could lose up to 50% of the shows we were expecting, and have gaps we couldn't fill, or could only fill with inferior shows. This in turn would mean that our venues wouldn't have full programmes, and that our deal would therefore not be profitable for the venues. So the whole Free Fringe concept would collapse.

This, incidentally, is the reason why universities have UCAS. And in UCAS an applicant can only hold two offers at any one time; one main and one as insurance. Same reasons. Universities need to know, with some accuracy, how many students to expect in September.

The other main reason is the protection of the Free Fringe brand. As I've mentioned before, not everybody has our quality control. Oh, yes, we've had some bad shows; our mistake for accepting them. And the others have had some excellent shows. But by and large our quality is higher, because we vet applications. And that's important because the public must not think that free shows are rubbish. It's a natural thing to think, and is true in many other circumstances. But we try to ensure that the standard of our shows is as good as the standard of the pay-to-play venues. And our brand guarantees that, in so far as one can guarantee something like that.

Right. So there was a challenge. Get more venues and fight off an obviously hostile campaign.

Of course I emailed all our existing venues, explaining Calum was no longer working with us. Several emailed back with the sentiment "good". To me it wasn't good. The first and best boss I had, in 1969, taught me not to give up on people, to move them around the organisation until the right niche for them could be found. Play to their strengths and minimise the effect of their weaknesses. His name was Hans Bruehwiler: he's probably dead now, but I won't forget him. Calum had many strengths. He interpreted my email as "they sacked me". Of course we didn't. You can't sack someone who isn't an employee. But we couldn't work with him while he was steering Freestival in direct opposition.

With Frank's help we could get more venues. He proved to be as good at finding venues as Calum, and considerably calmer.

Just as we could not have survived the coup of 2006 without Calum, so we probably could not have got through the 2014 season without Frank.

The Gang's threats proved mostly idle; we retained most of our major venues. The Canons' Gait remained our headquarters; we kept such venues as the Banshee Labyrinth, Whistlebinkies, Opium, Base/Beat, Bannermans and many others. We had done good jobs at all of these, and nobody could credibly promise a better deal. If we do a bad job at a venue (alas, it has happened) we lose it. And I hate it when that happens. But if we bring in the audience, and they buy drinks, and the acts are polite and co-operative with the venue staff, and indeed if they enjoy the shows, then we seldom lose a venue except where management changes. Or where money is waved at them.

And that, of course, is a big thing. The pay-to-play Fringe works by shows paying for their spaces, some money in advance, some as a percentage of ticket sales, and some in arrear. And that money is then the promoter's to spend as he/she wishes. And if the promoter wishes to spend it on offering hire fees to our venues, then we tend to lose them, for we can offer no money. And the sight of folding notes is a powerful motivator. Have I seen folding notes being offered? Well, no, of course not. These negotiations don't take place in front of me. But it's been reported to me. So, call it hearsay if you wish. It is beyond doubt that money in some form has been offered.

Now, of course, the Gang said they had sponsorship. They'd committed themselves to an enormous programme print and distribution bill, so if they got £50000, that would all be absorbed by printing and distributing their programme, if they kept their promise. Of course, it was unlikely that they would do what they promised, but almost any sponsorship money would enable them to offer money to our venues. Which made me anxious.

But we'd done a good job at most venues, so we kept them. I imagine that they didn't try payment. Such was the strength of our relationship with many of our venues that they may have said no even if offered. But I don't know what they tried.

We lost Fingers Piano Bar, and that was a pity. But the owner was particularly friendly with Calum, and that's how we got it in the first place. A lovely place; it had taken a lot of experimentation to find what sorts of shows worked there, but by 2014 we'd found the formula. We have it back now. This may be something to do with Freestival scheduling a show there by the holocaust-denier I mentioned as an applicant in 2012.

It took a long time for us to get enough venues. A lot of new things were tried. But we had Frank, and Frank is a hero. And occasionally venues would come to us and offer themselves.

But I wish things were as they were 20 years ago.

20 years ago there were shows all over Edinburgh, and audiences travelled to see them. But over the years the epicentre has shrunk, and there's now some danger of it becoming a black hole. Even without checking, I'm sure I've said this before.

So, the newer venues we were offered were often on the fringes of the critical area, or even outside it. And that made them more risky. Would audiences come? Would shows work hard enough to get them in? 20 years ago, they might have. But now some (not all) were just as likely to give up and blame us for giving them a venue that, in their thoughts, wasn't good enough for them.

We'd made the Fringe easier for performers, and now (some) performers wanted even more. I knew how difficult the Fringe was, 20 years before. But they didn't. They expected it to be easy, because we'd made it somewhat easier. But you still have to work unbearably hard to get people in, no matter where you are, no matter who you are.

And, as always, the early deadline for the Fringe Programme meant that we didn't have enough venues when the pressure was on, between January and March, and we had space later.

A nice thing nearly happened, but didn't. We were approached by the Footlights Bar. Now, this was the old Footlights and Firkin, where the Free Fringe had started. Oh, I thought, how nice it would be to come back to where we started, having grown immeasurably bigger. Well, not immeasurably bigger; it was perfectly measurable. What I meant was: much bigger. Much, much bigger. Why didn't I say that?

Anyway, we talked to the manager. But it turned out that he wanted in-bar comedy to fit around televised sport, avoiding certain days, and he didn't have the thick curtains that had provided separation of the space in 1996. After all, it wasn't a viable deal. Pity. I was so pleased with the beauty of it that I almost announced before the deal had been struck, and thank the gods I didn't. I did mention it, informally, to a few members of the team, and I shouldn't have done even that. Never announce before the deal is done, even informally.

More crucially, we lost Cowgatehead, the former Library storage, to the Gang, aka Freestival. I knew that would happen. They wouldn't have proceeded if Calum had not assured them of that. And that, at least, he could deliver. Come what may, they had a base and we lost four performance spaces. I thought that a serious problem.

But the solution, which only came in May or so, was under the same roof, if I had but known it.

The whole building (not the Library itself, which continues in public ownership, but the storage element), like many Edinburgh buildings, goes over several levels. The lower level has an entrance on Cowgate, where revellers revel and sunlight is seldom seen, due to the tall buildings. But it goes up four stories and has another entrance on George IV Bridge, in a shop space. And even above that there are two or three floors of flats. The flats don't concern us, but the rest does.

The building had been bought by Ricky Marino, as I mentioned in the 2013 section. Mr Marino is of a venerable age; he gave the building to his two sons to manage. The lower floors to Lorenzo Marino, who in 2013 had sublet them to Charlie Bruce, and thus we had them, and thus Freestival now had them. But the upper floors, the one on George IV Bridge and the floor immediately below that, he gave to Matteo Marino to manage. And we knew Matteo. In 2007 we had put shows on in his George Street venue, Madogs. One of our 2013 stages, with 11 shows, had been in Matteo's section, but we didn't know that at the time.

I say this as if I knew it at the time, but I didn't. Frank, however, did, or found out.

Now, I don't know the details of the rental arrangements between the Marinos and the Bruces. None of my business. Don't want to know; don't need to know. But I do know that the Bruces got Matteo's permission to run a bar on the George IV Bridge floor, and we got permission to put on shows in five rooms; two on the George IV Bridge floor and three on the floor below.

So, at the end of the day, we'd lost four stages in that building and gained five.

But late. We had to hustle to fill the spaces with shows. But of course we did. It was clear that the lower floor had only a last-minute change from office use, and had only two toilets. It was not luxurious. But it was the spirit of the Free Fringe, and I suggest the spirit of the Fringe itself, before it drowned in sponsorship and corporateness. This is where Art could happen, and yes, it deserves the capital A. This was almost the Lord Chamberlain's Men doing plays in inn yards. They had a decent writer, which made it easier for them. But we had decent writers too; perhaps not in Shakespeare's class, but still good at what they do.

Those five stages helped us to put on 501 shows with 8027 performances.

That, at least, was the figure (were the figures) on the last spreadsheet produced before the whirligig of the Fringe was released. I thought I was being clever, but I have to confess that I don't know what a whirligig is. I didn't want to say whirlwind, madness or maelstrom, and the Fringe has an awful number of gigs.

Digressed again. The point is: at that size you can't be completely accurate on figures. In olden days we could say with complete accuracy how many shows and performances we had. Now we can't. Always a couple of dropouts we wouldn't even know about, especially if the Venue Captain or the venue doesn't tell us. Sometimes Venue Captains would arrange a substitute without telling us; sometimes they wouldn't.

And dropout is annoying, because venues hate it, and we therefore lose the venues. Any dropout I've learned about I've always tried to fill. I get approached sometimes, during the Fringe itself, by shows let down elsewhere and looking for a venue. But if I don't know there's an unexpected hole in the programme, I can't do that, and everybody loses.

Dropping out, not finishing one's run, is one of the most disruptive things a show can do. It doesn't damage the pay-to-play venues; they have the money, or at least a contract making the show liable for the money. But it does do great damage to our model.

And dropout does happen. For understandable reasons. The Fringe is harder than anybody imagines who hasn't brought a show. Despite what we tell them, first-timers often think they'll beat the odds and come back stars. When that doesn't happen, they can give up. I understand that, but don't condone it. That it doesn't happen more at the Free Fringe is a tribute to the spirit of community we try to foster. Shows can turn to their more experienced peers for support.

The more I write, the more this is turning into propaganda for my own organisation. That wasn't my aim when I started writing. I promised myself I'd be honest and paint things as they were, and are. All those years ago, when I got an encore in the Bear Pit, I eventually walked home, a few inches off the ground, but with Kipling ringing in my ears:

If you can meet with triumph and disaster
And treat those two imposters just the same.

But I suppose that means that, when I'm genuinely proud of what we have achieved, I have to say that. And I am proud of what we have achieved, so I do say it. The trouble is that, in this world driven by Public Relations, everybody defends what they do, rightly or wrongly.

And I'm as guilty as many others. When we were under enormous pressure, I had to make confident statements. Did I feel confident? A lot of the time, no. When I got the Ultimatum, I had to think: are they right? Is there something wrong with my model? Would their way work better? Or is it my leadership that's the problem? Are they doing this because they simply don't like me? I can be pretty imperious, especially when time is short. I do tend to tell people exactly how I want things done.

Put all this together, and you have some very important factors. I was stressed to buggery. Normally the time between September and December is a time of low Fringe activity: almost a holiday. Not this season, not with the Ultimatum and its consequences. No break for me; 52-week stress. And such was the need to deal with every crisis, I couldn't enjoy the Fringe at all.

The only time I felt free of stress was when I was on stage. What a relief to just perform. Why did I ever aspire to do anything else? Sometimes, in Peter Buckley Hill and Some Comedians, I took wings and flew. Was this the year I got the whole audience singing Strawberry Fields Forever, with complete seriousness and gentleness? No, I didn't say "let's all sing this". That would be crass. I simply came on to start the second half, while some of the audience were still getting drinks and, without preamble, I started singing it, very quietly. They just joined in. Magic.

Another time I sang the Horst Wessel Song. I'm not proud of that. And they applauded. I shouted and screamed: no, no, you can't applaud that. That's the worst song in the world. And I translated the last two lines of the second verse to prove it. I hope they believed I wasn't a Nazi. I don't think I am. I just read a lot of German history. Why I sang that song, only the (Norse) gods know. One of the things that happen when you're compering. You have to trust the things that come out of your mouth; you can't do it from a script.

While I was happily compèring, I thought: I should never have expanded the Free Fringe. Should have kept to one venue. So I could come to the Fringe every year, get full houses and have fun, as I used to. Not like it is now.

This might have been diagnosed as depression, had I submitted it to medical scrutiny. But I didn't. Keep the front up and carry on.

A lot of things from the 2014 season came back to haunt me later. Health was one.

There was one major disaster in 2014. For the first time ever, and I hope the last, we lost a venue in the middle of the Fringe. Lola Lo's. The venue was well located, on George Street. Although when I went to find it, it was very difficult to find. It was a new venue; one of those venues I myself hadn't seen, negotiated by Frank. There had been a change in management since: seldom a good sign.

What they said to me was: you can stay if you cover the wages of our staff.

Even in a crisis, that was an offer we had to refuse. Once we start paying for venues, the whole Free Fringe principle collapses.

We did say to the shows: if you want to go independent and pay the venue yourself, you can, but we won't.

One show was very tempted, but finally didn't take that deal. The rest said no immediately.

So, we had to redeploy six shows. Not easy, in the middle of the Fringe, and when shows are quite angry at being displaced. Right; we could have taken the view that, if shows had worked harder to get people in, the whole affair might not have happened. But that would have been too harsh. In true Country style, we stand by our men. And women, of course.

One act arranged his own substitute, at the Royal Oak, a venue mostly concentrating on folk music but which we used Mondays to Fridays in the afternoons for Spoken Word. Unfortunately what he arranged overlapped one of our shows by 15 minutes, which caused further problems.

We found slots for the remainder. A lot of emails happened here and there; we had a couple of slots available at the George complex (which is what we called the top two floors of the ex-library-storage Cowgatehead building) because we got it late in the day. And we had had a dropout in a top venue — Whistlebinkies. A surprising one; an act running a variable-bill show, who was enjoying his third or fourth year with us. No compassionate reasons: he just said he was going. I compèred his slot myself for two days, on the first day at half an hour's notice, pulling in whatever acts I could find. So, this would have been a big source of rage, had not the Lola Lo problem occurred and given us more than enough shows to fill it. We ended up putting a Magic act in there, which was a piece of programming that would not otherwise have occurred to us.

I think one of the shows from Lola Lo's decided not to continue; this was an act hosting another variable-bill show, and she had a solo show at a more prestigious venue. She stayed with us in future years, which shows she wasn't too unhappy.

But this piled more stress upon stress.

I longed even for the days of 2009, when I left Edinburgh first-class, with a bottle of champagne on my table and an Edinburgh Comedy Award in my luggage, when even discovering that my car had been towed away on the day I left for Edinburgh and I had to pay £1300 to get it back, did not dampen my spirit.

Had we got too big?

I didn't think we had. Maybe this was because I wanted to be bigger than Laughing Horse. There was a time when they were bigger, and they boasted of it. We, of course, were better for acts and audience. Yes, I know I would say that. Our Wee Blue Book was sought-after: their printed programme was rubbish and not well distributed. Ours was, because of our system: nobody could leaflet for their show alone, but everybody had to offer the Wee Blue Book.

But yes, I was driven by thoughts of beating them on the one criterion on which they were, at one stage, in the lead. Perhaps I shouldn't have been. But also there was a vast surplus of applications over slots; I did want to satisfy as many of these applicants as possible. That's a much better motive, isn't it?

But it's no good satisfying applicants unless they came and behaved in the Free Fringe spirit. And not all of them did, or still do. And the bigger we get, the less easily we could inculcate new members with the spirit.

In order to combat pay-to-play, we have to be big. There'll always be pay-to-play. If acts can rent a venue and still make a profit, or break even, then one can't object to them doing that. And famous acts can do it that way. But it's the less-famous we want to rescue from deals that mean they make a massive loss at the Fringe, fuelled by their own dreams that somehow they won't. Gratified by seeing huge posters with their own faces on, they forget how much they've paid for them. For such shows, there's a better way, and it's us.

Yes, but how did 2014 go after all that?

When you win Best Newcomer, you're usually made as far as the industry is concerned. You're Box Office. You belong to the select band who can fill a reasonable-sized venue on your own name. So, the pay-to-play venues are keen on having you, and your agents and managers (you'll have them by that time, even if you didn't before) are usually keen that you should go to what they consider a prestigious venue. The manager-figures have usually not caught up with the reality of the Free Fringe.

But John Kearns, winner of Best Newcomer in the previous year, told us he wanted exactly the same venue and time he'd had the previous year. So he got that. (If performers ask for their previous slot back and they've done nothing to blot their copybook and they ask before New Year, they usually get it, so John didn't get any special deal). He stayed with us when he could have done otherwise, and I think that's admirable; the Free Fringe spirit embodied.

I mention that because John was nominated for the main Perrier prize in 2014. And he won it.

I was once again delighted. I said last year that his win as Best Newcomer had proved our quality to the world. But the main prize did so once again, and much more emphatically.

So, another good Saturday morning ceremony, and a nice name-check for me in the acceptance speech.

And the Best Newcomer winner, Alex Edelman, was also a Free Fringer.

Many PR-writing people would stop there. But that's spin. Yes, Alex won, and yes, Alex had a Free Fringe show that year. But the show that won it for him wasn't his Free Fringe show, but one he did at a pay-to-play venue.

Nevertheless, I was also pleased for him. And it made the same point.

Oh, and I got another tiny award, in the Barry Award series, which was called "Best Person".

Pretty ironic, in the light of what was to happen in the next year.

Well, I say I got it, and you'll have noticed that I didn't say 'won'. I must have known at the time what the selection process was, but I don't remember now. I think there was some voting involved, among Fringe shows.

In fact, I was joint winner. But the other winner was Robbie Slaughter. Yes, another pseudonym. I don't know why I persist with them.

Now, Robbie has featured before in this story. Looking back, I see I decided not to name him at the time. Oh well, another inconsistency for editors or me to sort out. He had started an organisation, based around a bus and a bookshop. I don't object to either buses or bookshops, just to be clear. I am regularly seen in both. But less in bookshops, because when I leave I'm still in the same place as when I arrived. Except perhaps mentally.

But having let us down in 2008, he was on the short list of people who will not get a show offer from us if they apply. Not that he will.

He was another person who was running a free-admission organisation. And he was pushing a model we'd considered, and emphatically rejected, many years before. It was the pay-for-priority model. A paid ticket guarantees you a seat; it's free for people without tickets after everybody who has paid has gone in.

Oh well. I don't like that model, and it would never work for us. Because we had dropped all the infrastructure of ticket booking, collection and checking. But I can hardly object if somebody else wants to try it.

If he charged his shows to play, I would dislike it more. But I simply don't know whether he does or not.

If this was business, I'd have somebody make false-flag applications to all other free-admission promoters, so I could see what their terms are and what promises, if any, they make to performers. In business, that's probably acceptable conduct. But it's slightly dodgy and, although tempted, I've never caused it to be done, and I won't. Of course, they could have done the same to us. They would have learned nothing that isn't public knowledge, I don't think.

So, 2013 was getting to be the routine story. Fear of failure, vast excess of applications before the deadline for the Big Fat Fringe Programme, not enough space, more space gained later, still enough applicants to fill it, various crises during the Fringe which took their toll, frequent full houses, some empty houses, some shows getting the Free Fringe spirit, others not, triumph snatched once again from the jaws of disaster, go home.

But what of Freestival, the Gang of Five and the coup? I had no information. Did they do well at Cowgatehead? They should have done. In that prime location, it would be quite difficult to fail. They must, I thought, have done enough to ensure their survival and even possibly growth, although we had done enough to ensure continuing at most of our venues. And they had a sponsor: an Edinburgh-based pizza company.

I have no quarrel with the pizza company; quite the reverse. They had a stand, among other places, outside the Tron Kirk, which did roaring business. I didn't use it; I thought it diplomatically best. Until the penultimate day of the Fringe, when I walked past and heard my name called.

Serving at the van was the owner, whom I'd met before. He offered me a free slice of pizza. This, at the Fringe, is not to be sniffed at. And it was very good pizza. Was I selling my soul? My soul is worth at least two slices. So he offered me another.

No, seriously, business was not talked. I gave him my business card and received his in return, as one does. I praised his pizza, and we talked of this and that. Nevertheless, I felt there was some significance in the move.

I proceeded to our venue, George on the Bridge, still clutching the half-eaten second pizza slice. At the Fringe, if you don't eat on the move, you tend not to eat at all. I arrived, and one of my members saw the pizza and was aghast. He said he'd been boycotting the pizza stand all Fringe, out of loyalty to the Free Fringe and to show solidarity against Freestival. And now, he said, I blatantly turn up clutching their pizza; his boycott had been in vain and he felt betrayed.

Oh, come on. I never asked him or anybody else to boycott the pizza stand. Or even the other free-admission promoters' shows themselves. I wouldn't go myself: that would be too provocative, but everybody else was free to. As for boycotting pizza: no. Completely the wrong target. Nothing I ever said could be construed as encouraging that.

Still, it was nice that the team was showing fierce loyalty, even if expressed in a way I didn't realise. I hope he went for a pizza after that, and enjoyed it.

I had a pizza when I got back to London. It wasn't as good. And I had to pay.

*

2015

In which we break the magic 9000 but things turn a trifle nasty.

I HADN'T HAD A WEEK WITHOUT STRESS, or even a day, for as long as I could remember. And this was all the Free Fringe. The major challenges, the minor irritations and the endless questions.

Free Fringers, as I keep on saying, aren't customers. But sometimes I felt like I was in a customer service role, or something similar. In that role, you answer people's questions as reasonably as you can. You may get the same question for the thousandth time, but to the questioner, it's a new question and it's only fair you give a reasonable answer.

And this has been, in the most recent era of conservative governments (the lower case c is deliberate; you can be conservative without being of the Conservative Party, and several governments have been) the problem with service businesses and public services.

They start out striving for efficiency. Cut out the dead wood. Identify slack and eliminate it, so you get maximum productivity.

That mentality comes from production lines. When jobs are purely mechanical, when humans are doing things only because machines can't yet, then maybe cutting out the dead wood works. Maybe. But I don't use self-checkouts in supermarkets. And I wish tube trains still had guards and buses still had conductors. These jobs would be more fulfilling work for the young than standing in the streets trying to sell charity subscriptions.

But the production line mentality doesn't work for the Free Fringe, and it doesn't work for many more important organisations.

Firefighters are employed to put out fires. So every hour they're not putting out fires is a waste of taxpayers' money, if you have a certain mentality.

So you look at the figures, and you say firefighters are over-equipped and under-employed, and you close down some fire stations to achieve economies, and sell off the land for luxury flats (what flats are not luxury flats nowadays? Apart from mine, that is.) And then two fires happen at once, and there aren't enough firefighters or engines to deal with both. And people die. Because there was a good reason for firefighters sitting around the station drinking tea, but you didn't realise it.

Even worse with the police. Cut out the slack in the police service and they have to prioritise. And naturally they prioritise the crimes that have happened rather than the ones that haven't happened yet. They deal with as much reported crime as they can, and to do that they cut back on being visible in the community, and keeping their information sources. Less proactive policing, and fewer crimes get stopped before they start. Which leads to even more reported crime, and thus to even less proactive policing.

If you cut away slack, you take away thinking time. And in thinking time, people think how they could do their job better, and if managers listen to the people who think, they may well find that things can indeed be done better, to everybody's benefit.

Take away slack in a service role, and you also lose the time people need to explain things to customers properly, to reassure them, to ensure they know everything they need to. And you get people who are more stressed, and therefore more abrupt with customers. They hear the same question for the thousandth time, and they snap.

Systems need slack. The sort of efficiency conservatives have sought is in fact very INefficient, measured by the quality of service provided.

What has all this to do with the Free Fringe?

I was mostly the service provider, and therefore I needed slack to do the job well and considerately. And the bigger the job became, the less slack I had and the more abrupt I was becoming.

I knew the time I should have taken to answer all our queries, to think about strategy and to improve our systems. And I didn't have that time. Even though I no longer had the day job.

I may also not have the patience. Tourette's sufferers often don't, and I often don't.

It became very necessary to think about how to rectify this. And the obvious answer was to spread responsibility; get more people on the job. Thus the Free Fringe could continue after I retired. I had not at that time considered dying; that came later.

Now, they system of Artistic Directors was already in place. In theory, I no longer made decisions on what show goes where (allocation decisions, as we call them).

Frank did the venue search and liaison, but I was often in Edinburgh showing my face and helping as far as I could.

Isla did the Wee Blue Book, and that's a huge task.

I did the data processing, and that was also huge. And I fielded all the enquiries and questions. I had to cut some corners so I could get the rest of the job done. For example, I made it policy not to answer the question "is it worth me applying to the Free Fringe?". That question came up a lot. But it meant double work. The question can't be answered with a simple 'yes' or 'no'. One needs to know a lot more about the show. In fact, one needs to know exactly the details that are asked on the application form. So, it was more efficient to make them apply, and then I or the ADs could make a reasonable assessment.

Processing the data was time-consuming but not excessively stressful, although late dropouts or changes often made me scream.

It was, however, only I who made the difficult decisions and who had to tell people things they did not want to hear.

And as long as it was only I who did those things, there could be no easy succession. More power had to flow from me to the team of Artistic Directors and the other members of the core team. And they in turn should bring more other members on board. And this would create slack in the system so we could do it better.

Let me start doing that now, in the 2014-15 season, while I'm still fit and in control. (That turned out to be prophetic).

Well, how?

Suppose I wasn't actually in Edinburgh in August? Then they'd have to deal with the crises themselves.

Perhaps drastic, but perhaps not, for I still would be steering things up to then, and still processing the data, so at least that would be right.

That was the tentative plan. It changed, as I shall hereafter relate (I always wanted to say that).

The plan was made easier from an unexpected source. The Canons' Gait. Our headquarters and number one venue; not the biggest, not the best equipped, but normally getting a very excellent bill of shows and having a good atmosphere. People liked playing there. I always did my own shows there. And we brought in big numbers; most shows filled every afternoon and night. Not a perfect venue, but good, and the centre of the Free Fringe. I would mostly be found there when I wasn't visiting other venues, and I had my own special small table in the bar, facing the entrance and the steps down to the performance room, keeping an eye on everything.

And yet it went strange. The owner declared himself dissatisfied with the amount of money he was taking in. This despite the staff's own reports. The owner, whom I had known for many years, and who should have been ecstatic at what we were bringing, was not. Yet we packed the place. Oh, years earlier I was bringing in over 100 people to my show every night, but that was before the fire limit was set at 70.

We could use it for one last year, he said. But the stage had to be in the middle of the long wall rather than at the far end of the room, and there had to be table service of drinks during the shows.

By that time, we'd booked shows already.

I found out later what his thinking had been. There was a bar in the performance room; there was a bar at ground floor level in the main pub. He was ascribing the takings from the downstairs till to us and the takings from the ground floor to not-us, to general pub traffic. But the overwhelming bulk of our audience bought their drinks on the ground floor, drank one while queuing and bought another to take down. Few bought at the downstairs bar. There was little time to do so before their show started. Especially as it got so hot we had to keep the audience upstairs while we had a ventilation break between shows.

But why we had to have the stage where the stage should not have been, I still don't know. Perhaps to him it made no difference, but to a performer it's very important.

Well, this ultimatum (another one!) came from nowhere. I felt quite annoyed by it, for we could do no better than we had already done over the years.

I worked out a plan which gave an alternative venue for each show. Some of the alternative venues were of equivalent standard to the Canons' Gait, but some were less sought-after. I put it to the shows. Do we pull out of the venue entirely? That would have been my preferred solution, but I wasn't going to impose that. They could choose. And they discussed, by email, and the discussion swung this way and that, but eventually all shows but one decided to stay with the venue under the altered conditions. The other show withdrew entirely, which was sad.

My memory is now confused. Did I decide not to do Peter Buckley Hill and Some Comedians for the 19th year because of this change to its customary venue, or had I decided not to come for other reasons before the Canons' Gait insisted on the change? I think perhaps the latter, but so many things have happened since that I can't be sure. PBHASC was a double slot, so that gave opportunity to two more shows.

Well, I thought, that's this year's major crisis over, and it'll be downhill from here.

Humph.

I mentioned that it had been difficult producing a redeployment plan for the Canons' Gait shows. This was because, as usual, we had many more applications than slots, and almost everything was full.

Cowgatehead, I thought, had continued with Freestival. I had, of course, tried to find out, by emailing Charlie Bruce, but there were no replies to my emails. I wasn't sure at first, but when the Big Fat Fringe Programme came out, I was sure, for they had booked many shows into it. And that was that. Or so anybody would have thought.

You may not believe the next bit. But it's true as I write it.

I got a message on Facebook. Which is not unusual. But this was from Charlie Bruce's son, also Charlie, asking me to telephone his father. Which I did.

And what Charlie said to me was: do you want any more venues?

Yes, I said. We have shows waiting.

And then I thought: what can he be offering? Perhaps something too far away from the psychological area, that I'll have to diplomatically say 'no' to. So I asked the question. What venues are you thinking of?

Oh, he said, the usual: Cowgatehead and Tron Kirk.

I was taken aback.

But surely, I said, you've given them to Freestival? They've booked shows in there. They're in the Fringe Programme.

No, said Charlie: I gave them no permission to do that. As far as I'm concerned, they're not booked.

Are you available tomorrow? I asked. He said yes, and I was on the first train to Edinburgh the next day.

(Pause for railway wheel effects, distance shots of trains speeding through countryside and Mallard's record-breaking run, even though that was in the other direction and my train was not a steam one).

No, it felt like that. Great speed was needed, because this could be big.

I met Charlie after I'd arrived in Edinburgh and Frank was there too. Charlie was indignant that shows had been booked in without his knowledge or consent, just as he had been on the telephone. And, at the time the shows must have been booked in, before the Big Fat Fringe Programme went to print, Charlie explained he had not yet acquired the lease, so he could not have given permission. Ricky Marino had, at that time, not decided what to do.

And this is also what Charlie said:

"I wouldn't have done it anyway. I'm not working with Sebastian Fisher again".

I didn't ask why. I didn't need to know.

(Just to remind you pseudonym-trackers: Sebastian was one of the main movers behind Freestival and their principal venue-liaison person.)

We looked at details. They had booked shows on nine stages in Cowgatehead. There could only be six stages (two more than 2013). They had booked shows in two stages in another building in Victoria Street for which Charlie had the lease: I was told that there would be no performances in that building other than live music. They had promised at least one fully-rigged stage with light and sound, as opposed to our more basic rig.

And they'd arranged a burlesque show for the Tron Kirk, just as we had before and as Charlie wanted. Only they had made it a charged, ticketed show, £10 a pop. And that show was also in the Big Fat Fringe Programme.

Did I want the venues? Of course I did.

But it was going to take a lot of work to sort out the chaos created by Freestival.

After the site meeting with Charlie was over, Frank and I went to a nearby hotel to think through the ramifications.

A lot of people who had applied to Freestival in good faith were going to suffer.

What were the options?

a. We keep all of Freestival's bookings where they were. Well, if you could fit eleven stages of bookings on to six stages, that might have been an option. But you can't. And anyway, what about our own waiting list? Do we give shows that didn't apply to us priority over shows that did apply to us? No, of course we don't.

b. We decline the venue in favour of Freestival, out of respect for the innocent victims of their foulup.

Not possible, as long as Charlie vows he won't work with Sebastian Fisher again. The result would be that nobody gets the space, Charlie makes a loss and never offers us anything again. Nobody wins.

c. We wash our hands of Freestival's problem. They made the mess; they can sort it out.

Tempting. But showing too much unconcern for the victims. Freestival, of course, charged for the space, as it said in their ultimatum. If I were one of their victims, I'd take them to the Small Claims Court, for by charging they have created a contract in Law. But most performers don't think like that. And we are the good guys. We ought to help, not wash our hands.

d. Inform the displaced shows and invite them to re-apply to the Free Fringe and receive positive consideration for their plight if they did so.

I didn't want any show on the Free Fringe that had not accepted our Ethos and Conditions. The Free Fringe relies on people doing what they promise to when they accept the Conditions. Any wholesale takeover of Freestival's unauthorised bookings would mean we had many shows who, at best, did not know what to do or, at worst, would simply not do it.

Option d it was, then. Carefully. Consideration of the plight of the innocent, equal rights for our own waiting list, insistence on the Free Fringe's Conditions, and all the time pouring eleven shows on to six stages, plus our own good people. Oh, and maintaining quality control. Because any show under our banner needs to have been checked for quality. We can make mistakes and certainly do from time to time, but we're not taking other people's shows as a job lot.

Right. Decision made. A lot of scheduling work needed in a short space of time. All hands to the pumps.

Firstly, there were people out there who were rehearsing, designing leaflets and posters, booking accommodation, all on the strength of something they had been promised by an organisation that couldn't deliver.

(And, yes, that had happened to our shows sometimes also. When venues closed down shortly before the Fringe started. But we'd always striven to find them another venue. And we had to do that again, later on in 2015, but I'll get to that.)

So, priority one: warn the affected shows what was happening.

Were Freestival going to nicely hand over their contact list? Of course they weren't.

There was only one thing to do, and even as I sat in that hotel considering these options and making the decision, I knew it would generate a storm. Not the sort of storm that happens six months after a butterfly flaps its wings in Argentina: an immediate one, like when Sun-reader vigilantes mistake a paediatrician for a paedophile. (Look it up; it happened).

The only way of telling the shows concerned was to tell everybody and hope, via social media and sharing, that they would see it.

So I posted:

This post is addressed to all shows who believe they have a Fringe slot in Cowgatehead organised by Freestival.

I regret to have to tell you that Freestival never had permission in 2015 to book shows into Cowgatehead. The slot you think you have is not real.

We have a confirmation from both the owner and the licensee of Cowgatehead. Freestival's bookings never had their approval, and these bookings are null and void.

I appreciate this will come as a shock to many of you. You will have proceeded on the basis that you had a confirmed performance slot. But you do not.

Even if you have paid Freestival, even if you have paid to be in the Fringe Programme, you do not have a slot.

Your first reaction will be not to believe this message.

But it is true.

The licensee has recently approached us, the Free Fringe, to book this space, and has explicitly stated that Freestival has no right to make such bookings. We, The Free Fringe, are now author-ised to book all performance spaces at Cowgatehead. No bookings other than those made by us are valid, and none will be honoured, whatever the circumstances.

I appreciate that many of you will be taken aback by this, and most of you will have acted in good faith in applying to Freestival. You are not to be blamed. Freestival, however, is to be blamed for taking bookings into a space which they were not entitled to book.

You could, of course, pretend this is not happening and turn up in August expecting to do a show. But you will not be able to.

The Free Fringe will entertain applications from you. You will have to accept the Free Fringe Ethos and Conditions, which you can read on [and here was a link].

These conditions stipulate that you should not be an applicant to any other provider of free-admission shows. This means that you should dissociate from Freestival forthwith.

By applying to the Free Fringe, there is a chance that your slot, or something close to it, may be given back to you. It depends on your application itself and the speed with which you make it.

We will look upon such applications as sympathetically as we can. You will need to mention the slot you thought you had and the length of the run you thought you had.

I have no doubt that Freestival, having been caught doing something they should never have done, will attempt to spin the situation in any way they think might exonerate them. But at the end of the day, they cannot deliver the slot they have promised you, and they have never been able to deliver that slot.

We are also informed that bookings at St John's are equally invalid, but in that case we have no power to rectify this. Such shows are also welcome to apply to the Free Fringe, but we cannot give you space at St John's. That is all the information we have about St John's.

We deplore the actions of Freestival. To run free shows, thus emancipating performers at a Fringe in which many organisations seek to exploit performers, one must be honest. It is difficult enough even if one is fully honest. But to promise you something *that they cannot deliver, and to charge you for it, is in our eyes deplorable.*

We do not know who you are. But we do know that (according to Freestival's web site) 171 shows have been promised space by them. The overwhelming majority of these applications are invalid. We urge you to spread this post so that all such shows can be reached.

No doubt they will call this venue poaching on our part. It is not. They never had the venue for 2015. Nothing has been poached. We, the Free Fringe, were contacted by the licensee and asked to programme Cowgatehead for 2015, as the sole programmers. If you thought otherwise, you have been deceived. We will help to the extent we can, giving weight also to our own unallocated applicants.

Free shows need to be honest. Even so, mistakes happen and are difficult enough. I regret that some of you have been the victims of what appears to be dishonesty on the part of Freestival.

Sincerely

Peter Buckley Hill

A difficult situation, certainly. But that's what they pay me £0 a year for.

But even the CEO of the Royal Bank of Scotland isn't paid enough to compensate for everything that was thrown at me in the aftermath. Typical response:

If it's true, Peter has shown himself as a very bitter and vindictive man that has just shat in a load of people's cornflakes. If it's not true, he's just shown himself to be bitter and vindictive.

and:

The acts who believe they have spots, should (at this stage) get their spots. Regardless of who is running it.

People take a month off work sometimes to do Edinburgh. They may have already paid deposits on their accommodation or booked onto a package show that they wouldn't have bothered with, without a solo spot.

Doing anything with those spots other than giving them to the people who think they have them would be truly "deplorable".

Freestival's initial reply:

To all Freestival Acts. It has been brought to our attention that Peter Buckley Hill has posted a statement claiming that he now has control of Cowgatehead and that St John's is no longer a valid venue. We have no idea what has lead him to this conclusion, and unless we are told otherwise by our Edinburgh partners these remain Freestival venues and your slots are secure. We are working to clarify the situation and will keep you posted.

Erm.. led, not lead, chaps.

Now, the one mistake I made here, unnoticed at the time as I was searching for forms of words that could be appropriate, was not to mention in my initial Facebook post that they had booked nine stages where there were only six, plus the two at St John's where there were zero. Hence the six-into-eleven problem. And hence the reply above that "the shows should get what they thought they had".

Dear reader: you might pause at this moment and think what you would have done, and how you would have communicated it.

If I had to do it over again, the only thing I would change would be to put the eleven-into-six factor into the post, as I said above. I think there was still some uncertainty over St John's, Victoria Street, as I wrote, so perhaps I should have written nine-into-six at the time. There were indeed no performances at St John's in the end, as Charlie had indicated.

This was late May. So now I have to question my own memory: did I in fact show Charlie the printed programme, or was it not out yet? Normally it comes out at the beginning of June. Perhaps I just knew their shows were in it; they'd certainly made it known on their web site that they had the venue, or thought they did. But why would they have thought that? And why did they book without confirmation?

The fallout was of Hiroshima proportions, or so it felt at the time.

It was, to the best of my recollection, three weeks before Freestival finally admitted they did not have the venue. During that time a lot of unpleasant things happened.

I received an email from Sebastian Fisher asking me to reconsider, otherwise the "whole free movement" was under threat. I baulked at that. Who was he to speak for the "free movement", whatever that is? If you levy charges on performers, you're not free. I felt, rightly or wrongly, that there was an element of threat to this: destroy us and we'll destroy your credibility. Well, I didn't destroy them; they did it to themselves. As for my credibility, yes. The attacks on me were hard to bear, and I bore them mostly by not reading them and getting on with the job.

For the job was difficult. The stages had to be programmed from among a mix of our applicants and ex-Freestival shows. The latter had to be given times close to those in the Big Fat Fringe Programme, or ideally so. But meanwhile those same shows were understandably looking round for other options, and we couldn't be sure they would accept even if we found them a suitable slot.

And of course, they wrote in all sorts of terms, some appreciating the situation, others not and demanding what they saw as their rights.

Many did not apply until Freestival finally admitted that they were not booking the space. Three weeks, as I said before, although that's a guess made two years later. Perhaps I should have made more notes at the time, but I was too busy sorting the situation out. And doing all the other things I had to do; even without the Cowgatehead problems, I would have been busy enough.

I'm not sure why it took them so long. Charlie would have confirmed in an instant. Perhaps they didn't ask, or perhaps he didn't return their calls.

I find it difficult to write coherently of the low-flying shit I had to dodge. From the recipient of a "Best Person" award in one year, I had turned into Adolf Hitler the next.

What shocked me most of all was the number of people who simply did not believe what I had said. I thought, obviously wrongly, that I had a track record of doing things openly and honestly for performers. Well, clearly I was deluded in that. To this day there are people who believe I stole the venue from Freestival. I find that extremely hurtful.

Of course, Freestival's propaganda machine was in full swing against me and us. And it was joined by many well-meaning people who were not aware of the facts, had not bothered to read my initial Facebook post, or simply did not believe it.

Among these was the then Director, or CEO, of the Fringe itself, who emailed me exhorting me to give up the venue and allow Freestival its "rightful" shows. I wish she had bothered to inform herself of the facts before making this judgement. I had a 20 year track record at the Fringe, so twenty times as much as Freestival. Did she pause to consider that things might not quite be as they had presented them? At one stage, I had to bring Charlie Bruce himself to the Fringe Office to vouch personally for our booking rights. (A year later, they started demanding written proof, and I had to ask Charlie to get a certificate from the owner, Ricky Marino. Neither of these gentlemen was happy about that. Business in Edinburgh is usually done on a handshake.)

And there was a petition, demanding I be stripped of my Edinburgh Comedy award. Although the petition was never formally presented to me, which spared me the trouble of re-sponding to it. If I had done, it might have contained the phase "out of my cold dead hands".

And one of our good acts in a major venue walked, in pro-test against what he felt was immorality. No discussion, no reading of our case. Pity. But on the other hand, another vacant space which helped us with the allocation problem.

Oh, they worked hard at spreading the poison. And they worked hard at trying to reverse the verdict. Calum went above Charlie's head and talked to the owner, Ricky Marino, in vehement language in his restaurant. He was asked to leave, and anyway he was talking to the wrong Ricky Marino. The Marino family of Italian-Scots is large and there is more than one Riccardo.

Pizza man, their sponsor, asked for a meeting with me, which I gave him when he was in London. The price of fizzy water at five-star hotels is astronomical, but fortunately he paid. Was there not a compromise? Could Freestival not have the top two floors? Er, no, because Charlie did not have the top two floors. No agreement had been reached. Substantial sums in rent were being asked for. Although Sebastian Fisher presumed we had those floors also (the ones off George IV Bridge, which I described in the 2014 chapter) we did not. Completeness demands that I say we subsequently got use of three stages on that floor, but at the time we did not and we were not planning for them.

And there was talk of picketing our fundraiser show at the Bloomsbury Theatre, which worried me. But in the end there were no pickets.

Possibly the nastiest was the burlesque show that had been booked for a £10 show at the Tron Kirk. They emailed with all sort of abuse. I've just re-read it and I shudder once again. But they wouldn't accept that their recourse could only be against the organisation that booked them in the first place. Had they been willing to do a free-admission show, we might have worked something out, but no: they insisted that they were too good for that. To quote them:

Freestival had the venue last year, and we did a free show then, and it was RUBBISH! The venue is a complete nightmare, bad sound, lights, stage, dressing area, it sucked, and the cheap arses that occupy free shows don't respect the artists. The only reason we agreed to do it was on the promise of better production specs, which I highly doubt will improve now that PBH is there. As far as I can see your a bully and squeezing out artists that deserve better in the first place, and whoever is controlling Tron are complete morons, as are you.

Oh well. I've been called worse, and at least this moron bully knows the difference between 'you're' and 'your'. As for audiences respecting the artists, there's such a thing as earning it.

All I could do was carry on. Well, I could have responded to every smear and snide remark on facebook, every blog post repeating Freestival's story, every mention. And that would have been so emotionally draining that I would have collapsed, I think. And it would have taken time away from the main task, which was to accommodate as many applicants as we could, providing they agreed the Ethos and Conditions and made the standard.

A few were grateful. Many were not.

When I started the Free Fringe, I thought I could enjoy it. Naïve visions of happy performers and me in their midst, an equal among equals, all sharing the work to a happy outcome and having fun on stage and off.

I didn't imagine this nastiness at all.

Is that what I'd given much of my life to?

So, when we got to the Fringe, I had Cowgatehead half-full of shows that wanted to be there and half shows rescued from Freestival's cock-up. Obviously I would have preferred to have a venue full of shows who had originally applied to us. Of course, the Freestival displacements had read the Ethos and Conditions and agreed to them, but, as it turned out, some would have agreed to anything to save their slot. It didn't mean that everybody actually did what they were supposed to, on the ground.

Especially not the show that propped a fire door open with a box of programmes after the Fire Officer had specifically told us not to. And then argued with the Fire Officer. We nearly got shut down.

Oddly, we ended up with a little spare space, even having tried to pour eleven stages into six. Other promoters on the pay-to-play side were active in trying to provide what they termed 'rescue space'. They cannot be blamed, I suppose, or it depends how much they charged.

For I must not lose sight of our main disadvantage. We are nomads. We are completely at the mercy of our venues, who can pull out at any time for good or bad reasons. Most of the pay-to-play venues have long-standing arrangements with the premises they use. And, of course, they pay rent, which gives them bargaining power we can never have.

You may recall the organisation who booked a venue we'd also booked, in 2013, and how they offered a lot of money to get that venue back. Well, that organisation was active in "rescuing" shows who had been misbooked in Cowgatehead. They could, said that organisation, come to them and still have free-admission shows. Several did. I leaned later that such shows were still charged rent for the space; their buckets were counted by the organisation and set against the daily rent. It appeared (I'm doing hearsay here) that the buckets were poured into a coin-counting machine by the promoter immediately after the show.

It continued to be a bad year for me. Cowgatehead had left me reluctant to be seen anywhere on the comedy circuit, lest I encounter people who believed Freestival's spin or that we had poached the venue. I hadn't scheduled a show for myself, because of that and the Canons' Gait problem; it was best I kept a low profile, and I kept away from Edinburgh entirely for the first ten days. I felt I was being forced into retirement. Perhaps no bad thing. The next generation could take over, unencumbered by the mud that had been flung at me. But for that to happen, they had to learn to run the Free Fringe.

In the whole history of the Free Fringe we have only had to terminate four shows before they had finished their run. But two of them were in 2015. I didn't need that, on top of everything else.

The first one was using his venue as sleeping accommodation. His venue contacted me and told me to get him out. It seemed that he had put no effort into his show at all, but had somehow — I still don't know exactly how — contrived to stay behind when the whole building turned into a nightclub, turn a sofa to the wall in a quiet area, and slumber on undisturbed. When the venue finally found out, they contacted me instantly and insisted something be done. I got there as soon as I could, but he had departed in a stream of curses before I arrived. And the curses were repeated in a text to me.

I'm not proud that we have to keep a 'do not book again' list, but this shows why we have to.

The second was worse.

This was an established comedian who had been given a full-run slot in one of our best venues. Like everybody else, he'd accepted the Ethos and Conditions.

And, pretty near the top, they say: you're either with us or another free-admission promoter, but you can't do free-admission shows with us and them. I've explained the reasoning for this earlier on.

So, there I was, walking down Cowgate on the perpetual circuit of touring all our venues and checking, or hoping, things were working (no matter how many times I call round during the Fringe, there are always some who say: we never saw you). Walking past, as one does, people leafleting for shows that aren't ours; there are many such leafleters, as you might expect. And, twenty paces past one of them, I had a 'what is wrong with this picture?' moment.

I hastened back and asked for a leaflet. And you will almost never see me doing that at the Fringe.

And my heart sank. For there was indeed the face of the comedian I described, featured as part of a Laughing Horse show.

This I did not need.

It's pretty much Rule One. Them or us; not both. And it was very clear in the Ethos and Conditions, and even if it wasn't, the whole comedy circuit knew it. This man was no stranger; it wasn't even his first Free Fringe. He knew.

What did he think would happen? Did he think it wouldn't be discovered? Did he think there would be no consequences?

What I hate most about this is that, by accepting the Ethos and Conditions, he had given his word; by accepting the other show, he had broken his word. Maybe it's a generation thing. Breaking one's word is something a gentleman simply does not do, or so I was brought up to believe.

What to do? After all the flak I had had to catch that year, why stick my head above the parapet for more?

What a mixed metaphor. Flak is anti-aircraft (*Flugzeugabwehrkanone* is what it's short for) and heads above parapets is trench warfare.

How tempting it would have been to pretend I hadn't noticed.

But then the precedent would have been set. People would think that, once you'd reached a certain level of fame, the rules didn't apply to you. And the floodgates would open. Right: by mentioning floodgates, I have now incorporated the Air Force, Army and Navy into my mixed metaphor.

I had to act.

I sent him a text message.

In it, I invited him to explain the situation. There was no reply, so after waiting for his response for three hours I cancelled his show.

No choice. Let one through, you have to let them all through. One precedent is enough. He'd given his word and broken it, so how could we trust him with anything else?

I texted him with the cancellation. It was in fact the Venue Captain who had to see that he didn't perform that night, but there was no trouble. The Canons' Gait were onside with it.

I received no answer to my text messages, then or later. Well, what could he have said? I think the phrase 'bang to rights' covers it. He couldn't deny the facts; he couldn't deny knowledge of the rule.

But after the Fringe was over, I received a letter in which he claimed £23000 compensation for loss of earnings.

Anybody who can earn £23000 from a single show at the Fringe in a 70-seater has my undying respect. It would mean completely full houses at every performance, and everybody putting an average of £14.20 in the bucket. Actually, more, for he had already done two weeks and therefore not lost that income. So to earn £23000 in the last week the average bucket contribution would have had to be £46.90. I wish I had an audience that generous.

Of course, that's just speculation. We owed him nothing. Had he not himself breached the conditions to which he had agreed, he could have finished his run.

Nevertheless, letters couched in legal phraseology are always a worry.

And it highlighted a problem of which I was not aware. We'd always said that our agreements were binding in honour only, as they used to say about the Football Pools. And, I thought, this was incontrovertible. There cannot be a contract. For a contract to exist, valid consideration must pass on both sides. We have to give them something of value (which we do); they have to give us something of value (which they don't; we don't charge them anything). There can be no contract in Law. No contract; nothing they can take legal action to enforce.

Or so I thought. This is the Law in all legal systems that are derived from English Law: US Law, Australian Law, much of Africa and so on. Anywhere where judges at one time wore wigs, even if they don't nowadays.

Except Scotland.

I should have known. Scots Law fiercely maintains its differences from English Law. In Scots Law, there can in some circumstances exist a unilateral contract with consideration on only one side. In certain circumstances, if I promise to give you money and don't deliver, I can be sued, even though you give me nothing in return for that money. I'll leave lawyers to go in to what those circumstances are.

So, in English Law, there was no contract between us and the performer. But in Scots Law, there might have been. It would take a massively expensive test case to find out.

However, even if there was a contract, the performer was clearly in breach of the terms of it.

It didn't, of course, come to that. I think somebody must have been advising him to try it on.

Our Free Fringers are a very disparate bunch. We have had everything from Peers of the Realm to ex-convicts and the homeless; every and no faith (as long as they don't prosyletise); all ages, races, sexual orientations and every other way in which people can differ. And all manner of former jobs and day jobs. Including lawyers.

I wrote a long and elaborate letter back to the performer explaining point by point why he had no case. Then I sent it to our lawyer-performer for comment. He told me to tear it up and write the shortest possible reply, just effectively saying 'no'. So I did. Trust the professionals.

That was the end of that issue. I worried unnecessarily about the Law. I should have worried about my own reputation. For the performer clearly still felt he'd been hard done by, and perhaps was not averse to telling other people how he felt. A few confronted me about it; I imagine others just filed me away as somebody not to deal with.

On top of the Cowgatehead troubles, I didn't need this.

What else went wrong in 2015? We lost a venue shortly before the Fringe. The way this usually happens is: the business owners, who lease the premises, decide they aren't being profitable and decide to shut up shop, or perhaps their creditors do that for them, I don't know. Just one day, they cease to open. And of course they don't tell us. Or any other future events they have in their diaries.

So unless somebody notices that a venue isn't open that should be open, and tells us, we simply don't know. In this instance, we don't know when they actually closed, but we found out very close to the Fringe.

I will say this: our track record in finding replacements when this horrible thing happens is excellent. In this case, we got a seventh stage in Cowgatehead partitioned off and moved the shows there. Oh, it was inconvenient, certainly; the shows had had their material printed and some were listed in the Big Fat Fringe Programme. But their new stage was more central and didn't let in water until 8 pm or thereabouts.

Lost another stage as well; the management of the Liquid Rooms were going to get a Portakabin-style space as a third stage. But something went wrong there, and behold: more displaced shows. However, the Liquid Rooms are professionals, and they didn't leave us hanging; instead, they converted their main music space into a venue for us, and the shows went ahead except on six nights when they had music gigs booked. Unfortunately three of those fell in the same week, particularly affecting our last show of the day, who was only doing a one-week run. He wasn't happy, and I can understand that. And then they wanted a fourth night, and he was even less happy, and I had to go in to bat for him. Hard to negotiate when one is holding no cards, but somehow I managed to salvage his show for that night, which few people attended. But it's the principle; one sticks up for the team. Unless they break rule one, as I agonisingly described above.

We brought mostly huge crowds to the Liquid Rooms, and happy to do so.

Cowgatehead was an exceptional set of problems, and not of our making. Loss of venues just before the Fringe had become, alas, routine. And it can always happen, especially in a bad economic climate.

Sneaky Pete's was a new venue for 2015. And a good one we were glad to welcome. We'd asked maybe ten years before, and received the reply that they only did rock'n'roll. Of which we approve. So we didn't ask again, until in 2015 they asked us. And we were very happy, and there was still rock'n'roll in the evening after we'd finished.

We had one nominee for Best Newcomer that year and one for the main Perrier prize, but alas neither won. There were other awards that I probably don't even know about. We'd come a long way from when we got our first Best Newcomer nomination and I rejoiced exceedingly; now it was almost routine to have one or two. No longer the cheapo cheapo cut-price almost-Fringe, the Fringe of the Fringe; we were, and are, right up there.

People asked me: did I not feel proud, looking at the size of the Free Fringe's achievement? And I made tactful answers, as far as I could, for I am very bad at tact and small talk. If somebody asks me how I am, I speak of my health at great length, which is not really the point of the question, although that's what it means.

I probably have a disease of some sort. Apart from the Tourette's, which is not what you think it is, unless you really know what it is, in which case, it is what you think it is.

When I was eight and in a class of over 50 children, as was usual in those days, the teacher taught the class the word 'eccentric'. And every head in the room looked at me. Why? I still don't know.

I have been called eccentric a lot since. I have challenged people as to why they described me thus. Nobody's given a satisfactory answer. Some have said "come on, you must know". No, I don't. It's annoying. Everybody can see it but me. It's like the card game where you hold a card up to your forehead and bet against others on your card's value, which everybody can see but you.

So, I'm bad at tact and diplomacy. And when people say I should be proud of what's gone right, I can only think of, and talk about, what's gone wrong.

So many of the team having a good time. So many not making the huge financial loss that was the norm before I started the Free Fringe. So many performers helping each other, rather than competing with each other. Friendships made, performing partnerships initiated, likewise writing partnerships. The Fringe made much more open to the citizens of Edinburgh, and good-value shows bridging the gulf between August visitors and the We-Live-Heres.

Much to be proud of. Was I proud? No. The vile unjustified things I was called over the Cowgatehead incident rang in my ears, and they still do.

If you ain't got self-esteem, you ain't got it. I went on a Positive Thinking course once. Failed it. Well, I knew I was going to.

September to December, if not an actual holiday, was usually a time of relative rest for me before the busy period when offers go out, in January. But for two years running this period had been interrupted by stress-crises.

I tried taking a real going-away holiday once, in 1995. It didn't work. The problems just come with you, and your familiar support-things aren't there. I never saw the point. Perhaps with a partner it might work, but never alone. No, performing is the only thing that relaxes me.

And I was spending so much time organising that I wasn't performing, or asking for gigs, for fear that the Cowgatehead accusations might stop promoters booking me.

I'd gone from a performer trying to do things for other performers, to a man who has to tell people what they don't want to hear. To a promoter malgré soi.

But the edifice I'd built, with help from others who may now feel unacknowledged but shouldn't, still stood. Not like a rock, but like a fairly firm but unduly large blancmange.

A big blancmange. In 2015 we scheduled 9268 total performances of 529 shows, a 15.8% growth on August 2014. That's huge. I cringe at things that go wrong, and blame myself as often as not, but at that size it's impossible for everything to go right. People were still saying "big four" to refer to Pleasance, Gilded Balloon, Underbelly and Assembly, but in 2015 we were bigger than any three of those put together. Although they say size doesn't matter. Missus.

If the Edinburgh Fringe is the biggest arts festival in the world, I think that year the Free Fringe was the second biggest.

I'm glad we've kept the personal touch that used to characterise the whole Fringe. Performers and audience mingle freely; nobody's aloof. We're big, but go to our venues and we look small. And decently humble; it's hard to be a prima donna holding a bucket. I think audiences appreciate that.

And with that bucket of mixed emotions, dominated by exhaustion and disillusionment, I entered the season of ...

*

2016

In which our hero attempteth to retire gracefully

EMAIL WAS INDISPENSABLE TO THE FREE FRINGE. I learned early that unless there was a written record of everything, misunderstandings would happen in April that wouldn't be noticed until August, and that would lead to problems. Like the show who insisted his slot was 75 minutes earlier than it actually was and had printed leaflets to that effect. This only happened once, but that was once too many.

So, by December 2015 the culture was firmly established. Everything confirmed by email. Which relied on me having a working email system and responding to everything promptly.

And that was fine, until I started flooding the Internet with porn.

Well, obviously I didn't. It wasn't me. But it was somebody. I woke up one morning to find my inbox overflowing with "no such user at this address" bounce emails. All directed to my personal email address; each with a different female name as the sender, each promising untold erotic delights. Thousands of them. I watched them come in; at least six a minute, often more. And these were just the ones that were bouncing back. How many had got through? How many had been sent? Who was sending them and how could I stop it?

It was difficult, almost impossible, to pick out my genuine emails from this forest of soft core. At least, I hoped it was soft core. I didn't investigate. I was curious, but I didn't want to give them the satisfaction, whoever they were.

This went on for a whole week. Every four or five emails, they'd change the name of the fictitious female sender, and the wording of the email. But it was always 'from' pbh@buckers.co.uk. In front of that address, I was Kristy Alvarez, Eloise Kim, Genevieve Graham, Desiree Hammond, Charlene Rice, Ann Murray, Nora Warren, Estelle Morgan, Paulette Palmer, Heidi Greer, Beulah Martin, and many many more. All wanting people to be their f#ckbuddy: their hash mark, not mine.

Jasmine Zimmerman. I was also Jasmine Zimmermen. She sounded lovely, like Bob Dylan's hippy daughter. I nearly fell in love with her until I realised she was me.

212 different names in the first four hours alone, and after that I gave up recording.

A few recipients emailed back indignantly: would I kindly stop sending them this vile stuff? Oh, if I had sent it, I would certainly kindly have stopped. It was strangling my ability to deal with the Free Fringe, and I could do nothing about it.

It stopped by itself after a week. But what a week it was. Still, I suppose it got me in touch with my feminine side, even if some of my feminine side was called Gertrude Briggs. And it would be just my luck if a real Gertrude Briggs sees this book and takes umbrage. Sorry, Gertrude, or Professor Briggs if you prefer.

My abiding memory of the 2016 season is the opening meeting for performers that we always have on the Friday evening, after everybody's helped rig their venues. Or didn't I mention that? That's the deal. We start on Saturday, and on Friday all shows (well, those performing on Saturday) go round to their venues and help rig them.

In some places, the management do all the work, where stages are already in place, like the Voodoo Rooms and Liquid Rooms and Bannerman's. (Does Bannerman's have an apostrophe? Oh well, it does now). Other places, especially the pop-ups, we have to rig the PA, put out the chairs, hang the backdrops, make sure we know where the fire extinguishers are, and so forth.

So after that's happened we assemble for a meeting, and pre-Fringe drinks, and the team get to know each other. And I chair that meeting.

There were, in 2016, a large number of performers present. And management hadn't put out the chairs yet, so it was mostly a standing meeting. So I took the mic, and theatrically declaimed: Welcome. Welcome to the Free Fringe 2006.

Only ten years out. Senility had crept up without my even noticing. And that rather set the tone for me, that Fringe.

I got a bit of it back when a loud emergency vehicle went past during my talk, and out came the standard emergency-vehicle - going- past-with-siren line from my standup set: "quick, it's the fuzz, flush the stash, man". Which almost none of them had heard, and it got a better laugh than it does at comedy clubs.

But those two incidents made me think: this isn't my generation any more.

I'd better fast-forward back (what? Another out-of-date reference. Ask your grandparents what a cassette was) to the beginning of the season, so September 2015. I almost wrote 2005 there.

For the first time in three years, I didn't have a crisis to deal with in September. I could rest. But I didn't. Like many other people, I listened to the negatives that surrounded me, not the positives. I didn't dare ask for gigs, lest I got the reply: oh, you shafted Freestival and then maliciously sacked an act mid-run. And this is one way of looking at it. Not the right way, obviously. We'd done our best; I'd done my best. But I felt alienated from the Comedy community and from other performing communities. Oh, if only one or more loyal Free Fringers had contacted me and said: we run a club, come and play for us. But they didn't.

So much, I thought, for community building.

Maybe I was like Name Redacted. Everybody loved Name Redacted. He ran a comedy club everybody loved to play. And was — how do I say this with love — a terrible comedian. And wasn't aware of that. I suppose he surfed on the support he was given. So maybe I was like him; all the laughter I'd got, the five-star reviews, the standing ovations, the individual gags getting rounds of applause: maybe all of this was for the Free Fringe, not my material and delivery.

When you're a comedian, you think like that. Twenty, twenty-five, thirty years ago, who knows how long, I was on a bill with Al Murray as The Pub Landlord. He was headlining, of course. So I'd done my set, and we were in the dressing room talking about something really quite profound and philosophical, I forget what, and the compère announced him, and in an instant he became the Pub Landlord and bounced on stage and stormed it. And when he came back, his first words were: bloke third in from the left on the fourth row didn't smile once. The fact that he'd blown the roof off the gig and everybody else had convulsed with laughter didn't, somehow, count.

So maybe my fundamental premise was wrong. Maybe performers couldn't organise themselves. Maybe we lack the detachment to do it.

And maybe, since I had by accident become a promoter of something huge, everybody thought I wasn't a comedian any more.

Well, maybe I wasn't. I certainly didn't get many gigs. Not even Robin Ince's Christmas shows, which I always loved doing. Did Robin, of all people, believe the mud that had been slung? He had, during Cowgatehead, emailed pleading that I should leave all the shows misbooked by Freestival in their slots, and I had to explain why that was not possible.

What had I become? A service-provider for acts, a figure they would otherwise have paid, but who was stupid enough to do the work and absorb the stress for no pay whatsoever?

And locked into it. Nothing to do but soldier on.

I feared, though, for my Artistic Directors, and still do. For they also had to work hard, and they also had to deal with prima donnas and awkward sods for no reward. How long would they stay in post? Oh yes, they believed in the Free Fringe, but clearly there are limits.

Something had to change, and I didn't quite know what. Or I did, but tried not to admit it to myself. So much mud had been flung; I had to make sure it stuck to me and only me, so that the Free Fringe itself remained unsullied and could carry on.

But we needed people who are as good at organising as I. And the secret to being good at organising is: you have to care passionately about what you're organising. You have to know about every aspect. You have to be motivated by something other than money. If you sell yourself to the highest bidder, you're not a true manager, no matter what your title is.

And if you don't listen to everybody in your organisation, you're a bad manager. They know more than you about the day-to-day interactions with the public.

You can't solve problems by devising systems from the top down and applying them rigidly. If you have to have systems — and at a certain size all organisations do — then they must stem from the actual needs of the people doing the work.

I needed to hand over, gradually, to a team who appreciated that.

But meanwhile I had to soldier on. Make sure Free Fringe 2016 was positive and good for performers and public. And if unpopular things had to be done, the responsibility had to be on me, and publicly on me.

My tables: meet it is I set it down

That one may smile and smile and be a villain.

Back in 1995 I remember I was down for a stint of compering at the Acoustic Music Centre's open cabaret, and I was testing the PA before the show started, and I broke into the opening speech of Richard III (Now is the winter of our discontent etc), and did the whole speech, hamming it up shamelessly, just for my own satisfaction. The early-arrivers gave me applause I hadn't expected. So maybe my vocation in life is indeed villain.

The first thing I had to deal with was the loss of my headquarters. The Canons' Gait wanted no shows. The owner called me in and told me that. We weren't making enough money for him. As before, he was counting only the downstairs till, and assuming the upstairs till takings were from pub visitors who weren't there for the shows. Which was rubbish. Everybody, almost, bought their drinks upstairs and took them down into the shows.

It was shaking; if we weren't bringing profit to the Canons' Gait, where we used to put the best acts and me, where were we bringing profit? And yet I knew we were. The staff told me so. It was just a question of knowing how showgoers actually behaved, and since the owner didn't visit during the shows, he could not know that. A man who had, in 2015, told us where we had to put the stage and that we had to have table service. After all the years we'd worked together, I thought he would have realised that we know something about running shows.

But fine. I was not going to grovel. I love the Canons' Gait, but all things must pass. We had many other good venues.

For the past ten years, I had effectively run the Free Fringe from a table in the Canons' Gait, facing the entrance so everybody could see me. When I wasn't on patrol around our other venues, or doing guest spots, people knew where to find me. Well, I'd have to be a nomad in future.

Later on in the cycle, they came back, saying we could have shows from 9pm. Well, we gave them some, including the midnight variable-bill show hosted by Kate Smurthwaite, and that was popular as always. But I wasn't going to bring Peter Buckley Hill and Some Comedians back, not unless the stage was back where it ought to be. It makes a gig twice as difficult if you're constantly turning from side to side to address the other half of the audience.

As usual, the Fringe Office excelled itself in negative customer service.

Charlie Bruce had acquired the use of a good venue opposite the old Holyrood Tavern. It would have made a good space for Comedy or Spoken Word, but Charlie wanted no access control. Fine; the only thing we can programme it with that doesn't need access control is Music. Agreed; we'll book music. Hands were shaken. Can we get it in the Big Fat Fringe Programme and therefore on the map?

By that time there were 24 hours to go before the BFFP deadline. Yes, I said, by registering a single show, it would be listed and therefore on the map.

I paid money to register a nominal show. I put in a portmanteau blurb saying there would be music.

They rejected the 'show'. You can't have a single show listing suggesting there will be more shows, they said. Otherwise everybody would do it.

Everybody's not doing it, I said. I am.

Well, you can't, they said. So, back came my money and the venue wasn't on the map.

I did argue that one, quite strongly, because I didn't want to let Charlie down. My money, my blurb: what right did they have to censor? It wasn't offensive to the public in any way. I asked them to list the show with the blurb "this blurb has been censored by the Fringe Office", but they wouldn't do that either.

This was also the year they made Charlie Bruce show them a signed agreement that he had the lease of Cowgatehead from the owner, Riccardo Marino. Mr Marino is over 80. He and KW for many years had done business, as is customary, on a handshake. But no; that wouldn't satisfy the Fringe Office. A written agreement had to be drawn up and produced. I believe a solicitor was paid to do it.

And to think the Fringe Office was formed to facilitate shows at the Fringe. That particular apple has fallen a long way from its tree.

We ended up with 767 applications, and there would have been many more if we hadn't closed applications for eight weeks between mid-March and early May. We didn't have enough venues by then; it seemed foolish to keep adding to the waiting list. We never have enough venues in March; if we did, we could become much bigger. And need a much bigger central team to look after all the shows and venues.

It's good to expand, but every performer new to the Free Fringe is a risk. Oh yes, they agree to the Ethos and Conditions, but do they mean it? Can we rely on them to come?

The one I remember not coming in 2016 was an American. OK, it's a big journey, and you're bound to make a loss at the Fringe when you factor in your travel costs and the fact you don't know where to go to find less-expensive accommodation. If we had more people on the team, we could help more. On the other hand, we never set out to be a nanny state. To be a successful Free Fringer you have to be a little bit self-sufficient. It's a delicate balance.

Anyway, I was already in Edinburgh when the news came through that this American wasn't coming and thus there was a gap to plug at a venue I wanted to keep.

I put out a call among our existing members, and Brendon Burns produced from his hat a fellow-Australian, who was along for the ride and to pick up spots. Did he have enough for a show? Well, said Brendon, what he has is good, and if it's not 50 minutes he can take on a guest spot every day. And I, Perrier-winner, will be the first guest spot and do several more.

That seemed good enough, so the deal was done. There's always some last-minute work, and that was 2016's. And it worked. Emergency posters, emergency fliers and they got people in. Always a difficult gig, when the first thing you say to an audience has to be: this is not the show in the programme and is in fact nothing like it whatsoever. For the American show was about the impending Trump versus Clinton election, in which people were interested.

The replacement comedian, Craig Quartermaine, was not only Australian, but much more Australian than most Australians, by which I mean he was, and is, an Aboriginal. So, interesting to Brits like me who'd never met any Aboriginals, and with a story to tell. But a different story to what anybody wanted to hear who'd come to hear about Trump and Clinton. Would it be funny if we merged the names and called them Trumpton? No. Cuthbert, Dibble and Grubb, possibly. I was at school with a Dibble and at University with a Cuthbert, but I've never met a Grubb. I can't die until I do. Unless Death himself is called Grubb. Enough of that. Terry Pratchett writes much better Death than I do.

We got an excellent new venue in the New Town, the Bourbon Bar, but it was being built when I saw it, and in the first week only one of the two spaces was ready. But the spirit was alive among the shows in the venue, and half of them did shows in the bar until the space was sorted out. I was under some pressure on that, but I couldn't make the building works happen any quicker. Everybody wanted them to; owners, managers, shows and the public. They were finished eventually and things ran as they should have.

Free Fringers have to accept that things like this do go wrong sometimes. You can't have a Fringe without threads hanging down from the fabric. It doesn't make me feel better when it happens, though. And because I can do nothing, people sometimes think I'm indifferent. The opposite of the truth; I seethe with impotent fury, but can blame nobody.

And this one: opposite the Bourbon Bar, there was Chiquito. Now, we'd used that for several years; downstairs, there was a room used for staff meetings and training, which didn't happen in August. Perfect for us, therefore, and I think they sold quite a few meals to people before and after our shows. They're part of a chain. And less than a month before the Fringe, the Frederick Street branch (ours) closed with 24 hours notice.

Why? Nobody knew. It wasn't that the chain went out of business. And it wasn't because of us; we only did shows in August. There it was, suddenly shut. And it remained shut all August, as if to mock us; we could have used our friends to put in a temporary bar and carried on. But no.

So, yet another emergency redeployment was needed, and this one came very close to the wire. Where else was there? Well, there wasn't, really. We'd played all the cards in our hand. In what universe are we going to keep a venue in reserve, unused, bringing no revenue to its owner, in case something like this happens? And yet it happened in most years.

One show in Chiquito had already been moved from Cowgatehead, when they told us "no shows on the first floor after 9pm". Oh, I haven't mentioned that yet? Yes, that happened. We were glad enough to have Cowgatehead, and to have it without problems or Freestival booking it without permission. If a licensee wants to do something, we don't have too much clout to argue, and in this case he wanted loud music in the ground floor bar after 9pm. So, no shows immediately above. They wouldn't be viable with the sound leakage. So, we moved all affected shows. That was earlier. And one went to Chiquito, and had to be moved yet again.

Now, there used to be a shop opposite the World's End. Which makes it sound like the Shop at the End of the Universe, a tribute to Douglas Adams. But the World's End is a pub, which I often drank in, since they always had Orkney Dark Island on draught, or most of the time. Graham (or is it Graeme; I never discovered which) always gave me the glad hello when I passed and told me news of obscure Scottish politics. And one night I was sitting in the World's End, alone, thinking and enjoying my Dark Island, when he walzed in and handed me a miniature of fine whisky from his shop, as a gift. And left. The staff asked me: did I want a glass for that? I came over all English. I said: I can't possibly sit in your pub and drink whisky that wasn't bought from you; that's not right. And to prove it, I ordered a different whisky from them. And had Graham's later, in the privacy of my own temporary home.

I don't know what the moral of that story is. But anyway, Graham had closed his shop. And opened, although I did not know it, an institution called the Natural Food Kafe (sic) on Clerk Street. Slightly out of the usual Fringe area. And he had a basement. Frank discovered this; I'd have had no idea.

The basement was small. But the Kafe was welcoming, and anyway we had no choice. I put it to the displaced shows. There was grumbling, as if I had personally shut Chiquito out of malice. But most of them took the move. Would it work, with no Big Fat Fringe Programme listing? We got it in the Wee Blue Book, and I congratulated myself once again for the policy of printing the WBB at the very last moment so things like this could be accounted for.

It worked. I had feared it wouldn't, but it did. So much so that some acts requested to return in 2017, even though they could have asked for a more mainstream venue. What made it work? It was interesting, homely and slightly eccentric. Whatever that means.

So, when I say it was a relatively quiet lead-up to the Fringe itself, I mean that chaos and panic like the above was becoming routine. Which is not good.

When I first devised the Free Fringe concept, people drank more. Our deal was more profitable to Edinburgh's bars than it subsequently became. And the economy was more buoyant. The crash of 2008 had not happened. The less money the public have to spend, the greater the danger to our model. And hotels were getting more numerous in Edinburgh, but no cheaper; visitors spent less.

Perhaps, when I got the year wrong in my opening speech, it was a Freudian wish to be back in those earlier years. And who doesn't want to be ten years younger, anyway?

One can never tell where the next bucket of mud is going to be flung from.

I got a message from a comedy publication: would I care to explain my homophobic behaviour? Well, indeed, I'd be happy to, if I had any such behaviour, but as far as I'm aware I didn't and don't.

It turned out that, in one of our venues which during the year is very gay-friendly, a gay act with another promoter put up a poster for his show. He did not ask permission to do so; he just did. The staff asked him to take it down, on the grounds that it wasn't a show in their venue. This is a rule many venues have. The performer concerned didn't contact me: he went straight to the media and accused me publicly of stifling publicity for his show in a venue where his target audience was likely to congregate. In this gay bar, he reasoned, all posters from gay acts should be welcome, and I was therefore showing anti-gay prejudice.

I had no idea this was happening, and I had done nothing. Policies on what posters are acceptable are made by our venues, not us. Fortunately the owner of the bar, on being made aware, wrote a very strong email to the act concerned. I simply copied that to the comedy publication, and received a rather grudging email back which almost said "we'll let you off this time".

Mud, mud, glorious mud.

And the charity awards show. One of our shows was invited to do an unpaid set in that show. They didn't want to. And why should they, if they didn't want? But no, because the show was held in a Laughing Horse venue, the organiser believed that I had prevented the act from performing. I hadn't. Our conditions do prohibit shows having other shows with other free-admission promoters, but one-off guest spots are specifically allowed. It's one of the joys of the Fringe, to play in as many places as you can. We wouldn't take that joy away. It was the act's decision that they did not want to play that gig.

And in the vitriol that was again thrown publicly in my direction, the allegedly- homophobic poster incident was brought up again.

Mud pies, mud baths, muddy waters but not Muddy Waters. (I saw his son play at a festival that year: Mud Morganfield. He's good.)

I was never a friend of the organiser of that charity show, or of the awards he had devised and named after a dead comedian. I have been nominated for two, and the second time I told him I did not wish to be considered. The same man has blogged against me and the Free Fringe on several occasions. Probably a lot more than I know about, since I don't read his blogs. I have better things to do, and if I hadn't, I'd find some. Nasty piece of work, in my opinion.

My job seemed to be increasingly to be a focus for others' hatred.

I did make two, or one-point-five, bad personal decisions in 2016.

It was our second year working with La Belle Angele. A venue with a long history, which had been gutted in the Great Gilded Balloon Fire of 2002. Most affected buildings didn't re-open and eventually became something else, but La Belle Angele held on and, thirteen years later, re-opened. And we were offered it, and took it. A large space by Fringe standards, so we'd need good-pulling acts to make good use of it. And we did that in 2015, and again in 2016, until they asked us: can you put on a show after 10pm Sundays to Thursdays?

We should have said no. Because the sort of act that can bring in 200 people at the Fringe is the sort of act that has a right to demand Fridays and Saturdays, the busiest and best nights.

But I'm always reluctant to say 'no' when it's a venue we want to keep. And we did want to keep it.

There was only one act foolish enough to attempt a show in La Belle Angele on relatively unpopular nights. Me.

In 1999, I had audiences of 140 and sometimes more coming to see Peter Buckley Hill and Some Comedians. At the smaller Canons' Gait, it was normally a full house. I didn't do it in 2015. Surely, thought my ego, I can bring these numbers back? The pause in 2015 will only have increased people's appetites?

All my years of Fringe experience, everything I've told other acts, should have told me otherwise. I tell them: don't listen to your ego. But, through fatigue and senility, I started listening to mine.

I can take these adverse conditions and pull it off, I thought.

I have a reputation that will work for me.

But it wasn't 1999; it was 2016. In 1999 I was one of the only three free shows in town, barring BBC and churches. Now there were many hundreds, and I had caused that.

I got very low numbers, and that was difficult to work with. Fortunately every other show in the venue packed 'em in, so the venue was still pleased.

The other reason I got low numbers was: I wasn't leafleting much. And at the Fringe, you have to leaflet a lot. You have to be visible.

I don't hold with paying people to leaflet. A lot of performers do precisely that. And some have whole armies of leafleters. I hate that, especially within the Free Fringe. We save people money; if they spend that money on extra promotion, then everybody else has to spend money on extra promotion as well, and nobody benefits. It's an arms race. I have probably said that before.

And for the first time ever, I had to cancel one Fringe performance, because I felt too ill to do it.

And the other thing was; my guest comedians have usually been well-known and first-class. But after the first couple of shows I felt I could not approach such acts, because I couldn't provide them a full audience and a good atmosphere. However, some excellent but less well-known Free Fringers stepped in and performed, so the shows themselves were good. But a satisfactory show has a full crowd, and we never had that.

Misjudged. Very low buckets. I was making a big financial loss on the Fringe, which I hadn't for some time. I suppose it reminded me of how difficult the Fringe is; in the Canons' Gait years, I had my regular audience and was comfortable. And now I wasn't.

Things were going wrong for me personally. Yes, I was spending most of the time troubleshooting for other people, as I always do, but in 2016 it seemed much more of a burden. I could barely climb the two flights of stairs to my flat, and more than once I had to terminate a meeting so I could lie down.

I hadn't the stamina to promote either of my shows. I was quite proud of the one-man show, which was only on for the last week; it was an hour done entirely in haikus. The first performance, one person turned up; Kate Copstick, the formidable critic for The Scotsman, who nevertheless generally likes my stuff. She loved the haikus. And gave it a wonderful writeup in Scotland on Sunday, which came out on the last day of the Fringe. I expected that to bring in a decent audience for the last day, at least. But it didn't. The paper printed no details of where and when it was on, and because it was a diary piece there were no review stars attached. So fulsome was the praise that I'm confident there would have been five, but there were none.

So, the one-man show also played to very small audiences, never more than ten. Like the other show, it reminded me of the Fringe heartbreak that prosperity and success had made me forget.

I couldn't go on like this. Losing money and getting little satisfaction from it. It was back to 1994, but at least in 1994 I got an encore in the Bear Pit. No Bear Pits in 2016, no bears, no encore.

I made a decision.

I'd spent the last three or four years trying to pass the management of the Free Fringe to the next generation. Make the problems visible to the core team; give them an idea of all the decisions that had to be made. But I knew, while I was there, the problems would eventually revert to me. I couldn't stop them coming; I couldn't stop myself intervening. It was my organisation, after all. I'd chosen to act like a CEO, albeit without pay; I was having to bear the consequent stress.

I had to be not-in-Edinburgh in 2017. At all.

I had to throw the team to the wolves at the deep end, to be devoured by the mixed metaphor monster.

I spent much more time in 'my' flat that year, not having the comfort of the Canons' Gait base, and wanting to lie down more than usual. I'd have a couple of pints in Stramash at midnight after my show, and then go home, shunning the bars where performers congregate and look for sympathy about their shows. Old age, as I thought, was striking.

So it was in that flat that I emailed all the Free Fringe shows.

(1). I intend not to attend Fringe 2017, either as organiser or performer.

(2). To achieve this, there must be new arrangements for the management of the Free Fringe.

(3). Everything below is based on The Free Fringe Ltd being solvent at the end of Fringe 2016. If, however, the costs of 2016 are not covered, then The Free Fringe Ltd will be formally insolvent and must by law cease to trade. That means the end of the Free Fringe.

(4). Assuming (3) above does not apply, arrangements for an orderly handover need to be made.

(5). We will start by having post-Fringe meetings/reunions in London and Edinburgh in September. These should be informal, happy occasions.

(6). A new management structure should be in place by December.

(7). Because of the scattered nature of our members (slightly over 50% in London, the rest elsewhere) most of the interaction between the new team will be virtual.

(8). It is intended, as now, that all members of the core organising group (let's call it a Committee) should have active roles and clear responsibilities. Nobody should just be there to give the benefit of their wisdom. The right to input on policy correlates with the duty to implement that same policy and to take responsibility for it.

(9). I see the following basic jobs as needing a person each, but this list is not exhaustive and some roles may be combined, as they are now.

Chair

Captain of venue-finding and retention

Captain of the WBB

Recorder of applications and decisions (Data Processor)

Public relations person

Link-person to Fringe Board

Artistic Directors to cover the following genres, sometimes jointly:

- Comedy
- Spoken Word
- Theatre
- Cabaret
- Magic
- Children's
- Music
- Science, Rationalism and Miscellaneous
- Dance (if we ever have suitable venues).

The size of Comedy is so great that it needs at least one Assistant Artistic Director, possibly more.

(10). This structure should not undermine the basic principle of the Free Fringe, that everything is everybody's responsibility. It is not intended that this Committee shall do everything while every other performer does nothing.

(11). Clearly this structure depends on volunteers coming forward. But if volunteers do not come forward, then the Free Fringe is doomed anyway. The important thing about volunteers is: they should see the task through to the end, no matter what difficulties arise. In the past, I have been there to pick up any role that has been dropped. But now I shall not be there.

(12). If more than one person puts him/herself forward for any of these roles, there should be an election.

(13). We lack the formal infrastructure for a proper election. You'll have to trust me. The electorate should be all shows performing at Free Fringe 2016 (i.e. WBB shows), plus Music represented by its venue captains. Any show not finishing its run without good reason should not have a vote. I do not immediately see a reason why shows who were Free Fringe in 2015 and not in Edinburgh in 2016 should not also have a vote.

(14). Nothing in this process should hold up the opening of applications for 2017, which should open as usual on November 1st.

(15). Nothing in this process should hold up retaining and finding venues for 2017. This, as before, is everybody's responsibility. Maintaining good relations with your venue is vital for all performers, even if you would rather be in a different venue. Spotting new venue opportunities is also everybody's job.

(16). I shall take a prominent role in liaising with current and new venues and in all things that belong to my current role, until replaced by the new structure. Where venues insist on negotiating with me and nobody else, I shall happily do that. Until replaced, I shall process the data using the current system. There will be a smooth takeover. It is important that venues and other bodies see this as a natural continuation of the work we have successfully done over the years.

Right. The decision was made. The die had been cast. The thousand ships had been launched by a single face. The Rubicon had been crossed. The Sudetenland had been annexed. The big red button saying "do not push this button" had been pushed.

And in the midst of the Fringe. Which gave everybody time to think about the situation and what they could do.

And in a year I could retire and breed worms and resentment.

I did get a few kind emails in reply, saying thank you for starting the Free Fringe. Which was nice. But when you're despondent, you're despondent.

Even when one of our shows won the Perrier main prize, for the second time in three years, and another was nominated. I was delighted for both, obviously. Richard Gadd, the winner, thoroughly deserved it, but so did Kieran Hodgson, our other nominee. Oh, I rejoice when our guys (and gals, of course) win, but anybody who gets nominated, whatever organisation they're with, is good and deserves praise.

It was a good note to go out on. And as I trucked folding chairs from one venue to storage, I saw how little strength I had left. Fortunately one act got the 'help needed quickly' message, and insisted I sit down while he did the lifting. The right spirit, although I felt very old.

Well, at least I had achieved something I never expected, ever: I got my picture in the Morning Star. And they got my name wrong: PHB's Free Fringe, they printed. It accompanied a flattering article by Attila the Stockbroker, who stopped doing the Fringe in the 1990s because it had become too corporate, and came back to join us in 2016, and was impressed by the spirit. We were still doing a lot of things right.

No restful September for me: I had to get the grand succession plan rolling in time for...

*

2017

In which our hero retireth in a way he did not expect, and turneth into a diarist

I ARRANGED THE MEETINGS WITH PERFORMERS to discuss the New Order. It doesn't really deserve capitals. One in Edinburgh on a Wednesday in mid-September, and one in London on the following Sunday.

I took the overnight sleeper to Edinburgh, to save hotel costs, discovered that the much-vaunted-in-the-brochure shower in the First Class Lounge in Edinburgh Waverley didn't exist, had never existed and was not going to exist. Which rather scuppered the plans. Never mind. A hard day's work with Frank, seeing venues, doing post-mortems and generally trying to set up 2017's venue offering as best we could. And then on to the meeting.

Decent attendance; lots of Edinburgh-based Free Fringers, good discussion, a number of tentative volunteers. And the question: did the idea of elections mean that existing Artistic Directors might not keep their jobs? Well, yes, in theory. But they'd have a big advantage, and I'd rather have collaboration than competition. Elections, however, showed that the people have the final say.

Good meeting. Another day's work on the Thursday, then back on the last train, and ready for the Sunday meeting with the London team, which should be a much bigger meeting.

Ha. Ha ha. Ha ha ha. Somehow I must have defied the gods. And they don't like it.

I didn't feel too well on the Friday evening. Never mind. Lie down. Take an indigestion tablet. It will pass. It has before.

It didn't. And then came the vomiting, and other disgusting bodily emissions. And the pain got worse, and I couldn't move even to vomit in a more tidy manner. By that time there was nothing more to bring up, but still I heaved.

I couldn't move.

The pain was worse than being booed off at the Bear Pit. Actually, at the Bear Pit, they used to boo you on as well as off. Anyway, not that sort of pain.

The gods had omitted to disconnect my bedside phone. I called my GP, expecting a referral service. It was by then 5am on Saturday. I left a message. Half an hour later, my GP himself rang back. Which was pretty amazing. He's a great GP.

Could he come round? No; he wasn't in London. And anyway, from everything I had told him, he concluded I needed to be in a hospital, quickly.

I can't move, I said. I can't get to the bus stop, let alone to the hospital.

I'll send an ambulance, he said.

And half an hour later an ambulance arrived. I didn't buzz them in, but they managed to get in anyway. There must be a secret ambulance word at which doors open.

I didn't think that at the time. I didn't think anything at the time except ouch. I couldn't speak for the pain. Took me several attempts to give the ambulance people my name.

Now, it's a straight run from where I live to University College Hospital. It's actually the same road, plus or minus the Camden Town one-way system. And ambulances call at hospitals all the time. You wouldn't think they could get lost. But this one did. Away I sped with blue lights flashing, in the wrong direction. A three-point turn almost at the doors of a different hospital, then down to King's Cross and eventually the Euston Road to UCH. By which time I was in a pretty bad way.

Things were somewhat of a blur after that. Needles were shoved in, drips attached, canulas and catheters and numerous other things that I know no names for, and doctors, prodded, poked, asked, measured, and sent me for scans, all in a blur. And they eventually wheeled me to a room, by myself, which was at least a substantial advantage.

Earlier that year I had abandoned my trusty Blackberry, which I loved, for an Android smartphone, which I hated and still can't work. But I'm glad I did. And glorious praise to the nurse who, from somewhere, found me a charger. Using these things I was at least able to send a message on Facebook that something untoward had happened.

Of course, not everybody got it. In the midst of Sunday's pain I got an indignant email. Why wasn't I at the meeting I myself had called? The sender had taken some trouble to get there, and my absence was most discourteous.

I don't know if the meeting went ahead as an informal gathering, or how many people were there. I hope not many; I hope the general facebook call I'd managed to put out had reached most people. I don't know. For the first time, I could look at something connected to the Free Fringe and say "that's not important".

Although what I really said was 'ouch'.

Yes, I know, childbirth, supposed to be the worst, and men can never experience or know, etc. etc. But if childbirth were as painful as severe acute pancreatitis, we'd die out within a generation.

I had offended a lot of mortals, although not half as many as had taken offence without cause. But I wasn't aware of having offended the gods. Not even Bacchus, by not having a final pint at the end of the Edinburgh meeting.

I should have. For I have had, on the orders of many doctors, no pints since.

Right. This is not a medical history. You get the basic idea. I was very ill. So ill, I couldn't think. Or walk. Or eat. Or do much of anything. It actually changes your taste facilities; nothing tasted palatable, so I ate nothing. When people finally started visiting, I asked them to bring me all the dishes I most liked, so I could at least eat something that did not taste horrible. And they kindly did. And it still tasted horrible.

I was in for over a fortnight, that first time, and had operations. And they seemed to achieve something positive; at any rate, the doctors started saying "you're lucky to be alive" which sort of meant the immediate danger was past.

They eventually let me out. I got the bus home. I lasted three days and then the pain came back with renewed force and I started trembling uncontrollably, so another ambulance was sent for and the blue lights again flashed for me. This time it was worse. I was put in a ward. With people. In the room they had given me first time out, I was able to get some tranquillity alongside the pain. They lent me a digital radio. I could watch the clouds and listen to Classic FM (my brain wasn't up to Radio 3, and pancreatitis makes you fall out of love with rock'n'roll). But the ward, banged up with strangers conversing about their mothers in the Blitz, or similar, was not tranquil.

I must stop bitching. After another two weeks they let me out again. I barely made it to the bus stop; I nearly fainted waiting. I got home, and for the next six weeks I couldn't walk more than 50 paces without a rest, or stand up for more than about two minutes. Or do much of anything. What I dropped, stayed on the floor. I had no energy even to pick it up.

This is not the portrait of a man able to run a large festival. Or one who could preside over the succession plan he'd sent out to members in August.

I thought, not then but later: if the same fate had befallen the chairperson of Laughing Horse (and I most emphatically do not wish it on him, or anybody), could that organisation have survived?

Well, the Free Fringe did.

The team took up the challenge. The idea of elections was quietly dropped. The existing Artistic Directors knew their roles well. They could operate without me. Frank, Isla and the Edinburgh team also knew what to do. Things could carry on, and they did.

I realised, in the later years, my role had been fourfold:
- processing the data
- telling people things they didn't want to hear
- being chief target of any mud that was to be slung
- doing any jobs nobody else wanted to do.

I was largely a figurehead, apart from the role in data processing. And that was a biggie.

How can I find words to explain how mindboggly huge and complicated processing data for the Free Fringe can be? When I was doing it, it was a full time job.

Take over a thousand applicants. A spectrum of venues with over 50 stages. Each stage having a series of time slots, agreed at negotiation but capable of varying. A set of shows receiving offers of spaces who then renegotiate them, politely or with contempt. Offers sat on for ages until you time them out to give somebody else a go, and then a week later the original offeree comes back accepting a slot that's no longer available. New venues coming on board; old ones dropping out. Filling day-off gaps with other shows, so the venues don't object that they're paying staff while no shows are happening. Climaxing the whole process in the production of the Wee Blue Book, as late as possible. Collecting a picture from each show and a blurb of about 50 words.

Oh, the blurbs. Amazing how many shows don't know the meaning of the number 50 and send in over 100 words. Amazing how many don't know the difference between it's and its. Or who put line feeds in their blurbs. Or, well, you get the idea. Every one has to be edited.

I still haven't given you the idea. How could this process possibly take up most of the week, even if you're not making the deployment decisions yourself?

And the tiniest mistake can have horrible consequences. In our system, every show has a number. But get your number wrong when you're sending in your blurb and you overwrite somebody else's blurb. Confuse your show number with your venue number, likewise.

It's got to be as right as possible. The Big Fat Fringe Programme comes out in June and its print deadline is early April. A lot of things change between April and June, and more change between June and August. The Big Fat Fringe Programme is inaccurate as soon as published: it has to be, by the very nature of things. The Wee Blue Book is printed very late July and delivered the day before the Fringe starts.

Which means it's less inaccurate. But never 100% accurate; things change, even during the Fringe itself.

Once we had two completely different venues with similar names. The Voodoo Rooms (which we still have) and the Voodoo Bar (which no longer exists). They were at opposite ends of Princes Street. And on our venue map we gave one the address of the other. I kept quiet about that and nobody else said anything; the Voodoo Rooms still pulled big audiences anyway. Maybe they noticed and kept quiet also. I hope they didn't notice.

To process the data, you have to know the data. Catch obvious mistakes and mismatches before they get out to the performer. If you offer the wrong show a venue by mistake, you ought in most cases to honour that offer, but sometimes you can't. The venues have views, sometimes strong ones, on what sort of shows they want.

Yes, data processing was the crunch point. It was here that I thought I would be most missed.

You have to keep in touch with shows. They apply, and then there's often a long wait until a suitable venue comes up. You have to keep telling them collectively what's going on. Without giving them the impression that they can demand service or that they're not co-responsible for the Free Fringe.

Oh, and days off. There are more complications to do with days off than you can shake a stick at. If you ever shake sticks at complications, which myself I've never tried. Initially, you offer them a full run (or whatever length they asked for on application) with an email saying 'if you want a day off, ask for it'. Sometimes they do. Often they don't, and you have to check the proofs of the Big Fat Fringe Programme to see if they've put days off in that programme that they haven't told you about. There's a golden rule. No show gets the same day off as the one before or the one after, or else venues complain there's too much dark space and no revenue. Sometimes venues want to be completely dark on a certain day, in which case shows can't take any other days off. Shows contact you in June with tales of having to go to friends' weddings. And you scream. Days off are nightmares.

And the time you spend answering questions that are already in the bumf you have sent them. Grrrr.

The whole data process takes a lot of personal engagement. The most dreaded words in the English language are "oh, we forgot to tell you that...".

So, data processing, crunch point. I needed to educate my successors on how to process the data. But I was in no position to. I did, a little, when I was at home but with very low mobility. I showed them the spreadsheets I used to crunch the data.

But, of course, these were designed to be used by me. No bits were written that showed anybody else how to use them. They were complicated. If I had foreseen the situation, they could have been re-written more simply and in a more user-friendly way. But you can only do that between September and late October. Once our applications are open, customarily on 1st November, you can't change the system that processes them.

Rewriting would have been an interesting task. But in September and October I couldn't rewrite my own name. Whatever it is.

I knew perfectly well that the control sheets could be written better. They had evolved over the years and, when something came along that the sheet couldn't do, I rewrote again so it could. Adapt, improve, etc.

Somebody else had to do it, and it is a dirty and time-consuming job.

Only I knew all the possible complications, and even in full health I couldn't list them without leaving something major out.

As it turned out, I wasn't consulted much. We have people from all sorts of backgrounds, as I have probably said many times. And among them were people with Information Technology jobs.

One of the nicest people you could meet had such a day job. And wrote us a complete new system.

My mind is now full of ancient commercials for Persil Automatic and their Complete New System dance. That was some time ago. It was a big campaign but I think they abandoned it when too many people asked them what papers had been published in refereed journals about this New System. For surely it couldn't just have been invented by an advertising agency, could it?

I remember the year the Fringe Office tried a Complete New System for their Box Office. Now, we don't use the Box Office, so I was a spectator on that one. But I do remember asking at the AGM: what arrangements have you made for system failure? And the answer I got was: the system won't fail. Last time we changed the Box Office system, the new one came in on time and within budget. Therefore this one will also.

Well, you can guess what happened. The system failed catastrophically, and had to be rescued by implementing a version of the Box Office system used by several of the large venues, thus giving them a stake in the central Fringe's data operation. Shows affected seethed with rage. But the Fringe has a short memory, possibly because it changes CEOs so frequently. In fact, this box office system fiasco did lead to the resignation of the then CEO. More heads should have rolled, but didn't.

Yes, that year I wore my 'told you so' hat proudly. And when you gloat like that, things come back to bite you.

I was invoking, then, the primary rule of data processing: never implement a mission-critical system without a fallback position.

And now the same thing was going to happen to my own organisation.

The system that was written, mostly while I was still in hospital, was a wonderful system. Much better than mine. It did all sorts of things that mine had not done.

It was all cloud-based. That technology is after my time. I was brought up on punched cards and COBOL. It dealt with shows' pictures in a much better way than we had in the past. It was updated in real time, so that Artistic Directors, when scheduling, could immediately see the effects of other Artistic Directors' decisions. It auto-acknowledged every application; when I was doing it, these acknowledgements were sent semi-manually, by mailmerge. It even showed pie charts of our applications by genre, updated in real time.

I didn't know that at the time. I didn't look at most of the system. I answered a couple of questions that were put to me, but the answers weren't always incorporated.

I remember fighting hard over the word 'any'.

For many years, we didn't have an application form at all. People emailed me asking to be part of it, and I/we worked from those emails. But after a certain size you can't do that; you need a system. You try to keep the system down to a human scale, but any system is more impersonal than no system. So, an application form there had to be, just so we could be sure we were keeping track of all applications. That was many years ago. On that first form, of course, we had to know about the show proposals. And one of the main questions was "How do we know your show will be good?"

I was happy with that question. It said fairly clearly: 'good' is the standard we expect. Not 'I'll try this and see if it works'. Not 'I've done 20 open spots and I think I'm now ready for a one-hour show at a tough festival'. But good. The already-famous had fun giving silly answers to that question, and we had fun reading those answers. But it wasn't aimed at the already-famous; it was aimed at people we didn't know. I thought it made a clear statement. And it stopped people giving formulaic answers.

In the rewritten form, the question became "How do we know your show will be any good?" Which is quite a different question. I pointed that out. It took a relatively long email exchange before I got my way.

Because the system designer was clearly also used to getting her way. Which is fair enough, but I was right. I may frequently dive in the lido of self-doubt, but I do know the data needs of the Free Fringe.

Perhaps my insistence here led to me not being consulted about the rest of the design?

Anyway, I wasn't. Applications opened rather later than normal, which worried me, but eventually they opened. And they came pouring in, as they had in previous years. Lots of people wanted to join us, as the Artistic Directors told me. I didn't, for the first year ever, look at the applications as they came in. I trusted the system. A second expert among our ranks checked it and was convinced of its viability.

Stirrings started happening in February, although I wasn't told about them then. One of our Artistic Directors made a series of offers, and looked the week after. The offers had disappeared from the system and the slots were occupied by other shows. The AD raised the issue, but was told it was being taken care of.

I didn't get involved until May, when the same Artistic Director contacted me and mentioned the problem.

By that time, various offers had gone out, and some shows had taken listings in the Big Fat Fringe Programme, clashing with other shows.

I raised the matter, and I too was told that a fix was on its way and that I should trust the data professionals.

I didn't get where I am today, wherever that is, by trusting people.

There were clearly problems. Among these was the inability to fill the gaps caused by shows taking a day off, with other shows.

And it appeared that having two consecutive days off meant that the system showed the show's run as finished. So show B would be booked in the space that show A thought it had.

And the clashes hadn't gone away.

The doctors had told me that stress could have been a major contributor to my pancreatitis. I was to take it easy. Avoid stress.

Getting involved at this stage would have been stressful. Having a programme in August with my name (well, initials) all over it which would have been riddled with errors, would have been even more stressful.

I couldn't avoid it either way. And the worst thing was: so much work had gone into this new system. And the person who did it was nice, consummately nice, much nicer than me. I was worn down by 20 years of telling people what they didn't want to hear, and fielding their reactions. I had trained myself to be Mr Nasty. Oh yes, perhaps I was born nasty and was certainly brought up nasty, but to be properly nasty you mustn't care about people's reactions. And unfortunately I did.

I wasn't going to tell the system writer that, despite all her effort, the system wasn't fit for purpose. Even though it wasn't. For once, that was somebody else's job.

But nobody took the job on, probably for the same reasons.

And this makes me fear for the future of the Free Fringe. Because somebody has to do the unpopular stuff.

I downloaded all the data, as far as I could, on to my old system. Difficult, because the format was very different. I sent it to Artistic Directors for checking. Even then, everybody was hoping I was wrong and that the spiffy new system would somehow be shown to work after all.

But I knew it wouldn't. After all those years of processing the Free Fringe bookings, I knew what they system had to be capable of. And it was capable of many things, but a few essentials simply couldn't be accommodated.

The system-writer disappeared for two or three weeks. We haven't talked about this. I don't think she wants an argument any more than I do. She must have got wind of what I was doing, even though never officially told, and taken some time to get her head around the reality. For it would be hard for her. After all that effort, you don't want somebody telling you you're fundamentally wrong, or rather that your data structures are. Especially not me, Mr Nasty, fossilised in ancient and out-of-date ways of processing data. The new system was much more modern, taking advantage of features that were too modern for me.

Oh, if only it had got the data right. We could have avoided so much stress on all sides. But it didn't. One-off shows, the sort we use to fill in day-off gaps, were hanging around in the system and the offers had not gone to the shows themselves. And there were still clashes. Gradually, picking my way through the new system, I understood why.

But it wasn't until the Fringe Office contacted us and pointed out a clash between two of our shows in a major venue, that the rest of the team started believing there was something fundamentally wrong.

(That's three times now I've used a comma like that, where I was taught a comma ought not to be. Something to do with the subject of the sentence coming in the middle? Well, it breaks the rules as I thought I knew them, but it still feels right. To-day I thought I'd call the whole book "How I done what I done and wether I should of done it". And then all sorts of people would be drawn to the book by the need to complain about the title, but they'd have noticed the book. I suspect this may not happen).

So, here I am at time of writing. And indeed, where else could I be at time of writing? We've worked very hard to clean the data, resolve the clashes, pick up a few other difficult problems and get the Wee Blue Book prepared.

June (when I'm writing this) is another crunch month. We need to use it to fill all possible full-run and part-run gaps, and as many day off holes as possible. And at this stage of the year, most of our applicants have gone elsewhere; you can't really blame them, although they should have emailed us and with-drawn. In June, as at several other points of the year, you have to make offers at least daily. Because half of them will be de-clined, because the show's gone elsewhere, and you then have to make another offer.

You can't do this by system. You have to know a lot about the venues and the shows, and spot aberrations.

One of the new system's problems was that it tried to auto-mate too much. The old system had an offer email, and it said: email back to accept or decline. We'd then enter that decision manually. Of course, automatic would be better and easier. But what about the statuses that are neither accept nor decline? These can be: wait for further information (can I get the time off the day job? Are all the people in the cast available at the offer time, or is one of them in a different and clashing play?) or renegotiate (try, for good reasons, for something different, whether the differences be major or minor).

Under the old system, renegotiate was the same as wait; they were given the contact details of the Artistic Director and could talk to him/her directly.

The new system gave them the three options: accept, decline or renegotiate. And clicking 'renegotiate' wiped the original offer from the system.

Now, sometimes that's the right thing to do, but sometimes it isn't. It depends entirely on the circumstances surrounding the renegotiation. We've offered them a time that clashes with something else they're doing? Yes, delete the original offer. We've offered them Venue A and they'd prefer Venue B? No, don't delete the offer for Venue A. There will probably be good reasons why they can't have Venue B. And when the system deletes their offer for Venue A because they want Venue B but can't have it, they end up with Venue Zero, and they'd certainly prefer Venue A to Venue Zero.

So, you see, if you try to automate too much, you miss the human element. In some cases, it's right to delete the original offer on renegotiation; in some cases it's wrong. And only a human can decide which.

This seemed to have been the cause of many of the clashes we found. 'Renegotiate' can mean something as big as a completely new offer, or as little as 'can we start on the Thursday rather than the Wednesday?'. The term wasn't defined.

But look on the bright side. Today is 28th June, and for the first time in several years we haven't had a venue close down on us. Fingers crossed. Ladders not walked under. Gods of various hues invoked. 'Macbeth' not said loudly in the theatre.

No, screw it. I'm not superstitious. MACBETH.

When the police broke in, a trail of slime was found, leading to the chalked outline of a body corresponding to mine, but no body itself. Who did the chalking?

Yes, now the other problem I had for the 2017 season was — can I call it yet another coup? Probably not; it wasn't aimed at me. At the most, it was a coupette. Little red coupette; baby you're much too fast.

Prone in my hospital bed, or do I mean supine? Can never remember which is which. Anyway, I was informed that the Artistic Director for Comedy did not wish to continue in office. But the person who informed me thus said he/she was prepared to take over and had brought two other people on board.

When I say he/she, I mean I know which he/she was. I just don't want you to know.

I believed this. Why should I not have? I knew that the Artistic Director was going through some stressful personal stuff at the time. And I was in no real position to intervene.

And it wasn't until a couple of weeks later, when I got back home, that I wrote the Artistic Director an email thinking him for his past service and wishing him luck in his troubled situation.

And then, of course, it came out. He had not wished to step down at all. But the person who informed me thought he ought to step down.

Ever since Laughing Horse tried to present me with a fait accompli in 2006, I have hated faits accomplis. Note correct French plural there.

Had he actually wanted to step down? No. Did he wish to carry on? Yes, but these personal problems might intervene. Very well, I said: you must have deputies. Comedy is the biggest portfolio anyway; it's too big for one person. In the past I myself had often stepped in and covered Comedy. Now I wasn't going to be able to. We agreed there would be at least a three-person team.

Now I want to tell you more about his problems, because they're all part of the story. But I think I won't. Sorry. They're not mine to share.

What I hated most was the manipulation. I had no reason to doubt what I had been sold as the truth. But it wasn't true, or at least the AD had not stepped down willingly or of his own volition. His continuing in office, it was thought, might bring the Free Fringe into disrepute. No. We stand by our men (and women, but that would mean a failure of the Tammy Wynette reference). And anyway, we were already in disrepute, or I was. The mud of Cowgatehead was still occasionally flung. Nothing for it but to carry on as we are.

And that's what we're doing. 1036 applicants as of right now, many of whom we haven't been able to find space for. The usual ups and downs. The usual passive-aggressive pleading for last-minute space, which we might well give if only we had it. The usual demands for early access to the venues so that shows can technically rig. No; that all has to happen on the Friday before. The usual demands for floor plans and stage measurements. No. If you want that sort of stuff, go where you have to pay for it. What resources do you think we have? A bunch of volunteers, each with other things to do as well.

It's like the Fringe itself.

You feel like packing up and going home at least once a day. You wonder why you do it. But it's addictive. I'm doing it right now, in defiance of doctors' orders.

And after I wrote that, another major problem cropped up. For the past few years, we've run a three-stage all-weekend gig at Balham. A famous comedy pub. This served as a benefit show but more importantly as a London showcase and a place where shows could give themselves a final run-through before the Fringe itself.

Today I saw the publicity and poster. No Free Fringe logo; no mention of the Free Fringe. Instead, it was billed as Alphonse Ladybird's Balham Free Fringe.

Well, of course his name isn't Alphonse Ladybird. I'm concealing his true identity.

I contacted him immediately by internet messenger. Surely some mistake, I said. No mistake, he said. I've taken on some shows that aren't Free Fringe. I thought it best. You can still have the money.

Fuck the money.

I'd rather have no money at all than take on a single Laughing Horse show. It's not about that. Any funds we raise are peripheral. It's about giving our own shows a chance for a run-through and keeping our brand known in London.

I didn't get enough shows when I asked for volunteers, he said.

What, with 499 shows on the books? For such was the figure today. It'll change.

If you don't want me to organise it in 2018, he said, you can get someone else. And I'll give the money to charity: Medicins Sans Frontieres was mentioned. Good destination.

I like the way he assumed he could screw us and still keep his 2017 shows. If I were not retired, he'd have lost them instantly. As it stands, I've put the matter out to consultation among the Artistic Directors.

I am stunningly angry. This whole "you're getting the money; I can do what I like" attitude.

If the Free Fringe were about money (it wouldn't be called the Free Fringe, obviously, but apart from that) we'd make money. We'd screw and we'd mulct and sell ourselves off to sponsors like the whores we would be. He can stuff the money up his arse and Doctors without Frontiers can extract it, euro-cent by eurocent.

Last year the Balham event yielded about £2000; the year before, if I remember rightly, £800. That might have been the year before that. I'll pay that myself rather than accept tainted money.

I bet if I emailed our 499 shows and asked "were you invited to play Balham?" a substantial proportion would say no.

No, what we have here is another coup. Limited in scope, but another coup. I don't know why people bother.

What I most fear here is compromise. My view has always been: if somebody has shown him/herself untrustworthy, don't work with him/her again. Let them get away with it and you're flagged as a pushover, and they, and others, will do it more and more.

Many other people don't think like that. They come back from Munich waving a piece of paper. They compromise. Breaking your principles a little bit doesn't do much damage, they reason.

I'll let you know how things work out. We've seen similar things before.

It's now two days later. And I'm still supposed to be off sick. I involved the team of Artistic Directors in the decision. After all, they're supposed to be taking over. And whatever message we were going to send was going to have to be signed by all of them, not just me. They have to take joint responsibility, and from next year they'll have to take sole responsibility. No more being slagged off as a mad egomaniac by the likes of Walter Walloon; this time there will still have to be a decision somebody doesn't like, but it will be seen to be a joint decision. A Cabinet decision, if you will. Too pretentious?

Anyway, it turned out they mostly didn't want to do it my way. My suggestion was simply to email all our members and tell them what had happened. If they were sufficiently indignant, they'd take action themselves. Power to the people, and all that.

But instead they decided to send an email to Alphonse Ladybird, emphasising evidence he already knew, since he wrote most of it. But they did find that things were even worse than I initially had feared. Acts from our direct competitors had been invited to perform, and there was a whole web site claiming the event as Alphonse Ladybird's ("every year I organise this, because I love you") with no mention of the Free Fringe whatsoever.

Truly is it said: you never know behind which corner the custard pie lurks.

I just sent the email; three pages of jointly-written recriminations, and a grammatical and stylistic bouillabaisse. Actually, my own writing can also be described thus, but this one genuinely has five hands in it.

I don't know how he's going to reply; I suspect with contempt. The question is: do we cancel his shows in Edinburgh? I would, but the others are more forgiving. They point out that he has broken the spirit of the rules but not the letter. Well, if we're going to have to write rules that think of every possible thing somebody can do against us, it's going to be a very long rule-writing session. We have no specific rule against sleeping in your venue, but we got rid of the show that did (at the venue's insistence).

It's strange, writing this in real time. Nothing more to say until we get a response, so I'll write something else while I'm waiting. Thanks to the power of word processing, you won't know what. I may have left something out of 1996, or 2007; who knows where the revising hand will strike?

He's replied now. Much more contritely than I expected. And he'll put the logo back and it can go ahead as a Free Fringe event and we can have the money.

Except we can't. We won't take it.

He booked too many acts from other free-admission promoters, mainly Laughing Horse. So, think it through. We can't unbook them. That would be unjust. As long as they're performing, we can't call it a Free Fringe show, because it highlights other promoters' acts as much as our own acts. Our policy is to put clear blue water between us and the others, and not to let the public think 'all free-admission shows are the same'. This would do the opposite.

So, we don't want the branding if the bill stays the same, and we're not going to remove acts, who themselves have done nothing to deserve it, from the bill. It has to go ahead unbranded.

Financially, our loss, Medicins Sans Frontieres' gain. They do good work. Good for them. But if we'd taken the money, it would have meant we were for sale. We'll manage without the money somehow.

Next year, we organise it. Or rather, my successors will.

Well, that was an exciting bit of trying to write in real time, like a diary. I thought I could keep it up. But I couldn't. It's now three and a half weeks later. The Free Fringe is in Edinburgh and in full swing. I'm in London, a week after the last operation, and lonely.

The money from Balham eventually went to the victims of the Grenfell Tower fire, and that was a worthy destination.

Since then, crisis has succeeded crisis, but then again it always does.

Because of the earlier data processing problems, we hadn't filled in people's days off with other shows as well as we should have. And several venues complained about that. So there was an intensive effort to plug the holes and present the venues with full programmes, or at least as far as we could manage.

And then we sent the Wee Blue Book off to the printer, and the day after that we lost two stages.

I had thought this would be the first year for some time in which we hadn't lost stages at short notice. But no. And in previous years, we had at least been able to adjust the Wee Blue Book.

Not this time.

Stop the press. Hold the Front Page. Follow that cab. No; 24 hours too late. The moving finger writes and, having writ, moves on. I applied all the Piety and Wit at my disposal, but they couldn't move it back to cancel half a line or blot out a word of it, with tears or anything else. The presses rolled. One hundred thousand pieces of partial inaccuracy were sequentially gilded with cyan, magenta, yellow and black, collated, folded, stapled, boxed and trucked, and a Golden Ticket placed within the pages of number 9764. Some of this is true. That number, incidentally, is my PIN.

The Wee Blue Book arrived in Edinburgh two days earlier than expected, which I'd normally be happy at, but I couldn't help thinking: two days to spare; maybe they could after all have stopped the press. But I don't think it works like that.

The beauty was, and all credit to Frank, that we got the shows themselves moved, from one of the two large popups to the other. The problem had been that the second floor of Bar Bados was not after all available for use, for fairly abstruse building reasons, but ultimately the Council and its inspectors had forbidden it. We lost three stages; one went to an extra room partitioned on the first floor, and the other two to new rooms at Black Market, in a section of the building that wasn't planned to be open. That made a total of eight stages in this new popup, just next to Waverley Station.

Nerve-racking enough. But under an excellent Venue Commodore, i.e. the captain of all the captains, the spirit was un-dimmed. The venue was rigged and, as of current reports, is going well.

Two shows dropped out in the week leading up to the start. It happens every year and I hate it every year. And they always say the same. "Due to unforeseen circumstances...". They should hire a better bloody soothsayer.

Although it doesn't take a soothsayer to predict they'll never do a show with us again.

And that's the sooth.

Then we had a third one. In one of our top venues. Didn't send the venue any posters, as I later learned, and didn't turn up for his first show. The day after, the Sunday, I got an email saying "I am cancelling all my shows". He cited some daytime work which we had no knowledge of, because we're not sooth-sayers either.

With some effort, we'd managed to plug the other gaps, but this was in a venue where there shouldn't be any gaps, ever. The Voodoo Rooms. And a very specific type of act, so anybody coming from the Wee Blue Book listing would have certain expectations. We simply couldn't get another act of that sort.

But we have temporary shows filling the gap until Thursday, when the permanent replacement takes over. One of our other shows who had been filling his own venue and was up for the challenge of extras. My fingers are firmly crossed, but I think he'll do well. Better, at least, than what he replaced.

A professional act, the original show was. Based in Australia and on several agents' books. All I could do was email those agents explaining how he'd let us down and suggesting that, if he let us down, he could equally dishonour any bookings of theirs.

Normally I'd have been among the maelstrom on rigging day and the first few days, as the venues and programme settled. Hell, this was only the second year in which we'd had over 9000 performances scheduled, and the only other over-9000 year (2015) was the only year in which we lost a venue mid-Fringe. So 9000 has its own omen-like quality.

But I wasn't there; I was at home, discharged from hospital late Thursday, with spare dressings and the instruction to lift no heavy weights for several weeks. The Free Fringe is not itself a heavy weight, but can be an enormous burden.

The rigging seems to have gone smoothly and good houses were reported on the opening Saturday. There will have been numerous minor crises on the Friday, with the chair-humping crews not being where the van with the chairs was, and the plaintive wails of "how do you turn on the microphone?".

Honestly. I don't expect everybody to be a sound technician, but you have to be a special kind of idiot not to check on-switch, leads, channel volume and master volume. Or get your soothsayer to do it for you.

Well, over the years, I'd seen everything.

No, never say that. Because yesterday (wow, I've caught up to real time again. It won't last) we had a 'how low can you stoop' moment. It wasn't us doing the stooping. Let me explain.

I have said, until you're sick of reading it, how important the Wee Blue Book is to us. The strategy of handing it out along with every individual show leaflet has paid great dividends in the past. People ask us for it now. And this year, such was the effort made to get it on the street, we'd called for a second delivery much earlier than we normally would have.

What we hadn't expected was the emergence of a pirate Wee Blue Book.

That, however, was what happened.

A blue book was produced, Same size and format as ours, Very similar cover. It had 'Old Town Festival' on it. It contained (so I'm told by people who are now in Edinburgh) listings of Laughing Horse's shows at three particular venues, all owned by the same large Glasgow-based Group.

And then another appeared, and that actually said "Free Fringe" on the cover.

Well, I say it said "Free Fringe". What it actually said was "FREE FRINGE". Somebody had been clever. If they say "Free Fringe", that's our Company name and they're passing off as us if they use it. But if they say "free fringe" that could be held to be a generic description, not a proper name. By using capitals and having all the surrounding text in capitals, that issue remains ambiguous.

Neither of them says Laughing Horse.

What I don't know as I write is whether this was arranged by Laughing Horse or the venue owners. Or who knew about it in advance. And I must not make baseless accusations. But somebody is attempting to deceive the public into thinking their shows are ours.

I don't know what we're going to do about this, if anything. I'll get back to you. I think what they're hoping is that I denounce this, loudly and publicly, and in the course of that make some unguarded statement they can hold against me. I have Tourette's Syndrome; I do that sort of stuff. But I'm not going to, this time.

I've already been asked, in all innocence, on social media whether we were a pirate Free Fringe. It would have been easy to blame the questioner, but he/she did not know and it was a genuine question. The answer is: no, we're not. They are.

But somebody's taking the bread out of our shows' mouths by producing these pirate Wee Blue Books. I can't imagine the shows are pleased.

Some of Laughing Horse's shows are pleased, though. They've been heard boasting of it in the Loft Bar. The pirate programme (they didn't call it that, of course) should receive the Cunning Stunt award, they're quoted as saying.

Well, if you should get an award for stealing somebody else's audience under false pretences, then by all means put that award on your mantelpiece. The Free Fringe, however, stands for co-operation between performers, not dirty tricks.

And still some people believe, or pretend to believe, there's no difference between us and them.

Even some people in the Fringe Office believe that. They forwarded us a complaint they'd received:

At tonight's (Aug 10) performance, hardly 10 minutes in, the performer started having an unduly nasty go at an audience member for nodding! Actually for nodding! how bullying is that? Even though the person explained that his nodding had been a sign of agreement, the performer refused to feel complimented and insisted the nodding was offputting, and several times mockingly asked if the person had a neurological disorder - itself not an attitude favouring accessibility, and otherwise than that the nodding had been unjustifiable. Then he switched his hostility to another audience member some distance from the alleged nodder, who had defended him. This person defended himself to banter rubbishing, which annoyed the performer, and rightly would not accept having bitingly worded fault or blame pinned on him by the performer. The performer would not drop it without having an insulting closing jibe at the person, yet started blaming this person for disrupting the show, by an exchange that the performer had started.

The exchange eventually stopped by mutual pacifying words, but not for long. The performer delivered a couple more lines of his act, then rounded them off with another jibe at this person. A total treacherous contradiction of having claimed to be disrupted, to go after the person again. Obviously rightly the person objected. Straight away another man at the back stood up in an apparently official capacity and ordered "Leave now".

I could not tell whether this man was a venue official, a worker for the performer, or spontaneous audience thug, but his action as seen was as the performer's hard mate, with the performer's approval. I walked out too in response to seeing it, and I was the first uninvolved audience member to declare solidarity with the victim.

The thrown out person had been targetted and bullied by the performer to this point of public humiliation, bren accused of disruption for taking the performer's own goading bait, then insulted by him again then thrown out for saying anything. I have never seen anything remotely like this hooligan abuse of audience before in Fringe-going spanning 26 years.

Now, I don't know what happened. I wasn't there. There are usually two sides to all stories. One would normally ask the performer what his/her version of events was, and check with other witnesses, and then reply to the complainant appropriately....

... except that this wasn't one of our shows at all. It was a Laughing Horse show. The Fringe Office just assumed it was ours.

We do advise all our shows, especially the Comedy section, not to make victims of audience members. These audiences have done the performers the great favour of choosing their show above all other shows they could have seen. All comedians have their own styles, but none can afford to alienate their audiences, unless the audiences start it.

Somebody, somewhere (the Fringe Office rightly protected his/her identity when forwarding the complaint) thinks that the Free Fringe has done this bad thing to them. And this is because Laughing Horse have tried to market themselves as the Free Fringe, rather than trade openly under their own name.

Do you understand why I resent this? I hope so.

Oh, I'm not saying our shows never have negative interactions with their audiences. Just that they shouldn't. And if it should ever come to an incident like the one above, we'll take responsibility and appropriate action.

Except when Calum barges in a dressing room to collect his Highland stick. That was sort of different. But I would say that.

There was a mood within the core team that we should take the business about the pirate Wee Blue Books to the Press. There's a lot of anger about it. But the majority view seems to be that, if we did, the Press would be uninterested in the substantive issue, but write it up (if at all) as a quarrel between two rival organisations. Quite probably using the term Free Fringe to describe both, without distinction. That's happened before.

Maybe we expect too much of the Press. And most of the Fringe Press and Media aren't professionals. Many reviewers are hired for the duration. without much expertise in the genre they're set to review. This year for example, one has been indignantly emailing me demanding I send her a picture of a performer she's reviewed. That's not my job. I don't have pictures. And the performer concerned is with Laughing Horse, not us.

As every year, venues joined and venues left. One venue I was particularly pleased to welcome was the Waverley, on St Marys Street. And I was pleased because I, and others, had been pitching for it for ten or more years. It was our sort of place; a nice informal function space upstairs, where Billy Connolly had performed in his banjo-playing days. And the owner had always told us no. No comedy. What about Spoken Word? No; no swearing. (At the Edinburgh Fringe??). And every year this lovely atmospheric space lay fallow. The owner, it was said, was rich; ran the place as a hobby, opened when he pleased and only then, didn't need us.

I wish no man's death. But wishing doesn't kill people anyway. The mechanisms are independent. And everybody dies. As did the owner. With, it appears, no close relatives to whom the pub could be left. It's now in the hands of our friends at Caledonian Heritable (the Heritable is quite ironic in these circumstances) and they were happy to have us in. It appears to be doing well.

I'm now writing this on a train. Most of the Fringe is over, but I couldn't resist going to have a look. The team are dealing with everything that's happened so far; I hope my visit will be stress-free. There seem to be a lot of extra performances scheduled for many shows. Perhaps that means that other shows have dropped out or gone home early. I hate that, although it happens every year. I nearly did that in my first year at the Fringe, as I described at the beginning. I wonder what my life would now be like if I had done?

But no; at the Fringe you tough things out. It can be worse than you imagine, but you stick to it. And eventually something nice happens. And I'm really glad that the team are arranging all these extra shows. Keep the venues as happy as possible, and we stand a better chance of retaining them.

By the magic of time passing in real life, but not in my computer, I'm now off the train and in Edinburgh. And depressed. Or despondent. Or both.

There are so many of our shows who haven't got the idea. You don't join a collaborative effort and then compete with the other members. But that's precisely what's happening. The system is clear. First offer the public the combined programme, the Wee Blue Book, and then offer them your leaflet as an ancillary attraction. This is the system that's been proven to work. And so many shows aren't doing it. And the pirate Wee Blue Book isn't helping. The public are being confused, as was clearly the intention.

And, to my mind, worst of all, fewer than 100 of our 520 shows voted in the annual election for the Fringe Board of Directors. This despite it being one of our conditions that they should. No, we don't tell them whom to vote for. That would be a subversion of the process. But we do tell them to join and vote. Conditions for performers can't improve unless performers take an active role in who runs the Fringe. And right now, that's not performers.

So, I have to ask: are enough shows taking the spirit on board, or are they taking the hard work of the core team for granted, and surfing on the resulting waves?

I have seen many that are doing the latter.

If we continue, perhaps the Ethos and Conditions should have a headline: "You are applying to join a collective. This means that, instead of paying, you do some of the work. And you follow the rules. If all you want is a venue, fuck off and pay for one."

I put that to the team. They said fine, but delete the fuck.

I think the 'fuck' gives it its emphasis; it says how important we consider this. We had the same phrase in an earlier version of the Ethos and Conditions. It said "if you think you're doing us a favour by joining us, fuck off". Several shows commented positively on that. I suppose anybody who didn't like it didn't mention it.

Anyway, it's up to the team. I'm really trying to retire, but it's very difficult to let go.

But at least I now know: it wasn't old age that caused me to do such a bad job in my 2016 shows. I was ill, but I didn't know I was ill. And it's taken over 18 months to get halfway better. Still, I'm so glad there was a reason. And I stared Death in the face, and stared him down. But he'll be back.

*

The Future

In which your humble author exhibiteth his crystal ball

BY THE TIME YOU SEE THIS, some of the future will have become the past.

Unless we give up, our story will never finish. My involvement will finish. I hope not by sudden death (that nearly happened in September 2016, and it's not fun). But by graceful retirement and a long slow descent into senility, in which my grandchildren will ask: what's that big purple Perspex block on your shelf? And I'll say "I don't remember. What's a shelf?" Or alternatively, "that was awarded to me at the ceremony they wouldn't let your mother attend". Or maybe they won't ask. Yes, that's more likely.

They gave the widows of World War I a bronze (?) plaque each, known as the Widows' Penny, with the phrase "He died for Freedom and Honour" and a space for the name of the deceased to be embossed. George Buckley, in the case of the one my grandmother had. And I never asked her about George, dead 31 years before I was born. I wish I had asked. But grandchildren often don't, and I don't suppose mine will.

That's nothing to do with anything, but I often wonder about George Buckley.

But never mind that.

Oh, the fun shows we've had over the years.

The tribute in which several comedians, including me, sang Half Man Half Biscuit songs with a live guitarist. No gimmicks, just joy.

The famous cult A Young Man Dressed as a Gorilla Dressed as an Old Man Sits Rocking in a Rocking Chair for 56 minutes and Then Leaves. Been going for seven years now. I know the identity of the gorilla, but I'd have to kill you if I told you. Which is difficult, because I'm just a book.

The show that consisted of our then Spoken Word Artistic Director saying nothing but "What the Fuck is This?" for 55 minutes.

The show in which the comedian attempted to pronounce the word "squirrel" and failed.

The world record attempt for the number of portraits painted in a day.

The show where Andrew O'Neill performed a Satanic ritual at midnight in a spooky venue (I insisted he took out Public Liability Insurance for that one, but it wasn't needed).

The two-handed standup comedy show with one Israeli and one Palestinian.

Trevor Lock's non-shows: "the (packed) audience sit in a circle around him and as he talks to them people write down what they think is going on in the room. He then reads out the writing."

Mr Methane; I mentioned him before.

The Bob Blackman tribute show: the late Bob Blackman was famous for banging his head with a tray while singing Mule Train.

The song cycle about the Medieval Papacy. Moon Horse versus the Mars Men of Jupiter. The Cheshire Liberation Front. Accident Avoidance with Cutlery.

We had many more strange and lovely shows, some of which I'll remember as soon as it's too late to edit this. And even more less-strange shows that were simply of excellent quality.

Over the years literally thousands of performers have played the Free Fringe, several of whom are now famous.

I think the point is: we gave people the chance to experiment, if we trusted them.

And somebody's now going to say: why did you qualify that? Why do you have to trust an act before you give him/her/ them the freedom to experiment?

Well, because we can still be hurt by people thinking that free equals rubbish. We have a quality reputation to uphold.

And some aspirant performers do suffer from Dunning-Kruger syndrome. But we always checked out the more bizarre proposals and tried to help.

It was common, and still is, for established acts to have a show in the pay-to-play venues and another one with us. And often they spoke of how much more receptive our audience was, freed from the pressure of payment.

Will the Free Fringe survive me? I always thought it would.

I grew up lonely and unsocialised, like many comedians.

And then when I went to University, I had a peer group for the first time. And four years after graduating, I did a Masters (Master's?) and I had a smaller but stronger peer group. And then I had jobs, and ended up lecturing, and that gave me a peer group also, although as time went on the group became weaker and less cohesive. If you're not careful, you start habitually drinking with your students. They make you welcome, yes, but they're not your peer group. I did that occasionally, but I was lucky not to get addicted and socially dependent on it. Many never got out of that pit. My cousin, who lectured in the North-West, died at 42 of kidney disease, which might have been exacerbated by the amount he drank with his students. My theory; could be wrong.

Anyway, comedians became my peer group and I was happy among them. And then I did things for them, and I became an organiser-figure without really planning to, and I lost the peer group. I became an outsider again. And now the doctors forbid me to drink, so the conviviality of drinks in pubs is lost to me.

If the same thing happens to my successor as CEO, that will be a problem for him or her.

Would anybody want the job?

Somebody's doing it at the moment, but I'm still in the wings, interfering. Whether I'm interfering too much or too little, I don't know. It's impossible that I should be interfering just the right amount. I hope not to interfere at all in 2018.

Could anybody else have built the Free Fringe as I did? Certainly. Just takes knowledge of the business, an endless willingness to learn the bits you don't know and a bucketload of stubbonness. Many people could have done it. But would anybody else have done it? Without hope of profit?

So, can other people take over?

There's a very good team in place. The data processing is complex, but we now have a better system that does all sorts of things my crude old system didn't. The Artistic Directors are doing excellent jobs, and Frank and Isla are indispensable on venue liaison and WBB production respectively.

But nobody wants to do the unpopular stuff, and eventually compromising with wrong will kill the Free Fringe.

Maybe we should let it fragment? Originally I thought that's what would happen anyway. Then Laughing Horse tried their coup and we had to stick together. There was a time when they were slightly bigger than us and boasted of it; we had the quality and the spirit, but they had the size. That's no longer true; we had over 9000 performances in 2017 and their press release gives them about 3500.

We've never objected to the Scottish Comedy Festival. They came to us and told us what their plans were, including free admission. They didn't try to take over, cannibalise, poach venues or anything. They behaved sensibly and ethically. Even if we had power to object, which of course we don't, how could we object? They wouldn't have done free-admission unless we'd blazed the trail, but since we did, they were welcome.

Another promoter we like is The Stand. Their model is different to ours, and they charge admission and there is a usage charge on their artists. But it's a fair one, and they say that if a show is seen to work hard, they will ensure that show does not make a loss. And, of course, they're an all-year-round comedy club in Edinburgh. Often we get applications which clearly say: if the Stand offers, we'll go there, otherwise we want to be with you. And that's fine; we're perfectly happy with that.

Oh, if only all other promoters were like these.

If they were, we could just let the Free Fringe fragment into smaller, more manageable groupings of venues. I don't think the Wee Blue Book could survive under such an arrangement, though, and the WBB is powerful.

Even the Wee Blue Book would be less powerful if the Big Fat Fringe Programme were less cumbersome, easier to search and read and didn't cost nearly £400 for a 40-word listing.

The future, I'm told, is apps. I hate the word. In my day, they were called applications and they were written in COBOL.

I exaggerate somewhat. We can't predict the future of technology. And Betamax was a better system than — what was the other one called? The one that won? But nobody uses either nowadays, and younger readers will be wondering what I'm talking about.

We have an app. So does the Fringe Office. But they charge to be on it. We don't. A chance meeting between one of my team and a professional app writer, a second meeting involving me in a station buffet near Birmingham, and the deal was done. We gave them a full-page ad in the Wee Blue Book; they gave us an app running on both platforms (not the platforms to which the station buffet was attached, although for all I knew about apps it might have been).

The world has been fantasising about paperless offices since the 1970s. And there's still as much paper as there ever was. I doubt there will ever be a time our app will replace the Wee Blue Book entirely. Several years ago, electronic books were supposed to be replacing real paper books. But there are still books. And, may the gods be thanked, still bookshops you can spend time in and walk out with something you didn't know existed until you walked in.

One can never have too many books. One can have too little shelf space. I have had occasional relationships in which the other half has suggested I should create space by getting rid of some books. It was easier to get rid of the other half.

They say cash is disappearing, and several 2017 performers say they encountered audience members who wanted to give to the bucket but didn't carry cash. Of course, it could have been the same couple going to a lot of shows. But some of our members are now looking at portable card readers for donations. Well, I prefer my donations crinkly, but I'm old, and things move on.

But if paper disappears, the Free Fringe need not.

The crisis points will come in the future as each individual in the core team discovers that he/she is putting in a disproportionate amount of effort to the Free Fringe, and thus not enough effort into his/her own shows and, more importantly, his/her enjoyment.

I reached that point some time ago. But I soldiered on until illness made me stop. I can't expect anybody else to soldier on to that extent, and they'd be foolish to do so.

So, we have to expect a rolling team of people, each generation handing on to the next. Passing on the knowledge and the torch. Erm, why do we say torch?

And if that happens, are the principles of the Free Fringe safe? I hope so. But perhaps only until somebody says: "look, we need money; let's get a sponsor". Or, even worse, a sponsor offers him/herself, and in the heady excitement, the then-committee forget why that's a bad idea.

And I won't be around to remind them.

And maybe that means the Free Fringe takes the first irrevocable step on the slippery slope (it can't be that slippery if you can take a step on it, can it? Sort your metaphors out, PBH) to becoming a full pay-to-play organisation.

When that happens, I hope that some younger version of me, festooned with future stuff (personal helicopter, Dan Dare wrist radio, helmet with aerial, mark of the Beast on forehead) has the guts to start a proper Free Fringe in opposition to the one that lost its way.

It's taken me a quarter of a century, almost. It will probably take him/her as long. And it will be more difficult. The healthier the population's consumption patterns are, the less profitable the Free Fringe is for its venues. Fortunately, Scotland will remain Scotland, in or out of the UK, in or out of the EU.

And that's if the Edinburgh Fringe survives.

It doesn't look moribund if you stand on the streets of Edinburgh in August. It looks anything but. But institutions, like trees, die from the heart outwards. Don't be deceived by the leaves.

Unless the people who manage the Fringe love the Fringe, it cannot thrive. And you can't achieve that love by paying people more. The Beatles knew that in 1963.

The Fringe has had six different Chief Executives since the Free Fringe has been established. If any of these had truly loved the Fringe, he/she would not have moved on to other jobs, in other countries.

If the Fringe Office is not the custodian of the spirit of the Fringe, who is?

Well, I like to think that we are. Or maybe — forgive the hubris — that I am. But having just condemned others for deserting their post, I'm about to desert mine.

How do you carry a spirit through a complete change of personnel?

Is it like the old brush, which has had six new shafts and four new brush heads, but is still somehow the same brush?

If Leeds United has a new manager and a complete new staff of players, is it still Leeds United? Yes, you say, they still play in white. Ah, but they didn't always; they used to be blue and yellow. What is it that ensures the continuity? Just being in Leeds? Is that enough? Is anything that happens in Edinburgh, the Fringe?

Why did I pick Leeds all of a sudden? Memories of a very bad school that thought itself a very good one. It got the results, so impressed the parents. It didn't give the deep education or inculcate the love of learning.

I'm writing about love a lot. You learn if you love your subject. You have a good Fringe if you love the things that make it a Fringe.

How many people do that?

And the people who think they hold the Fringe in trust: do they love the Fringe?

As an institution, I don't think they do. I think they're just carrying on for the sake of carrying on. Perhaps they think different. Perhaps I've missed the evidence.

Do the public still love the Fringe?

Well, there are nowadays plenty of other festivals that will take their money. When I started the Free Fringe, festivals were single-genre. There were music festivals (mostly), separated by type of music. There were theatre festivals, literary festivals and others, but few that combined the arts. But now there are. Latitude is one such, and there are many others. Comedy, music, theatre, dance, spoken word, literature, all on one site.

Perhaps Glastonbury was always like that also. I don't know; I've never been.

Edinburgh's big advantage is that you don't have to stay in a tent. Which is indeed a big advantage. Not to mention toilets.

There are Fringes and Comedy Festivals springing up all over the UK. Which is fine, as long as they too aren't pay-to-play for the performers. Some of them are.

Oh yes, ticket sales at the Edinburgh Fringe seem to go up every year. We're not part of that game. We don't count our audiences or our buckets. But are these genuine ticket sales? Mostly, they talk of tickets "issued". There's a lot of tickets issued that aren't actually sold. Audiences are boosted by giving away free tickets; it's called "papering the house".

I don't think anybody knows, really. And if anybody did know, it would probably be in their interest to put a spin on it, of some sort.

And spin is bad. Nowadays, we're so used to seeing spin that nobody expects unvarnished truth.

I mean, you should see some of our applications. The form says "write as one professional to another; don't give us your PR blurb". Most applicants ignore that and many promise what they can't deliver.

(The one I remember most was the one who claimed to have supported Van Morrison. Excellent, if true. But what he meant was that he played an open spot in the Club Tent at Cambridge Folk Festival in a year when Van Morrison was headlining the main stage. They didn't interact. I know; I was there, sporting a backstage pass our applicant did not have. Van Morrison left in a limo as soon as he'd finished his set.)

But it's worse than that. The Fringe suffers from the myth of level playing fields. Time and again, the answer from the Fringe Office is: "it's the same for everybody".

It's never the same for everybody. I could assemble a team of 11 footballers from the ranks of the Free Fringe performers, and that team could have a match against Manchester City on a level playing field. And our team would lose spectacularly. (Although we'd play in light blue to match the Wee Blue Book, so Manchester City would have to change).

So, how would my team stand a chance against Manchester City? Why, we'd buy or rent the best players we could afford. And if we paid an unimaginable amount of money, we'd stand a chance of winning.

Alas, we don't have an unimaginable amount of money. But those who do can always buy advantage, whether it's in stupid theoretical football matches or in the reality of the Fringe.

Level playing fields do not provide equal opportunity. Only positive support for the weak allows them to grow strong. If level playing fields worked, society would never have needed anti-discrimination laws. (Yes, anybody can apply for this job, but only white male middle-class candidates will get it. But you can apply, so it's not discrimination.)

Performers with resources, with powerful organisations behind them, have every advantage at the Fringe. They can buy large quantities of advertising; they can secure large venues in good time for the absurdly early deadlines of the Big Fat Fringe Programme; they can have PR firms working to place their stories in the national press. And yet any one of them, in his/her 400-seater venue at £15 a ticket for a one-hour show, pays the same Fringe Participation Fee (£391 including VAT) as somebody unknown doing a six-day run in a 25-seater.

Yes, that's a level playing field. But level does not mean fair.

It's about time those who manage the Fringe recognised that and introduced real fairness. But instead, over the years, they have abolished two of the major level playing fields: the Fringe Club and Fringe Sunday.

Money has talked too loud at the Fringe thus far; it needs to be quietened. There are many excellent performers who do not have money, and they should have the chance to be heard.

Not, I stress, that the famous and successful are not also excellent. You don't make it without talent and dedication. And most famous performers to whom I have spoken don't want to pull the drawbridge up after them. They support the equalisation of access; they remember the losses and difficulties they had when they first came to the Fringe.

The British class system is at work here. A performing career has become a middle-class luxury. And it shouldn't be.

I often get asked: why do you have relatively few BME (Black and Minority Ethnic) performers? And I appreciate that the question is asked. It should be asked.

Our shows are no worse in that respect than any other organisation's shows. And, as I hope you'll recognise, it's not because we actively discriminate, and nor does any other organisation. That would indeed be horrible.

No: it's a matter of what applicants come forward. And since, as I said before, a performing career is largely a middle-class luxury, the people who apply to us, and to others, will largely be middle class. And it is in the middle class itself that BME people are under-represented.

And now I think of Monty Python's dead bishop sketch:

"It's a fair cop, but society is to blame".

"Agreed. We'll be charging them too".

(Alright. A plug, and kudos to our member Che Burnley, who in 2017 organised the Fringe's first Black Comedy Showcase. His idea, not ours, but we were glad to host it.)

There used to be a joke that comedians told each other, until everybody knew it and it thus ceased to be a joke.

It went: In this game, if you can make just one, just one person laugh — you're rubbish.

At the Free Fringe, if we get an audience of one, we proceed. The show goes on. And maybe that's the difference between us and the ticket-counters.

That's got to be worth something, as long as it can carry on. And for it to carry on, performers themselves have got to keep the spirit alive. We live, more or less permanently, in deep mud. If you stay inside, you weigh the vehicle down. But if you get out and push, we get to our destination. It's the ratio of pushers to inside-sitters that determines whether we get anywhere. Yes, if you push you may get a little muddy. Mud is the fate of pushers. And sometimes the vehicle fails to move. But still you push.

*

I made a bold claim in the preface. I said the Free Fringe had saved the Edinburgh Fringe itself. Has this rambling and over-personal story proved the claim?

Well, you can't know what would have happened in alternate universes. But let me take a stab at it.

If there had been no Free Fringe, the price of ticketed shows would have risen steadily. The rents paid by promoters would have risen, and so would the costs of hiring PA and rigging venues, plus the (minimum) wages of box office and stewarding staff. That would have been passed on in ticket prices.

The stream of performers willing to back their dreams by paying ever-increasing venue rentals would eventually have dried up.

The supply of audience members willing and able to pay increasing ticket prices, several times a day, for one-hour shows, would also gradually dry up. Particularly in the economic times we have seen in the last decade.

The higher the ticket price, the more the Fringe falls out of the price range of lower income groups. Only the moneyed middle class are left.

And even they want value for their money. If you're going to pay, say, £20 for a one-hour show, however rich you are, you want to know it will be worth the money. Otherwise you'll feel personally affronted. Ripped off. Just like my grandfather a century ago, taking his best girl to a music-hall show that wasn't worth the shillings.

So, they'll only go to see safe shows. Ones put on by already-established names. And even those names won't do experimental material; they won't risk the disapproval of the audience.

The others, the non-established performers, would eventually realise that they couldn't win in that environment, and stop coming.

As the supply of performers dried up, the fixed costs would have to be shared among the remaining performers, and up go the ticket prices again.

You end up with a smaller number of expensive, safe shows, which the audience could probably see in their home towns anyway. Oh, still plenty of scope to have a good time in a wonderful city, but nothing unique any more.

It might have taken 20 years to get to that scenario; it might have taken 50. But to that scenario it would eventually have come.

And whatever survived might have still been called a Fringe, but wouldn't be a Fringe. It would be a festival. And there are plenty more of those, in other nice places.

There were four major points in the Free Fringe's story when we could have stopped, or been stopped, and I still wonder what would have happened if we had. Small changes have big outcomes; catastrophe theory.

But for a single incident in 1980, involving only four people, I might have given up performing and thus never got to Edinburgh in the first place. But that's another story.

If Eleanor had succeeded in making me charge for my show in 1997, there would have been no more free shows. Would somebody else have tried it, further down the line? It's possible. And just as it's taken us 20 years to get where we are, it would have taken them the same. Would they have persevered? Are they as stubborn as I? Or would they have needed, at some point, to make a profit on what they were doing? Because that would have killed the whole thing.

In 2003 when we had no venue, we might also have died. Had it not been for the three people who put on a show in the UCW Club on our behalf, the continuity would have been lost. But we might have recovered, because by then we had a following. Same question, though; if we hadn't carried on, would anybody else have taken up the reins?

2006/7 was, however, the crunch point. If we had not fought against the Laughing Horse takeover, what would then have happened? There would have been free-admission shows at the Fringe, just not ours. But the performers would have been charged to perform, or possibly to apply. Would the public have noticed, or cared? They might have noticed a loss of quality, but they might not: shows that would have come to us would probably have gone to them.

So, not much change on the surface. Below the surface? Yes. Once you start charging performers, you keep charging performers. And those charges creep upwards.

And would the venues have been happy with that? With the Free Fringe, they see a non-profit organisation, doing its best for its members. They, the venues, are part of the experience. But if they saw the show organisers making a profit, they'd want a slice. In would come venue rents, up would go costs to performers, and either they'd bring in tickets and admission charges or the performers would be even poorer.

You simply can't run free-admission shows at the Fringe for profit. Otherwise you're just exploiting.

So we had to fight back, after the 2006 coup, otherwise a major principle would be lost. But if Calum had not been there that day, if he had not heard what went on and if he had not decided to help — indeed, if I had not accidentally met him later at the Holyrood — all might have been lost. He saved us. He deserves every credit for that.

The same could be said for the Freestival breakaway in 2015; once you charge to perform, or charge to apply, you've undermined the whole thing. Nothing new there, so I don't count it as a possible break point. It only broke me, or my reputation, among some people, after the Cowgatehead fiasco. But the Free Fringe lived on.

No, the final point at which the Free Fringe could have died is when I nearly did, after the 2016 Fringe. And that was the triumph, because it didn't die. By that time, the spirit of community was so strong that it couldn't have died. The team of performers took over when I could do nothing. And if I had died, the Free Fringe would have gone on with barely a hiccup, and had a triumphant 2017. Which, of course, happened.

That team spirit is the Free Fringe's lasting achievement, and as long as it exists, the Free Fringe won't die. Without that spirit, if we had not existed, the Edinburgh Fringe would have become more expensive, more corporate and much less fun for the performers. And ultimately that would have killed the Fringe. I don't know how long it would have been a-dying, but I'm confident it would have.

Organisations have to reinvigorate to survive. We have been the force that reinvigorated the Fringe. Not to save the Edinburgh Festival Fringe Society Ltd, but to save the Fringe itself.

Quod erat demonstrandum. I haven't said that since O-Level Maths. But now I have.

*

At this point, the author laid down his pen. Or shut down his computer. I don't know which, even though I am the author. But I don't know how to end it.

Then he asked me would I yes to say yes my mountain flower and first I put my arms around him yes and drew him down to me so he could feel my breasts all perfume yes and his heart was going like mad and yes I said yes I will Yes.

But I reckon I got to light out for the Territory ahead of the rest, because Aunt Sally she's going to adopt me and sivilize me and I can't stand it. I been there before.

And it was still warm.

Write no more, Claudius, god of the Britons, write no more.

* *

*

Appendix

OH, COME ON, I wasn't going to write a book without an appendix, was I?

You'll be wanting a bibliography next.

The Free Fringe tries to stick to its principles. I wrote the Ethos Statement some years ago. It's here in case I haven't made it clear in the book what we're trying to achieve.

The Free Fringe was founded on a vision. Not everybody realises that. Perhaps that is because we have never spelt it out. It may help if we do.

These were the elements of the vision:

- *A Fringe where the artists who make it happen are (apart from the audience) the only important people.*
- *An end to the excesses of pay-to-play.*
- *An end to wasted resources which drain the artists' pockets.*
- *An end to the arms race under which more money is spent every year on publicity, at the artists' cost.*
- *An end to massive losses by shows.*
- *An end to unrealistic dreams of overnight success which lead artists to make inappropriate choices.*
- *A Fringe in which performers are free to enjoy performing with as little pressure as possible.*
- *A Fringe which does not bow to commercial pressures or sponsors, nor has to waste energy in pursuit of financeAn end to competition between shows.*
- *No more isolation of performers and no more performers feeling unsupported during the Fringe.*
- *An end to profiteering from the work of the performers.*

From this vision everything we do has followed, including the current Ethos and Conditions.

We support the election of the maximum possible number of performers to the Fringe Board of Directors, so that the Fringe shall consider first and foremost the interests of the performers without whom it could not happen. Performers are also venue managers and are also audience members.

Our existence predicates on a better and fairer deal for performers. For this to succeed, performers need to support each other. They also need to some extent to change the conventional thinking. The majority of people on the media and 'industry professionals' lists do not deserve the deference they appear to expect. There is nothing more important than entertaining the audience for each show.

*

The Free Fringe Ethos and Conditions get rewritten every year, and in 2018 were rewritten by much kinder hands than mine. They're now called the Ethos and Obligations, because my successors think that nobody reads Conditions. They're probably right. Here they are:

The Free Fringe:
Our Ethos and Your Obligations 2018

Our Ethos in one sentence is:
We are a movement for the emancipation of performers at the Edinburgh Fringe.

When you join us, you become part of a collective, so please read carefully before you apply.

As such, the Conditions of this agreement are also Your Obligations to your fellow performers within The Free Fringe.

Once you accept an offer, we expect you to adhere to the ethos and conditions below and in return the rest of the Free Fringe will do the same for you. If at any time you break these conditions, we reserve the right to terminate any agreement. We reserve the right to amend, rewrite and improve these as appropriate. These conditions do not constitute a contract; the relationship between us is non-contractual and relies on you and us keeping our word to each other. Our legal adviser asks us to add: if this were a contract, which it is not, English Law would govern it.

In layman's terms, we have rules and a particular way of working that benefits the whole collective. If at any time you break them, you may be be asked to leave that collective.

To quote a Free Fringer:

"If you expect the public to sit through 50 minutes. of your show, you can spend 20 minutes reading this"

Basic Principles

It's free. We don't charge the performers (unlike some other free admission organisations). We don't pay the venues. The shows are free to the public to attend and the venues benefit from the money spent at their bars and counters. Most performers make a 'bucket speech' at the end of the show to accept donations from the audience. Performers are asked to make voluntary contributions to the cost of running The Free Fringe (the main cost is printing The Free Fringe's programme — called the Wee Blue Book). More on our finances here [url]

We're a collective. Everyone shares the workload — before, during and after the Fringe. There isn't a paid team of people who work for you. We all work for the collective, and somehow between us we have to do everything.If for any reason you can't cover one of your responsibilities you must find someone to do it for you. And make sure they know what they're doing. Remember you're not applying to be a customer, you're applying to join a collective!

If you're just looking for a free theatre space with flashing lights and sound technicians; or to turn up, do your show and check out: this isn't for you.

Things do not always run smoothly. We can be let down by venues, by others we are working with in myriad ways, and by each other. When that happens we work together to solve the problem — finding new venues, talking to people, etc.

We believe that performers' voices should be at the heart of the whole fringe. In that sense our ethos is also political. We expect our members to participate in Fringe Society elections.

So if you still feel you're a PBH free fringe kind of person read our rules below and how to apply.

The Free Fringe rules:

Accepting your offer

Once you have accepted an offer with us, that's a firm commitment. Please do not accept an offer from us if you are still talking to other venues or not sure if you will have other commitments (including potential job offers), etc. In the event of serious illness contact us immediately and we will work with you to find a suitable solution. You may not pass your offer to somebody else nor change your show substantially from your initial application. In the event of a problem with the venue we will keep you informed at all times and do our utmost to find a suitable alternative. Do make sure our emails aren't going to your spam folder too please (check this early on — people have missed venue offers this way before!) Add our email address to your safe list to be extra sure.

If you are having an official day off you must tell us in advance and agree it in advance with your artistic director at the time that you accept your slot. If you haven't done that then the show must run.

Do your show.

Every day. Even if there's only one audience member. And if there's none — sit and wait for latecomers. When shows don't happen it damages our reputation because people think "why bother going, it might not even go ahead". If you are too ill to perform use the Free Fringe contact list to find a suitable replacement. Never leave your slot dark. Each year we have over 500 shows; one of them will be able to step in for you. Speak to your Venue Captain or Artistic Director if that is going to be a problem.

Flyering.

You MUST at all times that you are flyering, visibly carry and offer the Wee Blue Book to everyone you engage with. If you pay others to flyer your show or have friends and family helping, they must also do this. This actually makes flyering easier because the Wee Blue Book is widely recognised and people will often ask you for it. It also means at any given moment during the Fringe as many as 100 people may effectively be marketing your show by handing the book out. It's so easy, we made a video showing you how! Click here. Since there are Free Fringers all over Edinburgh we'll soon know if you're not doing it. If you run out of Wee Blue Books at your venue — go to one of our other venues and get some. Simple.

Door duty.

Someone from your show (if it's a solo show, that'll probably be you) must start your duty 15 minutes before the previous show finishes (normally 30 minutes before your show starts, possibly more).

They should be visibly and obviously on duty. In some venues they will be asked to wear a hi-vis vest to indicate this (as required by the City Fire Department).

Their first job is to stop audience members from walking into the performance space during the last 15 minutes of the previous show.

When their show finishes hold the bucket and offer the Wee Blue Book to the departing audience (depending on the needs of the show, they may prefer to do this themselves).

Ensure the space is clear and any litter or empty glasses are cleared.

Set up and do your show.

Finish your show on time. Even if the show before you over-ran. Otherwise the whole schedule slips and chaos ensues. If someone consistently over-runs, talk to (1) them, (2) the venue captain (3) the artistic director.

When your show finishes, help with clearing and tidying the venue, straightening chairs, etc.

Freeing the Edinburgh Fringe

Show the new audience in. Make sure you don't let in more people than the fire capacity of the room. If you have to turn people away suggest other Free Fringe shows they might like.

When the next show starts, remain on duty for 15 minutes and make sure latecomers are ushered in quietly (or turned away politely depending on space and on the wishes of the show in question).

More advice on door duty in our F.A.Q. here [url] Obviously before the first and after the last shows of the day the door duty is slightly different and you will need to make sure the space is set up or cleared and tidied, and electrical equipment switched on/off.

Be polite and respectful to venue staff. Wherever possible encourage your audience to buy drinks and food, etc. Do not allow your audiences to bring in their own food and drink (aside from water bottles). Do not hand out free snacks or drinks to your audience (within reason, if you're a magician who does a trick with a chocolate bar, fair enough, but handing out cans of lager to your audience etc is not ok. If you drink a pint or a coke during your show, buy it at the bar.) Don't damage anything at the venue, don't deface walls, don't assume you can use anything there without asking first. Don't leave equipment where it can be stolen. If you leave props at your venue, label them. If not, they may be thrown away unintentionally.

Do not apply for any other free-admission show, including the pay-for-priority-or-guaranteed-seat shows, e.g. Laughing Horse, Heroes of Comedy, Freestival, Just The Tonic shows, etc. Why? We explain in our F.A.Q here [url].

It's not a problem if you have done shows with other organisations in the past and it is also ok to do shows that are fully ticketed at paid venues in the same year as doing a Free Fringe show. If in doubt just check with us.

Do not make regular "billed" appearances at any other free-admission show, including the pay-for- priority- or-guaranteed-seat shows, e.g. Laughing Horse, Heroes of Comedy, Freestival, Just The Tonic shows, etc.

This one seems to cause the most confusion. So you CAN'T do one show (a solo show or a compilation show which you are in regularly and are listed in the brochure as being a part of) with us and another with another such "Free" organisation. BUT you can be a one-off guest at such shows should you wish to be and you can have acts from such shows on as one-off guests on your mixed bill show. Again, we have our reasons, all explained in our F.A.Q here [url].

Be honest; keep your word. If you're not willing to stick to the ethos and conditions, please don't apply. They all exist to strengthen the many, which is why we have occasionally had to remove shows from their venue midway through a run when they break these conditions. If you just send an email saying "due to unforeseen circumstances, I can no longer perform..." you will never be considered again. Talk to us, rather than give us an ultimatum. If there's a genuine problem, you should help us resolve any issues it has caused us (remembering that "us" includes every one of your fellow performers). We repeat: no exceptions.

If you choose to be listed in the big Fringe Programme produced by the Fringe Society then add "/PBH's Free Fringe" to your performer name (so i.e. "Vijay Patel/PBH's Free Fringe" or "Terrible Theatre Company/PBH's Free Fringe") and list your show as free and non-ticketed. Please remember that most of our venues are 18+ and if your venue does have an age limit you must include it on all listings and promotional material. When the Fringe Office asks for the age suitability of your show, you need to put 18+ if it is an 18+ venue. Ask if you're unsure and see our F.A.Q here [url] Help the Free Fringe in whatever of the following ways you can:

- Lend us any PA equipment you own
- Run benefits to help us cover our costs (note: saying "I'm happy to perform at a benefit" isn't much help unless you're really famous)
- Sell advertising in the Wee Blue Book
- Volunteer as a Venue Captain

- Be on hand to help move chairs and set up/take down venues, even if it's not your venue.
- Offer us whatever other specialist skills you have: IT? PR? Do you own a van? There's lots of stuff we need done and nobody but us will do it so get involved. Even if you are certain you have no useful skills at all let us know and we'll find you something easy to do!

Join the Edinburgh Festival Fringe Society (this applies to everyone who is regularly part of your show — on stage or behind the scenes). This costs £ 10 each and is the only money you are obliged to pay by the Free Fringe (and it doesn't go to us). You can do it at any time throughout the year at http://www.edfringe.com/about-us/membership. Join as soon as you accept an offer with us and forward your receipt, and those of your regular cast and crew, to pbhfringesoc@yahoo.com. And then VOTE in the elections to the Board of the Fringe Society. For our reasons, see F.A.Q here [url]. If you are interested in running for the Board itself, let us know.

Put the **Free Fringe logo**, including the QR code for our Free Fringe App, in its original colours, on both sides of your flyers and on your posters.

Write a blurb of 350 characters for the Wee Blue Book and send it to us together with a square show image when we ask and in the format we ask for them (it will be via an online form). Please remember the WBB only gives images, titles and blurbs so if your name isn't in the title, put it in the blurb if you want audiences to know who you are.

If your show runs the first day your venue opens (usually the first Saturday), be at your venue at 1pm the day before (usually the Friday) to set up. Similarly, if your show runs on the last day (usually the last Saturday or Sunday) be there at 1pm the day after (usually the Sunday or the Monday) to help pack away and tidy up. Bear this in mind when you make your travel arrangements.

Write a show report for the Free Fringe Forums after the fringe so that any problems can be addressed for future years, and so that future performers can be informed about the venue. You can find previous years' reports here [url].

Don't be a dick. There is undoubtedly some way to be an arsehole without technically breaking any of the rules we've listed. When you figure out what it is — don't do it. Examples from recent history would include: head butting an audience member, stealing wine from a venue, spraying graffiti around a venue and sleeping overnight in a venue despite it being a nightclub. Also, don't break the law!

Lastly — Make sure everyone else involved with your show has seen and read this document and understands that it also applies to them.

How to apply:

OK I have definitely read and absorbed 100% of the above information. Now I'm ready to apply:

Great. Now you know the deal, here's the application link to become part of our awesome collective. We hope the Fringe goes brilliantly for you and you wear your Free Fringe badge with pride. [application url here]

Our Advice:

We've been doing this a long time, if you're new to Edinburgh or to the Free Fringe please at least give our advice some consideration...

When you apply — just be honest and straightforward. We don't need to read your marketing spin. Just tell us who you are and what you do and what sort of space you want to perform in. We're all performers too so we won't be fooled by unnecessary guff.

Make sure you pick the genre that best suits your show. If in doubt have a look at the notes from the ADs below. Some short tips: if it has a script and characters, it's probably a play, and even comedy plays are still Theatre. If it's a series of loosely connected or unconnected funny sketches, it's a sketch show which is Comedy. If it's primarily aimed at children, then it's Children's regardless of what sort of show it is. If you're speaking directly to the audience and the primary intention is to make them laugh, it's probably Comedy. If you're speaking directly to the audience and the primary intention isn't necessarily to make them laugh, it's probably Spoken Word. If it's an hour of songs, it could be Comedy or Cabaret, the lines get a bit blurry here. If they're not funny songs and you're just looking for one off gigs, it's probably Music. If your show is burlesque, variety or includes several different genres it's probably Cabaret. Comedy magic is still Magic. If you're a band it's Music. If you're still confused talk to us.

When you get an offer, be realistic about it. All venues are imperfect. But shows have been incredibly successful in slots that others have turned down. The success will come down to your hard work. Of course if there's a real practical reason why your venue may not work for you, speak to your artistic director. Don't flypost around the fringe. It's illegal. Go to shops and venues and ask if you can put up posters.

Be realistic about the Fringe. You won't become famous. You won't meet The Man With The Cigar. You won't be discovered. Come to the Fringe to learn, and to become a better performer, not to become an overnight star as if by magic. The press, agents, industry people are less important than you think. Your job is to entertain audiences; focus on that.

Audiences won't come to your shows unless you go out and get them. Unless you're incredibly famous or have some alternative masterplan, you're going to need to print flyers (with our logo on) and distribute them (and the Wee Blue Book at the same time). The best person to flyer your show is likely to be you. If you do hire others, hiring directly (other Free Fringers is a good place to look) is a better idea than going through an agency who are working for lots of shows. Whoever does it, make sure they distribute the Wee Blue Book too.

We discourage hiring armies of leafleters. It's unfair to other performers who can't afford that. And the more you spend on publicity, the more you force other shows to spend.

The result is that everybody spends more and nobody gets any more audience. We didn't start The Free Fringe, thus saving you thousands of pounds, for you to spend those savings on publicity. The Free Fringe stands for reducing costs for all performers and eliminating massive losses at the Edinburgh Fringe.

The best way to do the Fringe is to do the full 22-day run (unless you're a music act which is different). We usually allocate full runs first. If you must do a part run don't pick the week in the middle. We might be able to squeeze you in for the first week or the last week. But because of shows that do the first two weeks or the last two weeks there is hardly ever a middle-week gap.

Doing a solo show is hard. If in doubt, don't. Put together a mixed bill show with a few other performers. These are easier to sell to audiences, means the workload is split and means you have the moral support of some fellow performers when things get tough (and at some point they will).

You will probably need a "bucket speech". This is a short pitch to the audience asking them to donate as they leave your show to your "bucket". It's up to you whether or not you ask audiences to donate as they leave your show. Most people do. If you're trying to cover your costs (1) do a great show and (2) ask nicely for donations. It is totally against the ethos of the Free Fringe to be rude to people who do not donate. There are people who just can't afford to and there are people who didn't like the show and don't want to. Thank them for coming. Smile.

Have a look at the forums to see how previous shows made the most of the Fringe. Ask other Free Fringers for advice at the many meetings and get togethers — official and unofficial — that happen year round.

If you've previously been at a paid venue you can expect things to be a little different. We don't have door staff or technicians or wardrobe assistants. If you need those things you'll have to bring your own. The venue staff work for the venue, not for you, so don't expect them to help when you have a problem with the sound desk or something. Although many do help us, it's not their job, it's ours.

No level of fame excuses people from door duty or sticking to the rules. If you're too busy to do these things, get one of your entourage to do it and make sure they have read this ethos and understand how important it is.

The Free Fringe supplies only a PA system, a backdrop, some signs and, in some cases, extra chairs. If your venue would benefit from extra lighting, a projector screen or a fold-out sign in the street, that's great that you spotted that. Contact the other shows at your venue and suggest clubbing together to buy or borrow or make the thing you have in mind. Make sure the venue will be ok with what you're planning and then go for it! Whatever it costs it'll be a lot less than the thousands you could be spending on a paid venue. And if you're sensible you'll hang on to the equipment so it can be used again next year.

If your show is super popular please make sure to clear the space for the next act before chatting to audience or friends who have come. But do take the time to chat to audiences if you can, make sure they have a Wee Blue Book and recommend some other Free Fringe shows to them.

If there's a problem speak to (1) Venue Captain, (2) Artistic Director and (3) Free Fringe Committee. Please don't make significant decisions without first checking that you're doing the right thing and consulting us. Keep us in the loop.

Keep your show simple. If you need more than ten minutes to set up your show — that's not going to work.

Almost all Free Fringe shows are 50-55 minutes long. If you want to do an irregular length show we need to know by December at the latest. After that slots will have been fixed.

Write something honest in your blurb about who you are and what the show offers. If we think you're misleading the public we reserve the right to change it. The Wee Blue Book has a reputation for offering trusted information.

Here's how the Free Fringe's money works: It costs about £28,000 to run the Free Fringe. Most of that is the Wee Blue

Book printing costs. It's worth it though; the book is in huge demand at the Fringe and brings in loads of of audience for us all. The rest is buying chairs, trips to Edinburgh to negotiate venues, printing signs and backdrops, extra PA equipment. No Free Fringer is paid to work for the Free Fringe.

We have three sources of income:

1. Benefit gigs
2. Sale of adverts in the Wee Blue Book (and we don't sell adverts to shows because we don't think that's fair)
3. Voluntary contributions.

Ideally we'd like to raise so much from (1) and (2) that we don't even have to ask for (3). Please help us by volunteering to run benefits and sell advertising. In recent years we've asked for £ 3-5 per performance, depending on room size, £2 per Music section shows booked by the gig. It's totally voluntary. No-one is chased or put at a disadvantage if they don't pay it. It's quite common for people who've had a great Fringe to share the love and chip in a bit extra.

It is always best to apply for shows on your own behalf. Obviously you may have an agent or manager who will be organising parts of your show but we would urge all agents and managers to ask their acts to read this ethos themselves before applying. Ultimately they will be the ones responsible for sticking to it.

Timings: The first round of offers will arrive in January. We usually allow a fortnight for people to reply before making another round of offers for the slots that haven't been taken up. Sometimes it takes longer than that. We don't make offers for venues until we are sure that we have the right to do so. Typically many bars and clubs don't start to think about the summer until well after Hogmanay.

That may not be convenient for other deadlines around the Fringe — especially the Edinburgh Fringe big programme. We consider that to be the fault of the Edinburgh Festival Fringe Society who should be able to assemble and print a brochure on a time scale of less than four months. Feel free to express this to them! And please try to be patient with us finding you a slot. It is very common for a great venue to contact us in May/June/July wanting to be involved. It's always better to contact us to check the state of play rather than panicking and paying a lot of money for a venue two days before we send you an offer!

At some point before/during/after the fringe you will hear someone say that the Free Fringe is free because it's not as good as other organisations. This is not true. We're free because we believe performers should not have to pay to perform and audiences should be able to see shows regardless of their financial circumstances. The Edinburgh Comedy Awards winners for 2014 and 2016 were Free Fringe shows. The Edinburgh Comedy Awards best newcomers for 2013 and 2015 were Free Fringe shows. Our acts have won dozens of other awards and accolades and hundreds of Free Fringers have racked up four and five star reviews and glowing praise. Numerical analysis of reviews suggests the quality of shows at the Free Fringe is at least as good as at most paid venue organisations and considerably better than some. Keep telling people this.

*